Intellectual Property Law in Hungary

Intellectual Property Law in Hungary

Second Edition

Levente Tattay

This book was originally published as a monograph in the International Encyclopaedia of Laws/Intellectual Property Law.

Founding Editor: Roger Blanpain
General Editor: Frank Hendrickx
Volume Editor: Hendrik Vanhees

Wolters Kluwer

Published by:
Kluwer Law International B.V.
PO Box 316
2400 AH Alphen aan den Rijn
The Netherlands
Website: www.wklawbusiness.com

Sold and distributed in North, Central and South America by:
Wolters Kluwer Legal & Regulatory U.S.
7201 McKinney Circle
Frederick, MD 21704
United States of America
Email: customer.service@wolterskluwer.com

Sold and distributed in all other countries by:
Turpin Distribution Services Ltd.
Stratton Business Park
Pegasus Drive, Biggleswade
Bedfordshire SG18 8TQ
United Kingdom
Email: kluwerlaw@turpin-distribution.com

Printed on acid-free paper

ISBN 97890-411-8748-2

e-Book: ISBN 97890-411-8771-0
web-PDF: ISBN 97890-411-8801-4

This title is available on www.kluwerlawonline.com

Printed and Bound by CPI Group (UK) Ltd, Croydon, CR0 4YY.

The Author

Levente Tattay was born in Budapest on 17 December 1943. In 1965, he was admitted to the Faculty of Law and Administrative Sciences of University Pécs, from where he graduated in 1970. In 1973, he took a special examination as law attorney and counsellor-at-law. After the special examination, he has worked as counsellor-at-law. During the years 1981–1986, he was employed as an expert of industrial property in Moscow in framework of cooperation of the countries socialist in the international organization, COMECON.

In 1983, he obtained a postgraduate diploma of Protection of Industrial Property. After his mission in Moscow, he worked in a Hungarian Patent Office as head of the department of trademarks. In 1988, he defended his candidate's thesis on 'Problems of Unification in Matter of Trademarks', and he has obtained a Ph.D. doctorate degree at University ELTE in Budapest (1989). Since 1995, he has been working in the faculty of Law and Political Sciences of Pazmány Péter Catholic University as an associate professor and later as a professor of the university. He habilitated in 2004 and was appointed as professor in 2006. He speaks Russian, German, and French fluently. He is author of fifteen books and circa 300 Hungarian and foreign publications and has appeared in recognized journals. In 1974, he married Agnes Baski. They have two children: Szilárd (1977) is a university assistant in Catholic University 'Pázmány Péter'; Enikő (1980) works as an architect in Budapest. He has membership in professional bodies: ALAI (Association of the Art and Literature, International); and German-Hungarian Association of Lawyers in Hungarian Trademark Association. His research area is private law, including personal law and the law of intellectual property as far as European Law.

The Author

Table of Contents

List of Abbreviations

Berne Convention	Berne Convention for the Protection of Literary and Artistic Works – promulgated by the Law Decree No. 4/1975
Chip Protection Act	Act XXXIX of 1991 on the protection of the topographies of microelectronic semiconductor products
Civil Code	Law No. V of 2013 on the Civil Code of the Hungarian Republic
Code of Civil Procedure	Act No. CXXX. of 2016 on the Code of Civil Procedure
Competition Act	Act LVII of 1996 on the prohibition of unfair trading practices and unfair competition
Computer Directive	Directive 2009/24/EC of the European Parliament and of the Council of 23 April 2009 on the legal protection of computer programs
Community Trademark Directive	Directive (EU) 2015/2436 of the European Parliament and of the Council of 16 December 2015 to approximate the laws of the Member States relating to trademarks (hereinafter: 'Community Trademark Directive')
Copyright Act	Act LXXXVI on the protection of copyright
Criminal Code	Law No. C of 2012 on the Criminal Code of Hungarian Republic
Design Act	Act XLVIII of 2001 on the legal protection of designs
European Agreement	The Association Agreement between Hungary and the European Communities signed on 16 December 1991 in Brussels
Design Directive	Directive 98/71/EC of the European Parliament and of the Council of 13 October 1998 on the legal protection of designs
E-Commerce Act	Act CVIII of 2001 on certain aspects of electronic commerce services and information society services
EPC	European Patent Convention 2000 (EPC 2000) – promulgated by Act CXXX of 2007
Film Law	The Act II of 2004 on motion picture
Firm Act	Act V of 2006 on Public Company Information, Company Registration and Winding-up Proceedings (hereinafter: 'Firm Act').
Gazette of Office	Official Journal of Hungarian Intellectual Property Office, that is Gazette of patents, trademark, and designs. etc.

Geneva Convention	Geneva Convention for the Protection of Producers of Phonograms against Unauthorized Duplication of Their Phonograms – promulgated by the Law Decree No. 18/1975
Hague Agreement	The Hague Agreement Concerning the International Registration of Industrial Design, Geneva Act of the Hague Agreement Concerning the International Registration of Industrial Designs – promulgated by Act XC of 2004
HIPO	Hungarian Intellectual Property Organization
IP Enforcement Directive	Directive 2004/48/EC of the European Parliament and of the Council of 29 April 2004 on the enforcement of intellectual property right
Lisbon Arrangement	Lisbon Agreement for the Protection of Appellations of Origin and their international Registration modified in 2015
Locarno Agreement	Locarno Agreement establishing an International Classification for Industrial Designs; Agreement signed at Locarno on 8 October 1968 – was promulgated by the Law Decree No. 29/1993
Madrid Agreement	The Madrid Agreement for the Repression of False or Deceptive Indications of Source on Goods – promulgated in Hungary by the Law Decree No. 29/1973
Madrid Agreement	Madrid Agreement for the International Registration of Marks (1891) – promulgated by Law Decree No. 29/1973
Madrid Protocol	Protocol Relating to the Madrid Agreement Concerning the International Registration of Marks (Madrid Protocol 1989) – promulgated by Act LXXXIII of 1999
Nice Agreement	Nice Agreement for the International Classification of Goods and Services for the Purposes of Registration of Marks (1957) – promulgated by Law Decree No. 29/1973
Office	Hungarian Intellectual Property Office, Hungarian Patent Office
Paris Convention	Paris Convention for the Protection of Industrial Property 1883 – promulgated by the Law Decree No. 18/1970 in Hungary
PCT	Patent Cooperation Treaty
Patent Act	Act XXXIII of 1995 on the patent protection of inventions
Rome Convention	The Directive 2001/84/EC of the European Parliament and Council of 27 September 2001 on the resale right for the benefit of the author of an original work of art Rome Convention for the Protection of Performers, Producers of Phonograms and Broadcasting Organizations – promulgated by the Act No. XLIV of 1998
Topography Act	Act XXXIX of 1991 on the protection of the topographies of microelectronic semiconductor products
Topography Directive	Council Directive 87/54/EEC of 16 December 1986 on the legal protection of topographies of semiconductor products (hereinafter: 'Topography Directive')

List of Abbreviations

Trademark Act	Act XI on 1995 on the protection trademarks and geographical indications
TRIPS Agreement	Agreement on Trade Related Aspects of Intellectual Property Rights promulgated by Act IX of 1998
UM Act	Act XXXVIII on the Protection of utility models
UPOV Convention	International Convention for the Protection of new Varieties of Plants of 2 December of 1961 as revised at Geneva on 10 November 1972, on 23 October 1978 and on 19
WIPO WCT	–WIPO Copyright Treaty – ratified by 57/1998 (XI29) OGY. Parliament resolution promulgated by Act LI of 2002 in Hungary
WIPO	World Intellectual Property Organization
WIPO WPPT	WIPO Performances and Phonograms Treaty – ratified by 57/1998 (XI29) OGY. Parliament resolution promulgated by Act LI of 2002 in Hungary

List of Abbreviations

General Introduction

§1. General Background

I. Geography

1. Hungary is a small country of only 93,000 square kilometres, 1% of the whole territory of Europe. Hungary, located in the centre of Europe in the Carpathian Basin, is surrounded by the Carpathian Mountains the Alps and the Dinaric Alps. Hungary lies in the temperate zone and is situated at the border confluence of three main climatic regions: Oceanic, Mediterranean, and Continental. The climate also varies greatly. The nation's mean annual temperature is 10 degree Celsius. January is the coldest month with a mean temperature of just above 2 degree Celsius, and in the summer, it can reach into the 30s. The annual average rainfall is about 650 millimetres.

The country is divided by the Danube, Europe's second largest river. The country's second largest river is the Tisza. Lake Balaton is Central Europe's largest lake and an important national and international tourism centre. The total length of Lake Balaton is 77 kilometres, its breadth varies between 1.6 and 14 kilometres, and its surface area is 598 square kilometres.

Nearly three-quarters of Hungary is lowland while one-fifth is composed of hills, less than 400 metres in height, and less than 5% consists of mountain ranges. The country's highest point, Kékesteto in the Matra Mountains, is only 1,014 metres high.

Hungary has six major geographical regions. These include the Hungarian Great Plain, the Western Lowland, the Transdanubian Hills, and the Transdanubian Mid-Mountains, which are commonly known as Transdanubia; the West Hungarian Border Region at the foots of Alps; and the Northern Mountains.

II. Cultural Composition

2. The Hungarian culture has more than 1,000 years of traditions. After the great Hungarian Conquest (896), King Stephen I (1000–1038) founded the Hungarian Kingdom. At Christmas in the year 1000, King Stephen (Stan) was crowned at Stardom. Stephen is revered as the founder of the Hungarian state. The birth of Hungarian national culture and literature, comprising both oral and the earliest examples of written culture, is obscured by the shadows of antiquity. Hungarian culture can be supposed to a have double root, namely the heritage of its pre-Christianity present in a later form, blended with Western Christian culture. By origin, Hungarian culture and literature of the Carpathian Basin is essentially of a Latin background. The first linguistic record that contains Hungarian words is the Deed of Foundation at Tihany Abbey, dating from 1055.

The golden age of medieval Hungarian culture occurred during the reign of King Matthias Corvinus (1458–1490) in the mid-fifteenth century. Hungary had a rich cultural life as evidenced not only by the many magnificent creations of European level Hungarian Romanesque and Gothic architecture, painting and sculpture, but also by the growth of Hungarian literature: the collection of codices, written in Hungarian, which regrettably have been destroyed by wars over the centuries. In the second half of the fifteenth century, the king's palaces in Buda and Visegrád emerged as influential centres of European Renaissance learning. The gems of Matthias library in Buda, Corvinus continue to be regarded as cherished examples of the Renaissance bookmaker's art.

3. Concerning the Hungarian culture today, it has intensified its presence in the 1990s, and its representatives have had international success. Hungarian participation at the World Exhibition 1992 in Seville was especially memorable. In 1999, Hungary was the guest of honour at the Frankfurt Book Fair of international renown.

In recent years, festivals presenting the whole of Hungarian culture have been organized in Belgium, France, Italy, and Great Britain. From among today's Hungarian writers Anna Jókai, László Krasznahorkai, Lajos Parti Nagy, Magda Szabó, and Géza Bereményi have attained remarkable popularity in the French, German, Italian, and English language areas. As an acknowledgement of universal Hungarian literature, in 2002, Imre Kertész received the Nobel Prize in literature for his novel titled *Fateless*. There is also continuous interest in the Western world concerning Hungarian masters of literature in the twentieth century, first all relating to the works of Dezsõ Kosztolányi, Zsigmond Móricz, Gyula Krudy, and Antal Szerb. Sándor Márai's novels, with their unique character, are having quite a renaissance in numerous countries.

From among Hungarian contemporary composers, György Kurtág, György Ligeti, and Péter Eötvös are the best known abroad. Hungarian pianists such as Zoltán Kovács, András Schiff, Dezso Ránki, and Gergely Bogányi are always welcome in great concert halls throughout the world. Hungarian movie directors of international renown include István Szabó, Károly Makk, Miklós Jancsó, Péter Gothár, and Béla Tarr.

4. The 1920 Trianon Treaty, signed as part of the Versailles peace process after the First World War, meant a loss of two-thirds of the territory and half of the population of Hungary.

However, the Hungarian political elite and the Hungarian people could not reconcile themselves to the injustices imposed by the Trianon Peace Treaty and reacted with bitterness to the oppression suffered by 3 million Hungarians who had become minorities. The situation of the Hungarian minorities living in neighbouring countries has also changed significantly. Nearly 2 million live in Romania, 600,000 in Slovakia, 200,000 in Ukraine, and 300,000 in Serbia, making a total of some 3 million Hungarians.

Having been liberated from the oppression of the respective communist regimes, these national minorities are now trying to establish their own political and cultural institutions. Political organizations have been formed in all regions with a Hungarian population, and in a number of instances, they have returned members to a national

Parliament and even participated in government. Many Hungarian schools, church organizations, and cultural institutions have also been set up.

The position of Hungarian emigrants in the Western hemisphere, traditionally imbued with a sense of national mission, has also changed: Nowadays, Hungarians living abroad have unrestricted access to their homeland and its institutions.

5. Hungary has several Nobel laureates. Although a small country in respect to its population, it is however, a major one in regards to the sheer number of scientists over the course of the twentieth century and no less than twelve Nobel Laureates – seven of them sons of Budapest – were able to trace their roots back to Hungary.

The Nobel Prize was awarded to Philip E. A. von Lénárd in physics in 1905; Robert Bárány in medicine in 1914; Richard A. Zsigmondy in chemistry in 1925; Albert von Szent-Györgyi Nagyrapolt in medicine 1937; George de Hevesy in chemistry in 1943; George von Békésy in medicine in 1961; Eugene P. Wigner in physics in 1963; Dennis Gábor in physics 1971; John C. Polányi in chemistry in 1986; George A. Oláh in chemistry in 1994; John C. Harsányi in economics in 1994; and Imre Kertész in literature in 2004.

III. Political System

6. Year 1989 was a turning point for Hungary in three respects. The change of the political system became irreversible and the preparations for the free elections in 1990 began to gather pace. Parallel with this, consensus gradually began to be established among the different political forces of Hungary's eventual full membership of the Western European organizations of integration. Also, Hungary played a role in launching changes that shook Europe, because it was actively involved in the peaceful but determined change of political system and through the winding-up of the Eastern Bloc.

The political system covers the following areas: the Constitution, Parliament, president of the republic, government, Constitutional Court, judicial power and jurisdiction, local government, and party system.

Evidence in respect to the principle of legality is demonstrated by the Constitution in its present form, and from the point of view of formal rights, it is a compilation and regrouping of the modifications of an earlier Constitution, that of 1949 into a coherent structure.

The new Hungarian Constitution, that is Fundamental Law, the country's Constitution was adopted on 18 April 2011, promulgated a week later and went into force on 1 January 2012. Hungary's first Constitution to be adopted within a democratic framework and following free elections, it succeeded the 1949 Constitution, adopted on 20 August 1949, and heavily amended on 23 October 1989.

The fundamental Law proclaims the following:

- We are proud that our people has over the centuries defended Europe in a series of struggles and enriched Europe's common values with its talent and diligence.
- We recognize the role of Christianity in preserving nationhood. We value the various religious traditions of our country.

- We commit to promoting and safeguarding Hungarian culture, the languages and cultures of nationalities living in Hungary, along with all man-made and natural assets of the Carpathian Basin. We bear responsibility for our descendants; therefore, we shall protect the living conditions of future generations by making prudent use of our material, intellectual, and natural resources.

According to the Constitution, Hungary is a parliamentary republic. The Hungarian system resembles that of a chancellery democracy. Its most important governmental organ and representative body, Parliament, is a unicameral structure consisting of 386 members, who are elected for four-year terms.

The Constitution regulating parliamentary elections prescribes a mixed constituency system with one round of a total of 199 seats, of which 106 are decided by individual constituency elections and 93 on the basis *of party-list seats including minority-list seats* allot.

According of the Constitution, the head of state expresses the unity of the nation and defends the democratic procedures of the governing institutions. The president is elected by Parliament. The president of the republic must be a Hungarian citizen and eligible voter aged 35 or older; he or she must be elected in Parliament with a two-thirds majority for a five-year term by secret ballot.

The traditional rights of the president, also set down in the Hungarian Constitution, have been defined in relation to legislative, executive and judicial authority, according to a system of the separation of powers.

The prime minister plays the dominant role in the executive branch of Hungary's government and is responsible for the government's activities, as the head of government is elected by Parliament on the basis of the majority principle and executive power. The election of the prime minister leads simultaneously to the adoption of the government programme. The government is formed with the appointment and swearing in of the ministers.

The two main executive functions in Hungary, as in other countries with similar political systems, are governmental decision-making and the direction of administration at the highest level.

The executive branch performs its governmental duties partly as an independent force and partly in conjunction with other governmental bodies both at the national and local levels: the former including Parliament and the president; the latter, local governments.

The Constitutional Court has existed as an institution of Hungary since 1989. The law defines the main tasks of the Constitutional Courts as the following: The Constitution provides normative standards and supervision over the Constitution, and it reconciles the differences between international and domestic law; it determines negligence in violations of constitutionality; it establishes the public responsibilities of the president and other public officials and interprets limitation on public referendums.

Judicial power and jurisdiction is essential guarantee within the Hungarian state structure; the courts are a separate, independent branch. Judicial recourse is considered as a fundamental human right.

The function of judicial power is exclusively to render justice. The courts of Hungary defend and guarantee constitutional order, the rights and legal interests of citizens, and punish those who commit crimes.

Hungary has a three-tier judicial system. Jurisdiction is exercised at the level of the Kuria (Supreme Court), county municipal courts, and also local (municipal district) courts, local government. Local administrative units include villages, 'large villages', cities, and cities which serve as county seats, the capital and its twenty-three districts.

The enfranchised residents of municipalities play a determining role in exercising the rights of local governments. Voting citizens exercise their right of governance indirectly by way of a body of representatives elected by them and directly through local referendums.

Local government has the right to own and regulate property, to earn income, and levy taxes; to freely associate with other local governments and establish and operate organs of local governments; and to establish and adopt symbols and local titles.

The central government directs the operation of local governments only through general guidelines.

Mayors are elected directly by local government.

Hungary's multi-party system emerged in the transition period of 1988–1990. The year 1949 marked the last multi-party elections which soon led, however, to a single-party dictatorship. The Hungarian Socialist Worker's Party (Hungarian Communist Party) was formed on 1 November 1956 following a decision by the Workers' Party (MSZMP) to disband. They declared their own dissolution in 1989. In its place, the Hungarian Socialist Party (MSZP) was formed, which defined itself as a social democratic party.

The former traditional parties began to reorganize themselves one after another; in 1988, Independent Smallholder Party (FKGP) re-emerged, and in 1989, the Hungarian Social Democratic Party (MSZDP) also re-emerged.

The parliamentary parties are linked to three markedly differing ideological centres, generally characterized as the 'Christian-conservative' political cluster, the liberal cluster, and the socialist social democratic cluster.

IV. Population Statistics

7. In January 2009, Hungary registered 10.031 million inhabitants, and according to the data of the previous year, the population decreased by 14,000. In terms of population, Hungary ranks thirteenth in Europe. Due to its low birth rate, but much more so to its rate of mortality, it stands at the end of the line of European countries with rapidly decreasing populations.

The country's population has not only gradually fallen but has become aged due to the widening gap between birth and death rates. There is a need for well-considered measures to temper this tendency and to shift it towards a more favourable long-term course.

According to the 2001 census, 98.5% of Hungary's present-day population almost 10 million people speak Hungarian as their mother tongue; the country can therefore be called a monolingual state.

With its population density of 111 persons per square kilometre, Hungary is considered to be a densely populated country even on a world scale and on an average one for Europe.

§2. Historical Background

8. The Hungarian history consists of four consecutive great ages. The great epochs of Hungarian History are as follows: the Hungarian Kingdom (1000–1526); the age of the Ottoman conquest (1526–1699); Hungary in the Habsburg Monarchy (1699–1918); and the independent Hungarian statehood (from 1918 to present day).

For centuries, the Hungarians wandered across the steppes of Eastern Europe before they came to the Carpathian Basin, which became their homeland. Following the Conquest in the year 896 under Chief árpád, the Hungarians left behind their nomadic lifestyle, dominated by animal herding, for the cultivation of land.

The Hungarians began to change and turn towards the nations and culture of Western Christendom. The Great Chief Géza (970–997) oriented towards western Christianity. He asked Otto I, the German Emperor, to send missionary priests, who arrived with German knights. Géza himself was Christian, and his son István (Vajk) received Christian education.

Géza's son Vajk, who received the name of Stephen (István) was brought up to be a Christian monarch, and Gizella, sister of Henry II, king of Bavari, was chosen as his bride-to-be. Stephen (1000–1038) found ten episcopates and several monasteries, had churches built, set up the administration of royal counties, crushed those tribal leaders who were seeking to maintain paganism, and opposed Europeanization, not to mention defending his country from attacks from the west. Stephen led his people to become a Christian nation of Europe and created the kingdom of Hungary.

The successor of Stephen I Ladislaus (László) enacted severe laws to restore internal order. It was in his reign (1077–1095) that King István, Prince Imre, and Bishop Gellért of Csanád were canonized.

St Stephen's day in Hungary is 20 August. The cult of Stephen is both rich and widespread in Hungary, particularly within the ecclesiastical traditions of Roman Catholic Church.

Despite making clear overall progress, from time to time, the medieval Hungarian state faced periods of serious decline, mostly as a result of the repeated destruction of previous achievements by hostile powers attacking Hungary from the east. In the middle of the thirteenth century, the Mongol (Tatar) invaded the eastern parts of Europe, which resulted in defeat for the army of King Béla IV at the Battle of Muhi in 1241 and laid Hungary to waste. As a result of this, the king had to flee. On his return, he had to carry out a so-called Second Founding of the Homeland.

Charles Robert (1308–1342) slowly restored order in the country and put royal revenues right. His son, Louis the Great (1342–1382), who was also the Polish king and ruled over an enormous empire played a similar role, and he helped make medieval Hungary into an international power.

The Hungarian Kingdom was important as a defensive bastion of Western Christendom during the Middle Ages, and indeed the country's eastern and southern borders marked the borders of the Western world.

In the fifteenth century, however, a new and more dangerous enemy than ever before appeared at Hungary's borders, the Ottoman-Turkish Empire, with its great military might was expanding rapidly at this time. This expansion was successfully curbed for a number of decades by the great military leader János Hunyadi. On 29 June 1456, on hearing of an imminent battle between the Hungarian and Turkish armies, Pope Calixtus III ordered the bells to be rung at noon in all Christian countries. By the time the decree had been issued, János Hunyadi's armies, which had gathered near Belgrade scored a magnificent victory over Mohammed II's numerically superior forces.

His victory saved Christian Europe from Turkish expansion for a longer period.

The timing of events prompted the subsequent belief that the pope had decreed the ringing at noon to celebrate the Hungarians' triumph at Nándorfehérvár.

The age of King Matthias Corvine (1443–1490), the son of General Janos Hunyadi, may be considered to be the golden age of the Hungarian state. He established a strong centralized system of government with financial and tax reforms, as well as a standing army ('the black army'). He bolstered royal power against the nobility, selecting his office holders and chief officials from the ranks of the lesser nobility, burgesses, and not infrequently, peasants. His education was excellent, enabling him to speak several languages, and he was cultured to a degree rarely seen amongst the aristocracy of his day. There are many sayings attributed to him, and in Hungarian popular poetry, he is often referred to as 'Mathias the Just'.

9. The battle of Mohács on 29 August 1526, when the Hungarian Army was beaten, may be considered as the beginning of age of the Ottoman Conquest (1526–1699). In 1541, II Suleiman I assumed the Hungarian royal set in Buda. For a long period, the western and southern parts of the country fell into the hands of the Habsburgs as a result of the dynastic treaties concluded with Hungarian Jagellos. The kingdom's eastern regions elected a sovereign later known as the 'Prince of Transylvania', from among the aristocrats and supported by the Turks. The country thus split into three parts: The Habsburg Dynasty took control of the western part; the centre of the country came under Turkish rule; while in the southeast, in Transylvania, an independent Hungarian principality emerged, marking the final outpost of national continuity. The Turkish occupation lasted for 150 years, and the state structure of the Hungarian Kingdom was slowly restored only after the reoccupation of Buda.

In 1686, in their second major attempt, allied forces reoccupied Buda Castle, the one-time seat of the Hungarian kings, which became the Turkish rule in Hungary. The Turks were expelled from Hungary within two years. In 1689, they were already at the borders of Serbia and Albania. The lengthy war was finally concluded by the Peace Treaty of Karlowitz (Karlóca) in 1699 in which the Ottoman Porte renounced all territorial demands on Hungary.

10. Hungary in the Habsburg Monarchy (1699–1918) lost its independence. The Habsburg government, after the expulsion of the Turks, immediately set out to abolish the feudal rights of the Hungarian nobility, because they were alleged to have obstructed efforts at unification. However, the anti-Habsburg uprising and struggle for freedom that followed led by reigning Prince Ferenc Rákóczi II (1703–1711) provided clear evidence that Hungary could not be governed without the Hungarian nobility, and certainly not in a way contrary to the interests of the noblemen.

The compromise that followed the failed uprising, the Szatmár Peace Treaty of 1711, restored and strengthened the dualistic division power that had formed over the previous century and a half.

Maria Theresa (1740–1780) and Joseph II (1740–1790), who was absolute sovereigns, managed to reassert Austrian influence to same extent in these areas. Maria Theresa was unusually with the nobility. Her son, Joseph II, who was unwilling to be crowned because he was opposed to ruling in Hungary, as emperor, had only a small group of supporters.

They looked upon the measures taken by Joseph II as the manifestation of spread of the enlightenment and the 'European' character, among simultaneously to abolish the county system, boost the role of legislature, unify public administration, address educational issues, and improve the conditions of serfs. However, the majority stubbornly adhered to the traditions.

Joseph II died as a broken leader, hawing withdrawn all his proposals except those allowing for the free movement of serfs and the freedom of religious practice of non-Catholics.

The first half of the nineteenth century was a golden age of Hungarian history. Parliamentary sessions of those decades laid down the groundwork of social change: The emancipation of the serfs and the development of the civil society began; the Hungarian language was made the language of state administration; and the Hungarian couture was able to catch up once again with the culture of Western nations.

The work, which was done during the so-called Reform Age to build up the country economically and politically, was spearheaded by Count Stan Széchenyi, a man of broad vision, and well educated in Western culture – he was also an excellent diarist – whose thinking was strongly influenced by the British model. His selfless organizing work led to the creation of the Hungarian Academy of Science, the construction of the Chaine Bridge connecting Pest with Buda, the beginning of the construction of Hungary's railway network, and the regulation of the flow Danube and Tisza Rivers.

In the early spring of 1848, a new revolutionary wave swept across Europe, which the people of Vienna joined on 13 March, followed by the people of Pest on 15 March. The 'twelve points' formulated by the radicals of Pest demanded at once: the setting up a responsible government; an annual parliamentary session; the establishment of a National Guard; the reunification of Hungary and Transylvania; the abolition of serfdom; equality in civil life, religion, and law; representative legislature; general and proportionate taxation; freedom of the press; and their introduction of a trial by jury. These were to have been implemented within the framework of monarchy, jointly with Austria under the leadership of then-emperor Ferdinand V (1835–1848), while Austria too, was undergoing a constitutional transformation. The revolution in Pest, unlike those in Paris, Berlin, and Vienna, was bloodless.

This revolution was headed by Lajos Kossuth, an outstanding political orator and thinker of international reputation. The bloodless revolution was followed by a bloody war of independence: First, the Viennese court incited some of Hungary's ethnic minorities against the Hungarian people and then intervened militarily. Ultimately, however, it was able to crush the Hungarian people only with Tsarist Russia, the most autocratic state in contemporary Europe. Popular Hungarian poet Sander Prettify gave his life in this war of independence.

The Austro-Hungarian Monarchy (1867–1918) started as a result of peaceful compromise between Austria and Hungary.

Vienna suffered a series of key military defeats, in 1859 by France, and in 1866 by Prussia, compelling the country to readmit its one-time partners, the Hungarian noble class into its system of rule. The Hungarian people did not break under the yoke of oppression, and when, in 1867, the joint efforts of the prudent reform Ferenc Deak and the Habsburg monarch,

Francis Joseph I sought to make peace for the Hungarian people. This culminated in the Austro-Hungarian Compromise, and the dual Austro-Hungarian monarchy – with one centre in Vienna and one in Pest-Buda – another age of progress, dawned in the turbulent history of Hungarian people, leading to a gradual increase in the importance of Hungary within the monarchy.

The two partner countries of the newly established Austro-Hungarian monarchy operated separate legislatures, governments, and capitals. Foreign affairs defence and all related financial matters were pursued in common, but otherwise the government conducted the affairs of their respective countries independent of each other. Coordination came in the form of the 'Council of Ministers' and what were called delegations. The Council of Ministers consisted of the foreign defence and the common finance ministers, the two prime ministers, as well as the ministers and authorities from various fields who were invited to attend cabinet meetings on occasion. Due to the dual system of governance, which emerged the period between 1867 and 1918 and is also known as the 'Age of Dualism', local executive power – today under of the interior minister – was exerted by the counties, thus providing shelter impoverished nobility and gentry. There ensued rapid development in both national and local administration with such areas as public health and education receiving particular attention.

Over the fifty years or so from the compromise to the First World War, Hungary underwent a fundamental transformation: Civil society grew stronger; industry and trade developed rapidly; the railway network increased in size; and the institutions' parliamentary constitutionality began to be put in place. At the same time, Hungary also had to face a number of difficult problems. Nearly half of Hungary's population consisted of non-Hungarian ethnic minorities – Germans, Romanians, Slovakians, Serbs, and Rutherians – nations that were calling for rights of autonomy, which the Hungarian government was unwilling to grant at the same time the country was in need of urgent social reforms. The system of large feudal estates was still in existence, while large masses of poor peasantry, well-organized industrial workers, and civic and industrial social groups were growing in strength and calling for radical changes.

However, conservative Hungarian governments consistently blocked all attempts at reform. The First World War broke out because of the assassination of Prince Francis Ferdinand.

In the First World War, the Hungarian people, along with the other nations of the Austro-Hungarian monarchy, fought and lost on the side of imperial Germany (1914–1918). The victorious powers in the First World War decided only on ending the monarchy, but not on the method to be used in this respect. The decision was left to the national minorities in Hungary, but more to Romania, Serbia, and the emerging Czechoslovakia. One after the other, the nationalities agreed to abolish the state frameworks within what was to be accomplished was greatly helped along by the Hungarian events of 1918.

11. The independent Hungarian statehood (from 1918 to the present day) began with the division of Hungary. A revolution broke out in Hungary on 30 October 1918. It also caused historical Hungary to fall apart. After the turbulence caused by democratic changes in the autumn of 1918, which steered Hungary towards civil development of a civil society – although this was restricted mostly to Budapest – came the communist coup d'état orchestrated by Béla Kun, and then the 'white' counterrevolution, led by Admiral Miklós Horthy. The newly independent Hungary was thereafter reduced to only one-third of its former historical territory by the peace treaty signed at the palace of Trianon near Paris. Croatia Hungary's territory decreased from 282,870 square kilometres to 92,963 square kilometres, and its population fell from 18 million to 7.6 million.

The Hungarian economy was badly hit by the damage caused along the way, and the political system introduced under the regency of Miklós Horthy did little to promote social modernization; on the contrary, it maintained the privileges of the traditional dominant social groups. Even so by the 1930s, one economic and cultural modernization, the litterbag linked to the diligent Minister of Culture, Count Kuno Klebelsberg. However, the Hungarian political elite could not reconcile to the injustices imposed by the Trianon Peace Treaty. In place of social modernization, Hungarian politics was dominated by the grievances caused by Trianon and by territorial revisionism.

Hoping for redress and respect for grievances incurred as a result of the Trianon Treaty, Hungary moved slowly towards an alliance with Germany and Italy, and with their assistance, was indeed able to regain control over some of its lost territories. The Hungarians populated section of the Felvidék in 1938, Kárpátalja in 1939, Northern Transylvania and Székelyföld in 1940, and Bácska 1941. However, these developments inevitably tied Hungary to the Axis powers, and so in 1941, Hungary entered into war on the side of Germany. In the winter of 1942–1943, the Second Hungarian Army perished in the bend of River Don. The Hungarian army – together with its German, Italian, Romanian, and Slovak allies – suffered a crushing defeat at the beginning of 1943.

German troupes invaded Hungary on 19 March 1944, Edmund Weesenmayer acting as commissioner with full powers. Horthy Regent of Hungary, forced by German pressure, bestowed the post of prime minister to Ferenc Szálasi, leader of Arrow-Cross Party, while Horthy and his family were deported to Germany. After 15 October 1944 following the Arrow-Cross takeover, persecution of the Jews also reached its peak. During the Holocaust, about 440,000–465,000 Jews from the war years' territory of Hungary perished in forced labour service or were killed in German extermination camps. The German occupation of Hungary and the terror imposed by the Hungarian fascists at the beginning of April 1945, to be replaced by a Soviet invasion, the whole of Hungary was occupied by Soviet troops.

The 1947 Paris Peace Treaty gave back those territories to neighbouring states that Hungary has reannexed between 1938 and 1941, while re-establishing the borders set by the 1920 Treaty of Trianon. Post-war communist party rule in Hungary was established in 1948–1949 only after three years of multi-party democracy and social and economic rebuilding. Only through intimidation and successful propaganda could the communist party take the 1947 parliamentary elections. What followed were indeed the dark days of dictatorship of forced industrialization, the knock on the door in the night. Indeed, the dictator of country was totalitarian Mátyás Rákosi general secretary of party (1945–1956). The abolition of the multi-party system was quickly implemented.

The institutions' characteristic of party dictatorship in totalitarian states were headed by party functionaries. The most fearful of institutions, the State Security Authority, also came into being at this time. It reported only to the leader of the party and committed every imaginable illegality against the exposed nation. In a country of 'socialist construction', everyone lived in danger. Also, the communist Interior Minister László Rajk was in danger, shown by the fact that he was executed in 1949. The communist dictatorship introduced into Hungary with Soviet assistance not only crushed the Hungarian people's desire for independence, but also put a stop to the freedom of thought. Tens of thousands of intellectuals were imprisoned or sent to labour camps, and the tyrannous rule of Mátyás Rákosi almost completely destroyed the intellectual foundations of Hungarian society.

12. History's only anti-communist revolution broke out on 23 October 1956. The communist dictatorship was swept away for a few days by the Hungarian Revolution to which Hungarian workers made a great contribution. The uprising started with a mass demonstration of university students and was transformed into a freedom fight as a result of the intervention of special armed police units, and later, Soviet troops. On 1 November 1956, the new government of Imre Nagy, complemented by representatives of the already reorganized parties, called upon the Soviet troops to pull out, declared Hungary's withdrawal from the Warsaw Pact and the country's neutrality, and asked for the assistance to the United Nations. Within a week, one of the cleanest revolutions in world history was carried out in Hungary. A new Soviet attack launched against Budapest in November swept away the scattered resistance of disintegrated army and armed civilian groups. The new government set up under leadership János Kádár dissolved the Imre Nagy government and declared latter's measures null and void. The crushed revolution was followed by unparalleled reprisals, in which 229 people were executed. Imre Nagy, the prime minister, was tried and executed in 1958.

What is paradoxically true, however, is that despite the fact that the uprising was crushed, everything began to change in Hungary after 1956. After the 1956 revolution was put down, the triumphant regime, which emerged with the help of Soviet tanks, consolidated in record time. A new government under Janos Kádár pursued a similar course to the initial communist dictatorship. The negative factors of Kádár regime (1956–1989) were: By the end of 1956, about 200,000 refugees had left Hungary and dispersed all over the world. Several thousand people suffered varying terms of imprisonment. The communist party was re-established and the single-party system restored. During 1959–1960, the Hungarian peasantry was largely forced back to cooperative farms that had been disintegrated during the revolution. This marked the end of the concept of private property, and thereby, the last basis of personal independence. In 1968, Hungary took part in invasion of Czechoslovakia, although with this move it seriously endangered the ethnic Hungarian minority living there.

Credits were taken from Western states, and the country ran deeply into debt. By the end of the 1980s, Hungary's foreign debt had increased to USD 21 billion; only a small part of this functioned as active capital while the majority of it was swallowed by badly designed huge industrial projects and attempts to maintain the average standard of living. That was the period of 'goulash communism'. Janos Kádár, the party chief who headed Hungary until 1989, although being placed in power by Soviet tanks in 1956, eventually oversaw the development of the most liberal regime of the former Eastern Bloc, particularly after 1968 ('soft dictatorship') when attempts were made to move, albeit very tentatively, towards a market economy. The 1980s saw increasing economic reform that eventually led to political change.

From the mid-1980s on, independent and opposition intellectuals became more active and organized into movements. As a result of the general decline of the Soviet empire, a process of political change and democratic reform started in the late 1980s. In January 1989, Imre Pozsgai a member of the political committee of the SUMP, publicly declared that the 1956 revolution was a popular uprising, and on 16 June, to a huge crowd, prime minister Miklós Nemeth paid his last respects at the coffin of Imre Nagy; it was clear to everyone that an era had closed once and for all. This resulted in the revival of such traditional political parties as the Small–holder's Party and Christian Democratic Party. However, it was the new political formations that proved very effective in generating mass support: the Hungarian Democratic Forum; the Alliance of Free Democrats; and the Alliance of Young Democrats. In September 1989, the Nemeth government opened the Hungarian border into Austria to East-German refugees, and Hungary declared that it would refuse to participate in any 'unprincipled partnership' with its Warszawa Pact allies. In 1992, the Soviet troops were withdrawn from Hungary. After the multi-party elections in 1990, a centre-right government formed under József Antall, with árpád Göncz as president. The democratic institutions underpinning the rule of law were developed. In 1997, Hungary became a member of OECD, in 1999 became a member of NATO, and in 2004, it acceded to the European Union.

Chapter 1. Copyright and Neighbouring Right

§1. Sources: Legislation

13. The current Copyright Act of Hungary, Act LXXVI of 1999, was adapted by the Hungarian Parliament on 22 June 1999.

The legal regulation of copyrights is more than a century-old tradition in Hungary. The first Hungarian legal regulation was enacted in 1884 (Act XVI of 1884), which settled the questions of artistic, scientific, and literary works. The amendment of first Copyright Act had been passed in 1922,[1] and the further Copyright Act of 1969 (Act III of 1969) entered into force on 1 January 1970. At the end of twentieth century, revision of the former Copyright Act was deemed necessary in view of technical and economic amendments.

The most important factor of Hungarian copyright is the process of association and accession of Hungary to the European Union. The Agreement of Association (hereinafter: 'European Agreement') between Hungary and the European Community was signed in Brussels on 16 December 1991. The European Agreement entered into force on 1 January 1994.[2]

By virtue of Article 65 of the European Agreement, Hungary was obliged to continue to improve the protection of intellectual, including industrial and commercial property rights in order to provide by the end of the fifth year entry into force of the mentioned agreement a level of protection similar to the existing one in the Community, including comparable means on enforcing such rights. This essential demand was concerned with the copyright too, and Hungary became a Member State of the European Union in 2004. The accession of the Hungarian Republic to the European Union on 1 May 2004 was promulgated by Act XXX of 2004. A revision of the former Copyright Act (Act III of 1969 was deemed necessary in view of the following considerations:

(a) the Republic of Hungary has several international commitments and international treaties as well as working towards European legal harmonization;
(b) the technological progress, (computers, databases, satellite broadcasting, Internet);
(c) passage to market economy;
(d) the need to eliminate the former regulation and their multi-level nature.

By virtue of Act CXLVIII of 2010, the name of Hungarian Patent Office was changed to Hungarian Intellectual Property Office (hereinafter: 'Office') as of 1 January 2011 to better reflect its competence extending to activities related to all form of industrial property protection as well as to the field of copyright.

The new Civil Code, the Law V of 2013 is one of the most significant achievements of the twenty-first century in Hungary. The Code omits detailed regulation of intellectual property. The new Civil Code shall apply in respect of intellectual property, if these

1. E. Lontai, *A szellemi alkotások joga* (Budapest: Eötvös József Könvvkiado, 2001), 18.
2. The European Agreement was promulgated by Act I. of 1994.

issues directly fall within its scope, which are not governed by the legislation on copyright and industrial property rights of Hungary.

The copyright was regulated by national and European laws and regulations as far as international treaties.

14. Hungarian laws and regulations:

- Act LXXVI of 1999 on Copyright.
- Act C of 2012 on new Penal Code Hungary.
- Act XVI of 2013 on the Amendment of certain Acts relating to Intellectual Property.
- Act CLIX of 2013 on the Amendment of certain Acts relating to Intellectual Property.
- Act No. CVIII. of 2001 on certain aspects of electronic commerce services and information society services (E- Commerce Act).
- Government Decree No. 156/1999 (XI 3) on Structure and Operation of the Council of Copyright Experts.
- Government Decree No. 158/2000 on the Determination on the Scope of Reprographic Equipments.
- Government Decree 117/2004 (IV 28) Korm. on the determination of the manner and conditions of the communication and making available to the public in the case of free use provided for in Article 38(5) of Act LXXVI of 1999 on Copyright.
- Act No. CXXX of 2016 on the Code of Civil Procedure.
- Law Decree No. 13/1979 on International Private Law (section 19).
- Government Decree 556/2013 (XII 30) on customs authority measures against goods, infringing certain intellectual property rights.
- Government Decree 138/2014 (IV 30) on the detailed rules related to the licensing of certain use of orphan works.
- Act No. LIII. of 1994 on judicial litigation (section 184/A).

15. Community laws and regulations:

- Directive 2004/48/EC of the European Parliament and of the Council of 29 April 2004 on the enforcement of intellectual property right, (hereinafter: 'IP Enforcement Directive').
- Directive 2009/24/EC of the European Parliament and of the Council of 23 April 2009 on the legal protection of computer programs.
- Council Directive 93/83/EEC aims at facilitating the cross-border transmission of audiovisual programmes such as, broadcasting via satellite and retransmission by cable.
- Directive 96/9/EC of The European Parliament and of the Council of 11 March 1996 on the legal protection of databases, (hereinafter: 'Database Directive').
- Directive 2001/29/EC of the European Parliament and of the Council of 22 May 2001 on the harmonization of certain aspects of copyright and related rights in the information society (INFOSOC-Directive).

- Directive 2001/84/EC of the European Parliament and of the Council of 27 September 2001 on the resale right for the benefit of the author of an original work of art (hereinafter: 'Resale Right Directive').
- Commission Recommendation (2005/737/EC) of 18 May 2005 on collective cross-border management of copyright and related rights for legitimate online music services.
- Directive 2006/115/EC of the European Parliament and of the Council of 12 December 2006 on rental right and lending right and on certain rights related to copyright in the field of intellectual property.
- Directive 2006/116/EC of the European Parliament and of the Council of 12 December 2006 on the term of protection of copyright and certain related rights.
- Directive 2011/77/EU of the European Parliament and of the Council of 27 September 2011 amending Directive 2006/116/EC on the term of protection of copyright and certain related rights.
- Directive 2012/28/EU of the European Parliament and of the Council of 25 October 2012 on certain permitted uses of orphan works.
- Regulation EU No. 608/2013 concerning customs enforcement of intellectual property rights and repealing Council Regulation (EC) No. 1383/2003.
- Directive 2014/26/EU of the European Parliament and of the Council of 26 February 2014 on collective management of copyright and related rights and multi-territorial licensing of rights in musical works for online use in the internal market.
- Commission Recommendation (2006/585/EC) of 24 August 2006 on the digitization and online accessibility of cultural material and digital preservation.
- European Parliament resolution of 13 March 2007 on the Commission Recommendation of 18 October 2005 on collective cross-border management of copyright and related rights for legitimate online music services (2005/737/EC) (2006/2008(INI)).[3]

16. Treaties, Conventions, and other International Norms:[4]

- Convention Establishing the World Intellectual Property Organization Signed at Stockholm on 14 July 1967 and as amended on 28 September 1979.
- Universal Copyright Convention as revised at Paris on 24 July 1971, with Appendix Declaration relating to Article XVII and Resolution concerning Article XI – promulgated by the Law Decree No. III of 1975.
- Berne Convention on the Protection of Literary and Artistic Works – promulgated by the Law Decree No. 4/1975[5] (hereinafter: 'Berne Convention').
- Geneva Convention for the Protection of Producers of Phonograms against Unauthorized Duplication of Their Phonograms – promulgated by the Law Decree No. 18/1975.

3. Pintz, *Találd fel magad,* 213.
4. P. Gyertyánfy et al., *A szerzői jogi törvény magyarázata* (Budapest: Complex, 2006), 458–498.
5. Pintz, *Találd fel magad,* 214.

- Rome Convention for the Protection of Performers, Producers of Phonograms and Broadcasting Organizations – promulgated by the Act No. XLIV of 1998[6] (hereinafter: 'Rome Convention').
- World Intellectual Property Organization (WIPO) Copyright Treaty – ratified by 57/1998 (XI 29) OGY. Parliament resolution; (hereinafter: 'WCT Treaty').
- WIPO Performances and Phonograms Treaty – ratified by 57/1998 (XI 29) OGY. Parliament resolution (hereinafter: 'WPPT Treaty').
- Agreement on Trade-Related Aspects of Intellectual Property Rights – promulgated by Act IX of 1998 (hereinafter: 'TRIPS Agreement').

§2. Subject Matter of Protection

17. The Hungarian Copyright Act provides protection for all literary scientific and art creations.

A creation shall enjoy copyright protection based on its individual, original nature originating from the intellectual activity of the author; the protection shall not be to any quantitative, qualitative, and aesthetic characteristics or to value judgments relating to the standard of the creation.[7]

The conceptual criteria of protection:

(a) literary, scientific, and artistic creations;
(b) intellectual activity of author;
(c) individuality;
(d) original nature;
(e) Independence of qualification of the work.[8]

18. The expression of literary and artistic works to be understood as a single legal and technical expression in the case of a given work, it is in general not necessary to determine whether it may be regarded as literary or artistic work.[9] It means all original intellectual creation irrespective of whether they may be regarded as belonging to the literary domain, to the artistic domain or to both of the same time.[10]

The traditional field of copyright in literature and artistic work shall include every production in the literary, scientific, and artistic domain.

However, some work may be regarded as being exclusively a literary work (short studies, novellas, or university studies) or exclusively artistic works (such as choreographic works and musicals). There are mixed works (e.g., encyclopaedias and multimedia works; these works contain literary and artistic works too).

6. L. Tattay, *A szellemi alkotások joga* (Budapest: Szent István Társulat, 2009), 405–409.
7. Article 1(3) of the Copyright Act.
8. Tattay, *A szellemi alkotások joga*, 90.
9. M. Ficsor, *Guide to the Copyright and Related Rights Treaties Administered by WIPO* (World Intellectual Property Organisation 2003), Index, Literary and Artistic Work.
10. In accordance of Art. 2(1) of the Berne Convention, the expression of literary or artistic works shall be deemed as works, protected by copyright.

When the Copyright Act additionally names science, this means protection of scientific books, conference materials, scientific studies, and not of scientific discoveries, ideas, or theories.

Scientific works means a category of literary and artistic work used in Hungarian copyright too. According to Article 2(1) of the Berne Convention, every production in the literary, scientific, and artistic domain are protected; thus, it is unnecessary and misleading since scientific subject matter of work is irrelevant from the viewpoint of copyright protection. For example, articles and books on scientific topics are protected not because of their topic but rather because they are articles and books, which are literary works.

The artistic and literary work shall be recognized irrespectively from qualitative, quantitative, and aesthetic factors. This, however, does not mean that any kind of creation is automatically eligible for copyright protection.

19. The intellectual activity of the author means personal intellectual activity, and only personal intellectual creations are protectable; it must concern a human protection. This is a conceptual criterion also in the case of joint authorship.

The work must be distinguished by its individuality from the mass of ordinary objects and reach a certain creative level. The work must have an imprint of personality of author or seal of personality of the author.

The originality of a work means that the author must subjectively create something new and not copy from another. It shall be understood that it is the author's own intellectual creation and is not copied from another work. The originality of work can derive from the form of contents of the work. The Copyright Act does not define the originality.

I. Different Categories of Protected Work

20. Article 1(2) a of Copyright Act lists the main categories of literary, scientific, and artistic works, such creations enjoy in particular the copyright protection:

(a) literary works (e.g., fictional works, technical works scientific works, journalistic works, etc.);
(b) speeches delivered in public;
(c) computer program creations and related documentation whether fixed in source code or object code or in any other form including application programs and operation systems,[11] (software protection);
(d) dramatic works, musical-dramatic works, ballets, and mimes;
(e) musical works with or without words;
(f) radio and television plays;
(g) cinematographic creations and the audiovisual works (cinematographic creations);
(h) creation produced by drawings, painting, sculpturing, and lithography or in other like manner, and designs thereof;
(i) artistic photographs;

11. Hungary was among the very first countries to recognize copyright protection for computer programs in 1983.

(j) maps or other cartographic creations;
(k) architectural creations and plans thereof, and plans of building complexes, and town planning projects;
(l) designs and engineering structures;
(m) applied art creations and designs thereof;
(n) costume, scenery and designs therefor,
(o) industrial design creations;
(p) databases rated as collections of works.[12]

The list is not exhaustive. For example, slogans, parodies, and puppet shows are not mentioned. This means that even though a category is not listed, it does not mean a work in that category is not protected.[13]

II. Works Excluded of Protection

21. Not all contents of production of the human mind are protected by copyright. Performances may be viewed as production of the mind, but they are not generally protected as such by copyright, but rather by a related right.

The Hungarian copyright laws exclude from protection official materials of government administration, judgments of courts, standards, and other official documents. By virtue of Article 1(4) Copyright Act:

> the protection provided by this Act shall not cover provisions of law, other legal instruments of state administration, judicial and authority decisions, authority or other official announcements and documents as well as standards an other like provisions made obligatory by legislative acts.

Official materials may be divided into primary or secondary categories:

(a) the primary category of official material includes the sources of law, acts, statutory instruments and regulations, judgment of courts, different documents of Parliament;
(b) the secondary category of official material involves the official translations,[14] decision of local governments, the announcements of authorities, the projects of regulation of law standards, etc.

No idea, principle concept, procedure, method of operation, or mathematical operation may be to the subject matter of copyright protection.[15]

The copyright protection shall not extend to facts and daily news that serve as a basis for press information.[16] The idea is not protected, but the expression of the idea

12. M. Ficsor, *The Protection of Copyright in Hungary*, in *International Copyright Law and Practice* 11 (P.E. Geller & M.B. Nimmer ed. Lexis/Nexis 2007).
13. In accordance with Art. 7 of the Copyright Act, the databases are protected as collective works.
14. This concerns only rough translation.
15. Article 1(6) of the Copyright Act.
16. Article 1(5) of the Copyright Act.

is protectable.[17] The exclusion of protection idea extends to any procedure process and discoveries.

In accordance with Article 1(7) of Copyright Act, the expressions of folklore shall not enjoy copyright protection. However, folk-art inspired works due to the author may be protected by copyright, if they have original and individual nature.

The expressions of folklore enshrine important aspects of the culture of a particular ethnic group. The expressions of folklore means characteristic elements of the traditional artistic heritage developed and maintained by a community, or by individual reflecting the traditional artistic exploitations of a community, including folk tales, folk poetry, folk songs, instrumental folk music, folk dances and plays, artistic forms of rituals, and other production of folk art. It has become an ever more generally shared opinion that copyright protection is not an appropriate means to protect expression of folklore, because authorship in general may not be established, and such expressions do not correspond to the concept of literary and artistic works.

The copyright shall not protect the expression of folklore due to the following circumstances:

(a) the expression of folklore does not recognize author by copyright;
(b) the works of folklore are not usually fixed or recorded;
(c) the expressions of folklore may be fixed and recorded in various considerably different forms.[18]

III. Special Categories of Works

A. Computer Software

22. Software has been protected in Hungary since 1983. Software program creations as specific genres of Copyright are regulated in Chapter VI, and Articles 58–60 of Copyright Act.

In accordance with Article 1(2)(c) of Copyright Act, computer program creations and related documentation, whether fixed in source code or object code or in any other form, including application programs and operation systems are protected.[19]

The computer program creation and its documentation may be recognized as software whether fixed in source code or object code[20] for being able to run on a computer. It may still be read and understood, at least by experts.[21]

A source code is the version of a computer program that has not been compiled yet being able to run in a computer. It may still be read and understood by humans at least, by experts. Where the copy of a computer program is obtained by a user, it is

17. The discoveries, ideas, methods of mathematical operations, methods of operations also shall not enjoy patent protection.
18. Ficsor, *Guide to the Copyright*, index, expression of folklore.
19. The TRIPS Agreement clarified in Art. 10.1 that computer programs, whether in source or object code, shall be protected as literary works.
20. Ficsor, *Guide to the Copyright*, index, computer software.
21. *Ibid.*, Index, Source code.

normally in the form of a compiled object code, and the source code (which may be read and understood by humans, at least by the experts) is not made available. This has made it necessary to permit de-compilation for the creation of interoperable programs under certain conditions.[22]

An object code is that version of a computer program which is already compiled from the source code of the program, and thus it is ready to be run on a computer. The object code files the Berne Convention and the WCT defines the software identically.[23]

The computer program means a set of instructions expressed in words, codes, schemes, or any other form, which is capable, when incorporated in a machine-readable medium of causing a computer – an electronic or similar device having information-processing capabilities – to perform or to achieve a particular task.[24]

The application programs (Microsoft, Office, Excel, and Cap) are important parts of computer programs.

The operation system (Windows, Linux) also shall belong to computer programs.[25]

The meaning of the expression 'computer software' is not precisely defined and is not used in a uniform way. In Hungary, it was a kind of synonym of a computer program and sometimes referred to everything that may be included in computers or in a machine in readable form. At that time, this basically meant the extension of the concept to databases and the first simple video games. With the widespread use of digital technology, this second meaning has become so broad that it has lost its value as *terminus technicus*. The expression – even more than before – cannot be considered a sufficient stable and precise term and can hardly be regarded relevant from the viewpoint of Hungarian copyright norm.[26]

The requirements for any work to be covered by copyright protection are that it should be original and of an individual creation. The law does not distinguish between creations based on their qualitative or quantitative level. This however, does not mean that any kind of software must be a creation, thus a program made by routine work that is not more than an obvious solution of a simple task cannot be regarded as a creation made by an original, individual act of intellectual activity.

The software with its documentation shall be able to form part of the program. The main task of software should be considered to enter into contact with the related parts of computer and the user and obtain the aimed task.

According to Hungarian Copyright Act, algorithms, mathematical expressions, principles, and laws underlie a program or a part or an element thereof is not protected by copyright.

The copyright belongs to the person who created the work.[27]

The software may be assigned, thus a legal entity may be the holder of economic rights of the software.

22. Ficsor, *Guide to the Copyright*, index, source code.
23. The WCT Treaty did the same in its Art. 4, with some wording differences. Computer programs are protected as literary works within the meaning of Art. 2 of the Berne Convention. Such protection applies to computer programs, whatever may be the mode or form of their expression.
24. Ficsor, *Guide to the Copyright*, index, computer program.
25. Tattay, *A szellemi alkotások joga*, 224.
26. Ficsor, 'The Protection of Copyright in Hungary', 10.
27. Article 4(1) of the Copyright Act.

As a derivative work may be recognized, the adaptation of the software from the original program language to a different program language.[28]

The software may be created in the framework of employment. The employer shall acquire the economic rights in following cases:

(a) If the program is created while the employee executes his or her duties.
(b) If the employee follows instructions given to him or her by employer.

Unless otherwise agreed in contract, the author who created the software under employment does not have the right to remuneration in the case of use and transfer the software. He or she receives only his or her salary.[29]

The author of the software has exclusive rights to use to transfer of use and assignment of software, any use of the software requires the consent of the author.

23. There are important limitations in respect of the exclusive use of software. If a contract defines the purpose of the transaction, e.g., the use of the program, the steps or operations required to accomplish that purpose will not require further consent from the author.

The ideas, principles, concepts, procedures, and methods of operation are not protected in computer programs.[30] In accordance with Article 59(1) of Copyright Act:

> unless otherwise agreed, the author's exclusive right shall not cover the reproduction, alteration, adaptation, translation and any other modification of the software, including the correction of mistakes, as well as the reproduction of the product resulting from these acts in so far as these acts of use are carried out by the person authorized to acquire the software in compliance with the intended purpose of the software.

24. The software may be copied in an exceptional case. No provision in the licensing agreement shall prohibit the user from making a back-up copy of the software if it is necessary.[31] Back-up copy means a machine-readable copy of a computer program made to prevent losing a program. Making a back-up-copy is permitted by the Hungarian Copyright Act if it is made by the lawful owner of the copy.[32]

In accordance with Article 59(3) of Copyright Act:

> the person entitled to use a copy of the software may, without the author's authorization, observe and study the operation of the software and may make a trial use thereof in the course of its loading, displaying on a monitor, running, transmission or storage in order to get to know the idea or principle serving as a basis for any elements of the software.

28. Article 4(2) of the Copyright Act.
29. Tattay, *A Szellemi Alkotások joga*, 225.
30. Article 58(2) of the Copyright Act.
31. Article 59(1) of the Copyright Act.
32. Making a back-up copy is an exception to the exclusive right of reproduction if it is made by the lawful owner of the original copy.

The economic rights relating to the software shall be assignable.[33]

25. From the viewpoint of software protection, the interface shall be mentioned. The interface is a surface of connection which makes the connection of software possible with other software or hardware. The interface may be indispensable for the acquisition of the information necessary to the combined operation of an independently created piece of software with another piece of software. In accordance with Article 58(1) of Copyright Act, the protection of software shall not extend to the idea, principle, concept, procedure, method of operation, or mathematical operation on which the interface of the software is based.

According to Article 60(1) of Copyright Act, no authorization of the author shall be required for the reproduction or translation of a code which is indispensable for the acquisition of the information necessary to the combined operation of independently created software with software supposing that:

(a) these acts of use are performed by the authorized user or another person entitled to use the copy of the software or a person put in charge of performing these acts by these persons;
(b) the information necessary to the combined operation has not been readily accessible to the persons referred to above;
(c) these acts of use are limited to those parts of the software which are necessary for ensuring the combined operation.

The so-called interface use may not be considered as the free use of the software.

B. Databases

26. Databases are regulated by the Copyright Act in Chapter VII (as specific genre of copyright) and in its XI/A Chapter (as neighbouring right). Databases as collection of works are protected under Article 1(2)(p) of Copyright Act.

A database shall mean a collection of independent works, data, or other material arranged in a systematic or methodical way whose materials are individually accessible by computer devices or other means.[34] Data consists of factual information, which as such, does not enjoy intellectual property protection.

The concept of database in Hungary has also been extended to all collections irrespective of whether they contain only works or only mere data. The concept of database has ceased to be connected to the use of electronic or analogous processes in Hungary, and it has been extended to all collections of information irrespective of whether they exist in printed form, in electronic storage, or in any other format.[35]

A collection (compilation) of data is to be protected by copyright, if it – by reason of the selection or arrangement of the data – is an intellectual creation. A collection of data shall be under copyright protection if the selection, arrangement, or

33. The software can be an exception from prohibition of the transmission of copyrighted works recognized use of the software.
34. Article 60/A(1) of the Copyright Act defines the database as collection of work.
35. Ficsor, *Guide to the Copyright*, index, database.

editing of its contents is of individual and original nature (collection of works).[36] The protection shall apply to the collection of works even if its parts or materials do not or may not enjoy copyright protection.

The copyright shall belong to the editor of the database. The copyright protection of a collection of works shall not extend to the materials of the collection of works. The regulations applying to databases shall not apply to the software used in the making or operation of databases having contents accessible by computer devices.

The authorized person, who has access to the use of a database, is free to carry out the necessary operation on the database. According to Article 62(1) of Copyright Act:

> The performance of acts necessary to get access to the contents of the database rated as a collection of works and to use the contents thereof in accordance with the intended purpose by a person authorized to use the database shall not be subject to the author's authorization.

The database may be:

(a) under copyright protection;
(b) under protection of neighbouring right;
(c) under copyright and neighbouring right protection equally;
(d) without legal protection.[37]

The economic rights relating to databases (as collection of works) shall be assignable.[38]

27. The databases may enjoy copyright protection on the one hand and, on the other hand, neighbouring right protection. The sui generis rights of databases protected since 1991.

The sui generis rights of database makers are instituted without prejudice to other rights, notably copyrights that may exist with respect to database or its content.

The economic rights shall belong to makers of a database. The maker of the database is the person who has a substantial investment in obtaining, verifying, or presenting concerning of database. The authorization of the maker of a database shall be required,[39] affecting of the contents of the database, for:

(a) its reproduction by making of one or several copies (extrication);
(b) making it available to the public through distribution of copies of the database or through communication to the public (utilization).

The distribution related to databases shall be understood to cover the following cases:

(a) release for commercial circulation through sale; or

---

36. In accordance with Art. 7(1) of the Copyright Act, the database may be protected if it is original and individual.
37. L. Tattay, 'Az adatbázisok jogvédelme', *Gazdaság és jog* 11, no. 5 (2003): 15–17.
38. Article 61(2) of the Copyright Act.
39. Article 84/A(1) of the Copyright Act.

(b) by the transfer of the right of ownership in a different manner; and
(c) import into the country for purposes of commercial circulation and rental.

The content of the database may be communicated to the public[40] may be by cable or any other means or any other manner so that the members of the public can choose the place and the time of availability individually.

The uses of database generally shall be subject to remuneration.

The right to database is subject to general limitations that apply to databases that have been made public. In accordance with Article 84/A(3) of Copyright Act, a lawful user of a database may not be prevented from extracting or reutilizing of substantial contents of database, but may not without the consent of maker of database, extract or reutilize such contents repeatedly and systematically, if such usage conflicts with the normal exploitation of the database or unreasonably prejudices the rights-owner's legitimate interests.[41] The Duration of protection of right to database (related right) is fifteen years.

28. By virtue of Article 84/A(7) of Copyright Act, the rights mentioned above shall belong to the maker of the database irrespective of whether the database is under copyright protection or any other legal protection. These rights shall apply to the maker of the database even if parts of, or materials in, the database are not, or cannot be, under copyright protection or any other legal protection.

As the maker of the database shall be recognized – the natural or legal person or business company – without legal entity at whose initiative, in whose name and at whose risk the creation of the database occurred and who/which provided the necessary resources therefore only in the case of obtaining verifying or presenting the contents of database have the investment of considerable resources.[42]

The protection of databases does not extend to the mere data or other unprotected material contained in them, and at the same time, their protection is to be without prejudice to the protection of works and objects of related rights included in them.

The rights of the maker of the database shall be without prejudice to the rights of the authors of the individual works included in the database as well as to other rights subsisting in specific materials of the contents of the database.[43]

The uses of the database shall be subject to remuneration, unless otherwise ruled by legislation.

29. There are several exceptions from the exclusive rights of use: These uses falling with the exception shall not be subject to payment of any consideration.

The databases made public may be used entirely or partly from third persons. No authorization of the maker of the database shall be required for the copying distribution or make a database available or its specific parts – whether repeated or regular – of an insubstantial part of the contents of the database by a person authorized for the use of the database made public.[44]

---

40. As provided for in Art. 26(8) of the Copyright Act, the communication to the public means the interactive or on demand communication.
41. Pintz, *Találd fel magad*, 122.
42. Article 84/A(6) of the Copyright Act defines the maker of database.
43. Article 84/A(8) of the Copyright Act.
44. Article 84/(3) of the Copyright Act.

Not even the person legally authorized for the use of the database made public may perform acts that conflict with normal exploitation of the database or unreasonably prejudice the legitimate interests of the maker of the database.

The use of a database without authorization of the maker of a database shall be without prejudice to the rights of the authors of the individual works included in the database as well as to the neighbouring rights applying to other materials of the contents of the database.

The following features of the use of the contents of databases may be considered as free use that is, the permission of author thereto is not necessary and remuneration shall not be paid:[45]

(a) an extract of even a substantial part of the contents of the database may be made by anyone for private purpose if it is not designed for earning or increasing income even in an indirect way. This provision shall not apply to databases operated by computer devices;[46]
(b) a copy of even a substantial part of the contents of the database may be made – in a manner and to the extent consistent with the use involved – for purposes of school education and scientific research subject to the requirements of reference to the source and avoidance of earning or increasing income even in an indirect way.[47] This use granted exclusively for purposes of school education and scientific research;
(c) an extraction or reutilization of even a substantial part of the contents of the database may be made – in a manner and to the extent consistent with the use involved – for purposes of evidence in court of justice, public administration, or other authority proceedings.[48]

C. Others: Cinematographic Works

30. By virtue of Article 1(2)(g) of the Copyright Act, cinematographic creations and other audiovisual works enjoy copyright protection; nevertheless, Chapter IX of Copyright Act regulates cinematographic creations and other audiovisual works. The film producers have neighbouring rights,[49] and the television broadcasters/organizations are also subject to neighbouring rights.[50]

In Hungary, a special Act concerning the cinematographic creations, named the Act II of 2004 on motion picture (hereinafter: 'the Film Law'),[51] regulates all domains of creative activity of the motion picture production. The Film Law establishes a legal background of Hungarian film industry and motion picture culture.

---

45. These uses falling with the free uses shall not be subject to payment of any consideration and to any authorization of the author.
46. Article 84/C(1) of the Copyright Act.
47. Article 84/C(2) of the Copyright Act.
48. Article 84/C of the Copyright Act.
49. Article 82 of the Copyright Act.
50. Article 80 of the Copyright Act.
51. The Film Law enhance and preserve the values of the Hungarian motion picture culture.

31. Audiovisual work is a shorter synonym of the expression of cinematographic work to which are estimated works expressed by a process analogous to cinematography appearing in the non-exhaustive list of literary or artistic works.[52]

The expressions 'cinematographic works', 'cinematographic creations', 'film works', 'audiovisual works', and 'films' are synonyms in international copyright literature.

By virtue of Article 64(1) of Copyright Act, the notion of cinematographic works (cinematographic creations) are defined:

> a cinematographic work shall be taken to mean a work which is expressed by motion pictures arranged in a predetermined order and accompanied or not by sound, irrespective of which carrier the work has been fixed on.

The Film Law also defines the notion of the cinematographic work (film):

> a cinematographic work means a work created by any technical procedure, which consists of a series of motion pictures set in a defined order without audio or connected by audio and is deemed to be an author's work under Copyright Act.[53]

The definition of a cinematographic work involved in Article 2 of the Film Register Treaty states: A cinematographic work consisting of a series of fixed related images, with or without accompanying sounds, susceptible to being made visible, and where accompanied by sound, susceptible to being made audible by means of appropriate devices.[54]

The conceptual criteria of a cinematographic work are as follows:

(a) a work consists of motion picture set;
(b) the motion picture set arranged in predetermined order;
(c) may be with or without sound;
(d) susceptible to being made visible by means of appropriate devices; in general, it is regarded to be an element of the concept of cinematographic works that when the series related images are made visible by means of appropriate devices, it imparts the impression of motion;
(e) irrespective of which carrier the work has been fixed on.

The feature films produced for movie projection, the television film, the publicity and documentary films as well as cartoons and educational films shall in particular be rated as cinematographic work.

32. The director of the film is the most essential person: he or she is author and represents all other authors. The other essential creators of films are as follows:

- the assistant director;
- the music composer;

52. Article 2(1) of the Berne Convention.
53. Article 2(2) of the Film Law.
54. Ficsor, *Guide to the Copyright*, index, audiovisual works.

- the sound director;
- the cameraman;
- creators of works of fine arts, designs, and authors of artistic photographs, script writers;
- composers and lyricists;
- producers of sound recordings.

The Copyright Act defines who may consider author of cinematographic work: The authors of the literary and musical works prepared for motion pictures, the director of the motion picture, and all other persons having made creative contribution to the production of the whole of the motion picture shall be taken to be the authors of the cinematographic creation.[55] This provision shall not prejudice the statutory right of the authors of other works used in producing the cinematographic creation. The Film Act defines likewise the notion of the authors of audiovisual work:

> Film authors means authors of literary and musical works produced for the purpose of the film, the director of the film, and all persons who have contributed creatively to developing the entire film, as well as authors of other works used in the film.[56]

33. In Hungary, the producer of the film is entitled to the use of a cinematographic work not automatically, but on the basis of a film contract.[57] The producer may exercise the rights due to him or her under the contract jointly with another natural or legal person, whether Hungarian or foreign.[58]

The Copyright Act defines the concept of producer of the film: The natural or legal person or the unincorporated economic organization who or which on their own behalf initiates and organizes the creation of the film and provides therefore the necessary financial and other conditions shall be taken to be the producer of the film.[59]

The Film Act also defines the status of the film producer. Film producer means a legal person or business company without legal personality who or which proposes and organizes the realization of the film in his or her own name, ensuring the financial and other conditions for the film production.[60]

34. The cinematographic works have several genre-specific rules. The so-called final cut right shall be first mentioned. The final cut means the acceptance of final version of cinematographic work. This right may be exercised by the director and the producer of the film jointly.

The Copyright Act contains the right to final cut:

---

55. Article 64(2) of the Copyright Act.
56. Article 2(3) of the Film Act.
57. Under some copyright laws following the common law tradition, the producer of an audiovisual work is the original owner of the copyright, and under some of those laws, he or she is even recognized as the author of such work.
58. Lontai, *A Szellemi alkotások joga*, 127.
59. Article 64(3) of the Copyright Act.
60. Article 2(4) of the Film Law.

> A cinematographic creation shall be considered as completed if its final version is accepted as such by the authors and the producer.[61] The final version may not thereafter be unilaterally altered by either party; that is the right to final cut concerns the right of integrity.

The director and producer of the film have the right to alter the film. The alteration of a completed film by addition, omission, or replacement or in any other form shall be subject to the authorization of the authors and the producer.[62] Except for the right to 'final cut' and the alteration, the producer may take action towards the protection of the moral rights of the authors.

The cinematographic creations shall not be subject to the general provisions relating to works created as duty under an employment contract.[63]

35. The genre-specific rules of the film agreement (synchronization agreement) are characterized by peculiar character of cinematographic works.[64]

Pursuant to the contract concluded on the production of a cinematographic creation, the author, that is, director of the film[65] shall assign to the producer the right of the use of the cinematographic creation and of the authorization of its use. The consent of the composer to conclusion of the film contract shall not be required:[66] The economic rights of composers cannot be assigned. The assignment of the right of use shall not extend to the economic rights to receive remuneration for copying film works to rental and to rebroadcasting of the cinematographic works. The organization performing the collective administration shall be entitled to receive the remuneration in these cases. The producer cannot acquire these economic rights.[67]

The economic rights, acquired on the basis of film agreement (synchronization agreement) by producer extend particularly:

(a) to the use of the title and figures of cinematographic work and to communication of the work to the public as following;
(b) to have his or her work communicated to the public by broadcasting; and
(c) to the communication to the public of an owned programme by cable or any like device or in any like manner, including the authorizing of another person therefore;
(d) to make available his or her work to the public in any other manner so that the members of the public can choose the place and time of the availability individually;
(e) the author shall also have the exclusive right to authorize the retransmission to the public of his or her work broadcast or transmitted in the programme of a radio or television organization or of an entity communicating its own programme by cable or by any other means to the public, simultaneously and in an unaltered manner via an organization other than the original one.

---

61. Article 65(1) of the Copyright Act.
62. Article 65(2) of the Copyright Act.
63. Article 30 of the Copyright Act.
64. Tattay, *A Szellemi Alkotások joga*, 231–237.
65. Article 66(1) of the Copyright Act.
66. Lontai, *A Szellemi alkotások*, 129.
67. E. Lontai et al., *A Szellemi alkotások joga, Magyar Polgári Jog* (Budapest: Eötvös József Könyvkiadó, 2004), 152.

The producer is also entitled to authorize others to the use of the above-mentioned rights.

36. According to Copyright Act regarding each manner of use, remuneration shall be due to the author (i.e., all authors of the film) separately.

The support made available to the producer for the creation of the film shall be considered as income related to the use.[68] It is the producer's obligation to pay the remuneration. The producer is obliged, at least once a year, to report in writing to the author on the incomes related to the use of the cinematographic creation by modes of use.[69] The term of performance of the synchronization agreement is absolutely important from the point of view of the risk and profitability of investments.

On the basis of the film agreement (synchronization agreement), the producer shall begin the cinematographic work within four years.

Pursuant to Article 66(6), should the producer fail to start the work of adaptation to the screen within four years from the acceptance of the work, or if such work is started but is not completed within a reasonable deadline, the author may unilaterally terminate the agreement and may raise claim to the payment of a proportional remuneration.

Any advance payment disbursed to the author shall be considered as due to him, and the author may freely dispose of his work.[70]

37. In the case of a film to be created in future, the producer may accept the work (the literary work, treatment of film, screenplay, etc.) and carry out the film. The producer of the cinematographic work may accept this within six months or return it for the author. If the producer returns the work for correction, the author shall be obliged to make changes a reasonable deadline.[71]

If the contract is concluded on a work to be created in the future for purposes of a cinematographic work, the delay of acceptation of the film is six months. The producer is obliged to notify the author in writing within six months from the delivery of the work whether he or she accepts it or requests it to be corrected. In case the work is returned to the author for corrections an appropriate deadline is to be set for performing those corrections.[72]

The producer is obliged to make it known whether he or she accepts the corrected work within three months from the delivery of the corrected work. Should the producer fail to meet his or her obligation to make a statement on the acceptance of the work or of the corrected work, the work shall be considered as accepted.[73]

38. The producer has the right to remake the film. The right to remake means that the producer of cinematographic production may create a new variety of the film. The author may not enter into another contract on the production of the new film in this period.

Within ten years from the completion of the production of the film, the author may not enter into another contract on the production of a new film unless it is consented

68. Article 65(3) of the Copyright Act.
69. Article 66(5) of the Copyright Act.
70. Lontai et al., *A Szellemi alkotások joga*, 152.
71. Article 66(7) of the Copyright Act.
72. Tattay, *A Szellemi Alkotások joga*, 235.
73. Article 66(7) of the Copyright Act.

to by the producer. This limitation shall also extend to characteristic figures in a cartoon or puppet film and – in case it is agreed between the parties – to another work of the author with the same topic as is that of the work created and utilized for the production of the film.[74]

39. Film distribution means making the original or reproduced copies of a film accessible to the public. The Copyright Act also defines[75] the concept of distribution.

The author shall have the exclusive right to distribute his work and to authorize others therefore. The making accessible to the public of the original copy or the reproduced copies of the work through putting into circulation or their offer for putting into circulation shall be taken to mean distribution. Accordingly, the distribution of film can happen:

(a) by marketing, or offers films for marketing;
(b) by operating cinemas;
(c) by publishing, selling, renting in usufruct films in any media particularly in video and DVD;
(d) importing films into Hungary for commercial purposes;
(e) possessing the copy of the film for commercial purposes.[76]

The film distributor or any other organization engaged in the distribution of film in a businesslike manner is a business company.

§3. Conditions of Protection

I. Formal Requirements

40. Pursuant to the Article 9(1) of Copyright Act, the entirety of authors' rights – moral rights and economic rights – shall belong to the author from the time of the creation of the work. Works become eligible for protection from the very first moment of their creation without any further condition.

The copyright protection of work is formality free in Hungary. All works of copyright are protected without filing of the applications[77] and registration that is without formal requirements.[78]

Under Article 5(2) of the Berne Convention, the enjoyment and exercise of rights must not be subject to any formality; such enjoyment and such exercise shall be independent of the existence of protection in the country of origin of the work. Consequently apart from the provisions of this convention, the extent of protection, as well as the means of redress afforded to the author to protect his or her rights, shall

74. Article 60(8) of the Copyright Act.
75. Article 23(1) of the Copyright Act.
76. Article 2(15) of the Film Law.
77. The objects if industrial property, i.e., patents, trademarks, industrial designs, and geographical indications shall registered by the Office.
78. This means that the fixation of work shall not be required to protection of copyrighted works.

be governed exclusively by the laws of the country where protection is claimed shall be granted.[79] Hungary, as a member of Berne Convention, does not impose formalities on copyright protection.

In Hungary, the general principle of copyright shall be considered the formality-free protection of copyrighted works. The works of authors are protected automatically once procedural and administrative requirements from the time of creation of the work have begun.

II. Substantive Requirements

41. The Hungarian Copyright Act provides protection for all literary, scientific, and art creations.[80]

In accordance with Article 1(3) of the Copyright Act, the creation shall enjoy copyright protection based on its individual, original nature originating from the intellectual activity of the author. The protection shall not be to any quantitative, qualitative, and aesthetic characteristics or to value judgments relating to the standard of the creation.

The literary and artistic works are to be understood as a single legal and technical expression in the case of a given work; it is in general not necessary to determine whether it may be regarded as literary or artistic work.

The intellectual activity of the author is an indispensable criterion of protection. The intellectual activity of the author means personal intellectual activity; only personal intellectual creations are protectable, as it must concern a human protection.

The work must be distinguished by its individuality from the mass of ordinary objects and reach a certain creative level, as the work must have an imprint of personality of the author. The creations of copyright are considerably dependent from the author's personality.[81]

The originality of a work means that the author most subjectively creates something new and not copies from another. It shall be understood that it is the author's own intellectual creation and is not copied from another work. The originality of a work can derive from the form of contents of the work. The Copyright Act does not define originality.

The artistic and literary work shall be recognized irrespectively from qualitative, quantitative, and aesthetic factors. This however does not mean that any kind of creations are automatically eligible for copyright protection.

---

79. Article 5(1) of the Berne Convention prescribes that the authors shall enjoy, in respect of works for which they are protected under this convention, in countries of the union other than the country of origin, the rights which their respective laws do now or may hereafter grant to their nationals, as well as the rights specially granted by this convention.

80. In accordance of Art. 2(1) of the Berne Convention, the expression of literary or artistic works means the traditional literature and artistic field of copyright which shall include every production in the literary, scientific, and artistic domain.

81. A. Szinger & P. B. Tóth, *Gyakorlati utmutató a szerzöi joghoz* (Budapest: Novissima Kiadó, 2004), 22.

§4. Ownership

I. The Author (Initial Authorship)

42. The authors, their successor in title, the copyright holder, and holders of neighbouring rights are usually mentioned in the Copyright Act. These persons are entitled to exploitation and protection of their copyrighted works. These persons may be called the beneficiaries of protection.[82]

The beneficiaries of protection are those physical persons who and legal entitles which may acquire, enjoy, and exercise protection of copyright or related rights under norms of Hungarian copyright and international norms.[83]

The beneficiaries may be classed as:

(a) authors;
(b) other initial beneficiaries of economic rights;
(c) secondary beneficiaries of economic rights.

43. By virtue of Article 4(1) of Copyright Act, the copyright shall belong to the person who has created the work. The entirety of author's right – moral and material rights – shall belong to the author from the time of the creation of the work.

The author is creator of a work, in general a physical person – the intellectual creator of the work. Special legal status such as individual legal capacity is not a precondition; even a child or legally incompetent person may be an author.[84] It follows from the nature of a work as a personal individual and original creation that copyright can only originate from a natural person and not a legal person. The author shall always be recognized as initial beneficiaries of copyright.[85] Hungarian copyright recognizes only natural person as author.

The Hungarian Copyright Act recognizes not authorship of legal titles – such as employers, producers, and so on – who take the initiative and responsibility for the creation of the work and who in general through determining the objectives and certain features of the work to be created, also have a direct or indirect impact on the nature, style, and contents of the work.

In the case of computer-assisted and computer-produced work and databases, only the individual or a physical person may be considered as author.

Computer-assisted work means a work for the creation of which a computer and appropriate computer program are used by the author as assistance,[86] e.g., for a

---

82. Economic rights can be assigned or transferred in the cases and under the conditions specified in law. The person who acquires economic rights is thereafter entitled to dispose them, unless otherwise stipulated in the contract concerning the assignment of the economic rights.
83. Ficsor, *Guide to the Copyright*, Index, Beneficiaries of protection.
84. F.K. Beier & G. Schricker (eds), *German Industrial Property, Copyright and Antitrust Laws* 42 (F.K. Beier, G. Schricker & W. Fikentscher eds , 2nd edn of IIC Studies, vol. 6 VCH Verlaggesellschaft 1989).
85. Articles 4 and 6 of the Copyright Act.
86. Article 4(1) of the Copyright Act.

computer-assisted musical work to produce and try out variant forms from which the computer selects one or more of his or her works.[87]

Computer-produced work means a work produced by means of a computer, in which the creative contribution of human beings are so indirect and merged into the whole of the work to such an extent that it is difficult or impossible to attribute authorship in respect of such contributors.[88] In the case of the computer-produced works, a physical person also may be considered as author. The initial beneficiary of copyright is the person by whom, or legal entity by which, the arrangement for creation of the work is made.

44. Employers, natural and legal persons, or business companies, may be the initial beneficiaries of copyrighted works in the case of works made for hire and related to collective works. In accordance with Article 30(1) of the Copyright Act, in respect of works created under employment or other service relations, the delivery of work to the employer shall imply the transfer of economic rights upon the employer as successor in title to the author.

By virtue of Article 6(1) of the Copyright Act, in the case of a collective work, the copyright shall be transferred by legal succession to the natural or legal person or business company without legal entity at whose initiative and under whose instructions the work was created and who published it in his or her own name.

45. Secondary beneficiaries of copyright protection may be a physical person or legal entity succeeding – by assignment, transfer, or by inheritance – the original owner of copyright or related rights as the owner of the rights concerned:

(a) the person who acquired the economic rights of author by inheritance of copyrighted work;[89]
(b) the licensee, the authors are generally the beneficiaries of works but there are the cases in which the initial beneficiary is some person other than creator of work;[90]
(c) the person who has acquired the work by assignment;[91]
(d) the phonograph[92] producer;[93]
(e) the radio and television organization;[94]
(f) the collective management organization;[95]
(g) the film producer.[96]

46. The derivative works enjoy copyright protection. The authors of derivative works are the persons who carried out the alteration by translation, adaptation, or

87. Ficsor, *Guide to the Copyright,* Index, Computer-assisted work.
88. *Ibid.*, Index, Computer-produced work.
89. Article 9(4) of the Copyright Act.
90. Article 42(1) of the Copyright Act.
91. Article 55 of the Copyright Act.
92. Ficsor, *Guide to the Copyright,* Index, Beneficiaries of protection.
93. Article 76 of the Copyright Act.
94. Article 80 of the Copyright Act.
95. Article 85 of the Copyright Act.
96. Article 66(4)-(7) of the Copyright Act.

arrangement of pre-existing work and have been created to form a new copyrighted work.[97]

In accordance with Article 4(2) of the Copyright Act: Without prejudice to the rights of the author of an original work, the alteration, adoption, translation of the original work, shall be under copyright protection if the work thus obtained is of individual, original character.

Original work means all work which by definition are original productions (intellectual creations), thus it would not be appropriate to use the adjective 'original' as reference to the works originality. The term 'original work' is not used in that way, but simply in contrast with the term 'derivative work' as a synonym of pre-existing work that is, the work which has been transformed through translation, adaptation, or other alteration, into a derivative work.[98]

The term 'original work' has a specific meaning in the provisions of the *droit de suite* (resale right) in the expression 'original work of art'. In this context, the expression has the same meaning 'original of a work'.[99]

47. The authors are entitled to publish their works anonymously or under pseudonyms.[100] The authors of anonymous and pseudonymous work shall enjoy in such works copyright protection generally established in the Copyright Act. By virtue of Article 8 of the Copyright Act, they are represented in the exercise of their rights by the editor or publisher until they reveal their identities.

Anonymous work means a work for which an author wishes to be anonymous, and who therefore does not indicate on the copies of his or her work, or in connection with communication to the public, either his or her name or pseudonym.[101]

Pseudonymous work means a work of an author who discloses and makes available the work under pseudonym.[102] The author's rights shall be exercised, until the author becomes known, by the person who first published the work if a work was published anonymously or under pseudonym.

In the case of a new, legitimate use of a work that has already been published under the author's name, the author is entitled to request that the work be used in the future without designating his or her name.[103]

There are specialized problems of identification of owner of right and term of protection in the case of anonymous and pseudonymous works.[104]

---

97. In general, this term i.e., derivative work refers to the translation, adaptation, arrangement, and similar alteration of pre-existing works which are protected under Art. 2(3) of the Berne Convention as such without prejudice to the copyright in the pre-existing works.
98. Ficsor, *Guide to the Copyright*, Index, Original work.
99. *Ibid.*
100. Article 12(3) of the Copyright Act.
101. Ficsor, *Guide to the Copyright*, Index, Anonymous work.
102. *Ibid.*, Index, Pseudonymous work.
103. Article 12(3) of the Copyright Act.
104. Article 7(3) of the Berne Convention contains specific provisions on the term of protection of anonymous work, and Art. 15(3) of the convention provides for a presumption that the publisher, whose name appears on such a work, is the representative of the author, and is entitled to protect and enforce the authors' rights. These provisions of the convention cease to apply if the author reveals his or her identity and establishes his or her claim to authorship of the work.

II. Joint Works/Works Created by Several Persons

48. Works may be created by several persons collectively or separately. Works done through cooperation that imply a creative collaboration between different authors shall be recognized as joint works.

The works created by several persons are as follows:

(a) joint work;[105]
(b) connected works;[106]
(c) collectively created works;[107]
(d) collection of works.[108]

Such authors do not merely add the results of their creative efforts, but rather direct and organize their work with a view towards a common result. The joint work means a work in the creation of which several individuals have participated. The joint work usually becomes the common property of its authors. In case of a joint work, if several persons created a work together, and their respective contribution cannot be separately exploited, they are joint authors. The moral and economic rights shall belong jointly to the joint authors.

The author of a joint work, the parts of which cannot be used independently, shall enjoy the copyright protection jointly and – in case of any doubt – in equal proportions; however, any of the joint authors may take action independently in the event of infringement of copyright.[109] In the case of joint work, several authors' work is created on the same material of the same genre (common painting, common sculpture).

Article 5(2) of the Copyright Act contains the concept of connected work:

> In case a joint work is made up of parts which can be used independently (connected works), independent copyright shall belong to each of the joint authors with regard to the respective individual part. The authorisation of all authors of the original joint work shall required if any part of the joint work wanted to be joined with a different work.

In the case of connected works, several authors combine their works for a joint exploitation, e.g., a book and its illustration. In this case, each author may require from the other authors consent to divulgation, exploitation, and alteration. In the case of connected works, several authors create works that belong to the creations of different genre (e.g., a building with one or more sculptures).

By virtue of Article 6(1) of the Copyright Act:

> In the case of collectively created works (e.g. national standard) the copyright shall be transferred by legal succession to the natural or legal person or business

105. Article 5(1) of the Copyright Act.
106. Article 5(2) of the Copyright Act.
107. Article 6(1) of the Copyright Act.
108. Article 6(2) of the Copyright Act.
109. Article 5(1) of the Copyright Act.

> company without legal entity at whose initiative and under whose instructions the work was created and who published it in his own name.

In the case of a collectively created work (e.g., national standard), the copyright shall be transferred by legal succession to the natural or legal person or business company without legal entity at whose initiative and under whose instructions the work was created and who published it in his own name – who or which becomes original owner of copyright – and in which the various contributors, because of their great number and indirect nature are merged into totality of work so that it is impossible, or at the least impracticable, to identify the individual works and their authors.[110]

A work shall be regarded as collectively created if the contributions of the authors cooperating in creation of the work are combined in the product of joint creation in a manner that makes the separate determination of the individual authors' right impossible.[111]

Collection of works or data means a work in any form is protected as a work if, by the reason of selection or arrangement of its content, it constitutes an intellectual creation.[112]

Pursuant to Article 7(1) of the Copyright Act:

> A collection shall be under copyright protection if the selection, arrangement or editing of its contents is individual and original nature (collection of works). The protection shall apply to the collection of works even if its parts or materials do not or may not enjoy copyright protection.

The protection shall apply to the collection of works even if its parts or materials do not or may not enjoy copyright protection (e.g., an anthology of contemporary poets) on one hand and cannot enjoy protection on the other hand (e.g., a collection of old postcards). Regarding the whole of the collection of the work, the copyright shall belong to the editor; however, this shall be without prejudice to the independent rights of the authors of the individual works selected for inclusion in the collection as well as of the holders of rights in neighbouring rights covered achievements.[113]

The copyright protection of a collection of works shall not extend to the materials of the collection of works.

III. Works Made for Hire

49. The expression 'work made for hire' does not exist in the Hungarian language. In harmony with international copyright law, works made for hire means a specific term covering both works created by employed authors under their employment, and certain works ordered or commissioned. The latter works are covered by the concept of works made for hire if they are specially ordered or commissioned for use as a contribution to a collective work: as part of a motion picture or other audiovisual work;

110. Gyertyánfy et al., *A szerzöi jogi törvény magyarázata*, 53–54.
111. Article 6(2) of the Copyright Act.
112. Ficsor, *Guide to the Copyright*, index, collection of works.
113. Article 7(2) of the Copyright Act.

as a translation; as a supplementary work; as a compilation; as an instructional text; as a test as an answer key for a test; or as an atlas, if the parties expressly agree, in a written instrument signed by them, that the work shall be considered a work made for hire.[114]

The work made for hire may be created:

(a) under employment;[115]
(b) on the basis of the contract of agency;[116]
(c) on the basis of contract of commission.[117]

The parties of contract of the commission are the commission agent and the principal. Anyone may include a contract in either position. There are important differences between the contract of agency and contract of commission:

(a) the agent makes a contract in name and on behalf of a principal; however, a commission agent makes a transaction in his or her own name for the principal's benefit;
(b) the contract of agency may be any activity, but the contract of commission is always aimed at concluding a contract;
(c) the contract of agency may be either onerous or gratuitous, while the contracts of commission are always onerous.

The prescriptions of works made for hire are included in the Copyright Act.[118]

50. The Copyright Act Article 30 regulates only the works created under employment and other service relations.

A work created under employment or other service relation is an artistic or literary work created by a person who by reason of his or her employment, is under the obligation to create achievements in the field of activity of the employer.

The provisions relating to a work created as duty under an employment contract shall be applied *mutatis mutandis* if the work has been created by a person employed as a public or civil servant belonging to the professional staff of the armed forces and police forces and being in active service, or a cooperative member employed under real relations similar to those of employment relations.[119]

The conceptual criteria of a work created under employment according to the Copyright Act are as follows:

(a) an existing relationship between author and employer;
(b) within the required labour relationship, the author shall be obliged to create original and individual new copyrighted works;

114. Ficsor, *Guide to the Copyright*, index, works made for hire.
115. Article 30 of the Copyright Act.
116. Article 6:272 of new Civil Code (Law No. V if 2013).
117. Article 6.281 of new Civil Code (Law No. V if 2013).
118. Articles 6:276 et 6:280 of new Civil Code (Law No. V of 2013).
119. Article 30(7) of the Copyright Act.

(c) the creation of new original and individual works to be realized by the author should be in the field of activity of the employer.[120]

In the case of works created under employment, the employer is the first beneficiary. A created work can be deemed to be a service nature only if it is unequivocally clear that it is within the very domain of employment, and the labour contract or the actual specification of the task laid down within the performance requirements so implies, thus obliging the author in terms of his or her labour relationship to create works within the scope of activity of his or her employer.

The employer or other person for whom the work is prepared is considered as first beneficiary of the copyright law of the country, and subject to written agreement to the contrary, owns all rights comprised in copyright, The employer shall be recognized as successor in title of author of a work, created under employment.

The contract to creation of a work and all declaration of legal nature relating to rights and obligations of parties shall be laid down in writing.[121]

Unless otherwise agreed, the delivery of the work to the employer shall imply the transfer of economic rights upon the employer who is successor in title to the author, if the creation of the work is the author's duty under an employment contract.[122]

The employee shall not be entitled to receive remuneration in case of works made under employment. The author receives only his or her salary.[123] However, the author shall be entitled to an appropriate remuneration if the employer authorized another person to use the work or transfers to another person the economic rights relating to the work. The author shall continue, even in the case of acquisition of rights by employer, to be entitled to the remuneration which is due even after the transfer of the right, e.g., the literary work transferred by the employer to film producer to make a film, pursuant to prescriptions of Copyright Act.[124]

51. The moral rights of the author are limited by virtue of a labour contract between employer and author. After delivery of the work, the divulgation may be made by the employer and not by author. After the divulgation of the works by the employer, the author may not withdraw his or her work. This prescription affects the author's moral right to withdraw.[125]

If the author is not entitled to withdraw his or her work, he or she may request that his or her name is left unmentioned. The employer may alter his or her work of service nature, and the author is not entitled to make alterations. This rule limits the authors' moral right of integrity.[126]

Article 35(5) of the Copyright Act prescribes as follows concerning the limitations of moral rights of authors:

120. Tattay, *A Szellemi Alkotások joga*, 122.
121. Article 30(6) of the Copyright Act.
122. Article 30(1) of the Copyright Act.
123. Article 30(3) of the Copyright Act.
124. Article 30(4) of the Copyright Act.
125. Gy. Csécsy, *A szellemi alkotások joga* (Miskolc: Novotni Kiadó, 2007), 49.
126. Lontai et al., *A Szellemi alkotások joga*, 63.

> If the creation of the work is author's duty under an employment contract, the delivery of the work to the employer shall be considered as an act of consent to the disclosure of the work to the public. In the case of the author's declaration aimed at withdrawing his work the employer is obliged to make no mention of the author's name. The author's name shall be likewise left unmentioned, at the author's request, if availing himself of his employer's rights the employer makes alteration in the work without the author's agreement.

The cinematographic creations shall not be subject to the general provisions relating to works created as duty under an employment contract.

52. The works made for hire can be achieved on the base of the contract of agency. The rules of contract of agency are involved in Articles 6:272–6:280 of new Civil Code (Law No. V of 2013).

Under a contract of agency, the agent shall attend matters entrusted to him or her. The agent shall perform an agency with the principal's instructions and in conformity with his or her interest.[127]

On the basis of the contract of agency, the author may submit a work of literature, cartoon and photography, article, or caricature, for deal as far as other intellectual creations. The agent may create a copyrighted work on the basis of the contract of agency (write a book or draw a caricature for a revue) on the one hand and conclude use of contract on the other. The contract of agency shall be in written form in the case of creation or assignment of a work.

Under Article 6:275 of the new Civil Code (Law No. V of 2013), a general rule may be considered, that the agent must act in person.[128] This obligation follows from confidential nature of agency. Provision of information is a necessary obligation of the agent, who must inform his or her principal at the latter's request – or even in absence thereof where necessary – of his or her activity or the state of affairs.

The agent shall inform his or her principal of his or her activities and the state of affairs upon request or, if necessary, even without a request, particularly if employment of another person has become necessary or if the instructions need to be changed due to the occurrence of new circumstances.[129] The agent shall notify the principal as soon as he or she fulfils his or her agency.[130]

On termination of the agency, the agent must give an account of his or her activity and hand over to the principal everything he or she has acquired in the course or as a result of performing the matter entrusted to him or her. On termination of the contract, the principal must pay remuneration for the agent. As a general rule, the remuneration falls due on the termination of the contract.[131] Remuneration is due even if the agent's activity was unsuccessful but was careful and businesslike.

---

127. Article 6:272 of new Civil Code (Law No. V of 2013).
128. In accordance with Art. 6:275(1) of the new Civil Code (Law No. V of 2013), the agent shall proceed in person; he or she shall, however, be entitled to employ other persons if the principal has agreed thereto or if it is implied by the nature of the agency. An agent shall be liable for the persons he or she employs as if he or she had carried out the matter entrusted to him or her.
129. Article 6:275(1) of the new Civil Code (Law No. V of 2013).
130. Article 6:275(2) of the new Civil Code (Law No. V of 2013).
131. Article 6:276(2) of the new Civil Code (Law No. V of 2013).

According to Article 6:276(1) new Civil Code (Law No. V of 2013), the principal may reduce the remuneration or deny payment thereof upon proving failure to obtain a result was due, wholly or in part, to cause for which the agent is responsible. It is usually in the case of the agency that the agent often undertakes an obligation towards the third person in the interest of the principal. Costs that arise in connection with the handling of a matter shall be borne by the principal. The agent is obliged to advance any costs.[132]

The contract shall be terminated even if the agency has not been fulfilled, if:

(a) either party cancels the contract by notice;
(b) either party dies or, if a legal person is dissolved, unless the dissolved legal person has a legal successor;
(c) the principal becomes partially or fully incompetent or if the agent becomes incompetent;
(d) the object of the agency becomes obsolete.

The contract shall terminate even without performance of the agency, if either party denounces the contract by notice. Accordingly, notice may be by the principal and may be by the agent.

53. The works made for hire may be created under commission agency contracts. The rules of commission agency contracts are included in Article 6:281–6:287 of new Civil Code (Law No. V of 2013.

The object of commission contract is always the conclusion of a contract.[133] In defining commission, the law refers to conclusion of a contract of sale or other contract but the closing provision of the contract of commission spell out that a contract by which the commission agent undertakes to conclude a contract other than a contract of sale shall also be deemed to be a contract of commission.

In framework of the commission contract, the commission agent may conclude a copyright license contract or copyright assignment. The commission agent's main obligation is to conclude a contract or sale of some other contract. He or she must make a contract with a third person, under the terms and conditions defined in contract of commission, in his or her own name, but for the benefit of the principal. Should the commission agent enter into contract of sale under conditions more favourable to the principal than those stipulated in the commission contract, the benefit resulting therefrom will be due to the principal.[134]

The principal has the right to determine the type and the content of the contract to be made with a third person constituting the object of the contract of commission.

In case the commission agent is unable to make a contract at the limit price, he or she must notify the principal and ask for instructions.

If he or she is able to sell below or to buy above, the price fixed, he or she is to ask for the principal's instruction.

A commission contract may be determined by its fulfilment in the prescribed manner or by notice. The contract is terminated by fulfilment in the prescribed manner

132. Article 6:276(3) of the new Civil Code (Law No. V of 2013).
133. Article 6:281(1) of the new Civil Code (Law No. V of 2013).
134. Article 6:286(1) of the new Civil Code (Law No. V of 2013).

if the contract of sale has been performed and the commissioner has settled account with the principal.

§5. Transfer

54. Under the international norms of copyright, the economic rights may be constituted as generally transferable or not transferable.[135] The moral rights of authors in contrast are not transferable.

In harmony with Hungarian copyright law, with certain exceptions, the economic rights may not be assigned, may not devolve on anyone else, and may not be renounced.[136]

In Hungary, generally neither the economic nor the moral rights are assignable. Hungarian copyright law recognizes only in certain cases the validity of assignment of copyrighted works.[137]

The economic rights shall pass on through inheritance, and the author is free to dispose of them to the end in the case of death. By virtue of Article 9(5) of the Copyright Act, the persons becoming holders of economic rights by inheritance may dispose of them to each other's benefit. Exceptionally under the conditions specified by the Copyright Act, the economic rights may be assigned or may pass on to another person.[138] Unless otherwise provided in the assignment contract, the acquirer of the rights may dispose of the economic rights he has acquired. The copyright owner has various options as to the way in which he exercises his rights. He or she may exercise them personally, or may give a license for their use.[139]

The main forms of transfer of copyright may be considered as:

(a) assignment of copyright;
(b) license.

I. Assignment of Copyright

55. The transfer of copyright means the assignment of copyright by the owner of such rights (assignor) to a physical person or legal entity (assignee) as a property. In contrast with a license, which includes only granting permission to perform certain specified acts of transfer (assignment) of a right – at least in the case of exclusive rights means that – the right of authorization or prohibition of acts covered by the right is transferred to the assignee. The assignor transfers the ownership of the work to the assignee.

135. In accordance with Art. 9(2) of the Copyright Act, the author may not assign his or her moral rights, not devolve on anyone else, and may be not renounced by the author.
136. Under Art. 9(4) of the Copyright Act, the economic rights shall pass by inheritance.
137. The software, the database, the film, as well as works ordered for publicity purpose.
138. Lontai, *A Szellemi alkotások*, 73–74.
139. Csécsy, *A szellemi alkotások joga*, 41.

The economic rights shall pass by inheritance, and the author is free to dispose of them to that end for the case of his or her death. The person becoming a holder of economic rights by inheritance may dispose of them to each other's benefit.[140]

The Copyright Act in exceptional cases allows the possibility[141] of assignment:

> In the cases and under the conditions specified by the Copyright Act, the economic rights may be assigned or may pass to (an) other person(s). Unless otherwise provided in the assignment contract, the acquirer of rights may dispose of the economic rights he or she has acquired.[142]

By virtue to Article 55 of Copyright Act, the provisions relating to license agreements shall apply *mutatis mutandis* to agreements aimed at assigning the author's economic rights and to licensing the use of performers' performances. The Copyright Act contains subsidiary special rules for the assignment of copyrighted works:

(a) the software,[143] that is, the economic rights relating to the software shall be assignable;
(b) database,[144] that is, the economic rights relating to the databases also shall be assignable;
(c) works ordered for publicity purposes,[145] the economic rights relating to a work ordered for publicity purposes shall also be assignable to the user;
(d) cinematographic creations and other audiovisual works acts.[146] In respect of films, the Copyright Act provides:

> Unless otherwise stipulated, pursuant to the contract concluded on the production of cinematographic creations the author – except the composer of a musical work with or without text – shall assign to the producer the right of the use of the cinematographic creation and of the authorization of its use.

The assignment of cinematographic works shall not extend to the following rights:

(a) to the copying of works for private purpose;
(b) the right of rental relating to cinematographic creations or to works or included in a sound recording;
(c) the right of rebroadcasting.

56. The author is entitled to conclude a license contract to transfer the use of his or her rights. The author cannot transfer his or her moral rights to another person. The rights of use may be transferred separately or divided between several persons.

---

140. Article 9(5) of the Copyright Act.
141. Article 9(6) of the Copyright Act.
142. The possibility of the transfer is in Hungarian Copyright an exceptional case.
143. Article 58(3) of the Copyright Act.
144. Article 61(2) of the Copyright Act.
145. Article 63(1) of the Copyright Act.
146. Article 66(1) of the Copyright Act.

From the aspect of the application of law, of great significance are the provisions of Copyright Act related to license agreements. On the basis of a license agreement, the author authorizes the use of his or her work and the user is obliged to pay remuneration therefore.[147]

Authorization is given by the owner of copyrighted work (licensor) to a person or legal entity (licensee) to perform a certain act in respect of the work. By a license, the ownership of copyright is not transferred; the right of further authorization is maintained by licensor.

The provisions of the Copyright Act relating to license agreement shall apply *mutatis mutandis* to agreement aimed at assigning the author's economic rights[148] and to licensing the use of performer's performances.[149]

II. Licenses

57. The license means authorization given by the owner of copyrighted work (licensor) to a person or legal entity (licensee) to perform a certain act in respect of the work. The rights of the licensee are limited depending on the form and extent of the license granted. There are two basic forms that are the exclusive and non-exclusive licenses.[150] The author should receive equitable remuneration related to license contract.

'It should be borne in mind that an author's license of a given use of his work presumed to pay him remuneration proportional to the revenues generated by licensed use.'[151]

The holder shall guarantee for the whole duration of the license contract that no third parties hold rights in the copyright preventing or limiting the right of use.

Legal warranty stipulated in license contracts only in case of an explicit provision of the license contract concerned.

The licensee may transfer the license or grant sub-licenses to third parties only with the express consent of the holder.[152]

If the contents of the license agreement cannot be interpreted unambiguously, the interpretation most favourable for the author shall be accepted.[153]

A license agreement is a typical juristic act, ensuring the lawful utilization of works protected by the copyright. Under Hungarian copyright law, the regulation of use contract is realized on three different levels:

(a) general rules of license agreements, Chapter V and Articles 42–55 of the Copyright Act include general provisions for license agreements and provisions for publishing agreements;

147. Article 42(1) of the Copyright Act.
148. Article 106(1) of the Copyright Act.
149. Article 55 of the Copyright Act.
150. Ficsor, *Guide to the Copyright*, index, license, licensor, licensee.
151. Ficsor, 'The Protection of Copyright in Hungary', 25.
152. Generally the assignment and the sub-license of license shall not be allowed by licensee.
153. Article 42(3) of the Copyright Act.

(b) specific rules concerning software program creation, databases, works ordered for publicity purposes, motion picture works, as far as creations of fine art, artistic photography, architecture, applied arts and industrial design, designs of engineering structures regulated by the Copyright Act,[154] taking into consideration the specific features and genres. As these rules stipulate only particular dispositions, rules of the Civil Code,[155] if these issues directly fall within its scope, which are not governed by the legislation on copyright of Hungary.

The applicable rules have to be complied from several fields related to given license contract. Essentially the contract aimed at the transfer of the material rights of authors, and the utilization of their performances also belong to this sphere as they are explicitly mentioned by the Copyright Act. Thus, they are of specific nature by comparison to the general use contracts. Nevertheless, complementary rules governing them have not been provided.

Relating to the stipulations of Chapter V of the Copyright Act, it contains general provisions applicable to all kinds of use contracts.

58. The general provisions of the Civil Code, covering all contracts are applicable to contractual conditions for which neither the general nor the genre-specific rules of the use contracts have stipulations.[156]

The use of contract set the conditions for utilization of copyrighted works belong to a particular, sui generis type, even if they are frequently related to other types of contracts within the greater family of the contracts.

The most important rules of the Copyright Act related to copyright agreements are as follows:

(a) conclusion of contracts;
(b) formal requirements;
(c) special features of copyright license contracts;
(d) exclusive and non-exclusive license contracts;
(e) rules concerning works to be created in future;
(f) the termination of license agreements.

59. The license contracts may be concluded on the basis of a work already completed at the time of contract or the purposes of the contract included the future creation of one or more works. License contracts concerning the works created in the future or those already existing have a common and essential feature in that the author or successor in title grants permission to exercise the right of use on the one hand, and a right arises for the user or its successor in title, on the other hand. Unless otherwise provided, the license agreement shall be drawn up in a written form.

The drawing up of the agreement in a written form shall be not obligatory if the agreement is designed for publication in a daily or periodical.

---

154. Chapters VI–X and Arts 58–67 of the Copyright Act.
155. Lontai et al., *A Szellemi alkotások joga*, 139.
156. The draft new Civil Code of Hungary contains the regulation of the license contracts.

Article 24 of the Code of the Hungarian Code of Private International Law[157] provides that in international relations, parties to a contract may freely decide which law governs contractual issues, such as interpretation and performance.[158] By virtue of Article 25(c) of the Code, the right of user shall be applied, when the parties have not chosen the applicable contract law.[159]

60. The Civil Code contains subsidiary rules concerning the conclusion of license contract. Article 6.73 of the new Civil Code (Law No. V of 2013) authorizes a preliminary contract with the author, and the user may conclude a preliminary contract, including in detail all substantial elements of contract on use to be concluded on different works. In the case of a preliminary contract (*pactum de contrahendo*), the parties agree to enter into contract at a later date. Preliminary contract gives rise to a contractual obligation; failure of the parties to make a contract may be a cause for the court to consummate one and to determine its content.[160]

In the case of a preliminary copyright license contract, the agreement must be made in written form. A breach of preliminary contract may be considered, if the author refuses to conclude a license agreement. The rule of *clausula rebus sic stantibus* comes into play in the case of preliminary contracts as well.[161] Notably, the parties do not make a final contract because some conditions is yet to be met, and if the particular condition is not satisfied, the parties may refuse to make a contract. The authorization of use shall cover the territory of the republic of Hungary, and its terms shall be in compliance with the period customary in agreements concluded on the use of work similar to subject matter of the agreement.

61. An option is known as a special kind of purchase applied by analogy, which grants a right concerning future performances and uses. The difference between an option contract and an agreement in principle is that the former does not establish a mutual obligation for future contracting; instead, it establishes a unilateral right of use so that, during the validity of the contract, the beneficiary may put into being a license contract by unilateral declaration. The option contract needs the indication of work, remuneration of the author, and rights and a form of use.

The author and user shall agree on an option contract. In accordance with Article 6:225 of the new Civil Code (Law No. V of 2013), the option grants a right concerning

---

157. Law-Decree No. 13 of 1979 on International Private Law.

158. The law selected by the parties on concluding the contract or at a later date shall apply to contracts. In the absence of a selected law, the law applicable to each contract shall be determined according to the Code of the Hungarian Code of Private International Law.

159. In accordance with Art. 25(c) of the Code of the Hungarian Code of Private International Law, the law relating to contracts shall be the law of the state in which the following persons have their place of residence, usual place of abode, central office or premises at the date of the conclusion of the contract) in the case of a contract relating to the utilization of rights falling under copyright protection, the user.

160. In accordance with Art. 6:73 (1)of the new Civil Code (Law No. V of 2013), parties may agree in principle on concluding a contract at a later date (preliminary contract). The preliminary contract shall be concluded in the form stipulated for the contract and shall be binding for the parties to conclude a contract.

161. Either party shall be entitled to refuse to conclude a contract if he or she provides proof of inability to perform the contract by virtue of a circumstance that has occurred after the conclusion of the preliminary contract pursuant to Art. 6:192 of new Civil Code (Law No. V of 2013).

of future performances and uses. In accordance with Article 6:225(1) of the new Civil Code (Law No. V of 2013), if an owner grants a right of purchase (option) to another person, the beneficiary shall be entitled to buy the thing with a unilateral statement. Agreements on options to purchase shall be put in writing with the thing and the purchase price specifically indicated.

Unless otherwise provided by law, the court may relieve an owner of his or her obligation deriving from the option to purchase if the owner is able to prove that, after granting the option, his or her circumstances have altered significantly, as a consequence of which performance of his or her obligation cannot be reasonably expected.[162]

62. The special regulation of license contracts as compared to the system of the new Civil Code has been justified on the basis of particular features of work protected by the copyright, and the amalgamation of personal and material rights, on the one hand, and on the typically weaker position of the authors within the process of contracting on the other.

One must keep in mind the concentration of works from the field of culture and the information industry.

The license contracts are aimed to bring into equilibrium the position of the bargaining parties.[163] The main specified rules of copyright license contracts are as follows:

(a) the author does not have the freedom to choose the type of license contract; the form of license contracts must be concluded in conformity with the concerned genre. Both parties agree they may deviate from the regulations pertaining to a licensing contract, to the extent that such deviation is not prohibited by law;
(b) the Copyright Act prescribes so-called unilateral cogency. This means that it is not possible to deviate from rules provided by the Copyright Act that protects the author's interests;
(c) principle of non-exclusivity;
(d) best-seller clause;
(e) prohibition of lifework-contracts;
(f) rules of performance of the contract.

63. The Copyright Act prescribes the rules of the performance of copyright licenses. Article 49(1) of Copyright Act stipulates:

> The user is obliged to make a statement on the acceptance of a work delivered to him under an agreement relating to work created in the future within two months from the date of delivery of the work to him. If the user returns the work to the author for the corrections to be made, it shall be counted from the date of delivery of the corrected work. If no statement is made by the user within the term available to him for that purpose, the work shall be considered as accepted.

The authorization of the reproduction of the work shall in case of doubt cover the distribution of the reproduced copies of the work. This shall not imply, however, the

162. The so-called *clausula rebus sic stantibus*: Art. 6.192 of New Civil Code (Act No. V of 2013).
163. G. Faludi, *Felhasználási szerződés* (Budapest: Közgazdasági és Jogi Könyvkiadó, 19.99), 32.

importation into the country of copies of the work for purposes for putting into circulation.[164] In a case in which the agreement was concluded on a work to be created in the future, the user shall be entitled to repeatedly return the finished work, with reference to justified grounds and setting appropriate deadlines, to the author for purposes of correction.[165]

In accordance with Article 46(3) of the Copyright Act, in a case in which the author refuses to make corrections without reasonable grounds, or fails to make the corrections by the deadline set, the user may rescind from the agreement without the payment of remuneration.

In a case in which work proves unsuitable for use even after the correction, only a reduced remuneration shall be paid to the author.[166]

64. The Copyright Act includes prescriptions concerning the exclusive and non-exclusive copyright licenses. By virtue of Article 43(1) of the Copyright Act:

> the licensee agreement shall provide the exclusive right to use only by an express stipulation to that end. In case an exclusive authorisation obtains, only the acquirer of the right may exploit. The author may not grant further authorisation for the use of the work, and even he himself remains entitled to use the work only if this is stipulated in the contract.

The Copyright Act disposes two kinds of exclusive license. In one of these, the copyright owner assumes only the obligation not to grant to anyone any right of use; however, he or she maintains the right to use the copyrighted work. In the other case, the owner not only renounces his or her right to grant further licenses of use but also agrees not to use the copyrighted work.[167]

In the case of works made for deals and reviews, the right of use shall not be exclusive. The authorization of use may be limited to a specific domain, period of time, manner of use, or extent of use. The holder may terminate the exclusivity of a license, subject to a proportional reduction in the royalty if the licensee does not begin the use of the copyrighted work within a reasonable period of time.[168]

65. By virtue of copyright legislation, it is not possible to conclude a license agreement for all future works.

Pursuant to Article 44(1) of the Copyright Act, the stipulation of the license agreement whereby the author authorizes the use of an indefinite number of works to be created in the future shall be taken as null and void.

Nullity of the life-work contracts underlined by the fact that specific causes for the nullity of its contents are applicable in this case.

This means that no contract may validly be concluded for the use of an indefinite number of works created in the future. If the contract provides for the use an indefinite number of future works, then it is null and void, and it is irrelevant whether the kinds of works to be created are formulated clearly and precisely. If an author obliges to

164. Csécsy, *A szellemi alkotások joga*, 71.
165. Lontai et al., *A Szellemi alkotások joga*, 139.
166. Article 49(4) of the Copyright Act.
167. Lontai et al., *A Szellemi alkotások joga*, 142–143.
168. *Ibid.*, 146.

create and transfer an indefinite number of works and to grant a license for their use on the basis of a contract concluded for a fixed duration, then the nullity is established.[169]

The declaration of nullity is a measure of protection for the weaker party, but it is not clear that it is the most efficient one. In this case, the legal consequences of nullity have to be examined and Article 3 of the Copyright Act, which makes reference to the new Civil Code (Law No. V of 2013) that is in the case of nullity, the provisions of the new Civil Code (Law No. V of 2013) shall be applied.[170]

Recourse to the new Civil Code (Law No. V of 2013) is not absolutely needed if the parties wish to conclude a license contract similar to a life-work contract, giving a preference to aspects of practicability and efficient functioning and requiring appropriate guarantees. The Copyright Act permits the author to conclude for more and precisely stipulated works to be created in the future even for an indefinite time.[171] In contrast to prohibition of life-work contract, a license agreement relating to works to be created in the future may be concluded so that the future works are referred to only by their genre or character of the work.[172]

66. In accordance with Article 46(1), the user may confer the authorization or may grant a sub-license to a third person for the use of the work only subject to the author's express consent thereto. An express term is needed to authorize a licensee to grant any sub-license to third party.

The authorization of use shall without the author's consent, be transferred to the successor in title in case of economic organization authorized for the use is winding-up or the affected organizational unit is withdrawn.

In case the user confers his or her rights or grants a sub-license without the author's consent,[173] or the authorization of the use is transferred without the author's consent, the user and the acquirer of rights shall be jointly and severely made responsible for the fulfilment of license agreement.[174]

The authorization of reproduction shall permit the user to fix in video or sound recording or copy it by computer or onto an electronic data carrier only on express stipulation to that end.

Under Article 47(3) of Copyright Act, the authorization of the distribution of the work shall permit the user to import copies of the work for purposes of putting them into circulation only on express stipulation to that end.

67. Performance, or set off with the same legal consequence is the most frequent case of termination of contracts. The license agreement shall cease to have effect:

(a) with the lapse of the time determined in the agreement;
(b) with emergence of circumstances referred to in the agreement;
(c) as well as after the expiration of term of protection;
(d) by the death of the licensee;
(e) by unilateral or bilateral declaration of parties.

169. Faludi, *Felhasználási szerződés*, 151.
170. Article 6:88 of new Civil Code (Law No. V 2013).
171. Article 52(1) of the Copyright Act.
172. Ficsor, 'The Protection of Copyright in Hungary', 26.
173. Ficsor, 'The Protection of Copyright in Hungary', 26.
174. Article 46(3) of the Copyright Act.

The license agreement may be terminated by the death of the licensee. As a general rule, a copyright license contract is not terminated by the death of licensee or licensor. Thus, there are those which terminate upon the death of either party. The licensor's death terminates any performance that can only be effected by author in the case of works to be created in future. It may happen that the contract will be terminated without performance having occurred at the will of the parties:

(a) by bilateral declaration (terminating or rescinding the contract);
(b) by a unilateral declaration of contract (renouncement, withdrawal).

The contract in these cases may be terminated: with effect for the future (*ex nunc*); or with retroactive effect to the conclusion of contract (*ex tunc*).

The licensee may terminate the agreement in the case of a work to be created in future by rescission (retroactive respect) in the cases:

(a) the author refuses to make corrections without reasonable grounds; or
(b) fails to make correction by the deadline set, the licensee may withdraw from the agreement without the payment of remuneration.

68. The author may terminate the license agreement with unilateral declaration if, with reference to any reasonable grounds, he or she withdraws his or her authorization to publish his or her work for the public or forbids the further use of his or her work having been published.

The exercise of right of termination is subject to the author providing a security for making up for the damage having arisen until the time of the announcement of the denunciation.

The right of termination of license agreement with unilateral declaration is limited. If the agreement of use is concluded with an indefinite term or for a period, longer than five years, the author may exercise his or her rights of termination with renouncement only after two years have passed from the date of the conclusion of agreement.[175]

The author may exercise his or her right of renouncement with the effect for future only after he or she has set a deadline for the licensee for the fulfilment of term of the terms and conditions of the agreement and that the deadline has expired with no result achieved.

An author may abrogate a contract containing a license of exclusive use:

(a) if the user fails to commence the use of the work within the period determined in the contract or a period that can reasonably be expected in the given situation; or
(b) if the user exercises the rights he or she has acquired through the contract in a manner that is obviously inappropriate for the implementation of goals of the agreement or in manner other than consistent with the intended purpose.[176]

175. Article 51(2) of the Copyright Act.
176. Article 51(1) of the Copyright Act.

This regulation entitles the author to terminate an exclusive license under either of the following conditions: if the license fails to start the use of the work within the period determined in contract or within a period that may be reasonably foreseen in the given case when the contract provides no specific period; or if the licensee exercises licensed rights in a manner that is obviously inappropriate for the fulfilment of the objectives of the contract or that is otherwise inconsistent with those objectives.[177]

Instead of abrogation, an author may terminate the exclusivity of a license while proportionally reducing the remuneration to be paid to him for use.[178]

69. If the agreement of use relating to the works to be created in future is concluded so that the future work is referred only by genre or character, either party may terminate the agreement with a six months 'notice after the lapse of five years' term.[179]

This prescription means that the licensor and licensee both have right to termination of use with unilateral declaration but only after the lapse of five years and with a notice of six months, which means the author may not in advance waive his right of determination.

If the author terminates the copyright license agreement with reference to any reasonable ground, or the author renounces the license agreement, he or she withdraws his authorization to publish his work to the public or forbids the further use of his work having been published[180] in harmony with a kind of *clause rebus sic stantibus* may be applied.[181] The exercise of the right of termination of license agreement is subject to the author providing security for making up for the damage having arisen till the time of the announcement of denunciation.

If the author terminates the copyright license contract with renouncement or cancellation and if following the termination of the license agreement, he or she wants again to consent to publishing his or her work to the public or to its continued use, the previous user shall have the right of first refusal of the license.

The Hungarian Copyright Act includes provisions in order to strengthen the contractual position of author. For example, the so-called best-seller clause provides that the court may alter the license agreement even if such an agreement infringes the author's substantive lawful interest in having equitable share in the income on use because of the considerable increase in the demand for the use of the work, following the conclusion of the agreement the difference in value between the services respectively provided by the parties becomes strikingly great.[182]

70. The official licensing of the use of orphan works: The Copyright Act and the Government Decree No. 138/2014 (IV 30) on the detailed provisions of the use of orphan works (hereinafter: 'Orphan Work Decree').

In Accordance with 41/A§(1) Copyrighted work and a performance of neighbouring right may be regarded as orphan work, if the rightholder is unknown, or the residence of the rightholder is unknown in spite of the fact that a diligent search needed to find

177. Ficsor, 'The Protection of Copyright in Hungary', 25.
178. Article 51(5) of the Copyright Act.
179. Article 52(1) of the Copyright Act.
180. Article 53(1) of the Copyright Act.
181. Article 241 of the Civil Code.
182. Article 48 of the Copyright Act.

the author or rightholder was carried out but with no success. (concept of orphan work includes important charcters of these works).

It is important to emphasize, a work can only be used as an orphan work when no other ways of legitimate use based on the rightholders license is possible. Given that in these cases the rightholders are unidentified or their location is unknown, therefore the use could not be licensed in any other way.

According to the 41/B. § (1) of Hungarian Copyright Act, the Hungarian Intellectual Property Office (hereinafter: 'Office') shall grant upon request a license in conjunction with the determination of a remuneration that is to be in compliance with the manner and extent of use to those who have taken measures that can generally be expected under the given circumstances for the search of the author with due consideration to the type of work and manner of use, and the search of the author was unsuccessful.

The license shall be effective for a maximum term of five years, within the territory of Hungary, non-exclusive, non-assignable, and shall not grant authorization for granting further licenses and for the adaptation of the work.

The orphan works shall be available to use:

- upon request of any user, following the licensing procedure determining the remuneration in the decision of the Hungarian Intellectual Property Office (HIPO);
- freely and free of remuneration by certain beneficiary organizations in accordance with the provisions of the Copyright Act and the Orphan Work Decree.

The procedure is free of charges, merely the user of orphan work shall pay administration fee of proceeding.[183]

Pursuant to the Article 41/F. § (1) of Copyright Act, the application form may be submitted by electronic means through the customer portal.

Different special forms are available for the licensing of use of literary works:

- visual creations;
- audiovisual works;
- and records;
- and of other types of copyright protected works.

The electronic application forms are available for download in PDF and RTF format from the menu bar on the right side.

In accordance with Article 41/A(9) of the Copyright Act, the Hungarian Intellectual Property Office (HIPO) cannot grant license for the use of works falling under collective management of rights. In these cases, the license shall be granted by the competent collective management organizations and there is no possibility to use them freely.

71. The use of orphan works by certain beneficiary organizations: As a result of the transposition of Directive 2012/28/EU of the European Parliament and of the

183. The administration fee of the proceeding is HUF 30,000, in case the permitted use is not intended directly or even indirectly to earn or to increase income;
– HUF 92,500, in case the permitted use is intended directly or even indirectly to earn or to increase income.

Council on certain permitted uses of orphan works, the Copyright Act provides the opportunity for certain beneficiary organizations to use orphan works contained in their collections or archives for certain purposes from the 29 October 2014 onwards. The prerequisite of such use is that a diligent search shall be carried out with good faith, with taking all necessary measures that can be expected in the given situation in order to find the rightholders remained unsuccessful, and certain information in regard to the work concerned shall be recorded in the unified online database maintained by the European Union.

In accordance with Article 38(5) of Copyright Act, the following organizations shall be regarded as beneficiary ones:

- publicly accessible libraries, educational establishments and museums;
- as well as archives, film or audio;
- heritage institutions; and
- public-service broadcasting organizations.

By Virtue of 41/F. § (1)of Copyright Act, the orphan works can be used by beneficiary organizations freely in order to fulfil their public-interest mission, in the following ways:

(a) by making the orphan work available to the public online;
(b) by acts of reproduction [to be digitalized for the purpose of making publicly accessible in accordance with point a), or indexing, cataloguing, preservation or restoration].

The rules of specific ways of 'free use' may be exercised by beneficiary organizations that apply to books, journals, newspapers, magazines or other works published in written form, as well as to cinematographic or audiovisual works and to phonograms. These provisions apply, furthermore, to the cinematographic or audiovisual works and phonograms produced by public-service broadcasting organizations and contained in their archives.

The first step, as prerequisite of starting the procedure, is a diligent search with good faith to be carried out by the beneficiary organization in order to reveal the identity and the location of the rightholder(s).

The use of the sources of information listed in the Orphan Work Decree specified for each type of works is a minimal requirement to allow the 'free use' of such works as orphan works.

The requested search for the rightholder shall be carried out with taking all necessary measures that can be expected in the given situation in good faith, thus in case the beneficiary organization has certain knowledge on the rightholder(s) identity or location, which could certainly be found by using a source of information not listed in the Orphan Work Decree, the work shall not be used as an orphan work, either.

72. The databases of orphan works: The orphan works recorded in the database and to being accessible in the collection of such organization can be used freely by any beneficiary organization, regardless of who was the one that carried out the search for the rightholders.

In accordance with 41/G. § (1) of Copyright Act, the beneficiary organization shall maintain records of all search carried out in order to find the rightholder(s). In these records, it is recommended to indicate detailed sources of information used during the search, thus it can be proved that the search in order to enable to prove the search was carried out with taking all necessary measures that can be expected in the given situation in good faith, once the rightholder(s) would oppose it.

By virtue of 41/G. § (2) of Copyright Act in case the diligent search for rightholders was not successful, the beneficiary organization shall submit the data of the work intended to be used to a single online record of the European Union. The single online record is maintained by the European Union Intellectual Property Office (hereinafter: 'EUIPO record or database'). The Hungarian Intellectual Property Office receives a notification about the report and takes measures for its transmission with no delay.

The report submitted to the EUIPO shall include the following data:

(a) the result of the search for rightholders;
(b) data on the use concerned (e.g., which use the beneficiary organization intends to exercise);
(c) any changes in the legal status of work (e.g., the rightholder(s) oppose(s) against the further use of the work);
(d) data enabling to contact the beneficiary organization.

The orphan work can only be used lawfully when the above-listed data – following their transmission to the The Hungarian Intellectual Property Office HIPO – are recorded in the database.

When a work to be found in the collection of the beneficiary organization is already recorded in the (HIPO) database as an orphan work, the beneficiary organization can use the work without carrying out the search for rightholders in this matter. In this case, in the database only the fact of the use shall be recorded by the beneficiary organization.

After the report of data conducted by the beneficiary organization, the Hungarian Intellectual Property Office receives an automatic notification of them. The reported data on the orphan work reported by the beneficiary organizations become visible via the European Union Intellectual Property Office (EUIPO) database for the HIPO and will be transmitted without delay by the H in order to record them in the database. The data on the use of the orphan work becomes recorded and made accessible and searchable for the public following the above steps. The recording of such data in the European Union Intellectual Property Office database is a prerequisite for starting the 'free use' of works exercised by the beneficiary organization.

Each beneficiary organization – following an online registration – can modify data recorded in the EUIPO database. Due to this right is provided, the beneficiary organizations can report the data regarding their search for rightholders through the EUIPO database to the HIPO as well, in order to ease fulfilling their duty to report such use and to reduce the administrative costs. Having regard to the new unified European regulation, all beneficiary organizations of each Member State shall use the same database; therefore, the HIPO does not maintain other online reporting surface.

The reported data on the orphan work reported by the beneficiary organizations become visible via the OHIM database for the HIPO and will be transmitted without delay by the HIPO in order to record them in the database. The data on the use of the orphan work becomes be recorded and made accessible and searchable for the public following the above steps. The recording of such data in the European Union Intellectual Property Office database is a prerequisite for starting the 'free use' of works exercised by the beneficiary organization.

73. The use of performers' performances are regulated by Article 55 of Copyright Act: In accordance with Article 55(1) of Copyright Act, the provisions relating to license agreement shall apply *mutatis mutandis* to agreement aimed at assigning the author's economic rights, and with derogations set out in paragraphs (2) and (3) to the agreement which aims to license the use of performers' performances and to assign the performers' economic rights,

Pursuant to Article 55(2) such publication fifty years after it was communicated to the public, calculated from the first day following the year when the publication or communication took place, the phonogram producer or any other person authorized by the producer does not offer copies of the phonogram for sale in sufficient quantity or does not make it available to the public by wire or wireless means or in any like manner in such a way that members of the public may access it from a place and at a time individually chosen by them, and the performer may terminate the agreement on the fixation of his performance made with the phonogram producer.

According to Article 55(3) of Copyright Act, the right to terminate the agreement referred to in paragraph (2) may be exercised if the producer fails to carry out both of the acts of exploitation referred to in paragraph (2) within a year from the notification of the performer about his intention to terminate the agreement on transfer or assignment pursuant to the previous sentence.

According to Article A 78/A of Copyright Act if the agreement on the fixation of a performance made with the phonogram producer is terminated by the performer pursuant to Article 55(2)-(3), all the rights of the phonogram producer related to the phonogram shall expire.

§6. Scope of Exclusive Rights

I. Moral Rights

74. All systems of copyright protection have as their prime inspiration their cultural value of authorship.[184]

The Hungarian copyright law recognizes that creative and intellectual efforts of authors are proper subject matter for legal protection divides that protection between economic rights on the one hand, and moral rights on the other. The moral rights have been accorded only to authors whose copyright rests on creativity rather than protected. The author has different moral rights.

184. W. Cornish & D. Llewelyn, *Intellectual Property*, 5th edn 452 (Sweet & Maxwell 2003).

The moral rights are also protected by the new Civil Code (Law No. V of 2013).[185]

The moral rights are non-assignable, that is, the right holder cannot transfer to another person the ownership of, say, the moral right to preserve integrity of the work. Moral rights shall belong to the concept of personal rights of the author and in consequence can only, be exercised by the author.

Chapter II and Articles 10–14 of the Copyright Act involve the provisions, concerning the moral rights of authors. The main varieties of moral rights in harmony within the Hungarian Copyright Act are as follows:

(a) right of integrity (right of respect);[186]
(b) right of acknowledgement of authorship (right of authorship, right of paternity);[187]
(c) right to indication author's name;[188]
(d) right to divulgation (disclosure) of work;[189]
(e) right of withdrawal;[190]
(f) protection of author's personality after death, (rights of reverence);[191] Article 14 of Copyright Act.

The term of protection of moral rights is practically seventy years, that is, the term related to author's moral rights falls under protection for the term of protection applying to economic rights. The moral rights are personal, but they are good against all who treat the work in a prejudicial manner. Since economic rights arising from a copyrighted work may be separated from the author's pecuniary rights, there is no simple dividing line between purely moral and purely economic rights.

75. The right of integrity is in connection with pecuniary rights of author namely with the right of alteration of a work. Alterations that are normally needed are authorized by the author of a protected work. The author shall have the exclusive right to alter his work and to authorize another person therefore. Authors have the right to oppose any alteration or modification in respect of their work.[192]

The right of integrity is the right to object to derogatory treatment of a work, or any part of it. Pursuant to Article 13 of Copyright Act, moral rights of the author are infringed by the distortion, mutilation, or any other alteration of or other derogatory action in relation to his work which prejudices the honour or reputation of the author.

The rule on the protection of integrity of the work has become more significant in comparison to the former Copyright Act by the specification that any alteration or mutilation of the work should violate the author's honour or reputation as provided for by the Berne Convention.[193]

185. Article 2.42, of new Civil Code (Law No. V of 2013).
186. Article 13 of the Copyright Act.
187. Article 12(4) of the Copyright Act.
188. Article 12(3) of the Copyright Act.
189. Article 12(3) of the Copyright Act.
190. Article 11 of the Copyright Act.
191. Article 14 of the Copyright Act.
192. Csécsy, *A szellemi alkotások joga*, 36.
193. §6*bis*(1) of the Berne Convention.

In harmony with the judicial practice considered only prejudicial alterations as such are ones that infringe the author's moral rights, thus inessential alterations have not been established as infringements of moral rights.[194]

76. The author may demand that the author's capacity shall not be called into doubt, that is, the author has the right to claim his or her authorship. The author has the right to determine whether the work is to bear an author's designation and what designation is to be used. The performers have also the right to claim to be identified as performers or their performances as regards their unfixed aural performances or performances fixed in phonogram.

The author's moral rights and particularly the right to acknowledgement of the authorship may be infringed by plagiarism. Plagiarism means presenting a work as the original creation of a person (the plagiarist) which is in fact the creation of another person (the author), either without change or in a more or less altered form or context. The concept of plagiarism is not restricted to a case of formal similarity, publishing a work, which is the adaptation of the work of another person, and presenting it as if it were one's own original work, is also plagiarism.[195] Generally, the name of the author contributes to identify the copyrighted works. The names of all natural and juristic people are under the protection of civil law.[196] In accordance with Article 12(1) of the Copyright Act, the author shall have the right to have an indication on his work or in the communication on his work – subject to the scope and nature of the communication – referring to him as the author; reference shall be made to the author in the event of including part of his work in another work, and citing or reviewing his work.[197]

The author may exercise the rights to have his or her name indicated subject to the nature of use and in a manner complying with it under a pseudonym. The author may require that his or her work having been divulgated to the public, with the indication of his or her name shall, in the case of a new authorized use; it may be further used, without the indication of his or her name.

The Copyright Act includes several prescriptions concerning the indication of the name of author. The owners of neighbouring rights are entitled to use their own names.

In the case of performances, the performer shall have the moral right to have his or her name indicated, depending on the nature of the use and in a manner consistent with it, in the case of ensembles of performers; this right shall apply to the indication of the names of the ensemble, the leader of ensemble, and the chief performers.[198]

In the case of phonograms, the producer of a sound recording shall have the right to have his or her name indicated on the copies of the sound recording.[199]

The radio and television organizations and the organization communicating by cable its own programme to the public shall have the right to have its name indicated.[200]

194. Gyertyánfy et al., *A szerzöi jogi törvény magyarázata*, 4–13.
195. Ficsor, *Guide to the Copyright*, Index, Plagiarism.
196. Article 2.43.f) of new Civil Code.
197. Lontai, *A Szellemi alkotások*, 54.
198. Article 75(1) of the Copyright Act.
199. *Ibid.*, Art. 79.
200. *Ibid.*, Art. 81.

The creators of fine art, artistic photography, architecture, applied art, and industrial design and designs of engineering structures are entitled to use their own names.

The designer shall have the right to determine where and how his or her name and the date of design should be indicated in building or engineering structure.[201]

However, the exercise of this right shall be the subject to the requirement that no unjustified and disproportionate infringement of this right and lawful interests of the owner, the user, or operator shall be caused.

In respect of cinematographic creations, the name of all creators (the authors of the literary of the literary and musical works for a motion picture, the director of the film, and so on) shall be indicated in an appropriate manner in the copies of audiovisual works.[202]

77. The law of divulgation of works is the most important moral right of author as he or she may also keep his or her work in secret.[203] The author shall decide whether his or her work may be made public. The author has right to determine whether or how his or her work is to be divulgated.

This law involves that neither the work, nor its essence, nor a description thereof has previously been publicly disseminated without his consent. Under Article 10(2) of the Copyright Act, before the disclosure of the work, any information on the substance if its contents may be provided for the public only subject to the author's consent.

By virtue of Article 10(3) of the Copyright Act, unless otherwise provided, the conclusion of a license agreement shall imply the author's consent to the user providing information on the contents of the work for the public in a manner complying with the purpose of the use.

As regards a work becoming known after author's death, it shall be presumed – failing other declaration by the author or his or her legal successor or the introduction of evidence proving the contrary – that the author intended his or her work to be divulgated to the public.[204]

78. Authors are entitled to withdraw their permission for the publication of works; the withdrawal must be in writing and for a well-founded reason. They are also entitled to prohibit the further use of those of their works that have already been published. They are obliged, however, to compensate for any damage that has been incurred prior to the statement. This does not concern employer's right to further use of the works; nor can this, in the case of the assignment of economic rights, obstruct the person who has acquired the economic rights in his or her use of the work on the basis of the assigned economic rights.[205]

Referring to the sound reason, the author may withdraw his or her authorization to disclosure of the work already divulgated; however, he or she is obliged to repair any damage having accrued until the time of such declaration. The exercise of the right of withdrawal in general goes together with the author's obligation to pay appropriate compensation to those who have copies to distribute, and this shall not

201. *Ibid.*, Art. 67(2).
202. Tattay, *A Szellemi Alkotások joga*, 232.
203. Article 10(1) of the Copyright Act.
204. Lontai, *A Szelleni alkotások*, 55.
205. Article 11 of the Copyright Act.

prejudice the employer's rights to exploit the work and shall not prevent in the case of assignment of the economic rights, the acquirer of rights from uses based on the economic rights.[206]

The author may make corrections after publication of his or her work. The right of withdrawal of work also includes the right of correction.[207] This right may be exercised against licensed uses; however, it may not be exercised prejudice the employer's right to exploit any work made on the job.[208]

79. The current Copyright Act does not provide for moral rights, that they are 'unlimited in time'. Rather, with one caveat, the current Act effectively fixes the term of protection for moral rights as identical to the term for pecuniary rights.[209]

After the author's death, actions against the infringement of the above-mentioned moral rights can be taken as remedies of civil law within the term of protection. The author's rights shall enjoy protection during the lifetime of the author and for seventy years following his or her death.[210]

The actions may be carried out by the person put in charge of the administration of the author's literary scientific or artistic legacy by the author, and if there is no such person or the one put in charge fails to take actions, it shall be the person having acquired the economic rights by virtue of inheritance.

After the expiration of the term of protection, that is, seventy years following the death of the author, the organization performing the collective administration of rights or the association representing the author's interests may take action, with reference to offence against the author's memory, against a behaviour which would be taken under the term of protection to infringe the author's right to have his or her name indicated on his or her work or in a communication related to work.[211]

In the special literature of copyright, the acronym 'p.m.a.' (*post mortem authoris*) is commonly used. The abbreviation p.m.a. is a Latin expression meaning 'after the death of author'. This term is frequently used in Latin, sometimes in abbreviated form as p.m.a., referring to a term of protection lasting during the life of an author and seventy years after his or her death.[212]

II. Exploitation Rights

80. The economic rights of authors are as follows:

(a) to obtain remuneration;[213]
(b) the right to use;[214]

206. Csécsy, *A szellemi alkotások joga*, 35.
207. Tattay, *A Szellemi Alkotások joga*, 114.
208. Ficsor, 'The Protection of Copyright in Hungary', 37.
209. Ficsor, 'The Protection of Copyright in Hungary', 39.
210. Article 14(4) of the Copyright Act.
211. Article 14(2) of the Copyright Act.
212. Ficsor, *Guide to the Copyright*, index, post mortem authoris.
213. Article 16(4) and (5) of the Copyright Act.
214. Article 16(1) of the Copyright Act.

(c) the right to authorize the use;[215]
(d) the right to assignment;[216]
(e) the right to use the original title of the work;[217]
(f) the right to the commercial utilization of any characteristic and original character in the work.[218]

81. The right to remuneration is a fundamental right of authors.

The right to obtaining remuneration means payment to be made by those who perform an act in respect of a work on the basis of an exclusive right of authorization; the owner of rights is in opposition to subject of authorization of any act covered by the right to the payment of an appropriate remuneration.[219]

Remuneration shall be due to the author against the license he or she has given for the use of his or her work, which remuneration – unless otherwise agreed – shall be in proportion to the revenue earned by the use of the work.[220]

The author may waive his or her claim to remuneration by an express representation to that end. Should he or she stipulate a specific form for the licensing agreement to be valid, the waiver of remuneration shall itself be valid in the specific form only.

The remuneration means the payment to be made by those who perform an act in respect of a work or object of related right. On the basis of an exclusive right of authorization, the owner of rights is in a position to authorize any act covered by the right to the payment of an appropriate remuneration.[221]

In the specified cases, remuneration shall be due to the author for the use of his or her work even if he or she has no exclusive right to authorize the use. The law may exclude the right to waive such remuneration, and should such provision fail to obtain, the author may only waive the remuneration by an express representation to that end.[222]

The right to remuneration may be qualified as the main essential economic right of the author. The free use shall be recognized from mandatory payment of remuneration. Uses falling within the scope of the free use shall not be subject to payment of any consideration and to any authorization of author.[223]

82. The remuneration shall be due to the author against the commercial utilization of the title, any characteristic and original character in the work. In the case of unlawful utilization, remuneration shall also be due against the use concerned and infringement of copyright.

The employee shall not be entitled to receive remuneration in the case of works made under employment. The author receives only his or her salary, but the author shall be entitled to an appropriate remuneration if the employer authorized another

215. Article 16(1) of the Copyright Act.
216. Article 55 of the Copyright Act.
217. Article 16(2) of the Copyright Act.
218. Article 16(2) and (3) of the Copyright Act.
219. Lontai, *A. Szellemi alkotások*, 59–74.
220. Article 16(4) of the Copyright Act.
221. Ficsor, *Guide to the Copyright*, Index, Equitable remuneration.
222. Article 16(5) of the Copyright Act.
223. Csécsy, *A szellemi alkotások joga*, 37.

person for the use of the work or the economic rights transfer to another person relating to the work.

The employee shall receive the appropriate remuneration, if the employer concludes license agreement or assigns the copyrighted work:[224]

(a) Authors are entitled to appropriate remuneration if the employer authorizes a third person to use the work or assign the economic rights in connection with the work to a third person.[225]
(b) Authors are entitled to receive the remuneration that they are due after the assignment.[226]

Under Article 30(4) of the Copyright Act, the author shall continue, even in the case of acquisition of rights by employer, to be entitled to the remuneration which is due even after the transfer of the right, e.g., a literary work is transferred by the employer to a film producer to make a film.

83. The most frequent cases of the remuneration are the payments based on mandatory collective administration of copyright and related rights.

In the cases of mandatory collective administration of the works, regulated in the Copyright Act, remuneration shall be due to the author for the use of his or her work even if he or she has no exclusive right to authorize the use. The law may exclude the right to waive such remuneration, and should such provision fail to obtain, the author may only waive the remuneration by an express representation to that end.

In the cases of compulsory obligatory collective management (collective administration) of the works, the author shall have the right only to remuneration. The right holders may exercise their rights only through collective administration and may waive their remuneration only with effect following the date of its distribution and to the extent of the amount due to them.

The cases of compulsory obligatory management are as follows:

(a) reproduction and distribution of musical works;[227]
(b) the private copying of copyrighted works, performances, and sound records;[228]
(c) reproduction of works (works reproduced in photocopying or in like manner);[229]
(d) rental relating to a cinematographic creation or a work included in a sound recording;[230]
(e) lending to the public of works except of cinematographic creations, sound recordings, and software;[231]
(f) terrestrial broadcasting of literary and music works;[232]

224. Tattay, *A Szellemi Alkotások joga*, 103–105.
225. Article 30(3) of the Copyright Act.
226. Article 30(4) of the Copyright Act.
227. Article 19(1) of the Copyright Act.
228. Articles 20(1), (2) and 95 of the Copyright Act.
229. Article 21(1), (3), (5), (6), and (7) of the Copyright Act.
230. Article 26(6) and Arts 85–93 of the Copyright Act.
231. Article 26(7) of the Copyright Act.
232. Article 27(1) of the Copyright Act.

(g) the simultaneous and unaltered retransmission to the public of works and performances by cable;[233]
(h) the transfer the ownership of an original work by any dealer in works (droit of suite);
(i) the transfer of the ownership of an original work of art by a dealer in works after the expiration of term of protection.[234]

84. The most problematic features of remuneration of this kind are as follows:

(a) royalty against reproduction of works;
(b) royalty against the private copying of copyrighted works, performances, and sound records, that is, royalty paid for use of blank audio and video carriers;
(c) royalty against lending;
(d) royalty against droit de suite.

85. The authors of the works and the publishers thereof in the form of book, or in periodicals that are reproduced by photocopying or in like manner on paper or on like carrier – as by reprography – shall be due to be paid fair and equitable remuneration on private-purpose copying.

The remuneration shall be paid by the manufacturer of the device suitable for reprography, in the case of manufacture abroad by the person obliged under the law to pay customs duties, or – in the absence of obligation to pay customs duties – by the person who imports the device and by its first domestic distributor under joint liability. For the payment of the remuneration, all domestic distributors of the device concerned shall be jointly liable. In addition, the person operating the reprographic device for a consideration is also obliged to pay remuneration. The remuneration referred to above shall be set by the organization performing the collective administration of rights. When determining the said remuneration, it shall take due account of, in particular, the manner of the use of the device and its output characteristics, as well as the place of the operation in the case of its use for a consideration.[235]

The remuneration referred to in above-mentioned paragraph shall not exceed 2% of the manufacturing issue price of the device suitable for reprography, or, in case of a device manufactured abroad, 2% of the value for customs according to applicable legal regulations.

The remuneration shall be paid:

(a) by the manufacturer of the device suitable for reprography;
(b) in the case of manufacture abroad by the person obliged under the law to pay customs duties;
(c) or by the person who imports the device and by its first domestic distributor under joint liability. For the payment of the remuneration, all domestic distributors of

233. Article 28(2), (3), (4), (5) of the Copyright Act.
234. Article 100 of the Copyright Act.
235. Article 20(2) of the Copyright Act.

the device concerned shall be jointly liable. In addition, the person operating the reprographic device for a consideration is also obliged to pay remuneration.[236]

The remuneration shall be determined by the organization performing the collective administration of rights of other interested right holders. At the determination of the remuneration, it shall be taken into account whether effective technological measures for the protection of copyright and related rights are applied on the works, performances, films, and sound recordings concerned.

In accordance with Article 20(3) of the Copyright Act, the remuneration for repeated reproduction shall be set by the organization performing the collective administration of rights. When determining the said remuneration, it shall take due account of, in particular:

(a) the manner of the use of the device;
(b) and its output characteristics;
(c) as well as the place of the operation in the case of its use for a consideration.

The obligation to pay remuneration shall not apply to the case where the device is put into circulation for export purposes. The publishers shall have the greatest share (40%) of royalty in respect of reprography.

86. The most important feature of private copying is the reproduction copying of performances, films, and sound recordings for the private purposes that a fair and equitable remuneration shall be due, for the private purpose of copying of works, performances, films, and sound recordings, that are broadcast in the programmes of radio and television organizations, included in the programmes of the entities communicating their own programmes to the public by cable, and released for distribution on audiovisual or audio carriers:

(a) to the authors of works;
(b) the performers of performances;
(c) and the producers of films and sound recordings.[237]

The remuneration shall be paid:

(a) to the manufacturer of blank video and audio carriers;
(b) in the case of manufacture abroad by the person obliged under the law to pay customs duties;
(c) or – in the absence of obligation to pay customs duties – by the person who imports them and by their first domestic distributor, under joint liability, to the organization performing the collective administration of rights in literary and musical works.

For the payment of the remuneration, all domestic distributors of the carriers concerned shall be jointly liable.

236. Article 21(1) of the Copyright Act.
237. Article 20(1) of the Copyright Act.

In accordance with Article 20(3) of the Copyright Act, the obligation to pay remuneration shall not apply to:

(a) putting into circulation for export purposes furthermore;
(b) video and audio carriers applicable with devices (e.g., studio equipment, dictaphone) which are not used in their regular application for the private purposes making copies of works, performances or performers of sound recordings.

87. The right holders may enforce their claims to remuneration only by the organizations performing the collective administration of their rights, and they may renounce the remuneration only with effect following the date of the distribution and to the extent of the amount due to them.

Under Article 22(1) of the Copyright Act, the commercial manufacturer of the blank audiovisual and audio carrier, the person obliged under the law to pay custom duties for importing such a carrier, as well as the importer and the first domestic distributor of such carrier is obliged to inform the organization performing collective administration of rights on the quantity imported or put into circulation.

The organization performing the collective administration of rights may request further information on the figures relating to putting into circulation and on the sources of procurement for determining the fair amount of remuneration.

88. Public lending right means rights granted in respect of lending of copies of work usually books and other publications by non-profit libraries open to the public. The right of distribution also extends to Hungary in public lending:

> By virtue of Article 23(7) of the Copyright Act, in the case of the lending to the public of radio and television plays, performances, databases, maps, other cartographic creations, and other works – as far as architectural, applied art, and industrial creations are concerned, of their design, a fair and equitable remuneration shall be due to the authors. This claim to remuneration may be enforced only via the collective administration of rights and the right holders may waive such remuneration only following the date of its distribution and to the extent of the amount due to them.

The exhaustion of rights does not concern the right to lending of cinematographic works and sound recording.

89. In the case of resale, right royalties must be paid when the ownership rights to an original work of art are transferred for valuable consideration with the involvement of an art dealer. This provision applies only after the first time the ownership rights to a work of art are transferred by the author. This type of remuneration may not be waived.

The author has the right to receive a royalty based on the sale price obtained for any resale of the work subsequent to the first transfer by the author. The dealer shall not be subject to royalty if the sale price does not exceed HUF 5,000.[238]

Article 70(4) precisely defines the amount of royalty:

---

238. Article 70(6) of the Copyright Act.

> The royalty shall be set on the basis of exchange value, which is or can be expressed in money. The work of art is valued at the net rate of tax and of the public dues (e.g., cultural contribution).

The amount in HUF shall be calculated on the basis of the official exchange rate of the national Bank of Hungary, valid on the first day of the calendar quarter of the conclusion of the contract.[239]

90. Article 17 of the Copyright Act includes the exemplificative list of features of use. The use may be carried out in any tangible or intangible form. The tangible forms of use of copyrighted works are: reproduction, distribution, rental, public lending, and exhibition. The intangible form of use is: the public performance, communication to the public by broadcasting or any other manner, or retransmission of the broadcast work to the public with the involvement of another organization than the original one.

Reproduction and alteration may be equally in tangible and intangible form.

The economic rights of authors may be divided into copy-related and non-copy-related works. The term of copy-related rights means those rights that relate to the making and distribution of copies, in particular in right of reproduction: the right of distribution, the right of rental, and the right of public lending.

The term of non-copy-related rights means those rights that relate to the making available of works and objects of neighbouring rights without using a copy. These are: right of broadcasting or other communication to the public, and the right of public performance.

91. The following, in particular, are considered uses of a work.

(a) reproduction of a work (Articles 18–22 of the Copyright Act);
(b) distribution of a work (Article 23 of the Copyright Act);
(c) public performance (Articles 24–25 of the Copyright Act);
(d) presentation to the public by broadcast or some other manner (Articles 26–27 of the Copyright Act);
(e) retransmitting broadcast works to the public through an organization other than the original (Article 28 of the Copyright Act);
(f) alteration (Article 58 of the Copyright Act);
(g) exhibition (Article 69 of the Copyright Act).

A. Reproduction Right

92. The Copyright Act defines of notion of reproduction: Authors have the exclusive right to reproduce their works and to authorize other persons to do so. (First sentence of Article 18(1) of Copyright Act) Reproduction constitutes the following:

- the (direct or indirect) recording of a work on any medium in any manner, whether final or temporary; and
- the preparation of one or more copies of the recording.

239. Article 74(7) of the Copyright Act.

Reproduction is a fixation[240] of the work or object of related rights sufficiently stable in that way that the work or object of related rights may be perceived[241] further reproduced and communicated on the basis thereof.[242] Storage of works in an electronic form (computer) since it fully corresponds to this concept. Pursuant to the Article 18(2) of the Copyright Act, as reproduction of the work shall be rated the storage of the work in a digital form on electronic devices.

The main features of reproduction:

(a) the method, manner, and form of the reproduction are irrelevant;
(b) it is relevant whether the copy of the work may be perceived directly or only through a device;
(c) it is irrelevant whether or not the copy is embodied in a tangible object that may be distributed;
(d) it is irrelevant whether the reproduction is made directly e.g., on the basis of a tangible copy or indirectly e.g., off air a broadcast programme; and
(e) the duration of the fixation whether it is permanent or temporary.

In accordance with Article 18(1) of the Copyright Act, it shall be within the author's exclusive right to reproduce his work and to grant authorization therefore.

Reproduction shall be taken to mean the direct or indirect fixation of the work in any manner on a tangible carrier, whether definitively or temporarily, and the making of one or several copies of the fixation of the works.

The right of reproduction extends:

(a) to the fixation of the work in a mechanical manner;
(b) to the cinematographic fixation;
(c) to the fixation in magnetic way;
(d) in making copies of it by printing;
(e) to the production of audio or video recording of the work;
(f) to the fixation if works for purposes of communication to the public by broadcasting or by cable;
(g) to the storage of the work in digital on electronic devices; and
(h) to the production in a tangible form of the work transmitted by the computer network.

In the case of architectural creation, the primary or secondary construction of creation laid down as a design shall be likewise rated as reproduction.

In accordance with Article 19(1) of the Copyright Act, the reprographic reproduction means reproduction of works by photocopying or an analogous procedure in the form

---

240. The Rome Convention contains an explicate definition (Arts 3, e 9.): reproduction means the making of a copy or copies of fixation. The reproduction may be direct or indirect as this conception differs from the above-mentioned concepts.
241. Article (1) of the Berne Convention states that owners of copyright must enjoy exclusive rights to authorize the reproduction of the work in any manner or form. In harmony with this, from the viewpoint of the concept of reproduction and the coverage of the right of reproduction.
242. Ficsor, *Guide to the Copyright*, index, reproduction.

of facsimile copies, making reduced or enlarged facsimile copies is also reprographic reproduction.[243]

93. The reproduction has specialized features: the producer of a sound recording, the creator of a multimedia work, and the maker of an electronic database may require that the repeated reproduction of non-dramatic musical works and lyrics for music and parts of musical-dramatical works against the payment of a fair and equitable fee shall be authorized.[244]

The obligation of payment of royalty for rightholders concerns the users of works mentioned which are fixed on sound recordings and video recordings, in a multimedia work or an electronic database distributed on digital carriers, and the distribution by copies of such reproductions.

The licensing agreement shall be concluded with the organization performing the collective administration of rights related to literary and musical works.

The foregoing provision shall not apply to the right of adaptation and the exercise of this right, that is, for adaptation of a work, the authorization of the author shall be required.[245]. According to Article 19 (1) of Copyright Act the producer of a sound recording, the creator of a multimedia work, and the maker of an electronic database to may require that the repeated reproduction of already disclosed non-dramatic musical works and lyrics for music and parts of musico-dramatical works fixed on sound recordings and video recordings, in a multimedia work or an electronic database distributed on digital carriers, and the distribution by copies of such reproductions against the payment of a fair and equitable fee shall be authorized for them too. The licensing agreement shall be concluded with the organization performing the collective administration of rights related to literary and musical works.

B. Performing Rights

94. Performing rights is a commonly used term, mainly in the context of collective management of copyright and of the related rights, to mean more or less all non-copy-related rights. The right of public performance involves the right of public recitation, the right of broadcasting, and the right of communication by the cable (wire).

It is to be distinguished from communication to the public because this makes works perceptible to people at a distance.

According to 24(1) of the Copyright Act, the author shall have the exclusive right to perform his work to the public and to authorize another person therefore. The making of the work perceptible to those present shall be taken to mean performance.

---

243. Article 18(2) of the Copyright Act clarifies the concept of reproduction: As reproduction of the work shall be rated in particular the fixation of the work in a mechanical, cinematographic or magnetic way and making copies of it by printing, the production of audio or video recording of the work, its fixation for purposes of communication to the public by broadcasting or by cable, the storage of the work in a digital form on electronic devices, and the production in a tangible form of the work transmitted by the computer network. In the case of architectural creations, the primary and secondary construction of a creation laid own as a design shall likewise be rated as reproduction.

244. Article 19(1) of the Copyright Act.

245. Gyertyánfy et al., *A szerzői jogi törvény magyarázata*, 115–116.

As performance shall be rated in particular:[246]

(a) the performance of the work to the public by a performer in person, including stage performance, concert, recital, reading out (live performance);
(b) making the work perceptible by any technical device or manner, including the projection of a cinematographic creation, making the work communicated or distributed (as a copy) to the public become audible by loudspeaker or visible on a screen.

A performance shall be taken to be public if it occurs in a place accessible to the public or in any other place where people other than the members of the family[247] of the user and their acquaintances gather or may gather.[248]

An exhibition of creations of fine art may be qualified as public performance of works. The owner of a fine art, photographic, or applied art work is obliged to make the work temporarily available to the author so that he or she can exercise author's rights, if in so doing the author does not infringe the owner's equitable interest.[249]

The author's approval is required for the exhibition of fine art, photographic, architectural, and applied art works. It is not necessary to obtain the consent of the author or remunerate the author for displaying a work in a public collection.

The owner of a fine art, photographic, or applied art work is obliged to make the work temporarily available to the author so that he or she can exercise his author's rights, if in doing so the author does not infringe the owner's equitable interest.[250]

C. Adaptation Right

95. Adaptations are covered by the generic category of derivative works.[251] By adaptation, it is understood to be the transformation of work into another form. The adaptation belongs to category of alteration.

The alteration means the act of any modification of a work.[252] A generic term that covers both those modifications which, due to their original nature, may enjoy independent copyright protection (also including adaptations and arrangements) and those that do not amount to the level of new, creative contribution.

The Copyright Act in Hungary grants protection to alterations that are recognized as derivative work. Pursuant to Article 29 of the Copyright Act:

> The translation of the work, its dramatic or musical adaptation, its adaptation for a cinematographic production, the adaptation of the cinematographic creation,

---

246. Article 24 a) and b) of the Copyright Act.
247. Article 24(3) of the Copyright Act.
248. Ficsor, 'The Protection of Copyright in Hungary', 42.
249. Article 69(1) of the Copyright Act.
250. Article 69(2) of the Copyright Act.
251. According to Art. 12 of Berne Convention, the author has exclusive right to authorizing adaptation, arrangement, or other alteration of work.
252. The alteration is a feature of derivative works in accordance with Art. 2(3) of the Berne Convention.

> and any other alteration of the work as a result of which another work is derived from the original one shall be taken to mean alteration.

The Copyright Act gives an exemplificative list of derivative works:

(a) translation of the work;
(b) dramatic or musical adaptation of (literary) works;
(c) adaptation of the work for the cinematographic creations;
(d) any other alteration of the work as a result of which another work is derived from the original.

At the same time, such an alteration is submitted to the right of adaptation of the owner of copyright in the original work. Alteration also means the modification of original work that does not amount to the level of new creative contributions.[253]

96. Adaptation generally means the act of altering a pre-existing work (either protected in the public domain) or an expression of folklore, for a purpose other than for which it originally served, in a way that a new work comes into being in which the elements of the pre-existing work and the new elements – added as a result of the alteration merge together. The purpose may be to produce a work in the form of a new genre or to make it suitable to use in another context. There are specific terms for the alteration of a musical work for the purpose of a new way of performing it, and for the expression of a literary work in another language 'arrangement' and 'translation'.[254]

The alteration means any modification of a work, a generic term that covers the modifications which, due to their original nature, may enjoy copyright protection.[255]

Alterations are normally needed for authorized uses of protected works; if these alterations are not of an original nature, they do not result in the creation of a derivative work.

They do not require separate authorization of the owner of copyright in such works. For example, the assignee of the software may carry out certain alterations. The author's exclusive right shall not cover the reproduction, alteration, adaptation, translation, or any other modification of the software, including the correction of mistakes, as well as the reproduction of the product resulting from these acts insofar as these acts of use are carried out by the person authorized to acquire the software in compliance with the intended purpose of the software.

D. Translation Rights

97. The Hungarian Copyright Act does not define the concept of translation. The Copyright Act lists the translation of work between the varieties of derivative works as outlined in paragraph 95.

The translation is generally considered to mean transformation of a text sometimes written or spoken in one language into another language. The right to translation

253. Ficsor, *Guide to the Copyright*, Index, Alteration.
254. Under Art. 6*bis* of the Berne Convention, authors have right to oppose any alteration of their works, which would be prejudicial to their honour or reputation.
255. The Art. 29 of Copyright Act concerns the alteration of works.

extends to the transformation of a computer program from one programming language into another one.[256]

Translation is a kind of the adaptation that shall be protected as an original work, without prejudice of the copyright in the original work.[257]

As an object, it is the result of an act of translation. The translation of a right shall be protected as original works without prejudice to the copyright in the original work.[258]

The alteration is mentioned in the Copyright Act in respect of special genres.

The user of industrial design and interior design creations (intended for industrial production purposes) shall have the right of exclusive use and alteration within the scope covered by the contract; however, the designer shall be consulted before the execution of any alteration.[259]

In the cases of creations of fine art, artistic photography, architecture, applied art, and industrial design and designs of engineering structures, the alteration without the author's consent of the design of an architectural creation or engineering structure that influences the appearance or the intended ordinary use shall be taken to be an unauthorized alteration of the work.[260]

The arrangement of the musical work may be recognized as translation. Arrangement of a musical work means the act of altering a musical work (either protected or in the public domain) for a new way or form of performing it (such as the transcription for a piano piece of a work originally composed for an orchestra) and the result of an act of arrangement mentioned in paragraph above.

Arrangements are covered by the generic category of derivative works, and are to be protected under Article 2(3) of the Berne Convention. At the same time, an act of arrangement is covered by the right of adaptation of the owner of the copyright in the original work.

E. Other Rights

1. Droit De Suite

98. The majority of countries in the European Union had already introduced the *droit de suite* before 2000 in their national law, but with different provisions, as well as a need for harmonization. Directive 2001/84/EC of the European Parliament and Council of 27 September 2001 on the resale right for the benefit of the author of an original work of art (hereinafter: 'Resale Right Directive') was implemented in Hungary in 2006 (Act CVIII of 2005).[261]

256. Ficsor, *Guide to the Copyright*, Index, Translation right of Ficsor.
257. Under Art. 8 of the Berne Convention, owners of copyright must be granted an exclusive right to permit creation of the derivative works from its works.
258. Article 2(3) of the Berne Convention.
259. Article 71 a) of the Copyright Act.
260. Article 67(1) of the Copyright Act.
261. Pursuant to Art. 14 of the Berne Convention, granting such a right is optional, and its application may be subject of reciprocity.

With economic reform leading to a market economy in Hungary, *droit de suite* to be seen as a pre-eminent element of pecuniary rights of creator in the fine arts, thus Article 70 of the Copyright Act incorporates the regulation on *droit de suite*. It usually takes a form of a specific percentage of the sale price or the difference between the sale price and previous sale price.[262]

Droit de suite is a French expression meaning resale right that is not used in Hungarian copyright. Article 70 includes prescriptions of resale rights. *Droit de suite* is the inalienable right of the author or after his or her death, the persons or institutions authorized by national legislation, to an interest in any sale of his or her original work of arts – much more rarely – his or her original manuscript, subsequent to the first transfer by him or her.[263] The *droit the suite* concerns particular paintings, drawings, graphic and design materials, sculptures, or tapestries marked with the initials of author that are transferred through the dealers of art.[264]

The classic case of Vincent van Gogh may be mentioned who sold none of his paintings during his lifetime, and whose works are now worth millions of dollars.

It takes the term of specific percentage of the sale price or the difference between the sale price and the previous sale price in Hungary. The applicability of the right is restricted to public actions and to sales through a dealer.

Droit de suite may be characterized as follows:

(a) *droit de suite* is an unassignable and inalienable economic right of an author;
(b) *droit de suite* is intended to ensure that authors of fine arts, applied arts, and photographic arts share in economic success of their works;
(c) *droit de suite* shall be qualified as an integral part of copyright;
(d) the prescriptions of *droit de suite*, which are laid down in the Copyright Act shall apply if the author is a national of any of the Member States of the European Economic Area, or a national of any of the countries outside of the European Economic Area, and also authors who are not nationals of any of the Members States of the European Economic Area, but who have habitual residence in Hungary[265] (Article 70(12) of the Copyright Act).

99. Royalties must be paid when the ownership rights to an original work of art are transferred for valuable consideration with the involvement of an art dealer. This provision applies only after the first time the ownership rights to a work of art are transferred by the author. This type of remuneration may not be waived.[266]

The term 'original work' has a specific meaning in the provisions of *droit de suite* in the expression 'original work of art'. In this context, the expression has the meaning 'original of art'.

An 'original work of art' means works of fine art (pictures, collages paintings, drawings, engravings, prints, lithographs, or sculptures); works of applied arts (e.g., tapestries, ceramics, glassware); and works of photographic art provided they are made

262. Ficsor, *Guide to the Copyright*, Index, Resale right.
263. Article 70(1) of the Copyright Act.
264. Lontai, *A Szellemi alkotások*, 73.
265. Article 70(12) of the Copyright Act.
266. Article 70(1) of the Copyright Act.

by the author or are copies considered to be original works of art. Copies of works shall be considered to be original works if they have been made in limited number by author or under his or her authority. Copies of work of art which are numbered, signed, or otherwise authorized by the author shall be considered to be such copies.[267]

The Copyright Act also defines the notion of dealer: The dealer in works of art shall mean any natural or legal person or business organization without legal personality marketing works of art.[268]

100. The author has the right to receive a royalty based on the sale price obtained for any resale of the work subsequent to the first transfer by the author. The dealer shall not be subject to royalty if the sale price does not exceed HUF 5,000.[269]

Royalty shall be set on the basis of the official exchange rate of the National Bank of Hungary, of the work of art (sale price) net exclusive of taxes and other public dues (e.g., cultural contribution) at the following rates:[270]

(a) 4% for the portion of the sale price up to EUR 50,000, or its equivalent in forints;
(b) 3% for the portion of the sale price from EUR 50,000.01 to EUR 200,000, or its equivalent in forints;
(c) 1% for the portion of the sale price from EUR 200,000.01 to EUR 350,000, or its equivalent in forints;
(d) 0.5% for the portion of the sale price from EUR 350,000.01 to EUR 500,000, or its equivalent in forints;
(e) 0.25% for the portion of the sale price exceeding EUR 500,000, or its equivalent in forints.

The total amount of royalty cannot exceed the amount in HUF which is equivalent to EUR 12,500.[271]

Pursuant to Article 70(7) of the Copyright Act, the amount in HUF shall be calculated on the basis of official exchange rate of the National Bank of Hungary, valid on the first day of the calendar quarter on the conclusion of the contract.

101. When a museum obtains the ownership of an original work of art from a person other than a dealer in works of art, there shall be no obligation to pay the royalty concerning *droit de suite*, provided that the activities of the museum do not generate or increase incomes in any way or form.[272]

The dealer in works of art shall pay the royalty to the collecting society performing the collective management of fine art applied arts. The collecting society shall be paid the collected royalty to the author of the work or his or her successor in title.

The dealers shall have joint and referral liability, if more than one dealer in works of art is involved in the transaction of the transfer of the ownership. In such a case, unless the dealers agree otherwise, the seller is obliged to pay royalty.[273]

267. Article 70(2) of the Copyright Act gives interpretation of an original work of art.
268. Article 70(3) of the Copyright Act.
269. Article 70(6) of the Copyright Act.
270. Article 70(4) of the Copyright Act.
271. Gyertyánfy et al., *A szerzöi jogi törvény magyarázata*, 368–369.
272. Article 70 of the Copyright Act.
273. Gyertyánfy et al., *A szerzöi jogi törvény magyarázata*, 367.

If none of the dealers involved in the transaction participates in the transfer as a seller, the royalty shall be paid by the buyer.

In accordance with Article 70(11) of the Copyright Act, for a period of three years after the conclusion of contract related to the transfer of the original work, the collecting society may require from the dealer in works of art to finish all the information that may be necessary in order to collect the royalty.

The term of protection of *droit de suite* corresponds to a general term of protection laid down in the Copyright Act. In accordance with this provision, copyright lasts for a term of seventy years after the death of the author, as well as through the life of the author.[274]

2. Public Lending Right

102. The distribution right is recognized in Hungary and regulated in the Copyright Act.[275]

In accordance with Article 23(1) of the Copyright Act, the accessibility to the public of the original copy or the reproduced copies of the work through putting into circulation or their offer for putting into circulation shall be taken to mean distribution.

The distribution right is generally accepted as acts relating to the author of control dissemination of physical copies of the work and covers the right of lending and the rental. The right is recognized by several international treaties by Berne Convention,[276] WCT,[277] and WPPT[278] as far as by the Phonograph Convention.[279]

In the broader sense, the distribution is making available to the public. The distribution means in a broader sense making available of the original or the copies of a work or an object of related rights to the public by sale or other transfer of ownership or rental, lending as far as other transfer of possession.[280]

In a narrower sense, it is the making available of the original or copies of a work or an object of related right to the public by sale or other transfer of ownership.[281]

103. Public lending right means rights granted in respect of lending of copies of work usually books and other publications by non-profit libraries open to the public. The right of distribution also extends to Hungary in public lending.

By virtue of Article 23(7) of the Copyright Act, in the case of the lending to the public of radio and television plays, performances, databases, maps, and other cartographic creations and other works – as far as architectural, applied art, and industrial creations are concerned, of their design, a fair and equitable remuneration shall be due to the authors. This claim to remuneration may be enforced only via the

274. Article 31(1) of the Copyright Act.
275. Article 23 of the Copyright Act.
276. Article 14(1) and 14(1)*bis* of Berne Convention.
277. Article (6)(d) WCT Agreement.
278. Articles (7) and (12) WPPT Agreement.
279. Article 1 d), c) of the Phonogram Convention.
280. Ficsor, *Guide to the Copyright*, Index, Distribution.
281. *Ibid.*

collective administration of rights and the right holders may waive such remuneration only following the date of its distribution and to the extent of the amount due to them.[282]

The exhaustion of rights does not concern the right to lending of cinematographic works and sound recording.

3. Rental Right

104. The rental right means the transfer of the possession of the work or an object of related rights for a limited period of time, and for direct or indirect economic or commercial advantage, under some conditions and with some exceptions.[283]

The rental right is an important feature of the right of distribution. Distribution means in a broader sense, making available of the original or the copies of a work to the public by sale or other transfer of ownership or rental.

In Hungary, rental is regarded to be covered by a broader concept of distribution, and a general right of distribution also extends to rental rights.

The rental right is regulated by the TRIPS Agreement[284] and WCT Agreement[285] as far as by WPPT Agreement.[286]

In accordance with Article 23(6) of the Copyright Act, if the right of rental relating to a cinematographic creation or a work included in a sound recording has been transferred, or otherwise licensed, by the author to the producer of the film or sound recording, the author shall retain a claim to the producer of the film or sound recording for a fair and equitable remuneration regarding the distribution of the work through rental. This right may not be waived by the author; however, he or she may enforce his or her claim to remuneration only via an organization performing the collective administration of rights.[287]

The principle of exhaustion of rights is not applied when rental becomes one of the basic means of exploitation of certain works (such as cinematographic works and works included in sound recordings).

In such cases, a right of rental, as subcategory of the right of distribution survives the first sale. The exhaustion of rights in the work and object of related rights embodied in the copies in respect of which the right of distribution is exhausted does not extend to any other right (interactive) making available of works and objects of related rights to the public, irrespective of how the 'umbrella solution' is applied in a given country.

4. Right of Communication of a Work to the Public

105. The right of communication of a work to the public means generally making work perceptible to the public at a distance, that is, to absentees.

The right of communication of a work to the public means the transmission, by wire or by wireless means, of the images or sounds, or both, of a work or of an object

282. Lontai, *A Szellem alkotások*, 71–73.
283. Articles 9 and 13 of the Copyright Act.
284. Articles 11 and 14.4 of TRIPS Agreement.
285. Article 7 of WCT Agreement.
286. Articles 11 and 14 of WPPT Agreement.
287. Articles 85–93 of the Copyright Act.

of related rights, making it possible for the images and sounds to be perceived by persons outside the normal circle of family and the closest social acquaintances of the family, at a place, the distance of which from the place where the transmission is started is such that without the transmission, the images or sounds, or both, would not be perceivable at the said place, irrespective of whether the said people can perceive the images and sounds at the same place and the same time, or at different places and at different times.[288]

The author shall have the exclusive right to have his or her work communicated to the public by broadcasting and to authorize another person or persons therefore.[289]

The communication to the public is a notion collective, which includes the following kinds of communication:

(a) broadcasting;
(b) other varieties of communication recognized as broadcasting, communication by cable or any other means;[290]
(c) making available to the public.[291]

The communication to the public of an own programme by cable or any like device or in any like manner shall be subject, *mutatis mutandis*, to the provisions relating to broadcasting.[292]

106. Broadcasting is communication of a work, an object of related rights by wireless transmission. It covers terrestrial broadcasting and satellite broadcasting.[293] The concept of broadcasting is defined in the Rome Convention[294] and in WPPT Treaty.[295]

Articles 26 and 27 of the Copyright Act regulate broadcasting. The author shall have the exclusive right to broadcasting and to authorize other persons therefore. This right involves also the right to fixation of the programme permitting its repeated broadcasting. The fixation of the work permitting its repeated broadcasting is subject to the author's special license. Each and every use of the recording is subject to the payment of remuneration.

The Copyright Act defines the concept of terrestrial and satellite broadcasting: not only terrestrial broadcasting, but also satellite broadcasting, provided that the broadcast programme can be directly received by the public.

---

288. Ficsor, *Guide to the Copyright*, Index, Right of communication to the public.
289. Article 26(1) of the Copyright Act.
290. Gyertyánfy et al., *A szerzöi jogi törvény magyarázata*, 155–162.
291. Lontai et al., *A Szellemi alkotások joga*, 70.
292. Article 26(7) of the Copyright Act.
293. Ficsor, *Guide to the Copyright*, Index, Broadcasting.
294. The Rome Convention in Art. 3(f) contains an explicit definition of broadcasting, which reads as follows: Broadcasting means the transmission by wireless means for public reception of sounds or of image and sounds.
295. The definition of broadcasting is contained more precisely in Art. 2(f) of WPPT Agreement. It reads as follows: Broadcasting means the transmission by wireless means for public reception of sounds or images and sounds or of the representations thereof. Such transmission by satellite is also broadcasting. Transmission of encrypted signals is broadcasting when the means for decrypting are provided to the public, by the broadcasting organization or with its consent.

Terrestrial broadcasting means the making of a work perceptible to people at a distance by the transmission of sounds or pictures and sounds or the technical presentation of these without the use of cable or other like devices.

Satellite broadcasting shall be taken to be covered by the broadcasting of the work in case the programme broadcast can be directly received by the public.

The programme broadcast by satellite shall be regarded to be accessible to direct reception by the public if, under the responsibility and control of the radio or television organization, signals carrying the work are up linked to the satellite and from there back to the ground by uninterrupted transmission with the purpose that the signals can be received by the public.[296]

In the case of broadcasting by satellite, the place of the use of work shall be solely in the Member State of the European Economic Area when under the control and responsibility of the radio or television organization, the programme-carrying signals are introduced into an uninterrupted chain of communication leading to the satellite and down towards the earth for reception by the public.[297]

The presumption concerning the place of the use by satellite broadcasting shall be considered as irrefutable presumption.

107. The broadcasting may be divided into four features:

(1) the communication by local cable television;[298]
(2) the provisions pertaining to broadcasting must be applied appropriately to the transmission of own programming to the public by cable or other similar means or in another similar manner;[299]
(3) The transmission by AM microwaves which may be perceptible only at distance of thirty kilometres;
(4) the technology of Internet, that is, webcasting.[300]

Broadcasting should not to be understood as including interactive making available of works and objects of related rights over computer network.

Webcasting is still an evolving concept without any generally accepted legal characterization. Webcasting means making accessible for reception by the public of transmissions of sounds, images, or sound and images or the representation thereof, by wire or wireless means over a computer network. Such transmissions, when encrypted, are supposed to be considered as webcasting where the means for decrypting are provided to the public by webcasting organization or with its consent.[301]

The fixation of the work permitting its repeated broadcasting is subject to the author's special license. Each and every use of the recording is subject to the payment of remuneration.

---

296. Article 24(2) of the Copyright Act.
297. *Ibid.*
298. The communication to the public also occludes the transmission of works by cable or like media by the organization originating these programs.
299. Article 24(7) of the Copyright Act.
300. Lontai, *A Szellemi alkotások*, 109.
301. Ficsor, *Guide to the Copyright*, Index, Webcasting.

108. The broadcasting and cablecasting and other varieties of broadcasting may be made by encryption. Encryption means placing a work or object of related rights in digital format into a secret code (encoding), as a result of which it cannot be perceived or, at least, it becomes unreadable or unintelligible, without the key to the code necessary for its decryption (decoding). Encryption is a technological protection measure.[302]

An encrypted broadcast means the communication to the public in which the signals carrying the programme are transformed in any manner in order to restrict the access thereto to a limited part of the public shall be considered as an encrypted broadcast.[303]

Broadcasting also includes coded broadcasting that can be directly received by the public only after the programme signals have been made suitable for it – on the basis of agreements signed with the original radio or television organization and with the device (decoder) obtained from it or, with its approval, from other persons – by an organization that transmits to the public.

Broadcasting is coded whenever the programme signals are altered in any manner in order to limit access to a smaller section of the public.[304,305]

The original radio or television organization and the organization that uses the decoder and transmits to the public bear uniform responsibility for such uses.[306]

The two essential features of the encrypted broadcasting are defined in the Copyright Act. On the one hand, the decryption is made centrally by the broadcasting organization or with its consent, and on the other hand, the decoding may be carried out by the members of the public with consent of a broadcasting organization.

As broadcasting of the work shall also be rated if the signals of the broadcast programme are encrypted by the organization concerned with communication to the public and the work is accessible for undisturbed perception by the members of the public only by the use of a device for decryption procured from the said organization on the basis of an agreement concluded with it or from another organization authorized for the sale of the said device by the original organization.[307]

The special permission of the author is required for recordings that make repeated broadcasting possible. Fees have to be paid for each and every use of a recording.[308]

109. The WPPT has extended the concept of communication to the public to interactive making available to the public for performers and producer of the phonogram.[309] Pursuant to the solution of the Geneva Diplomatic Conference,[310] the right of communication to the public as an umbrella solution covers the interactive digital transmission.

The so-called umbrella solution contains the following elements:

302. Ficsor, *Guide to the Copyright*, Index, Encryption.
303. Article 26(5) of the Copyright Act.
304. Article 26(3) of the Copyright Act.
305. Article 26(7) of the Copyright Act.
306. Article 26(3) of the Copyright Act.
307. Article 26(4) of the Copyright Act.
308. Article 26(6) of the Copyright Act.
309. Articles 10 and 14 of WPPT Agreement.
310. Geneva Diplomatic Conference of 1996 which adopted the WCT and WPPT Agreements.

(a) describing such interactive digital transmission in a neutral, legal characterization-free manner as making available to the public of works/performances fixed in phonograms, by wire or wireless means, in such a way that the members of the public may access them from a certain place and at a time individually;
(b) providing an exclusive right to owners of copyright and related right to authorize such acts;
(c) leaving to possibility for legal characterization of such acts – whether they are qualified as communication to the public or distribution or both – and the choice of rights to be applied, as long as the same acts are covered by the same kind of right (exclusive right).[311]

According to Article 26(8) of the Copyright Act, the author shall further have the exclusive right to make available his or her work to the public. This right shall in particular cover the case when the work is made available to the public by cable or any other means or in any other manner so that the members of the public can choose the place and time of the availability individually.

110. The protection of broadcasted works (including authorization of works and pay of remuneration for authors) shall be carried out by collective management organizations.

In the name of writers, composers, and lyrics the organization performing collective administration of rights in literary and musical works shall conclude licensing agreements with the user on the authorization of the broadcasting of an already disclosed work and on the remuneration to be paid for it.[312]

The use of literary works written for dramatic purposes and musical-dramatic works, or scenes or overviews thereof, and of non-fiction works and longer fiction works written for non-dramatic purposes (such as novels) shall not be object of collective management.[313]

In the case of satellite broadcasting, the provisions of the collective administration[314] shall apply only if:

(a) the programme is simultaneously communicated to the public by the same radio or television organization through terrestrial broadcasting; and
(b) the author has not made a declaration against collective administration of his or her works.

In the name of composers and lyricists, the organization performing collective administration of rights in literary and musical works shall conclude licensing agreements with users on the authorization of uses covered by the right to communication of work – and in case of already disclosed non-dramatic musical works with or without words and on the royalty due to be paid, unless the author has made a declaration against collective administration of his or her work.[315]

311. Ficsor, *Guide to the Copyright*, Index, Umbrella solution.
312. Article 27(1) of the Copyright Act.
313. *Ibid.*
314. Article 27(2) of the Copyright Act.
315. Article 27(3) of the Copyright Act.

This collective management does not extend to use musical-dramatic works or scenes or overview thereof.[316]

It shall be mentioned and emphasized that authors cannot assign or waive their moral rights or have these rights assigned to another person in any other manner.[317]

The right of broadcasting is an essential variety of related rights, as outlined in paragraphs 145–146 below.

5. Right to Retransmission

111. Authors have the exclusive right to retransmit (by way of broadcasting) those of their works that have been transmitted to the public by broadcasting as well as the exclusive right to authorize other persons to do so.[318]

Retransmission means the simultaneous and unchanged broadcasting by one broadcasting organization of the broadcast, cablecast or webcast of another broadcasting, cablecasting, or webcasting organization.[319]

Cablecasting means the communication to the public of a cable-originated programme. Transmission by cable of encrypted signals carrying a cable-originated programme is 'cablecasting' where the means for decrypting are provided to the public by the cablecasting organization or with its consent.[320]

In accordance with Article 28(2) of Copyright Act, the author shall also have the exclusive right to authorize the retransmission to the public of his or her work broadcast or transmitted in the programme of a radio or television organization or of an entity communicating its own programme by cable or by any other means to the public, simultaneously and in an unaltered manner via an organization other than the original one.

The right of retransmission is regulated by the Berne Convention. The owner of the copyright enjoys the exclusive right to authorize a rebroadcast when it is done by an organization other than the original one.[321]

Broadcasting organizations enjoy the right to authorize or prohibit the rebroadcast of the broadcasts.[322]

In respect to rebroadcasting, the right holder involves an organization other than original for transmission of its programme. The right to rebroadcast may be exercised through collective management.

The right holder shall also have the exclusive right to authorize simultaneous, unaltered, and unabridged retransmission by cable or other means for reception by the public of an initial transmission (with the involvement of an organization other than the original) by wire or other means of television or radio programmes intended for reception by the public.[323]

---

316. *Ibid.*
317. Article 29 of the Copyright Act.
318. Article 28(1) of the Copyright Act.
319. Ficsor, *Guide to the Copyright*, Index, Rebroadcasting.
320. *Ibid.*, Cablecasting.
321. Article 1 of the Berne Convention.
322. Article 13(a) of the Berne Convention.
323. Article 28(2) of the Copyright Act.

Right holders can only enforce their rights of retransmission through collective copyright management. They are only entitled to waive their fees to the extent of the amount that is due to them, and such waivers can only take effect after the date on which the fees are distributed. The fees are determined by the organization concerned with the collective management of copyrights in literary and musical works in accord with the collective rights management organizations of other right holders. The transmitting organization shall pay the fee as charged to the organization concerned with the collective management of literary and musical copyrights.[324]

The right holders may exercise their rights referred to retransmission only through collective administration and may waive their remuneration only in effect following the date of its distribution and to the extent of the amount due to them.

6. The Right to Exhibition

112. The right to exposition (right to public display) is also regulated in Hungary. This right means showing, exposing, or exhibiting the original or copy of a work in a static (non-sequential) form, either directly or indirectly, that is by means of a side view, an image on a screen, or any other similar way, or, in the case of an audiovisual work, showing individual images non-sequentially.[325]

The Hungarian Copyright Act provides for an exclusive right of authorizing public exhibition of work of art. The Hungarian Copyright Act qualifies the right of exhibition as a legal feature of use of a copyright work in tangible form.

The owner of fine art, artistic photographic, applied art or industrial design creation is obliged to make the work temporarily available to the author in order that he or she can exercise his or her author's right, if such action is without prejudice to the owner's equitable interest.[326]

The exhibition of fine art, artistic photographic, architectural, and applied art creations shall be subject to the author's authorization.[327] The exhibition of a work forming part of a public collection shall not be subject to the author's consent, and no remuneration shall therefore be due to the author. In accordance with Article 69(3) of the Copyright Act, the author's name shall be indicated in the case of the exhibition of the work.

§7. Limitation and Exemptions to the Scope of Copyright Protection

113. The limitations and exceptions in respect to exclusive rights of copyright owners may be permissible so as:

(a) to create and maintain a balance between the interests of authors and other right holders, users and the public at large;

324. Article 28(3) of the Copyright Act.
325. Ficsor, *Guide to the Copyright*, Index, Displaying, display.
326. Article 69(1) of the Copyright Act.
327. Article 69(2) of the Copyright Act.

(b) to take into account the requirements and demands of education, culture and scientific research;
(c) to permit free access to information; and
(d) diminish the monopoly law of authors.

Limitation and expression covers all kind of free uses, non-voluntary licenses as well as other possible limitations (such as subjecting the right to obligatory collective management). Free use means cases where in spite of some general provisions granting an exclusive right or a right to remuneration, shall not be subject to the payment of any consideration and to any authorization of the author.

The main kinds of exceptions and limitations are as follows:

(a) the free use;[328]
(b) the territorial limit and the term of protection of copyright;[329]
(c) the right of the collective management;[330]
(d) the exhaustion of right to distribution.[331]

114. Uses falling within the scope of the free use shall not be subject to payment of any consideration and to any authorization of author. Only works disclosed to the public may be used freely.[332]

The use under the provision relating to free use is permitted and not subject to the payment of a fee only so far as it does not conflict with a normal exploitation of the work, does not unreasonably prejudice the legitimate interests of the author, is in compliance with the requirements of fairness, and is not designed for purpose incompatible with the intention of free use.[333]

The main practical criteria of free use are as follows:

(a) does not conflict with a normal exploitation of work; it is to be understood that the free use is permissible only for the purposes (and may extend to the manner) laid down in the Copyright Act;
(b) does not prejudice the legitimate interests of author;
(c) shall be in compliance with requirements of fairness;
(d) is not designed for purpose incompatible with the intention of free use;
(e) the free use may concern only a divulgated work;
(f) is not intended for earning or increasing income even in an indirect way;
(g) the provision relating to free use shall not be interpreted in an extensive manner.

The three-step test means the basic test for determining whether or not an exception or limitation is permissible under the international norms on copyright and related

328. Articles 33–41 of the Copyright Act.
329. Articles 2 and 33(1) of the Copyright Act.
330. Articles 85–93 of the Copyright Act.
331. Article 23(6) of the Copyright Act.
332. Article 33(1) of the Copyright Act.
333. Article 33(2) of the Copyright Act.

rights. The Hungarian Copyright Act uses the so-called three-step-test provided in the Berne Convention,[334] as far as in TRIPS,[335] WCT,[336] and WPPT[337] agreements.

The three elements of the three-step test that is, an exception or limitation:

(a) may cover only certain special cases;
(b) must not conflict with a normal exploitation of the works and objects of related rights;
(c) must not unreasonably prejudice the legitimate interests of the rights of owners.

115. The purposes of free use permissible by the Copyright Act are as follows:

(a) copying for private purposes;[338]
(b) school education;[339]
(c) scientific information and research;[340]
(d) actual information on current political, cultural events for mass media purposes;[341]
(e) to meet demands of disabled persons;[342]
(f) in court, public administration and other authority proceedings.[343]

116. The most frequent and most significant variety of free use is private copying.

It is well known that many people regularly copy from sound records onto audio cassette or from sound records onto CD and DVD, or sound and audiovisual recordings from MP3 onto CD, and sound and audiovisual recording on DVD, and so on.

From this viewpoint of private reproduction, it must be taken into account that copying for private purposes is under control of the three-step test. This means, that, also in the case of such reproduction, any exception and limitation may only be granted in special cases, and it must not be with a normal exploitation of the works and objects related rights concerned, and must not unreasonably prejudice the legitimate interests of owners of rights.

Private use means use of work and objects of related rights for private, personal, and non-commercial purposes, such as scientific research, education, media, and entertainment. The right to private copying is granted exclusively for any person concerned, his or her family, and circle of acquaintances. In these cases, generally free use is permissible. In certain cases of private use, however, the exclusive right involved (such as the right of reproduction in a computer program) must not be limited, because it would be a normal exploitation of the work. In other cases of private use, the exclusive

334. Article 9(2) of the Berne Convention.
335. Article 13 of the TRIPS Agreement.
336. Article 10 of the WCT Agreement.
337. Article 16 of WPPT Agreement.
338. Article 35(1) of the Copyright Act.
339. *Ibid.*, Arts 34(2), 38(1)b and 38(5).
340. *Ibid.*, Arts 34(2), 35(4).
341. *Ibid.*, Arts 34(7), 36.
342. *Ibid.*, Art. 41(1).
343. *Ibid.*, Art. 41(2).

right involved may be limited to a right of remuneration (as in the case of private copying of phonograms and audiovisual works).

Private copying through the global computer network leads to a specific situation. Due to the great number of people connected to the network, who may make 'private' reproduction, e.g., through the swapping system, allowing this to continue freely would seriously conflict with a normal exploitation of the rights in the works and objects related rights concerned.[344]

In accordance with Article 35(1), a copy of a work may be made by a natural person for private purposes. The private copying shall not be intended for earning or increasing income even in an indirect way.

This provision shall not apply to architectural works, engineering structures, software, and databases operated by a computer device, as well as the fixation of the public performance of a work on video or sound carrier. It shall not be allowed to reproduce sheet music by means of reprography[345] even for private and other purposes.[346]

A complete book as well as the whole of a periodical or daily may be copied even for private purpose only by handwriting or typing.

It shall not be considered as free use to have a work copied by someone else by means of a computer and/or on an electronic data carrier, even if it is done for private purposes.[347]

117. Free use connected to school education is precisely detailed and regulated in the Copyright Act. The possibilities of the free use of school education are as follows:

(a) citation;
(b) borrowing;
(c) making copies for purposes of school education;
(d) making a copy for internal institutional purposes;
(e) the works may be performed for purposes of school education and at celebrations held at school;
(f) the works may be altered for the purposes of school education and within the framework of teaching. The author shall permit in this case the alteration of his work;[348]
(g) free display on the screens and dedicated terminals libraries, educational establishments, museums, archives, as well as audio and audiovisual archives;[349]
(h) the picture of a fine art, architectural, applied art and industrial design creation, furthermore artistic photographs may be used without the authorization of the author and paying remuneration to him or her.[350]

118. For use of the rules of free use shall be taken to serve the purposes of school education if it is implemented in accordance with the requirements of education and

344. Ficsor, *Guide to the Copyright*, Annex, Private copying.
345. Article 21(1) of the Copyright Act.
346. Article 35(2).
347. Lontai et al., *A Szellemi Alkotások joga*, 66–67.
348. Article 34(4) of the Copyright Act.
349. Article 38(5) of the Copyright Act.
350. Article 68(2) of the Copyright Act.

with the curricula respectively used in kindergarten, primary school, secondary school, industrial school education, the primary education of arts, as well as in higher education falling under the scope of the law of higher education.[351]

The Copyright Act permits the right to citation and borrowing.

From a work, any part may be cited by indication of the source and naming the author indicated therein. Such citation shall be true to the original, and its scope shall be justified by the nature and purpose of the borrowed work.[352]

The notion of borrowing defined by the Copyright Act means the use of a work in another work to an extent that goes beyond citation.[353]

Part of a literary or musical work or such a type of an entire work of a minor volume disclosed to the public may be borrowed for the purposes of illustration for teaching and scientific research, with the indication of the source and the author named therein, to the extent justified by the purpose on condition that the borrowed work is not used for commercial purposes.

By virtue of Article 35(1) of the Copyright Act:

> The non-commercial reproduction and distribution of the borrowed work shall not be subject to the author's authorisation where the borrowed work is, pursuant to the relevant legislation, qualified as a textbook or a reference book and that the school education purpose is indicated on its front page.

It is permissible to make copies for purposes of school education and the non-commercial reproduction of the copies.

A complete book as well as the whole of a periodical or daily may be copied even for private purpose only by handwriting or typing.[354]

The publicly accessible libraries, educational establishments museums and archives as well as audio and audiovisual archives shall be allowed to make a copy for internal institutional purposes – outside the scope of entrepreneurial activity – to the extent and in the way justified by such a purpose if it is not intended for earning or increasing income even in an indirect way[355] and if the copy is:

(a) required for scientific research;
(b) made for archiving from an own copy of such an institution for scientific purpose or for public library supply;
(c) made of a minor part of a work made public or of an article published in a newspaper or periodical; or
(d) the copying is allowed by a separate law under certain conditions, in exceptional cases.

For purposes of school education in a number corresponding to the number of pupils in a class, or for purposes of exams in public and higher education in a number necessary

351. Article 33(4) of the Copyright Act.
352. Article 34(1) of the Copyright Act.
353. Article 34(2) of the Copyright Act.
354. Article 35(2) of the Copyright Act.
355. Article 35(4) of the Copyright Act.

for the said purpose, specific parts of a work published, as a book, as well as newspaper and periodical articles may be reproduced.[356]

The works may be performed for purposes of school education or at celebrations held at school, for purposes of scientific educational lectures, as well as of school education, the picture of a fine art, architectural, applied art and industrial design creation. Furthermore artistic photographs may be used without the authorization of the author and paying remuneration to him or her.[357]

119. Free use is also admissible for purposes of the media. The information society may be characterized by necessity of the quick diffusion of the information.

By virtue of Article 37 of the Copyright Act:

> Particular works may be used freely for the purpose of information on current events to the extent justified by this purpose. In the case of such a use, the source – along with the name of the author – shall be indicated, unless it proves to be impossible.

The parts of publicly presented lectures and similar other works, and political speeches may be freely used for the purpose of information to the extent justified by this purpose. In the case of such a use, the source – along with the name of the author – shall be indicated.[358]

Free use in this case is also limited. The authorization of the author shall be required for the publication of collections of publicly presented lectures, political speeches, and similar other works.

Articles published on current economic or political topics or works broadcast on the same topics may be freely used, provided that the author has not made a representation prohibiting such a use.

The free use for the purposes of media extends to:

(a) reproduction;
(b) communication to the public;
(c) making available to the public by cable or any other means or in any other manner so that the members of the public can choose the place and time of the availability individually. In the case of such a use, the source – along with the name of the author – shall be indicated;[359]
(d) any fine art, photographic, architectural, applied art or industrial design creation may freely be used in a television programme as decor. In this case, the indication of the author's name may be dispensed with;
(e) however, the use in a television programme of works made for purposes of decor or costume is strongly limited. In these cases, the authorization of the author shall be required and the indication of his or her name is also prescribed;[360]
(f) ephemeral recording.

356. Article 35(5) of the Copyright Act.
357. Article 68(2) of the Copyright Act.
358. Article 36(1) of the Copyright Act.
359. Article 36(2) of the Copyright Act.
360. Article 36(4) of the Copyright Act.

Ephemeral recording means the recording or fixation of a work or object of related rights made by a broadcasting organization, for a limited period, for broadcasting by the same organization.[361]

Under Article 35(7) of Copyright Act, the ephemeral recording of a work lawfully used by a radio or television organization for the broadcast of its own programme, if made by its own facilities, shall be free.

The term 'ephemeral recording' is limited. Unless otherwise provided by the contract authorizing the broadcasting of the work, such a recording shall be destroyed or erased within three months counted from its making.

The Copyright Act prescribes the possibility of the recording for an indefinite term. The ephemeral recording may, however, be for an indefinite term, preserved on the grounds of their exceptional documentary character in audiovisual and audio archives qualifying as public collections.

120. The free use for the purposes of scientific activity and research allowed by the Copyright Act for the purposes:

(a) right to copying and;
(b) right of the publicly accessible libraries, educational establishments, museums and archives as well as audio and audiovisual archives shall make a copy of a work for internal institutional purposes;
(c) the right of reproduction for purposes of scientific research may be admitted;
(d) ephemeral recording shall be without prejudice to the rights to remuneration for reproduction.[362]

121. The free use for the purposes of scientific activity and research shall be allowed in the following kinds of use:

(a) citation;
(b) borrowing;
(c) making a copy for internal institutional purposes, a copy of the work be made by a natural person;
(d) the picture of a fine art, architectural, applied art and industrial design creation, furthermore artistic photographs may be used without the authorization of the author and paying remuneration to him or her;[363]
(e) under Article 39 of the Copyright Act, libraries providing public services may freely lend individual copies of a work. This provision shall not apply to software and to databases operated by computer devices. The copies reproduced within the scope of free uses shall not be distributed without the author's authorization, except for lending between libraries;
(f) free display on the screens and dedicated terminals libraries, educational establishments, museums, archives, as well as audio and audiovisual archives.

The conceptual criteria of this free display are as follows:

---

361. Ficsor, *Guide to the Copyright*, Index, Ephemeral recording.
362. Article 35(7) of the Copyright Act.
363. Article 36(3) of the Copyright Act.

(a) the free use is permissible only in institutions mentioned;
(b) only in the absence of a contractual provision to the contrary;
(c) only for the purpose of research or private study;
(d) on the screens of dedicated terminals on the premises of such establishments;
(e) provided that this is not for direct or indirect earning or increasing income.

According of the Article 33(4) of the Copyright Act, in the absence of a contractual provision to the contrary, works forming part of the collection of publicly accessible libraries, educational establishments (Article 33(4)), museums, archives, as well as audio and audiovisual archives, may be, for the purpose of research or private study, freely displayed to individual members of the public on the screens of dedicated terminals on the premises of such establishments, and, in the interest of this, they may be in a way and on conditions as provided for in separate legislation communicated, including making available to such members of the public, provided that this is not for direct or indirect earning or increasing income.[364]

122. The free use is allowed to assure the equality of chance. Any non-commercial use of a work shall be free if the purpose of the use is to meet demands of disabled persons that are directly related to the disability and it does not exceed the extent justified by the purpose.[365]

123. The free use is also allowed in the authority proceedings. In court, public administration and other authority proceedings a work may be used for purposes of evidence, in a manner and to the extent consistent with the purpose.[366]

124. The free performance may be considered as a specific case of the free use.[367]

In the cases of free use, the performance shall not be designed to earn or increase income even in an indirect manner and the participants of the performance shall not receive remuneration.

In Article 38(2) of Copyright Act, the given interpretation of increase of income states:

> If a use is suitable for increasing the number of customers (e.g. that of a shop or a place of amusement) or for entertaining the customers of a shop or other types of consumers, it shall be taken to serve the purpose of increasing income. The collection of entrance fees, even if a different name is used for these, shall be taken to mean earning income. Payments exceeding the incurring and justified costs in connection with the performance shall be taken to mean remuneration.

The works may be freely performed in the following cases:

(a) if the performance is not designed to earn or increase income even in an indirect manner;

364. Article 38(5) of the Copyright Act.
365. Article 41(1) of the Copyright Act.
366. Article 41(2) of the Copyright Act.
367. The kinds of free use of the performances regulated in Art. 38 of the Copyright Act.

(b) by amateur theatre groups if a dramatic work is involved and it is performed on the basis of a text published or a manuscript lawfully used, supposing that this is not to prejudice any international agreement;
(c) for purposes of school education or at celebrations held at school, a dancing party held at a school shall not be taken to mean performance for purposes of school education;
(d) within the framework of the care of those of social disadvantage and of aged people;
(e) at religious ceremonies or on religious holidays;
(f) for private use and at occasionally held private social gatherings.[368]

The private social gathering (event) means a party held by an economic organization or a legal entity other than an economic organization exclusively for its members, officers, and employees.

125. The special feature of free use the temporary act of reproduction concerns the use on the internet. In accordance with Article 35(6), a temporary act of reproduction that is transient and incidental – and is an integral and essential part of a technological process with no independent economic significance – shall be free if its sole purpose is to enable:

(a) transmission in a network between third parties by an intermediary, or;
(b) a use of the work authorized by the author or permitted pursuant to the provisions of the Copyright Act and accordingly the linking, browsing, and cashing in on the Internet shall be considered as free use.

126. There are several exceptions under rules of free use laid down in the Copyright Act.[369] A copy of the work may be made by a natural person for private purposes if it is not intended for earning or increasing income even in an indirect way.

This provision shall not apply to:

(a) architectural works;
(b) engineering structures;
(c) software;
(d) and databases operated by a computer device; as well as;
(e) the fixation of the public performance of a work on video or sound carrier;
(f) sheet music.

A complete book as well as the whole of a periodical or daily may be copied even for private purpose only by handwriting or typing.

It shall not be considered as free use to have a work copied by someone else by means of a computer and/or on an electronic data carrier, even if it is done for private purposes.

The performances may be qualified as free use, if these are not designed to earn or increase income even in an indirect manner and the participants do not receive

368. Article 38(1) of the Copyright Act lists the cases of the free performances.
369. Article 35(1) of the Copyright Act.

remuneration, however, a dancing party held at a school shall not be taken to mean performance for purposes of school education.

According to Article 39 of the Copyright Act, libraries providing public services may freely lend individual copies of a work.

This provision shall not apply to software and to databases operated by computer devices.

The copies reproduced within the scope of free uses shall not be distributed without the author's authorization, except for lending between libraries.

Ultimately, it shall be emphasized that the prescriptions of free use shall not be interpreted in an extensive manner.

127. The territorial scope and the term of protection laid down in Copyright Act may be considered as limitation or frontier of copyright. The territorial force of the Hungarian Copyright Law extends exclusively to the Hungarian Republic.[370] The term of copyright protection is acknowledged as a limitation of copyright. In accordance with Article 31(1) of the Copyright Act, the author's economic rights shall be enjoyed during the lifetime of author and for seventy years following his or her death.

128. Compulsory obligatory collective management is a considerable limitation of copyright, in which cases the author shall not conclude a contract of use. The author shall have the right only to remuneration. The right holders may exercise their rights only through collective administration and may waive their remuneration only with effect following the date of its distribution and to extent of the amount due to them.

The cases of mandatory collective management[371] are as follows:

(a) reproduction and distribution of musical works;[372]
(b) the private copying of copyrighted works, performances and sound records;[373]
(c) reproduction of works (works reproduced in photocopying or in like manner);[374]
(d) rental relating to a cinematographic creation or a work included in a sound recording;[375]
(e) lending to the public of works except of cinematographic creations, sound recordings, and software;[376]
(f) terrestrial broadcasting of literary and music works;[377]
(g) the simultaneous and unaltered retransmission to the public of works and performances by cable;[378]
(h) the transfer of the ownership of an original work or article by any dealer in works (droit de suite);[379]

370. Article 2 of the Copyright Act.
371. Lontai et al., *A Szellemi alkotások joga*, 157.
372. Article 19(1) of the Copyright Act.
373. Articles 20(1)(2) and 95 of the Copyright Act.
374. Articles 20(1), (3), (5), (6), and (7) of the Copyright Act.
375. Articles 26(6) and 85–93 of the Copyright Act.
376. Article 26(7) of the Copyright Act.
377. Article 27(1) of the Copyright Act.
378. Articles 28(2), (3), (4) and (5) of the Copyright Act.
379. Article 70(9) of the Copyright Act.

(i) the transfer of the ownership of a original work of art by a dealer in works after the expiration of term of protection.[380]

129. The exhaustion of right may be considered as special limitation of right to distribution. Exhaustion of rights means losing the enjoyment of rights (in fact, the very right itself) by exercising them in certain way.[381] In accordance with Article 23(5) of the Copyright Act:

> If the copy of the work has been put into circulation by the right holder or by another person expressly authorized therefore by the right holder through sale or the transfer of proprietary rights in any other manner in the European Economic Area, the right of distribution – with the exception of the right of rental, lending and importation – shall further be exhausted with regard to the copy of the work, thus put into circulation.[382]

In the field of copyright and related rights, the principle of exhaustion of rights is applicable to the right of distribution. As a rule, the right of distribution, in respect of a copy, is exhausted with the first sale of that copy, or with other first transfers of the intellectual property right in that copy. Therefore, the doctrine of which the principle of the exhaustion of the right of distribution is based, called the 'first sale doctrine'.[383] The purchaser of a copy of a work and object of related rights is free to do certain acts regarding that copy, such as resell it, and in some cases, rent it (but not reproduce it), because the right of distribution of the owner of copyright and object of related rights in respect of the given copy has been exhausted.[384]

The right of exhaustions does not concern the right to lending of cinematographic works and sound recording.

In accordance with Article 23(6) of the Copyright Act, if the right of rental relating to a cinematographic creation or a work included in a sound recording has been transferred, or otherwise licensed, by the author to the producer of the film or sound recording, the author shall retain a claim to the producer of the film or sound recording for a fair and equitable remuneration regarding the distribution of the work through rental. This right may not be waived by the author; however, he may enforce his claim to remuneration only via an organization performing the collective administration of rights.[385]

The principle of exhaustion of rights is not applied when rental becomes one of the basic means of exploitation of certain works (such as cinematographic works and works included in sound recordings); in such cases, a right of rental – as subcategory of the right of distribution – 'survives' the first sale. The exhaustion of rights in the work and object of related rights embodied in the copies in respect of which the right

380. Article 100 of the Copyright Act.

381. Ficsor, *Guide to the Copyright*, Annex, Exhaustion of Rights.

382. The exhaustion of right concerns not only the copyright, but also affects the objects of industrial property (patents, trademark, designs, plant varieties, and utility models).

383. Ficsor, *Guide to the Copyright*, Index, Exhaustion of rights.

384. *Ibid.*

385. Articles 85–93 of the Copyright Act.

of distribution is exhausted does not extend to any other right, e.g., (interactive) making available of works and objects of related rights to the public, irrespective of how the 'umbrella solution' is applied in a given country.

§8. Duration of Protection

130. The term of copyright required by the Berne Convention for the classic form of copyright is the author's life and fifty years thereafter. The Hungarian copyright law prescribed an identical term from 1922 to 1999. Following the Duration Directive, the general term for copyright is the author's life and seventy years thereafter.[386]

The Copyright Act with the amendment of former copyright law have been reinforced by a seventy-year term of protection for authors' rights and one of fifty years of neighbouring rights. It is that in view of the European Union's unquestionable wish the terms of protection are reviewed with retrospective effect.

The duration of protection is the period of time during which copyright in works is and related rights in objects thereof are protected. The basic provision on the duration of copyright protection is Article 31(1) of the Copyright Act. In accordance with this provision, copyright lasts for a term of seventy years after the death of the author, as well as through the life of the author, that is, the authors' rights shall enjoy protection during the lifetime of the author and for seventy years following his or her death.

The seventy-year term of protection shall be counted from the first day of the year following the death of the author; however, there are certain cases in which another prescription can be applied.[387]

In the case of joint authors, the seventy-year term of protection shall be counted from the first day of the year following the death of the joint author who died last. This rule aims to apply to a longer period of protection.

In case of connected works, which made up of which independently can be exploited (volume of poetry and its illustrations) from the first day of the year following the death of the joint author who died last.

In a case in which the author is unknown, the term of protection shall be seventy years and shall be counted from the first day of the year following the first disclosure of the work. In this case, the copyright (only economic rights) belongs to institutions, societies, corporations, or legal entitles.[388]

However, if the author should become known during this period of time, the term of protection shall be counted from the first day following the death of the author.[389]

The duration of copyright protection may depend upon the date of publication. In cases in which the work consists of several volumes or parts, the term of protection is calculated with respect to each volume or part. In the case of a work disclosed to the public in several parts, the year of the first disclosure shall be counted part by part.[390]

386. Tattay, *A Szellemi Alkotások joga*, 116–118.
387. Article 31(2) of the Copyright Act.
388. Article 31(3) of the Copyright Act.
389. *Ibid.*
390. Article 31(4) of the Copyright Act.

The term of the protection of a collective work shall be counted from the first day of the year following the first disclosure of the work.[391]

The term of protection of a cinematographic creation shall be calculated from the first day of the year following the death of the last of the following persons to survive, whether or not those persons are designated as co-authors: the director of the film, the author of the screenplay, the author of the dialogue and the author of the music specifically created for the use in cinematographic creation.[392]

In this case, the term of protection shall be counted from a date other than the first day from the divulgation of creation, and the work is not disclosed to the public within a seventy-year period following its creation, no copyright protection shall further on be due to the work.

According to Article 32 of the Copyright Act, copyright protection of a scope consistent with the author's economic rights shall be due to the person who, following the expiration of the term of protection or the period of time (if the work is not disclosed to the public within the seventy-year period following its creation, no copyright protection shall further be due to the work) discloses according to the law a work previously not disclosed to the public. The term of such protection shall be twenty-five years from the first day following the first disclosure.

With the expiry of the term of protection, the work or the object of related neighbouring rights falls into the public domain.[393]

The duration of copyright protection for motion picture works must be calculated from the first day of the year following the death of the author who dies last.

131. The term of protection of neighbouring rights is generally fifty years. Article 84 of the Copyright Act regulates the duration of all neighbouring rights.

Pursuant to the Article 84(1) of Copyright the subject matters of related rights – with the derogations set out in Article 84(2) – shall enjoy protection for the following periods of time:

(a) unfixed performances, for fifty years from the first day following the year in which the performance was held;
(b) performances fixed not in phonograms, for fifty years from the first day following the year in which the performance was first put into circulation, or for fifty years from the first day following the year in which the recording was fixed if it had not been put into circulation during that term;
(c) performances fixed in phonograms, for seventy years from the first day following the year in which the phonogram was first put into circulation, or for seventy years from the first day following the year in which the phonogram was fixed if it had not been put into circulation during that term;
(d) phonograms, for seventy years from the first day following the year in which the phonogram was first put into circulation, or for fifty years from the first day following the year in which the phonogram was fixed if it had not been put into circulation during that term;

391. Article 31(5) of the Copyright Act.
392. Article 31(6) of the Copyright Act.
393. Lontai et al., *A szellemi alkotások joga*, 84.

(e) broadcast programmes or in own programmes transmitted by cable to the public, for fifty years from the first day following the year in which the programmes were first broadcasted or the transmission occurred;
(f) films, for fifty years from the first day following the year in which the film was put into circulation, or for fifty years from the first day following the year in which the production of the film was completed if the film was not put into circulation during that term.

By virtue of Article 84(2) of Copyright Act the fifty years provided in paragraphs (1) b) and f), and the seventy years set out in point (c) shall be calculated from the first day following the year in which the first communication to the public occurred, if the subject matter of related rights was not put into circulation within fifty years from when the subject matter of related rights was made, but it has been communicated to the public or its communication to the public was prior to its putting into circulation. In the case of phonograms, the seventy years term shall be calculated from the first day following the year in which the first communication to the public occurred if the phonogram was not put into circulation within fifty years after it was made, but it was communicated to the public during that time.

132. The term of duration of protection of databases is generally protected during the fifteen years.

In accordance with Article 84/D, the duration shall run for fifteen years from the first day of the year following the year in which the database first made public or for fifteen years from the first day of the year in which the database was completed in case it was not made public during the term referred to.[394]

In the case of substantial alteration, the term of protection shall recommence that is, the term of protection applying to the database in case the contents of database have undergone a substantial alteration. This substantial alteration as a result of which the altered database, as such, shall be rated as one completed with substantial resources.

A substantial alteration of the database may be the result of successive additions, deletions, and modifications.[395]

133. The term of protection of *droit de suite* corresponds to the duration of copyright society, that is, the authors' rights shall enjoy protection during the lifetime of the author and for seventy years following his or her death.[396]

§9. Neighbouring Rights

134. Chapter XI and Articles 73–84 of the Copyright Act include the prescription in respect of neighbouring rights.

In the traditional narrower sense, the term 'related rights' means the right of performers in respect of their performances, the right of producers of phonograms in

394. Article 84/A(1) of the Copyright Act.
395. Article 84/A(2) of the Copyright Act.
396. Articles 31 and 70 of the Copyright Act.

respect of their phonograms, and the right of broadcasting organizations in respect of their broadcasts.[397]

The broader meaning of the expression extends also to the rights of publishers in typographical arrangement of their published editions (only in certain countries, but these typographical arrangements are not protected in Hungary), and of the generic rights of makers of databases.[398] In particular, in the context of neighbouring rights, it must be noted: scientific edition of works or texts in public domain and the first printing and bequeathed works; phonographic works; performing artists (musicians, singers, conductors dancers, actors, directors); producers of sound recording (records, tapes, and so on.); broadcasting companies (radio, television and so on.); film makers; and owners of databases.

Copyright law accords a more or less reduced protection, similar to copyright, to certain accomplishment that by nature approaches the creation of works of which are closely related to the performance of a work.

The achievements of performers, producers of sound recordings, radio and television organizations, and film producers as far as the makers of databases shall enjoy protection specified by the Copyright Act. The 'neighbouring rights' are synonymous to 'related rights'.[399]

There are organic contacts between the copyright and related rights; however, the protection of the neighbouring rights stipulated in XI Chapter of the Copyright Act may not prejudice the protection of author's in literary, scientific, and artistic creations.[400]

No authorization of the right holders under neighbouring rights shall be required in cases in which the author's authorization shall not be required for the use of statutorily copyrighted creations.[401]

Remuneration shall be due to the owner of related rights against the license he or she has given for the use of his or her related rights, which remuneration shall be in proportion to the revenue earned by the use of the work. The author may waive his or her claim to remuneration only by an express representation to that end.[402]

In the cases of use of related rights, remuneration shall be due to the owner of related right for the use even if he or she has no exclusive right to authorize the use.[403]

397. Ficsor, *Guide to the Copyright*, Index, Related rights.
398. *Ibid.*
399. Article 1(8) of the Copyright Act.
400. Article 83(1) of the Copyright Act.
401. Article 83(2) of the Copyright Act.
402. Lontai et al., *A Szellemi alkotások joga*, 120–123.
403. Article 83(2) of the Copyright Act.

In accordance with Article 74(1), remuneration shall be due to the performer for the uses mentioned in Article 73(1).[404]

Article 74/A regulates the supplementary remuneration for performers.

Where an agreement on the fixation of a performance made with the phonogram producer provides the performer a right to claim a non-recurring remuneration, the performer shall have the right to obtain an annual supplementary remuneration from the phonogram producer for each full year directly following the 50th year after the phonogram was published or, failing such publication, the 50th year after it was communicated to the public.[405]

The right to obtain such annual supplementary remuneration may not be waived by the performer. The right to claim a supplementary remuneration shall only be exercised through collective management of rights.

(2) Following the 50th year, the phonogram producer in order to pay the remuneration determined in paragraph (1) shall transfer to the collective management organization the amount that corresponds to 20% of the revenue which the phonogram producer has derived during the preceding year from the reproduction, distribution and making available[406] of the phonogram in question not reduced with costs. The phonogram producer shall provide any information which may be necessary for the distribution of the supplementary remuneration to those who are entitled to it and to their collective management organizations.[407]

(3) Where a performer based on the agreement of the fixation of a performance made with the phonogram producer is entitled to recurring remuneration proportionate to the income resulting from the use of a performance, the performer shall have the right to obtain a remuneration following the 50th year after the phonogram was published or, failing such publication, the 50th year after it was communicated to the public. The provisions aiming the reduction of this remuneration either by advance payments or deductions defined in the agreement shall be null and void.[408]

135. The performer, the producer of sound recording and broadcasting organization shall have right to authorize or prohibit the use of their performance.

Under the criteria of protection of related rights, the fixation must be first mentioned: The fixation of neighbouring right is capturing an object neighbouring rights in some material form (including storage in an electronic or computer memory)

---

404. In accordance with Article 73, the performer's consent shall be required for:
a) the fixation of his unfixed performance;
b)the broadcasting or the communication in another manner to the public of his unfixed performance, unless the performance broadcast or communicated in another manner to the public is itself a broadcast performance;
c) the reproduction of his fixed performance;
d) the distribution of his fixed performance;
e) making his performance available to the public by cable or any other device or in any other manner in a way that the members of the public can choose the place and time of access individually.
405. Article 74A(1) of Copyright Act.
406. made available to the public by cable or any other means or in any other manner in a way that the members of the public can choose the place and time of access individually.
407. Article 74A(2) of Copyright Act.
408. Article 74A(3) of Copyright Act.

in sufficient stable form in a way that on the basis of the neighbouring rights may be perceived, reproduced or communicated to the public.[409]

The performers, phonogram producers, and radio and televisions organizations have the right to use and particularly to public performance and licensing their performances.

The user of the neighbouring right is a physical person or legal entity who performs an act covered by economic right under related rights. In the broader sense, the user of the related rights is anyone who performs an act of using related rights in any manner or form, including using a lawful copy by the owner, such as reading a book, listening to a phonogram, or watching an audiovisual work.[410]

The use of related rights may be interpreted as follows: in the broader sense, using an object of related rights in any manner and for any purpose including any use by a lawful owner of a copy, such as reading a book, listening to a phonogram, or watching an audiovisual work.

The neighbouring rights may be transferred and assigned. Transfer of the neighbouring rights is the assignment by owner of such rights (assignor) to a physical person or legal entity (assignee) as property. In contrast with a license, which involves only granting a permission to perform certain specified acts, the assignment of a right – at least in the case of exclusive rights – means that the right of authorization or prohibition of acts covered by the right itself is transferred to the licensee (assignee).

136. The Copyright Act includes the exhaustive list of neighbouring rights, which are as follows:

(a) right of performers;[411]
(b) rights of producers of phonogram;[412]
(c) rights of radio and television (broadcasting) organizations;[413]
(d) rights of film producers;[414]
(e) rights of the makers of databases.[415]

The questions of databases are outlined in paragraphs 27–30.

137. In accordance with the Copyright Act, the performer, the producers of sound recording, and radio and television organizations are entitled to make available performances or programmes to the public by cable or in any other manner so that the members of the public can choose the place and time individually.

Programmes communicated to the public by cable may be:

(1) programmes of broadcasting organization simultaneously with original broadcast without changes (broadcast originated programmes);
(2) own programmes of the cable organizations;

409. Ficsor, *Guide to the Copyright*, Index, Fixation of the work.
410. *Ibid.*, Use of related rights.
411. Articles 73, 74 and 75 of the Copyright Act.
412. Articles 76–79 of the Copyright Act.
413. Articles 80 and 81 of the Copyright Act.
414. Article 82 of the Copyright Act.
415. Articles 84/A), B), C), D), E), and F) of the Copyright Act.

(3) programmes of broadcasting organizations not transmitted simultaneously;
(4) programmes of broadcasting organizations transmitted simultaneously with the original broadcast with changes (e.g., the original broadcast may have subtitles).

138. Making available to the public means offering a work or a object of related rights to the public by any means, such as by distribution of copies, public display, public performance, public recitation, broadcasting, or other communication to the public, or by interactively making available to the public, that is, through acts covered by the copy-related rights and acts covered by non-copy-related rights.[416]

On demand transmission is a synonym of making available to the public in a sense, in which that term used in the provisions on the right of making available to the public.[417]

139. As performance shall be rated in particular:

(a) The performance of a work by means of a live performance before an audience, such as stage performances, concerts, recitations, and readings.
(b) Making works perceptible by any technical means or method, such as projecting motion picture works, amplifying the sound of works that are broadcast or distributed (on a particular copy) to the audience, and projecting them on screens.

The performer is the person who recites or performs a work or participates as a performer in the recitation or performance of work.[418]

The performer is not a creator, and what he or she does is only to give an execution of something that has been created by the author.

Performing a work means the act of a performer concerning a work as a result of which, the work becomes audible and/or visible for those who are present at the place of the performance. Furthermore, it means the making audible or visible of an audiovisual work or a work embodied in phonogram through appropriate equipment.[419]

If works are made audible and/or visible to those who are not present at the location from where this takes place, in other words from where the work originates, it is not a performance but a communication to the public, and provided it is given to the public by cable (wire) and in certain cases, making available the work to the public.[420]

It is well known that before the first technological revolution and of mechanical instruments, like performances of music were the occasion in which performers in music earned their money. At the end of nineteenth century, musicians, singers, and

416. Ficsor, *Guide to the Copyright*, Index, Making available of the work to the public.
417. Making available of the work to the public is essential feature of the broadcasting which defined in Art. 26(8) of the Copyright Act.
418. Lontai et al., *A Szellemi alkotások joga*, 69.
419. Ficsor, *Guide to the Copyright*, Index, Right to performing.
420. Under Art. 11(1) of the Berne Convention, owners of copyright must be have the exclusive right of authorizing public performance of their dramatic, dramatico-musical, and musical works. The provision clarifies the concept of such public performance and extends to public performance by any means of process, which means that the public performance of such works fixed in audiovisual fixates or in phonograms is also covered.

other performers lost the position of effective protection of performing rights. The performers have established communities of right owners – joint management organizations – to reinforce their positions.

The right of performers may be considered a commonly used term mainly in the context of collective management of copyright and neighbouring rights, to mean more or less all non-copy-related rights. The performing rights include:

(a) the right of public performance;
(b) the right of public recitation;
(c) the right of broadcasting; and
(d) the right of communication to the public by cable. Performing rights organization is an organization[421] acting as a collective management organization in respect of performing rights.[422]

140. According to Article 73(1) of the Copyright Act, the performer's consent shall be sought for:

(a) the fixation of his or her unfixed performance;
(b) the reproduction or his or her fixed performance;
(c) the broadcasting or the communication in another manner to the public of his or her unfixed performance, unless the performance is broadcast or communicated in another manner to the public;
(d) distribution of his or her fixed performance;
(e) making his or her performance available to the public by cable or any other device or any other manner, so that the members of public can choose the place and time of the availability individually.[423]

In the case of an ensemble of performers, the performers may exercise their rights of performance via their representative.

Article of 73(3) of the Copyright Act provides that after authorizing the fixations of their performances in an audiovisual work, performers may no longer exercise the rights just set out.[424] However, performers retain residual rights of remuneration for home taping, rental, lending, and cable retransmission.

141. The performers also have moral rights.

Under Article 75(1) of the Copyright Act, in a case of the uses, the performer shall have the moral right to have his or her name indicated depending on the nature of use and in a manner consistent with it.

In the case of ensembles of the performers, this right shall apply to the indication of the names of the ensemble, the leader of the ensemble, and the chief performers.[425]

421. Usually an author's society, union or association of owners of related rights.
422. Ficsor, *Guide to the Copyright*, Index, Performing rights organization.
423. Lontai et al., *A Szellemi alkotások joga*, 125–126.
424. The performances may be fixed in cinematographic creations and radio and television programmes.
425. Article 75(1) of the Copyright Act.

The performer also has the right of integrity. The distortion, mutilation, or any other alteration of a performance that prejudices the honour or reputation of performers shall be deemed as infringement of moral rights.[426]

142. The protection of producers of phonograms is also extended to the digitalized phonograms.

The concept of producer of a phonogram, which means the person or legal entity, who or which takes the initiative and has the responsibility for the first fixation of the sounds of a performance or other sounds or the representation of sounds. This definition also extends to electronically[427] generated sounds.[428]

The Rome Convention in Article 3(c) also defines the concept of the producer of phonogram as being the person who or legal entity which first fixes the sounds of a performance or other sounds.

By virtue of Article 76(1) of the Copyright Act, the consent of the producer of a sound recording shall ensure that the sound recording is:

(a) reproduced;
(b) distributed;
(c) made available to the public by cable or any other means or any other manner, so that the members of the public can choose the place and time of the availability individually.

Performers whose performances are recorded in commercially distributed phonograms share, with the producers of these phonograms.

A simple remuneration that parties must pay when broadcasting or otherwise communicating such phonograms to the public.[429]

In Copyright Act, the term is outlined for 'commercial purposes'.[430]

The use of sound recordings for commercial purposes may be considered, if the user of a performance or sound recording makes it available to the public by cable or any other means or in any other manner so that the members of the public can choose the place and time of availability individually.

The retransmission and rebroadcasting and broadcasting or the communication in another manner unfixed performance of performer, broadcasting and the communication to the public sound recording in any other manner shall be regarded as communication to the public.

In the case of the broadcasting or communication to the public of a sound recording released for commercial purposes, rights holders may enforce their claim

426. The performers have moral rights to name, to integrity and to reputation.
427. Digitally distributed.
428. Article 2 d) of WPPT Treaty.
429. By virtue of Art. 77(1) of the Copyright Act, in the case of the broadcasting or communication to the public of a sound recording (or of its copy) released for commercial purposes, the user must be paid an additional remuneration, in addition to the royalty to be paid for the use of the works under copyright protection. This remuneration shall be due to the producer of the sound recording and the performer on an equal basis.
430. Article 77(2) of the Copyright Act.

to remuneration through the organization performing the collective administration of their rights.[431]

143. The producers of sound recordings are entitled to authorize to public lending[432] or rental.[433] In the case of public lending and rental, in addition to that of the author of the work embodied in the recording, the phonogram producer, and performer shall give the authorization. The rental right provided by TRIPS, WCT, and WPPT is in respect of audiovisual programmes and phonograms.

The questions of rental right and lending right outlined on Article (4), (5), (6), (7) of Copyright Act. The lending and rental shall be subject to the payment of remuneration.

144. Pursuant to the Article 79 of the Copyright Act, the producer of a sound recording has the right to have his or her name indicated on the copies of the sound recording.[434]

145. A programme transmitted broadcast as such is an object of related rights granted to the broadcasting organization. Broadcasting is communication of a work of an object of related rights by wireless transmission. It covers terrestrial broadcasting and satellite broadcasting.[435]

For the broadcasting or the communication in another manner to the public of unfixed performance broadcast or communicated in another manner is a broadcast performance.

The definition of broadcasting is contained more precisely in Article 2f of WPPT Treaty. It reads as follows:

> Broadcasting means the transmission by wireless means for public reception of sounds or images and sounds or of the representations thereof. Such transmission by satellite is also broadcasting; transmission of encrypted signals is broadcasting where the means for decrypting are provided to the public, by the broadcasting organization or with its consent.

Broadcasting is not to be understood as including interactive making available of works and objects related rights over computer networks.

The decrypting (encryption, encrypting, decoding) is an important technological protection measure.[436]

The decrypting of a work or of object of neighbouring right into digital format into a secret code (encoding) as a result of which it cannot be perceived or, at least, it

431. Article 77(3) of the Copyright Act.
432. Public lending right means rights granted in respect of lending of copies of work, usually books and other publications, by non-profit libraries open to the public.
433. The rental right means the transfer of the possession of the work or an object of related rights for a limited period of time, and for direct or indirect economic or commercial advantage under some conditions and with some exceptions.
434. Between the moral rights for the author and owner of neighbouring rights, the most essential is the right to name.
435. Article 3(f) of the Rome Convention contains an explicit definition of broadcasting, which reads as follows: Broadcasting means the transmission by wireless means for public reception of sounds or of image and sounds.
436. The terms 'decrypting' and 'decryption' are synonyms of 'decoding'.

becomes unreadable or unintelligible without the key to the code, necessary for the decryption (decoding).[437]

Decoding means the process and the device, respectively, used for the removal or circumvention of the coding, of a work or an object of related rights – which is a technological protection measure – and thus, for its making available for human perception, for reproduction or of (further) communication to the public.[438]

It is usually to publicly communicate its television broadcast by broadcasting organizations in places accessible to the public against payment of an entrance fee.

146. By virtue of Article 80(1) of the Copyright Act, the radio and television organization shall give authorization that its programmes can be:

(a) broadcast or communicated to the public by other radio and television organizations or by entities concerned with communication by cable to the public;
(b) fixed;
(c) reproduced after fixation, if the fixation was made pursuant Article 83(2) of Copyright Act, that is, when no authorization of the right holder under neighbouring rights shall be required, in cases and the reproduction is made for a different purpose than license agreements and, when the author is not entitled to accord exclusive right of use;
(d) made available to the public by cable or any other means or any other manner so that the public can choose the place and time of the availability individually;[439]
(e) to rebroadcast its broadcast;
(f) to fix its broadcast on visual or sound records, naked photographs of its broadcast, and reproduce such records or photographs;
(g) to publicly communicate its television broadcast in places accessible to the public against payment of an entrance fee.[440]

The radio or television organization and the organization communicating by cable its own programme to the public shall have the right to have its name indicated in the case of fixation, communication to the public, reproduction after fixation, making available to the public of their programme.[441]

The use of broadcasting programmes shall be subject to the payment of remuneration. The right to remuneration extends to:

(a) fixation;
(b) communication to the public;
(c) reproduction after fixation;
(d) making available to the public of broadcasting programmes;[442]

437. Ficsor, *Guide to the Copyright*, Index, Decoding, decoder.
438. *Ibid.*
439. Interactive or on demand communication to the public.
440. The publicly communicate its television broadcast in places accessible to the public against payment of an entrance fee may also be considered as broadcasting, and the authorization of radio and television organization shall be required thereto.
441. Article 81 of the Copyright Act.
442. The cases mentioned in Art. 80(1), a, b, c, d of the Copyright Act.

(e) communication broadcasting programme in places accessible to the public against payment of an entrance fee.[443]

147. The producers of the films may enjoy related rights. The neighbouring rights have new aspects received by the Copyright Act. The changes in this regard have great practical impact. The essence of this regulating is that film producers enjoy neighbouring rights. The right of reproduction, distribution, and access in the case of films which are not rated as cinematographic creations and hence do not feature individual, original characteristics that could be considered to originate in the author's own intellectual activity.

By virtue of Article 82(1) of the Copyright Act, the authorization of the producer of a motion picture is required for the motion picture to be reproduced; distributed, inclusive of lending to the public; made available to the public by cable or any other means or in any other manner so that members of the public may access the motion picture from a place and at a time individually chosen by them.

Unless otherwise provided by statute, remuneration must be paid for the use of film in framework of related rights. The questions of cinematographic creations are outlined in paragraphs 64, 65, and 66 of Copyright Act.

§10. Infringement and Remedies

148. The Hungarian Copyright Act defines the types of activity which constitutes infringement of the various forms of copyrighted works generally the right to use (reproduction, distribution, lending, and so on) may be infringed.[444] The Copyright Act also includes further provisions[445] related to the following consequences of infringement:

(a) infringement of moral rights: Under the forms of infringement of moral rights of author, the most dangerous is plagiarism. Plagiarism means presenting a work as the original creation of a person which is in fact the creation of another person either without change or in more or less altered form or context;[446]
(b) unauthorized use of copyrighted works;
(c) circumvention of technological measures[447] shall order that the seizure be carried out at the expense of the infringer. Circumvention of technological measures means avoiding, bypassing, removing, deactivating, or otherwise impairing of technological protection measure;
(d) infringement of the rights management data;[448]
(e) the case of infringement of license agreements;[449]

443. Article 80(2) of the Copyright Act.
444. Chapter II and Arts 10–15 of Copyright Act.
445. Lontai et al., *A Szellemi alkotások joga,* 108.
446. Article 84 of the Civil Code.
447. Article 95 of the Copyright Act.
448. Article 96 of the Copyright Act.
449. Article 8 of the Copyright Act.

(f) infringement of related rights.[450]

Infringement of copyright is an act carried out in respect of a work protected by copyright or an object of related right without authorization of the owner of copyright or neighbouring rights concerned when such authorization is required. The liability for infringement may exist not only on the basis of direct liability but also on the basis of 'contributory liability' or 'vicarious liability'.[451] Liability of those who have the right and ability to supervise the infringing action of another person along with an obvious and direct financial interests in the exploitation of works or object of related rights concerned (e.g., the owner premises hiring). Such liability may exist even in the absence of actual knowledge, because it is connected to the direct infringers, and not necessary to the carrying out infringements.[452]

The author may according to the circumstances of the case have recourse:

(a) on the basis of the Copyright Act;
(b) on the basis of Hungarian Penal Code;
(c) where copyright is infringed, the holder may request – under the provisions of special legislation – measures by the customs authorities to take measures for preventing the goods affected by infringement of rights from being put into circulation.

149. The new Penal Code (Law C. of 2012) contains the provisions concerning the infringement of copyright and certain rights related to copyright. The new Penal Code (Law No. C of 2012) defines in Article 385 certain acts of infringement as criminal offences if they cause material loss to the right holder. Criminal infringement may be constituted even in cases in which it is committed by negligence and on non-commercial scale, albeit with differing sanction.

The new Penal Code also provides for the seizure and confiscation of instruments, such as goods, tools, or devices, that result from, or are used for the commission of offence. Seizure and confiscation are admissible, even when the owner of the instruments is not the offender but is aware of the commission of the offence. The Article 385 of new Penal Code (Law No. C of 2012) prescribes to apply following sanctions:

(a) up to two years imprisonment in the case of infringement committed for profit causing economic prejudice;[453]
(b) up to two years imprisonment in the case of failing to pay the blank media fee or reproduction fee that is due to the author or the holder of a right related to copyright;[454]
(c) up to three years of imprisonment in the case of infringement causing substantial economic prejudice or committed on a commercial scale;[455]

---

450. Article 99 of the Copyright Act.
451. Ficsor, *Guide to the Copyright*, Index, Vicarious liability.
452. *Ibid.*
453. Article 385(1) of the new Penal Code (Law No. C of 2012).
454. Article 385(2) of the new Penal Code (Law No. C of 2012).
455. Article 385(3) of the new Penal Code (Law No. C of 2012).

(d) up from one year to five years imprisonment in the case of infringement causing particularly considerable financial injury;[456]
(e) up to from two to eight years imprisonment in the case of infringement causing particularly substantial financial injury.[457]

The Penal Code has introduced, defined, and prohibited the following copyright crimes:

(a) Compromising or defrauding the integrity of technological measures for the protection of copyright and certain rights related to copyright.[458]
(b) Falsifying data related to copyright management.[459]

150. The amendment of the Copyright Act,[460] effective since 15 April 2006, has introduced changes in the legal system, whereby compliance with the Directive 2004/48 of the IP enforcement (hereinafter: 'IP Enforcement Directive') has been implemented. The main elements of IP Enforcement Directive were adapted by the Copyright Act.

The Copyright Act provides further civil remedies.[461] According to the Copyright Act, the author has recourse to the civil remedies:

(a) he or she may demand that the infringer give information on the identity of persons involved in the protection and distribution of the infringing goods or the provision of infringing services and of channels of distribution;
(b) he or she may require surrender of the enrichment obtained by the infringement of the trademark;
(c) the seizure of goods resulted from the infringement or the delivery up thereof to a particular person, or the recall or definitive removal thereof from commercial circulation, or the destruction thereof.

The important question of the court proceedings is who can be acknowledged as author.

The Copyright Act states presumptions:

(a) for the author to be regarded as such it shall be sufficient for his or her name to appear in the work in the usual manner;
(b) where foregoing subsection does not apply, pending proof to the contrary, the person under whose name the work is registered by the office in the voluntary register.

Seizure of the means and material used in infringing activities and of the infringing activities and the infringing goods shall be admissible even though they are not in the

456. Article 385(4) p.a) of the new Penal Code (Law No. C of 2012).
457. Article 385(4) b) of new Penal Code (Law No. C of 2012).
458. Article 386 of the new Penal Code (Law No. C of 2012).
459. Article 387 of the new Penal Code (Law No. C of 2012).
460. The Act CLXV of 2005 on Amendment of the Copyright Act.
461. Article 94(1) of the Copyright Act.

possession of the infringer, but the holder knew or had reasonable grounds to know about infringement.[462]

The Copyright Act has the rule according to which the infringer can be obliged to provide information against a person or persons whose services are in connection of copyright infringement. In case of copyrighted works, the obligation to provide information is an obligation that can be imposed against any third person, who:

(a) was found in possession in the infringing goods on a commercial scale;
(b) was found to be using the infringing services on a commercial scale;
(c) was found to be providing services on a commercial scale of infringing activities;
(d) was indicated by the person referred to in (a), (b), and (c) as being involved in the production, manufacture, or distribution of the goods or services or the provision of the services.

The delivery of the information can be claimed on an objective basis against third parties as well, thus the obligation can be imposed irrespectively of the fact whether he knew or should have known that their corresponding activity was connected with an infringement.

The following information[463] can be requested:

(a) the names and addresses of the persons involved in the manufacture, production, distribution, supply, and performance of services other holders of the goods affected by the infringement involved in infringement, as well as of wholesalers and retailers involved or intended to be involved and suppliers and holders of the infringing goods or services, as well as the intended involved wholesalers and retailers;
(b) the quantities produced, manufactured, delivered, received, or ordered, as well as the price paid or received for the goods or services in question.

151. The Copyright Act prohibits the infringing acts on commercial scale. Actions on commercial scale should be understood as the acts in which it is obvious from the nature or quantity of the infringing goods or services that these acts carried out for direct or indirect economic advantage.[464]

At the request of the author, the court may order that the materials, implements, goods seized, or recalled and removed from the channels of commerce be deprived of the implements infringing nature and that they be destroyed if such removal is not possible. In justified cases, the court may order, instead of destruction, that the materials seized be auctioned according to the procedure of judicial execution; in such cases, the court shall decide how the sum obtained is to be used. The court shall order the seizure and other measures at expense of infringer.[465]

152. Preliminary injunctions could be requested after the copyright infringement proceeding was started. This is a very substantial measure, as owners of rights can

462. Article 94(8) of the Copyright Act.
463. Article 94(6) of the Copyright Act.
464. Article 94(5) of the Copyright Act.
465. Article 94(7) of the Copyright Act.

obtain such basic information well before the infringement proceeding is finished if they succeed in having the courts order preliminary injunction.

In accordance with Article 94/A(1) of the Copyright Act, in court actions instituted due to infringement of a copyright, temporary measures shall be considered required for the special protection of claimants' rights. If the claimant can prove that the work is under copyright protection and that he or she is the author, the author's heir at law or such a licensee of the work, or a collective management organization is entitled to file an action due to the infringement in his or her own name.

This rule shall not apply if the copyright infringement has commenced more than six months and/or if a period of sixty days has passed since the claimant gained knowledge of the infringement and of the identity of the infringer.[466]

In a copyright infringement case, a request to order provisional measures may be lodged before the filing of the statement of claim and it shall be adjudged by the court in lodging a non-litigious proceeding.[467]

153. The author – beyond the civil law claims available in connection with infringement – may request the court to order, under the conditions applicable to provisional measures:

(a) protective measures in accordance with provisions in the Act on Judicial Enforcement, if able to substantiate that any subsequent attempt for the recovery of enrichment made via the infringement or the payment of damages is in jeopardy, and the infringement is committed on a commercial scale;
(b) the infringer to give notification of and to present bank, financial or commercial information and documents for purpose ordering to protective measures;
(c) the provisions of security if in exchange – in lieu of demanding the cease and desist from infringement – the author gives consent to the continuation of the alleged acts of infringement.

The court shall pass a decision on the provisional measure in expedited proceedings, not to exceed fifteen days following the lodging of the petition for such measures. The court of second instance shall adjudge appeals against court decision on provisional measures also in expedited proceedings, not to exceed fifteen days following the date of lodging the appeal.[468]

154. When one of the parties in a copyright infringement has already substantiated a lawsuit in his or her statement to a reasonable extent, upon the request of party providing evidence, the court may order the other party:

(a) to present and allow for the review of documents and other material proof in his or her possession;
(b) to give notification and to present, bank, financial and commercial information, and documents in his or her possession if the infringement is carried out in commercial scale.

466. Article 94/A(2) of the Copyright Act.
467. Article 94/A(3) of the Copyright Act.
468. Article 94/A(6) of the Copyright Act.

When any delay is likely to cause irreparable harm, it shall be treated as a case of extreme urgency, and provisional measures may be ordered without the other party having been heard.[469]

155. Concerning the circumvention of technological measures, the legal consequences of the infringements of copyright shall apply. Theoretically, a person who circumvents a technical device applied to protect a work or furnishes the means or services necessary for doing so may be held liable for copyright infringement under the Hungarian Copyright Act.

The circumvention of technological measures may be made exclusively in bad faith. Bad faith acts means the person, whoever produces, sells, imports, promotes, installs, modifies, or uses, either for personal or public use, with fraudulent purposes, devices or parts of devices meant to decode conditional access to audiovisual transmissions which have been broadcast by air, satellite or cable, whether in analogue or digital form.[470]

According to Article 95(2) of the Copyright Act, the legal consequences of the infringement shall apply to the manufacture, import, distribution sale, rental, advertisement for sale or rental, or possession for commercial purposes or devices, products or the components or the provisions of services used for infringing:

(a) are promoted, advertised or marketed for the purposes of circumvention of; or
(b) have only a limited commercially significant purpose or use other, than circumvent; or
(c) are primarily designed, produced, adapted or performed for the purposes enabling or facilitating of the circumvention of any effective technological measures.

The technological measures in the Copyright Act are as follows: any device, component, method, or technology that, in the normal course of its operation, is designed to prevent or restrict acts, in respect of works that are not authorized by the copyright holder. Technological measures shall be deemed effective when the use of a protected works is controlled by the right holders through application of an access control or protection process in particular encryption or other transformation of the work or a copy control mechanism, which is suitable to achieve the protection objective.[471]

The legal consequences of infringement shall not apply in respect reproduction, alteration, adaptation translation, and any other modification of software and reproduction or translation of its code by authorized person, but the above-mentioned special legal consequences shall apply relating to the distribution or possession for commercial purposes of any technology, device, or component whose sole intended purpose is to facilitate the unauthorized circumvention or removal of a technological measure applied for the protection of the software.[472]

156. Article 95/A includes provisions concerning the conflict between the circumvention technological measures and free use. The conflict may be arisen particularly in the following cases, namely:

469. Article 94/A(8) of the Copyright Act.
470. Article 95(1) of the Copyright Act.
471. Article 95(2) of the Copyright Act.
472. Article 60 of the Copyright Act.

(a) relating to copying of literary, musical, or scientific works by a natural person for private purposes;
(b) in respect to borrowing of literary works;
(c) copying a work for internal institutional purposes. This kind of use concerns the libraries, educational establishments, museums, and archives as well as audio and audiovisual archives;
(d) ephemeral recording of a work used by a radio and television organizations;
(e) use related of the disabled persons and the free use in court, public administration, and other authority proceedings.

Beneficiary such as free use may demand that the right holder in spite of the protection, granted against the circumvention of technological measures make the free use possible for him, provided, that the beneficiary of the free use has got access to the work lawfully.

The foregoing exceptions shall not apply when the work made available to the public, on a basis of the contract in such a way that the members of the public may access it from a place and time individually chosen by them.

157. By virtue of Article 98(1) of the Copyright Act, the infringement of a license agreement has also consequences:

> In the case of the infringement of authors' economic rights the exclusive licensee may call the author to make necessary measures to stop the infringement. The licensee is entitled to initiate such as legal action in his own name, when the author fails to make the measures within thirty days of the notification.

The licensee is entitled – in the case of a non-exclusive license – to initiate legal action in case of infringement only on express authorization given in the license agreement.

§11. Overlapping and Relations to Other Intellectual Property Rights

158. The admissibility of the parallel protection of different objects of intellectual property belongs to the fundamental principles of Hungarian intellectual property right. According to this basic principle, the cumulative protection of several objects is generally permissible. The protection of copyrighted works may overlap with protection of trademarks, patents, and designs. The cumulation of different rights may be occurred particularly, if these have identical functions.[473]

The overlap between the protection of copyrighted works and trademarks is considerable.

Several subject matters protected by copyright under Hungarian law may also be protected by other intellectual property rights, particularly by industrial property rights. However, there are certain objects in which the limit between the subject matter of copyright and other intellectual property rights is considerably vague. The disappearance of distinctive criteria between the various features of intellectual property creates the

473. For example, the main function of trade marks and geographical indication are identical.

possibility of protection claims under different intellectual property rights for the same subject matter.

In accordance with Article 1(3) of the Copyright Act, the creation shall enjoy copyright protection based on its individual, original nature originating from the intellectual activity of the author.[474] Not only the copyrighted works, but also the designs shall have individual character.

159. Cumulative protection of the copyrighted works and trademarks is possible in Hungarian intellectual property rights.

The extent and function of protection can also be different. Copyright law protects against the reproduction (copying and adaptation) of the work. Trademark law protects a trademark against confusion, but a trademark's power of identification can differ strongly, depending on the intensity of use over time. In other words, while copyright law defines the extent of protection of the protected object by its creation, the extent of protection of the trademark can vary and must be examined in each individual case.

In Hungarian Trademark Law, there is no rule that would exclude works from trademark protection if they are already protected by copyright. Of course, if the applicant or owner of the trademark is not the same person as the copyright owner and has acted without his or her consent, the latter is entitled to claim copyright infringement and cancellation of the trademark registration.

160. The following creations of copyright may be filed and protected as trademarks:

(a) The titles of books films, and, the names of fictitious (e.g., cartoon) characters of copyrighted works as words and combinations of words may be protected as trademarks.
Work titles may be granted independent copyright protection if they are original, but that occurs very seldom by virtue of Article 16(2) of the Copyright Act. The use of the title of the work, if it is unique, shall be subject to the author's authorization, too. Far more important in practice is the specific protection granted for work titles under the Trademark Act, in which titles are not mentioned as a particular category of distinctive signs. Their function of identifying a work is analogous to that of trademarks or other distinctive trade symbols, that is, the function of indicating the origin and the identity of a product. Accordingly, the titles of books and films may be registered as trademarks. Names of fictitious characters can be protected as trademarks for specific goods and services, but they will normally not be eligible for copyright protection due to a lack of originality.
(b) Short works of literature such as slogans can enjoy trademark protection.
Slogans may be protected by the copyright if they are original and individual, and these creations are generally protected as trademarks.
(c) The appearance and other aspects of fictitious (e.g., cartoon) characters of copyright and the emblems as figures and pictures.
(d) The applied art creations or creations produced by drawing, painting, sculpturing as the two or three-dimensional devices (emblems, labelling) may also be protected.

474. The individual character also is the criterion of protection of the industrial designs.

Emblems can be protected both under trademark and copyright law, provided that the respective requirements (distinctive character/originality) are fulfilled. In practice, emblems of a more complex nature, containing not only very plain and banal graphical elements, will often be eligible for cumulative protection. However, in some cases, the external rules define the form of expression so that the emblem cannot be a result of one's creative work so as to be eligible for copyright protection.

Labels are certainly protectable as trademarks if they are sufficiently distinctive, and they can also be protected by copyright if their graphical elements are original.

(e) The works of visual art such as the shape of goods or packaging may be filed as trademarks.

Three-dimensional articles as such can enjoy trademarks after becoming established. Subject to the certain exclusion clauses, the shapes and packaging of consumer goods are protected as trademarks.

Pursuant to Article 2(2)(b) of the Trademark Act, signs exclusively consisting of a shape which are excluded from trademark protection:

- results from the nature of the goods;
- is necessary to obtain a technical result; or
- gives substantial value to the goods.

The Hungarian Intellectual Property Office regularly registers bottles of spirits, wines, perfumes, crates, and containers, if they differ substantially from other shapes of packages available on the market. Whether those packages will also attract copyright protection appears somewhat doubtful in the light of the strict standards generally observed in respect of protection for works of applied art:

(a) musical works as sound signals may be protected as trademarks;
(b) appearance of books or periodicals have distinctiveness thus may enjoy trademark protection.

The appearance of books or periodicals would be protected as 'artistic works' under Article 1(1) of the Copyright Act and generally have distinctive character.[475]

475. The copyright creations shall have originality and individuality; the trademarks shall have distinctive character.

Chapter 2. Patents

§1. Sources: Legislations

161. The current statute of patent regulation in Hungary is the Act XXXIII of 1995 on the protection of inventions by patents (hereinafter: 'Patent Act').

Patents and their regulation have more than a century-old tradition in Hungary. The first Hungarian patent regulation was Act XXXVII of 1895 on the Protection of Patents, which settled questions concerning patent protection of inventions by following the Austrian and German Acts. This Act – with several amendments and complements – was in force until 1 January 1970. The next Hungarian regulation was Act II of 1969, whose first supplementary amendment was carried out in 1993. The intergovernmental Agreement on Intellectual Property concluded in 1993 with the USA, exerted a direct and substantial influence on Hungarian patent law. This agreement demanded – in addition to the recognition of imports as an act of utilization, and the modification of authoritative rules of compulsory license permits – the introduction of patent protection for pharmaceuticals, chemicals, and food products.

The most important factor of the development of Hungarian patent law is the process of association and the accession of Hungary into the European Union. On 16 December 1991, the Association Agreement (hereinafter: 'the European Agreement') between Hungary and the European Communities was signed in Brussels. The European Agreement was entered into force on 1 January 1994. The European Agreement was promulgated by Law I of 1994. The Agreement in its Article 65 prescribed: Hungary shall continue to improve the protection of intellectual, industrial, and commercial property rights, in order to provide by the end of the fifth year from the entry into force of the agreement a level of protection similar to that existing in the Community, including comparable means of enforcing such rights. Finally, within the mentioned time limit, Hungary shall apply to accede to the European Patent Convention (hereinafter: 'EPC') and to other international treaties. Hungary has been a Member of the European Union since 1 May 2004. Thereby all directives and regulations of the European Union are directly valid in Hungary.

The new Law XXXIII of 1995 on the Protection of Inventions by Patents (hereinafter: 'Patent Act') meets the conditions of accession to the Munich Convention: (EPC) The criteria of patentability and the revocation of protection are defined in harmony with the provisions of the convention. The implementation of the application procedure in stages is also in line with the logic of the Munich Convention.

The Patent Act took into account the rules of the Luxembourg Convention on Community Patents, which has not yet come into force, and the EC Directive on the protection of biotechnological inventions and the protection of plant varieties. The Patent Act satisfied also the requirements that were formulated by the multilateral commercial agreement on the settlement of questions related to the trade in intellectual property in the Uruguay Round of GATT (hereinafter: 'TRIPS Agreement'). The Patent Act puts an end to the previous two-levelled regulation and creates a unified codification on a global with reference to rights and obligations related to the patent protection of inventions. The Patent Act – supported by intellectual property theory – retains the civil law character of the Hungarian patent law and the civil law links of the regulations.

The most important new provisions of the Hungarian Patent Act are as follows:

(a) the subject of patent protection;
(b) rights and obligations resulting from invention and patent production;
(c) provisions of license agreement;
(d) invention and patent infringement;
(e) expiration of patent protection;
(f) court proceedings in patent case.

Hungary became a member of the EPC on 1 January 2003. The main legal effect of this fact is that, following this date, a European patent can be claimed and granted with an effect that extends to the territory of the republic of Hungary. The fitting rules and the correcting rules were created by amending the Patent Act with several modifications.

The Hungarian regulations on patents have been reviewed and amended by Act CII of 2003. The new Act entered into force on 1 May 2004, which was the accession of Hungary to the European Union, and introduced the regulations of obtaining a supplementary protection certificate in Hungary based on the Council Regulations (EEC) 1768/92 of 18 June 1992, concerning the creation and protection of medicinal products and amended the rules of exhaustion of patent rights.

The Implementation of the IP Enforcement Directive (2004/48 EC) adopted in Hungary according to Law CLXV of 2005 have been fully effective since 15 April 2006. This law has changed the main elements in the enforcement of patent rights:

> By virtue of Act CXLVIII of 2010 the name of Hungarian Patent Office was changed to Hungarian Intellectual Property Office (hereinafter referred as Office) as of 1 January 2011 to better reflect its competence extending to activities related to all form of industrial property protection as well as to the field of copyright.

The new Civil Code, the Law V of 2013 is one of the most significant achievements of the twenty-first century in Hungary. The Code omits detailed regulation of intellectual property. The new Civil Code shall apply in respect of intellectual property, if these issues directly fall within its scope, which are not governed by the legislation on copyright and industrial property rights of Hungary.

The regulation of patents contains the national laws and regulation and the European laws and regulations, as far as international treaties.

162. National laws and regulations:

Hungarian laws and regulations

Enforcement of decision on intellectual property rights infringement:

– Act LIII of 1994 on Judicial Execution [184/A. §].

- Act XXXIII of 1995 on the protection of inventions by patents (hereinafter: 'Patent Act'). Act VII of 1994 on the amendments to certain laws of industrial property and copyright (concerns the patents).
- Act XXIII of 2009 on the accession to the Agreement, dated 17 October 2000 in London, on the application of Article 65 of the Convention on the Grant of European Patent.
- Act XVI of 2013 on the Amendment of certain Acts relating to Intellectual Property.
- Act CLIX of 2013 on the Amendment of certain Acts relating to Intellectual Property.
- Government Decree 556/2013(XII 30) on customs authority measures against goods, infringing certain intellectual property rights.
- Government Decree No. 147/2007 (VI 26) on the detailed rules concerning electronic filing of certain documents in industrial property procedures.
- Decree No. 19/2005 (IV 12) on the fees for administrative services in industrial property procedures before the Hungarian Patent Office.
- Decree No. 20/2002 (XII 12) on the detailed formalities for patent applications, documents filed in relation to European patent applications, European patents and international patent applications for plant variety protection. Act VII of 1994 on the amendments to certain laws of industrial property and copyright. Government Decree No. 26/2004 (II 26) on the rules necessary for the implementation of the European Community Regulations concerning the creation of a supplementary protection for certain products.
- Government Decree No. 141/2008 (V 16) on the detailed rules of the procedure to declare a patent application of state secrets.
- Government Decree No. 61/2006 (III 23) on the deposit and handling of biological materials for the purposes of patent procedures.[476]

163. Community laws and regulations: Following the date of the accession of Hungary to the European Union, all Community law and Regulations are directly valid in Hungary. The most important European Union rules related to patents are as follows:

- Regulation (EC) No. 816/2006 of the European Parliament and of the Council of 17 May 2006 on compulsory licensing on patents relating to the manufacture of pharmaceutical products for export to countries with public health problems.
- Directive 2004/48 of the European Parliament and of the Council of 29 April 2004 on the enforcement of industrial property rights.
- Directive 98/44 of the European Parliament and the Council of 6 July 1998 on the legal protection of biotechnological inventions.[477]
- Regulation 1610/96 EC of the European Parliament and of the Council of 23 July 1996 concerning a supplementary protection for plant protection products.
- Regulation (EC) No. 469/2009 of the European Parliament and of the Council of 6 May 2009 concerning the supplementary protection certificate for medicinal products.

476. Lontai et al., *A Szellemi alkotások joga*, 183.
477. Tattay, *A Szellemi Alkotások joga*, 405–409.

164. Treaties and conventions: Hungarian patent law was always characterized by the following up of international legal developments and by the taking into consideration of the pertinent international conventions in force. Hungary joined the Paris Union Convention for industrial property in 1909. Since that time, Hungarian patent acts have developed in harmony with the Paris Convention as well as with the important international agreements linked to it.

The most significant international treaties in which Hungary is a member:

- Paris Convention for the Protection of Industrial Property – Promulgated by the Law – Decree No. 18/1970 (hereinafter: 'Paris Convention').
- European Patent Convention 2000 (EPC 2000) – Promulgated by Act CXXX of 2007.
- Implementing Regulations to the European Patent Convention 2000 – Promulgated by the Government Decree No. 319/2007 (XII 5).
- Agreement on the application of Article 65 of the Convention on the Grant of European Patents (London Agreement) – Promulgated by the Act XXIII of 2009.
- Act LI of 2002 on the Promulgation of the International Convention for the Protection of New Varieties of Plants 2 December 1961, as revised at Geneva on 10 November 1972, on 23 October 1978, and on 19 March 1991.
- Patent Cooperation Treaty – Promulgated by Decree No. 14/1980 (hereinafter: 'PCT Treaty').
- Regulations under the Patent Cooperation Treaty – Promulgated by Decree No. 34/2002 (XII 25) IM.
- Patent Law Treaty – Promulgated by Act CXXXI of 2007.
- Regulations under the Patent Law Treaty – Promulgated by the Government Decree No. 320/2007 (XII 5).
- Budapest Treaty on the International Recognition of the Deposit of Micro-organisms for the Purposes of Patent Procedure – Promulgated by Decree No. 1/1981.
- Regulations under the Budapest Treaty on the International Recognition on the Deposit of the Micro-organisms for the Purposes of Patent Procedure – Promulgated by Decree No. 21/2002 (XII 13).[478]

§2. Patentable Subject Matter

165. The Patent Act defines the notion of patentable invention: patents shall be granted for any inventions in any field of technology which are new, involve an inventive activity, and are susceptible to industrial application.[479]

Pharmaceutical products, chemical products, and foodstuffs for human or animal consumption as such can be patented since 1 July 1994. Processes for the manufacture of any of these were patentable already before that date.

Biotechnological inventions are patentable in accordance with Directive 98/44/EC of the European Parliament and of the Council on the protection of Biotechnological Inventions.

478. Tattay, *A Szellemi Alkotások joga*, 405–409.
479. Article 1(1) of the Patent Act.

The Patent Act established the protection of biotechnological inventions when the subject matter of the invention is a biotechnological material, possessing specific characteristics as a result of the invention, and the exclusive right of exploitation shall be extended to any biological material derived from that biotechnological material through propagation or multiplication in an identical or divergent form and possessing those same characteristics.[480]

In accordance with Article 20/A(2) of Patent Act, when the subject matter of the invention is a process that enables a biological material to be produced possessing specific characteristics as a result of the invention, the exclusive right of exploitation shall extend to any biological material directly obtained through that process and to any other biological material derived from the directly obtained biotechnological material through propagation or multiplication in an identical or divergent form and possessing those same characteristics.[481] However, inventions that concern microbiological or other technical processes or products obtained by means of such processes and, furthermore, elements isolated from the human body or otherwise produced by means of technical processes, including sequences and partial sequences of genes, may constitute patentable inventions.[482]

166. Plant varieties and animal varieties and essentially biological processes for the production of plants or animals shall not be patentable.[483]

Inventions concerning plants or animals may also be patentable if the technical feasibility of invention is not confined to a particular plant or animal variety.[484] The amended Patent Act introduced a new independent protection for plant varieties. In accordance with Article 105 of the Patent Act, a plant variety is a plant grouping within a single botanical taxon of the lowest known rank, which grouping, irrespective of whether the conditions of protection are fully met can be:

(1) defined by the expression of the characteristics resulting from a given genotype or combination of genotypes;
(2) distinguished from any other plant grouping by the expression of at least one of the said characteristics;
(3) considered as a unit with regard to its suitability for being propagated unchanged.

Plant variety protection shall be granted for varieties that are distinct, uniform stable, and new.

167. The first medical or veterinary use of a substance already known per se may be patented.

The second or subsequent medical or veterinary use of a substance already known in the treatment of another disease[485] may be patented.

168. The following are not deemed inventions and therefore cannot be patented: methods for treatment of the human or animal body by surgery or therapy, and diagnostic

480. Article 20/A(1) of the Patent Act.
481. Csécsy, *A Szellemi Alkotások joga*, 96.
482. Lontai, *A Szellemi Alkotások joga*, 158–160.
483. Article 6(4) of the Patent Act.
484. Article 6(5) of the Patent Act.
485. 'Second medical indication'.

methods to be carried out on the human or animal body.[486] This provision shall not apply to products, in particular substances (compounds) and compositions, for use of such methods.

169. The following types of biotechnological inventions are explicitly excluded from patentability:[487]

(a) processes for cloning human beings;
(b) processes for modifying the germ line and genetic identity of human beings;
(c) uses of human embryos for industrial or commercial purposes;
(d) processes for modifying the genetic identity of animals which are likely to cause them suffering without any substantial medical benefit to man or animal, and also animals resulting from such processes;[488]
(e) biological processes for the productions of plants or animals; the human body, at the various stages of its formation and development, and the simple discovery of one of its elements, including the sequence or partial sequence of a gene.[489]

170. Inventions shall be considered unpatentable when their commercial exploitation would be contrary to public order or morality; however, this type of exploitation shall not be deemed to be so contrary merely because it is prohibited by law or regulation. However, the use of an invention may not be deemed contrary to public order only because it is prohibited by law or regulation.[490] The Act outlines the sphere of inventions excluded from patent protection in the narrowest way possible, and only those are listed whose publication or utilization could offend against public order or public morality. There is an important regulation that makes it unambiguous that utilization should not be considered as violating public order simply because it contradicts a given real regulation.

171. Pursuant to Article 5(2) of Patent Act, therapeutic or surgical processes for the treatment of the human or animal body shall not be considered as susceptible of industrial application. This provision can be mentioned as an exclusion of patentability:

(a) discoveries, scientific theories, and mathematical methods;
(b) aesthetic creations;
(c) schemes, rules and methods for performing mental acts, playing games or doing business, and programs for computers;
(d) presentation of information.

172. Computer programs as such cannot be patented, but may be protected under copyright law. Computer-related inventions, namely inventions involving the use of a computer program,[491] may not be patentable due to a lack of the required technical nature as referred to above.

486. Article 6(10) of the Patent Act.
487. Csécsy, *A Szellemi Alkotások joga*, 97–99.
488. Article 6(2) of the Patent Act.
489. Article 5/A(3) of the Patent Act.
490. Article 6(2) of the Patent Act.
491. Pintz, *Találd fel magad*, 22.

Computer programs are covered under the Copyright Act.[492]

§3. Conditions of Patentability

173. The Patent Act sets out the concept of patentable invention, as well as the conditions under which the patent may be protected, in harmony with several international treaties.[493] The Patent Act does not include a legal definition of the concept of an invention or patent; it only states the criteria for patentable invention.

By virtue of Article 1(1) of the Patent Act, a patent shall be granted for any invention in that is new, or that involve an inventive activity and are susceptible to industrial application in any field of technology.

Under this definition, the conditions of patentability have been substantially changed because the Patent Act imposes only three conditions of patentability, instead of the original four requirements imposed by the earlier Act (Act II of 1969) that were: novelty, progress in the art, technical character, and practical applicability. Thus, out of the earlier requirements, novelty alone has actually been retained. Inventive activity is a new requirement. As a consequence of the requirement of technical character and practical application, strictly speaking, industrial application had also been earlier.[494] The concept of advancement is not included in the former Patent Act. However, this requirement was indirectly retained, because inventive activity in general supposes a solution of advancing character.

The aim of the requirements of the conditions of patentability is to create legal security for a third person, who, acting in good faith makes use of different technical solutions, and to exclude any double or parallel patent protection.

The Patent Act sums up the conditions that make it possible, once they are satisfied, for the applicant to have a patent granted for his or her invention. Through its formulation, it is made unambiguous that the patent authorities do not have discretionary competence as to the granting of patents. These conditions correspond to the necessary and sufficient conditions of patentability. In case of the absence of any of them, the invention cannot be protected by a patent; however, if they all exist, a patent has to be granted – without consideration of any point of view – for the invention.

174. The novelty is the most essential criterion of patentability. The Patent Act defines the requirements of novelty. By virtue of Article 2(1) of the Patent Act, an invention shall be considered new if it does not form part of the state of the art. The sense not forming part of the state of the art has been prescribed in Article 2(2) of the Patent Act: The state of the art shall be held to comprise everything made available to the public by means of a written description or oral communication, by use or any other way, before the date of priority. The state of the art deemed to comprise everything made available, to the public anywhere in the world, before the filing or priority date,

492. Article 1(2) c) of the Copyright Act.

493. Article 52 of the Munich Agreement (EPC) and Art. 27 of the TRIPS Agreement, Art. 1 of the third Strasbourg Agreement.

494. Lontai et al., *A Szellemi Alkotások joga*, 184.

through written description or oral information, by use in any other way (absolute novelty requirement).

The state of the art is also deemed to comprise the contents of patent applications and utility model applications filed in Hungary before the filing or priority date and published after that date. Furthermore, the state of the art is deemed to comprise the content of international patent and utility model applications filed under the PCT or a European Patent application designating Hungary, provided that the national phase of PCT applications before the Office has been properly entered into and the European patent application published. Under Article 2(3) of the Patent Act, the content of such a European patent application and international (PCT) patent application shall only be considered as comprised in the state of the art on special conditions laid down in Patent Act. For the purposes of these provisions since 2003, the whole contents of European patent applications designating Hungary should be considered as belonging to the state of art.[495]

The contents of a patent application or a domestic application for design protection with earlier priority shall be deemed to comprise part of an existing technology, provided it has been published or announced following the priority date in the application procedure.[496] Under the Hungarian patent law, the whole contents of earlier applications as mentioned in the foregoing paragraph are to be taken into consideration, and not only claims of a valid Hungarian Patent or utility model based on an earlier filing date would be detrimental to novelty.[497]

The EPC has empowered the Member States to regulate the content and conditions for provisional protection, which comes into effect by the publication of European patent application in a way different from the final protection. For this purpose, the Patent Act provides that rights conferred by the publication of a European Patent application shall be affective in Hungary when the Office has given official information in the Gazette on the filing of the Hungarian translation of the claims.[498] The content of this provisional provision identical to the final protection of Hungarian patents laid down in Patent Act.[499]

The abstract shall not be interpreted as the content of the application from the point of view of patentability and the proof of novelty or inventive activity. The contents of earlier applications as mentioned in the foregoing paragraph are of relevance only for the determination of novelty of an invention, and not for deciding upon whether the invention based on an inventive step when determining the novelty an invention.[500]

It may not be considered to comprise a part of an existing technology in the disclosure of the invention, that occurred no earlier than six months, preceding the date of priority if it was due to an abuse of the rights of the applicant or his legal predecessors in title or display of the invention[501] – within six months preceding the priority date – by applicant or his or her legal predecessor at an exhibition specified

495. Article 84/D(2) of Patent Act.
496. Article 2(3) of the Patent Act.
497. Csécsy, *A Szellemi Alkotások joga*, 94.
498. Article 84/E of the Patent Act.
499. Article 19 of the Patent Act.
500. Pintz, *Találd fel magad,* 25.
501. Article 3 a) and b) of the Patent Act.

in an announcement by the president of the Hungarian Patent Office published in the Hungarian Official Gazette.[502]

175. Inventive activity is regulated under Article 4(1) of the Patent Act.[503] According to the Patent Act, only solutions representing determined creative performance can obtain patent protection.

The law defines two criteria to judge inventive activity, namely, the state of art and the person skilled in the art, because it prescribes that the invention cannot be concluded obviously from the state of art by a person skilled in the art. The criterion of the inventive step allows such a creative requirement to prevail. The inventive step can be established if the solution, compared with the state of art is not obvious.[504] When judging such evidence, it is the knowledge of a person skilled in the given technical field that will be the norm, that is, will serve as guidance. If the knowledge belonging to the art gives sufficient guidance to the skilled person enabling him or her to carry out the invention, that is, using such knowledge as a basis, it would be possible to reach the solution for which a patent application has been filed without any inventive step – no patent protection can be granted.[505]

Pursuant to Article 4(2) of the Patent Act, patent and utility model applications with earlier priority but later publication included in the state of art under Article 2(3) are not to be considered in the examination of inventive activity.[506] Today, an ever-greater number of solutions based on inventive activity are being developed in spheres of sciences such as chemistry, bioengineering, plant cultivation, engineering, and electronics. These solutions are the results of extensive experimental series and pre-planned work processes as such inventive character cannot be denied solely because they are based on pre-planned experiments.

When inventive activity is examined, the state of the art should be considered in its totality, that is, mosaic like manner.[507] Whereas all interiorities accessible to the public should be viewed commonly as a sum of experiences, which are freely available to every person skilled in the art endowed with an ordinary capability to combine them to solve the task. Such a person skilled in the art and who possesses average theoretical knowledge and practical skill shall be considered in the professional art relating to the invention.

The inventive level is not influenced by the method of invention, because an invention may be based on a conscious chain of ideas, fortunate intuition, systematic design of work, or even an accidental recognition. Similarly to the novelty examination, retrospective judgment on the state of art with knowledge of the invention should by all means be avoided, when examining inventive activity.[508] This means that one should beware of declaring a solution to be obvious that appears simple based on the first

502. Magyar Közlöny.
503. An invention appears to involve an inventive activity if it is not obvious to an expert relative to an existing technology.
504. Pintz, *Találd fel magad*, 26.
505. Csécsy, *A Szellemi Alkotások joga*, 95.
506. From the perspective of an inventive activity, the provisions contained in Art. 2(3) pertaining to existing technologies shall not apply.
507. Cornish & Llewelyn, *Intellectual Property*, 201.
508. Lontai et al., *A Szellemi Alkotások joga*, 187.

impression received from the invention. That is, simple solutions are not always obvious; inventive activity is not excluded by the simplicity of an inventive idea. It can even be stated that achieving the same result through the development of a simple solution instead of a more complicated one is much more difficult. Thus, the simplicity of an invention may actually be proof of inventive activity when no one has previously suggested a solution despite a long-established demand.

When judging inventive activity, care should be taken that the judgment is not influenced either by technical development following the date of the application or knowledge due to the invention. A decision about whether or not a technical teaching is based on an inventive activity must be made only by evaluating all circumstances of the case.

The fact that the invention significantly influenced technical development may be proof in itself of inventive activity.

In a well-developed field, improvements can be considered as the result of inventive activity.

A finding of inventive activity is often supported by the unexpected surprising properties of a product. This is the case of analogous chemical processes resulting in new compounds, in which the new product of an obvious process known per se shows properties or activities that could not be expected with the knowledge of products similar in structure in the present state of science.

Significant technical progress can be the mark of an inventive performance but in itself cannot be substituted for inventive activity. However, if the technical teaching was obvious under the knowledge of the state of art, patentability is not established even by a high-level technical advancement that achieves significant economic success.

Commercial success can also represent as proof of inventive activity; however, the presence of inventive activity cannot be concluded from commercial success if it can essentially be attributed to business, economic, and organizational factors.[509]

Inventive activity is also present in the prevailing opinion of professionals who, have not discovered the technical teaching based on the invention, despite a long-established demand. However, inventive activity cannot be based on a long-established and insufficiently satisfied demand in itself when the solution was obvious and did not require the invention to overcome particular difficulties. Nevertheless, overcoming a commonly established technical misconception is proof of inventive activity.

Recognition of a way to achieve a decisive advantage by deviating from commonly used routes is an unequivocal proof of inventive activity. Such a case occurs when professional prevailing opinion has become accustomed to particular solutions and is not inclined to assume the risk, accompanying a deviation, while the new teaching leaves the accustomed way and so provides important advantages.

In the case of inventions relating to an application, inventive activity can be judged on the basis of whether the novel application of a known substance, equipment or process is an obvious solution for a person skilled in the art on the basis of the state of art and the average knowledge of a person skilled in the art. The novel application must be a performance exceeding the average, and which cannot be expected from a person skilled in the art.[510]

---

509. Cornish & Llewelyn, *Intellectual Property*, 204.
510. Pintz, *Találd fel magad,* 27.

In the case of transfer inventions, inventive activity cannot be found if an average person skilled in the art could have achieved the same, because inventive activity is usually absent when a known teaching transferred to a related technical field.[511] It is to be decided whether there is a need to examine other technical fields when the same task presumably would have been obvious to a person skilled in the art of a technical field seeking the same goal. However, a transfer can be considered the result of inventive activity in the case of related technical fields, if technical difficulties exist that can be overcome only by creative activity.

Examination for inventive activity of an invention using a combination should be commenced with an investigation of the combination of all characteristics. In the case of such inventions, inventive activity should be recognized when, due to the combination, a cooperation of the individual components occurs, or due to the simultaneous use of the components known per se forming the combination an unexpected surplus appears. Inventive activity should also be recognized when the combination is based on a new recognition and gives a novel instruction to the state of art.[512]

176. Industrial applicability is the practical criterion of patentability. By virtue of Article 5 of the Patent Act, an invention shall be considered susceptible to industrial application if it can be produced or used in a branch of industry or agriculture.[513]

In harmony with international practice[514] – from the point of view of industrial applicability – the industrial character must be understood in the broadest sense possible. The industrial character is a criterion of patentable invention; however, the task solved must not fall absolutely within in the field of industry. For example, products, devices, and equipment used in processes for surgical or therapeutic treatment or examination of the human or animal body are qualified to be industrially applicable.[515]

It is sufficient that it is possible to begin exploitation the subject of the invention in such a field; that is, the patenting of an invention is not excluded if the subject of the invention can be used in another unpatentable field in addition to the industrial or agricultural use. The inventor has to prove only the possibility of the industrial or agricultural use, therefore he or she is not to exclude the possibility of an industrial or agricultural use, and so he or she is not obliged to exclude the use of the subject of his invention in an unpatentable field. Thus, a cosmetic treatment is not unsuitable for patentability owing to the fact that the chemical substance used for the treatment of the human or animal body can be used both for cosmetic and therapeutic purposes, e.g., to decrease or increase weight and simultaneously, for the treatment of pathological obesity.[516]

The substances (compounds) and compositions for methods of treatment of the human or animal body by surgery or therapy and diagnostic methods practised on the human or animal body are industrially applicable.

---

511. Tattay, *A Szellemi Alkotások joga*, 246.
512. Csécsy, *A Szellemi Alkotások joga*, 96.
513. In accordance Art. 5(1) of the Patent Act, an invention is deemed susceptible of industrial application if it can be produced or used in a branch of industry or agriculture.
514. Article 2(2) of the Paris Convention.
515. Cornish & Llewelyn, *Intellectual Property*, 206.
516. Pintz, *Találd fel magad*, 22–23.

Any self-supporting activity carried out for the purposes of profit-making are considered as industrial. The preparation, commercialization, and transportation of economic and consumer goods belong to this category. Most services rendered for fees, such as the activities of hairdressers and beauticians as well as the activities of mining, gardening, forestry, fishing, and the like can be classified in this category.[517]

However, the pursuit of liberal professions such as the activities of physicians, pharmacists, lawyers or architects as well as examination and measurement processes aimed exclusively at scientific establishment cannot be classified as industrial activities.

A finding of industrial applicability cannot be refused for chemical intermediates that can be transformed to useful final products because these are produced in industrial plants. All products, including equipment, devices, and substances prepared in an industrial plant can be considered to be industrially applicable.

Inventions that are aimed at modifying an area or construction works placed thereon, e.g., the establishing of dams channels, bridges, silos, roads and the like, are industrially applicable.

A process can be considered as not industrially applicable, if all possibilities of use of any industrial field are excluded. A process of this art, e.g., a surgical process to inhibit and alleviate baldness, is therefore not patentable.[518]

The irradiation of the human body with X-rays, ultrasound or electrical waves and similar processes carried out to obtain criminal data on the dead human or animal body are not excluded by Article 5 of the Patent Act.

In particular, the therapeutic or surgical procedures for the treatment of the human body or animals, as well as diagnostic procedures to be carried out on the human body or animals shall not be deemed susceptible of industrial application. However, this provision shall not apply to any product used in such procedures, in particular to any material (compound) and mixture.[519]

Diagnostic processes carried out on the human or animal body cannot be considered to be industrially applicable. Such a process may be present when the aim of the examination is to obtain data or symptoms relating to the health state or the patient as well as to determine the therapeutic process required. Thus under common conditions, both establishing facts to recognize and systematically identify a disease as well as evaluation, that is, a statement of diagnosis, belong to the scope of diagnostic methods. However, diagnostic processes are only excluded from patentability if the results can be directly utilized to determine the appropriate medical treatment, such as an allergy test carried out on the basis of skin alteration.[520]

Processes relating to the treatment of the human or animal body, which do not serve therapeutic purposes, are also industrially applicable. In addition to cosmetic processes, such processes include those relating to the detection of pregnancy and contraception, since pregnancy is not a pathologic state; and processes regarding aging, because aging is a natural physiological process and not an anomalous state of the organism.[521]

---

517. Lontai et al., *A Szellemi Alkotások joga*, 188.
518. Tattay, *A Szellemi Alkotások joga*, 255.
519. Article 5(2) of the Paris Convention.
520. Lontai, *A Szellemi Alkotások joga*, 159.
521. Csécsy, *A Szellemi Alkotások joga*, 96.

Treatment processes enhancing the performance of useful animals, e.g., processes increasing the output of meat, milk, egg, or wool, are not therapeutic treatments and therefore, are industrially applicable. Processes for the artificial insemination of animals as well as for killing pests are considered to be patentable.

§4. Formalities (Procedure of Grant and Obtaining Patent Protection)

177. In a fashion similar to that of the previous Patent Act (Law II of 1969) the 1995 Act delegates patent procedures partly to the public administration and partly to the competency of the courts. The so-called patent affairs listed in Article 44 of the Patent Act belong to the areas of public administration whereas the competency of the courts extends to a procedure for legal remedy concerning public administrative resolutions adapted in patent affairs and patent lawsuits.

By virtue of Article 44(2) of the Patent Act, the Office shall have authority in the following matters:

(a) granting of patents;
(b) decisions on the lapse of patent protection and the restoration of patent protection;
(c) revocation of patent;
(d) decisions on lack of infringement;
(e) interpretation of patent descriptions;
(f) keeping the registers of patent applications and patents, including matters concerning their maintenance;
(g) official information on patent matters;
(h) the Office shall have authority in matters, deriving from the application of provisions relating to European patent applications and European patents and to international patent applications;
(i) the Office shall also proceed in matters relating to supplementary protection certificates;
(j) the Office shall also proceed in matters relating to compulsory licenses.

The decisions of the Office in patent matters shall be reviewed by the court in non-contentious civil procedure.[522]

The Office shall proceed in the patent matters referred to its jurisdiction in accordance with the provisions of Act CXL of 2004 on the General Rules of Administrative Proceedings and Services.[523]

Unless otherwise prescribed by law, the Office shall open proceedings in the patent matters referred to its jurisdiction upon request.[524]

178. Concerning subjective, objective and formal requirements of the patent procedure the following should be mentioned. The person who has created an invention

522. Article 53/A(2) of the Patent Act.
523. Article 45(1) of the Patent Act.
524. Article 45(2) of the Patent Act.

shall be deemed to be the inventor. The right to patent shall belong to the inventor or his successor in title.[525]

Unless a final court decision or other final decision rules on the contrary, the right to patent shall belong to the person who filed the application with the earliest date of priority.[526] The date of filing an application for a patent shall be the day on which the application is received by the Office.[527]

Patent protection shall be granted for an invention if it satisfies the conditions of the patentability (novelty, inventive step and industrial applicability) and is not excluded from patent protection. The relevant application shall comply with formal requirements related to patent applications and patent procedure.[528]

Inventors are granted patents if they disclose their inventions. Nothing that is not described in a patent specification can enjoy patent protection. The Patent Act strengthened the application of this principle by providing legal grounds for cancellation, which include the case when the subject of the patent is wider than the contents of the original application.

The prescriptions of patent procedure are very applicant friendly. The Office accepts papers in foreign languages but may require verified translation of the official documents.

The Patent Act prescribes a four-month period, counted from the filing date, the specification, claims an abstract in Hungarian along with the drawings. After filing the application, the priority claim of an application filed not earlier than twelve months before may be accepted and the priority is to be submitted within four months from the acknowledged filing date.

During the examination procedure, the Patent Office may object both to the unity[529] and the merits of the application. The objections are expressed in a written action, and the applicant is given the opportunity to respond to the objections within an extensible term of at least thirty days. If no answer is filed, the Office deems that the applicant has revoked the rights previously acquired on the basis of publication. This means that any amendment of the application documents originates from the applicant. The term is usually three months for applicants from abroad, and it can be extended three times.

The principle of priority plays an important role in the patent procedure. One cannot exclude the possibility that several inventors will come up with the same idea. Under the Hungarian Patent Act, a patent is granted to the one that filed the earliest patent application (the principle of 'first to file'). The Hungarian patent law has always applied the principle of 'first to file'.

The date establishing priority shall be:

(a) generally, the date of the filing of the patent application (application priority);

---

525. Csécsy, *A Szellemi Alkotások joga*, 125.
526. Article 7(1) of the Patent Act.
527. Article 45(1) of the Patent Act.
528. Article 7(2) of the Patent Act.
529. In accordance with Art. 59 of the Patent Act, patent protection may only be claimed for one invention, or for a group of inventions which are connected by way of a single and common concept of invention.

(b) in cases defined by the Paris Convention, the date of filing of the foreign application (convention priority);
(c) the date of the filing of previously filed and pending patent application for the same subject matter, which is not earlier than twelve months prior to the current filing, provided that it has not served as a basis for claiming a right of priority (internal priority).

179. Convention priority shall be claimed within sixteen months from the date of the earliest priority, making a declaration to this effect. Correction of the declaration of priority may also be requested within this time limit. The Patent Act defines the convention priority.[530] Priority within the Community, under the conditions set out in the Paris Convention for the Protection of Industrial Property, may be claimed if the application was submitted in a country that is a member of the World Trade Organization but not a party to the Paris Convention for the Protection of Industrial Property, or in another country under the principle of reciprocity. As to whether reciprocity applies shall be determined on the basis of the opinion of the president of the Office.[531]

The filing date of an application shall be the date on which the application filed with the Office contains at least:

(a) an application that patent is sought;
(b) indication identifying the applicant or permitting contacts with the applicant;
(c) a description or a document that can be regarded as a description, even though it does not comply with other requirements, or in place of it reference to an earlier application.[532]

If in place of the description reference is made to an earlier application for according a date of filing, a copy of the earlier application shall be filed within two months from receipt of the application containing this reference and – if it was made in a foreign language – the Hungarian translation thereof.

The document underlying convention priority within the Community (priority document) shall be submitted within also sixteen months from the date of application.[533] Correction of the declaration or priority may be requested within this time limit.

The priority document – the copy of the origin of foreign application – shall be deemed to be filed if it is available to the Office in any other way and if it is considered as an annex of the patent application, without filing it separately, on the basis of an international treaty or a decision of the President of Office taken with regard to the international cooperation and published in the Gazette of Office.[534] Convention priority may be claimed on filing or within two months of filing the application, stating the country, the filing date, and of the serial number of the first Convention application.

530. Article 61(9) of the Patent Act.
531. Article 61(4) of the Patent Act.
532. Article 58 of the Patent Act.
533. Articles 61(2) and (4) of the Patent Act.
534. *Official Journ*al of the Hungarian intellectual Property Office.

If the application is made in the name of someone other than the applicant in the basic case, an assignment of priority rights is required.[535]

The priority document shall be submitted by the applicant. The priority document – copy of a foreign application – shall be deemed to have been submitted if it is made available to the Office by other means, and if it is deemed to have been accompanying the patent application under international treaty or by decision of the president of the Office made under international commitment, and published in the Gazette of the Office.[536]

180. The admissibility of the parallel protection of different objects of intellectual property belongs to the fundamental principles of Hungarian intellectual property rights. According to this basic principle, the cumulative protection of several objects is generally permissible. The protection of patents may overlap with protection of utility models. The patent applications may be transformed utility model application and vice versa.[537]

Internal priority may also be claimed from the earlier patent application filed in Hungary, for an application filed within twelve months of the filing date of such an earlier application.[538] For claiming internal priority, it is required that publication of whose priority is claimed is still pending, and that it has not yet served as a basis for claiming priority right. If an internal priority has been claimed, the earlier application whose priority was claimed shall be considered withdrawn. Derivation from utility model application is allowed, when the applicant has already filed a utility model application at an earlier date, and he or she may, in his or her declaration of priority filed within two months after the date of filing of patent application for the same subject matter, claim the filing date of the utility model application and the right of priority relating to such application.[539]

Under Article 62(2), derivation of a patent application shall be admissible within three months from the date when the decision on the grant of utility model protection becomes final, but not later than twenty years from the filing date of the utility model application.

Partial priority may also be allowed.

Multiple priorities are also allowed. Multiple priorities may be claimed for any one claim in a patent application.[540] If one or more priorities are claimed with respect to an application, the priority right shall cover only those elements that are disclosed in a sufficiently clear and detailed manner in the application whose priority is claimed.

Overlapping between the protection of utility models and designs is a regular phenomenon. Protection may be granted to a technical invention by utility model relating to the construction, structure or arrangement of components of an article,

---

535. Lontai, *A Szellemi Alkotások joga*, 246.
536. Article 61(5) of the Patent Act.
537. Tattay, *A Szellemi Alkotások joga*, 292–293.
538. According to Art. 61(6) of the Patent Act, internal priority shall be claimed within four months from the date of filing the patent application. If claiming internal priority, the earlier patent application shall be deemed to be withdrawn.
539. Article 62(1) of the Patent Act.
540. Article 61(5) of the Patent Act.

provided that they are new, involve an inventive step, and are capable of industrial application. Only one article is registerable in one application.

A design shall be protected to the extent that it is new and has individual character. Design means the appearance of the whole or a part of a product resulting from the features of, in particular, the lines, contours, colours, shape, texture, and/or materials of the product itself and/or its ornamentation.

The shape and appearance of a product may be protected simultaneously by utility model and design.

181. Article 57 of the Patent Act includes the main requirements of patent application. Relating to patent-granting procedure, the procedure for the grant of patent shall begin with the filing of the patent application with the Office.

According to Article 57/A of Patent Act, patent application can also be filed electronically by using an electronic form drawn up by the Office for this purpose.[541]

The patent applications, requests for the recording of the changes in the facts may also be filed electronically:

By virtue of Article 53/D(1) of Patent Act Intellectual Property Office shall not be obliged to communicate with the party by electronic means in writing.

The patent application shall contain a request for the grant of a patent, a description of the invention with one or more claims, an abstract, drawings when necessary, and other relevant documents.

A patent application shall be subject to the payment of the filing fee and a search fee; the fees shall be payable within two months after the date of filing.

When the documents making up the patent application have been prepared in a foreign language, the patent description with the claims, the abstract and the drawings shall be filed within four months after the date of filing.

The request, the description with claims, the drawings, and the abstract must commence on a new sheet and must all be numbered separately as consecutive numerals. The contents of all these parts must be in accordance with each other.

In accordance with Article 57(1) of the Patent Act, following the submission of the patent application, the Office examine whether:

(a) the application meets the requirements for the accordance of the date of application (Article 58 of the Patent Act);[542]

---

541. In accordance with Arts 57/A(1) and (2) of Patent Act, patent applications may be filed by way of electronic means, using the standard electronic form prescribed for this purpose by the Office and the Office shall confirm receipt of patent applications by way of electronic means by sending a notice to the applicant – in accordance with specific other legislation – by way of an automated reply system containing an electronic file number.

542. Article 58(1) prescribes that the date of filing an application for a patent shall be the day on which the application is received by the Office and it contains *inter alia* the following:

(a) reference to a claim to the patent;

(b) data that can be used to identify the applicant or make contact with the applicant possible;

(c) description or a similar document, regardless of whether or not it complies with the prescribed requirements or a reference to an earlier application submitted in lieu of a description.

(2) The reference to claim to the patent and the data identifying the applicant shall be indicated in Hungarian for having the date of application acknowledged as well.

(b) the application and research fees[543] have been paid;[544]
(c) the patent description, extract, and drawing have been submitted in Hungarian.[545]

The person whose name is shown in the application submitted on the registered date of application as the inventor shall be deemed the inventor.

This examination is called preliminary examination of patent.

182. The main requirements[546] of a request for the grant of patent are the following:

(a) petition for the grant of patent;
(b) the full name and address of the applicant;[547]
(c) if there are several applicants the proportion of their entitlement must be mentioned;
(d) title of the invention;
(e) indication of subject matter of invention;
(f) declaration that the applicant is the inventor or successor in title of the invention;
(g) indication of name and address of inventor, if there is more than one inventor;
(h) proportion of authorship must be mentioned;
(i) name and address of patent attorney, if any (power attorney);[548]
(j) claim to priority rights;
(k) list of documents attached to the request;
(l) signature of applicant or agent.[549]

183. The description must disclose the invention in such manner and with such details so that the invention can be carried out by a person skilled in the art on the basis of the specification and drawings.

The description and claims may not contain any drawings, but they may contain tables and mathematical formula denoted by numbers or letters.[550] The description must include:

(a) claims;
(b) all the reference signs indicated in drawings;
(c) the title of the invention;
(d) a short specification of the subject matter;

543. Article 58 of the Patent Act.
544. According to Art. 57(4) of the Patent Act, patent applications filed by electronic means shall be considered submitted when the automatic confirmation is sent to the applicant containing the electronic file number, unless the Hungarian intellectual Property office declares the document received unworkable, and notifies the party accordingly by electronic mail.
545. By virtue of Art. 57(5) of the Patent Act, if the appendices to the application are prepared in a foreign language, the Hungarian version of the patent description, the claim or claims, the extract and the drawing shall be submitted within four months from the date of the application.
546. Article 58(1) of the Patent Act.
547. Csécsy, *A Szellemi Alkotások joga*, 128.
548. Manuel of Patent Applications (Budapest: Hungarian Patent Office, 2009), 11.
549. Pintz, *Talál, fel magad*, 39–44.
550. Csécsy, *A Szellemi Alkotások joga*, 128.

(e) indication of the prior background art, by describing the known solutions that are the closest to the invention and citing the documents that reflect this prior art, and description of the shortcomings the invention intends to improve;
(f) indication of the technical problem to be solved by the invention;
(g) mentioning of the most usual mode for carrying out the invention in accordance with the main claim;
(h) description when necessary, of the advantageous modes in accordance with the dependent claims;
(i) enumeration of the figures in the drawings by indicating their subject;
(j) one or more examples supporting the scope of protection claimed;
(k) statement of the advantages of the invention with reference to background art;
(l) chemical and mathematical formula and foreign characters, if necessary;
(m) the claims may only contain tables if there are indispensable;
(n) the claims may refer to the specification or drawings only by the reference signs;
(o) the description and the claims must be signed at the last page by applicant or agent.[551]

In the claims, the extent of the patent protection applied for must be defined unambiguously, and in accordance with the description. Depending on the nature of inventions, claims may be for a product, an apparatus a process or a use. The claims must be numbered consecutively in Arabic numerals. A claim must consist of one sentence. It must consist of a first part (statement) and a second part (characteristic portion); the first part must indicate the subject matter of the invention and when appropriate, and its features common with the solution forming part of state of the art which is closed to the invention.[552]

The second part must indicate the features that distinguish the invention from the solutions already known and, in particular, from the solution closest to the invention.[553]

184. Drawings, if necessary for a clear understanding of the invention shall be annexed to the filing. The drawings must be executed in dark, well-defined durable and informally thick lines without colourings, folds, or cracks. The different figures of the drawings must be arranged on the sheet or sheets clearly separated from each other. Each reference sign used in the drawings must be simple and clear. The drawings may not contain text matter, except, for short and simple words being indispensable for understanding (water, open, closed, and great and small, etc.).

185. The abstract must be filed in the Hungarian language. The abstract must contain the title of the invention and the short summary (preferably in fifty to hundred fifty words of the invention as disclosed in the specification, claims and drawings, so as to allow a clear understanding of the gist of the solution of the technical problem concerned through the invention, and the principal use of the invention.[554] The abstract shall serve for the purpose of technical information only. The abstract may in particular

551. Pintz, *Talald fel magad*, 39–44.
552. *Manuel of Patent Applications*, 8–10.
553. Pintz, *Talald fel magad*, 42.
554. *Manuel of Patent Applications*, 14–15.

not serve for the interpretation of the extent of the protection claimed, and may not be taken into consideration when determining the state of the art.[555]

186. Procedure for processing patent application[556] has three main periods (period of the filing-period of novelty search-period of substantive examination) and may be divided into eight sections:

(a) preliminary examination;
(b) formal examination;
(c) novelty search;
(d) publication of application;
(e) observations;
(f) substantive examination;
(g) preparations of grant, amendment;
(h) grant of patents.

A patent application shall be subject to the payment of filing fee and search fee and before the grant of a patent, the fee for the grant shall be payable.[557]

The Gazette of the Office shall be given information to the public relating to the patent application and certain data and facts relating to the grant of patents after obtaining of patent.[558] A patent application shall also be published after the expiry of eighteen months from the earliest date of priority in the Official Journal of the Office.[559]

187. The section of the patent filing includes preliminary examination and formal examination of patent application. Upon filing of the application, the Office will examine whether the minimum requirements for obtaining a filing date have been meet, the application fees, including the search fee has been paid and the description, drawings, and abstract have been filed in the office to be complied with, then the applicant will be given thirty days within which to comply therewith. If the required documents are filed within this period, the date that these are received will be considered as the filing date. If the required documents are not filed within the thirty-day term, the application will be deemed withdrawn.[560]

If the required fees have not been paid, the applicant will be informed to the effect that payment within two months from filing the application is a necessity, and failing to do so will incur forfeiture of application. If the requirements for obtaining the filing date have been met, the following will be published in the Gazette of the Office including the name and address of applicant and the agent, the file number of application, the application date, and the priority date and the title of invention

If the applicant fails to respond to the request within the prescribed time limit, the patent application shall be considered withdrawn.[561]

---

555. *Guide to Patent Protection* (Budapest: Hungarian Office, 2004), 26.
556. Lontai et al., *A Szellemi Alkotások joga*, 214.
557. Lontai, *A Szellemi Alkotások joga*, 214–221.
558. *Guide to Patent Protection*, 11.
559. Article 70(1) of the Patent Act.
560. *Guide to Patent Protection*, 56.
561. Article 68(2) of the Patent Act.

188. Pursuant to Article 68(1) of the Patent Act, after the preliminary examination, the application will be examined as to compliance with the formal requirements.[562,563] If the formal requirements are found not to meet the appropriate standard, the applicant will be notified and be invited to remedy the defects. If the applicant's reply is considered insufficient, the application will be rejected. If the applicant fails to reply, the application will be deemed withdrawn.[564]

189. The novelty search follows the formal examination of patent application.[565] If the formal requirements are found complied with, the Office will carry out a novelty search, and will prepare a novelty search report on the basis of the claims, with due regard to the description and drawings[566] (if any). In this report, the documents and data will be mentioned which may be taken into consideration when judging novelty and inventive step.[567] The report will be sent to the applicant, with copies of the documents cited therein. Information on the novelty search will be included in the publication of application, or if the search report is not yet available at the date of publication, it will be published separately in the Gazette of the Office.

In accordance of Article 69/A(1) of Patent Act at the request of the applicant, the Hungarian Intellectual Property Office shall draw up a search report supplemented with a written opinion.

The written opinion – containing also reasons – is a preliminary establishment whether the invention, taking into account the documents and the information cited in the search report, appears to meet the requirements of novelty, inventive activity, and industrial application.[568]

The request for a search report supplemented with a written opinion shall be filed within ten months from the accorded filing date.[569]

In accordance with Article 69(1a) of Patent Act, if the patent application with regard to all the claims or certain claims is unsuitable for a proper novelty search, the search report shall only contain a statement to it and the reasons thereof. If the patent application also contains claims suitable for novelty search, the Office shall prepare a partial search report with regard to such claims.

Pursuant to Article 69(1b) of Patent Act, if the patent applications does not satisfy the requirements of unity of the invention (Article 59), the Office shall prepare a partial search report concerning the invention mentioned in the first place among the claims, or concerning the inventions constituting a uniform group with this invention. The

562. Special formal requirements of application, request for the grant of patent, description, claims an abstract and the drawings.
563. Tattay, *A Szellemi Alkotások joga*, 280–281.
564. *Guide to Patent Protection*, 14–15.
565. By virtue of Article 69(1)of Patent Act Intellectual Property Office shall carry out a novelty search and shall draw up a search report on the basis of the claims, with due regard to the description and any drawings.
566. According to Art. 69 of the Patent Act, if the patent application is in compliance with the conditions set out in s. 65, the Hungarian Intellectual Property Office shall conduct a novelty search and shall prepare a novelty search report on the basis of the claims, with regard to the patent description and the drawing.
567. Lontai et al., *A Szellemi Alkotások joga*, 220.
568. Article 69/A(2) of Patent Act.
569. Article 69/A(3)of Patent Act.

Office shall invite the applicant for the division of the patent application during the substantive examination

According to Article 76(2) of Patent Act, the search report shall mention those documents and data, which may be taken into consideration in deciding whether the invention to which the patent application relates is new and involves an inventive activity.

By virtue of Article 76(3) of Patent Act, the search report together with copies of any cited document shall be transmitted to the applicant.

In accordance with Article 76(4) of Patent Act, information shall be published in the Gazette of Office on the search carried out simultaneously with the publication of the application, or separately if the search report is available at a later date.

The written opinion containing also reasons is a preliminary establishment whether the invention, taking into account the documents and the information cited in the search report appears to meet the requirements of novelty, inventive activity, and industrial application.

In accordance with Article (6), the request for a search report supplemented with a written opinion shall be rejected if it does not comply with the requirements mentioned.

In accordance with Article 69/A(6) of the Patent Act, the Hungarian Intellectual Property Office shall draw up the search report supplemented with a written opinion--with the exception for an accelerated research-- on the basis of the description, claims and drawings at its disposal on the last day of the fourth month from the filing of the request to this effect and shall send it to the applicant within six months from the filing of the request for a search report supplemented with a written opinion.

190. A patent application will be published after expiration of eighteen months from the filing date.[570] Publication shall be made by publishing following data in Gazette[571] of the Office:

(a) the name and address of applicant and the agent;
(b) the application file number;
(c) the application date;
(d) the priority date;
(e) the title of the invention;
(f) the name of the inventor;
(g) the international classification of the invention;
(h) the abstract with the most characteristic drawing (if any);
(i) and a statement as to whether publication is to be made after preparation of the novelty search report.[572]

In accordance with the publication of the application, a provisional protection starts. Upon publication of the application, the entire file will be open to public inspection. Until the publication of the application, only the applicant, his or her representative and the body of experts can be called upon to give an expert opinion (if any) and will

570. Article 70(1) of the Patent Act.
571. Article 70(2) of the Patent Act.
572. *Guide to Patent Protection*, 29.

have access to the files. The inventor also has access to the files and is entitled to make remarks, even if he or she is not the applicant.[573]

The applicant may withdraw his or her application before publication of application.

191. Any person may file with the Office observations[574] with regard to the patentability of the invention, after the publication of an application. Such observations will be taken into consideration during the substantive examination.[575]

192. The substantive examination shall include inquiries:

(a) whether the invention meets the requirements of patentability, set out in sections 1–5/A and is not deemed unpatentable pursuant to subsections (2)–(4) and section (10) of section 6 of the Patent Act;[576]
(b) whether the application therefore is in compliance with all the proceedings conditions.[577]

Each patent application is to be examined as to novelty, patentability per se, inventive step, and applicability in industry and unity of invention. The substantive examination is not taken up automatically, but only on specific request thereto being made by the applicant. The examination request may be made on filing the application, or thereafter, but may not be made later than six months after the day that information on the novelty search is published in the Gazette of the Office.[578] An examination request once made cannot be withdrawn, but the application may be withdrawn. The required examination fee must be paid on filing of examination request or within two months thereafter, failing which the application will be deemed withdrawn.[579]

193. If the requirements of patentability are found not to be met, the applicant will be invited to remedy the defects, to file his or her comments or the file divisional application, as the case may be. If the applicant's reply is found unsatisfactory, the application will be rejected entirely or partly; however, a second Office action may be issued if deemed.

In accordance with Article 77(1), if the patent application and the invention to which it relates meet all the requirements of the examination, the office shall grant a patent for the subject matter of the application.

If, during the examination, it is found that a patent may be granted, the Office will send the applicant the version of the description, claims, and drawings for which it is intended to grant a patent. The applicant may then within a period of three months inform the Office whether he or she agrees with that version.[580] Within the same three-

573. Pintz, *Talált fel magad*, 50.
574. Article 71(1) of the Patent Act.
575. Csécsy, *A Szellemi Alkotások joga*, 130.
576. Article 74(2) of the Patent Act.
577. *Guide to Patent Protection*, 91–92.
578. Article 75(1) of the Patent Act.
579. Article 75(5) of the Patent Act.
580. In accordance with Art. 77(2) of the Patent Act, prior to granting the patent, the versions of the patent description, the claim and the drawing, upon which patent will be granted shall be sent to the applicant for agreement. The applicant shall communicate his decision concerning such agreement within three months.

month period, the fee for grant and printing must be paid.[581] If the applicant agrees with the said version, providing that the grant and printing fee are paid in time, the patent will be granted. If the applicant proposes an amendment, or files a new description, claims, or drawings, the Office will make the decision as to whether the amendment or new version will be taken into consideration when establishing final version.[582]

After granting of the patent, a patent certificate will be issued with the printed specification, claims and drawings attached thereto. The invention, as patent will be registered[583] and published in the Gazette of the Office which includes:

(a) the registration number;
(b) name and address of patentee;
(c) name and address of the agent;
(d) the file number;
(e) the application date and priority date;
(f) the title of the invention;
(g) the international classification, the name and address of the inventor; and
(h) the date of decision of grant.

194. If the application is rejected, an appeal with the Office is not possible, but a request for reconsideration of the decision of the Office by the Metropolitan Court of Justice can be filed within thirty days of the notification of a decision. The request may be submitted to the Office, which will forward it to the Court with the documents of the patent case within fifteen days. The Metropolitan Court shall act through a division of three members, two of these members having a technical university degree or equivalent qualification. An appeal to the decision of the Metropolitan Court can be lodged with the Metropolitan Appeal Court within fifteen days.

195. Annual fees are due for the maintenance of patent protection, both in respect of a published application and for a granted patent. The first payment of annuities is due on the date of the publication of the patent application. Further annuities are payable on the anniversaries of the filing date.

Pursuant to Article 53/A(1) of Patent Act against the decisions of the Office appeals, rehearing and supervisory procedures and notice of the prosecutor under the Act of Prosecution shall not be admissible.

The decisions of the Office in patent matters shall be reviewed by the court in non-contentious civil procedure.

In the absence of a provision of this Act to the contrary, the Office may withdraw or modify its decisions terminating the procedure taken in the following matters only if a request for review is made and only until such request is transmitted to the court:

---

581. In accordance with Art. 77(4) of the Patent Act, before granting the patent, a granting fee defined in specific other legislation shall be paid within the three-month time limit set for the statement of applicant. Failure to do so shall be construed as the applicant's surrender of temporary patent protection.
582. Article 77(3) of the Patent Act.
583. In accordance with Art. 78(2) of the Patent Act, the granting of the patent shall be registered in the patent register and official notice shall be published thereon in the *Gazette* of the Office.

(a) grant of patents;
(b) decision on the lapse of patent protection and the restoration of patent protection;
(c) revocation of patents;
(d) decision on lack of infringement;
(e) grant, modification and review of compulsory licenses to which Regulation 816/2006/EC;
(f) publication of the translation of the claims of the published European patent application, filing of the translation of the specification of a European patent and correction of the translation.

According to Article 53/A(4) of Patent Act, in the absence of a provision of this Act to the contrary, the Office may withdraw or modify its decision terminating the procedure taken in the matters:

(a) decision on lack of infringement;
(b) grant, modification and review of compulsory licenses to which Regulation 816/2006/EC;
(c) publication of the translation of the claims of the published European patent application on the basis of a request for review only if it establishes that its decision infringes the law or if the parties request unanimously the modification or withdrawal of the decision.

Pursuant to Article 53/A(5) of Patent Act, in cases where no opposing parties are involved, the Hungarian Intellectual Property Office may – according to the request for review – withdraw or modify the decisions defined in Article 85(1)(b) to (e)[584] if the decision does not infringe the law; however, the Hungarian Intellectual Property Office agrees with the content of the request for review.

In accordance with Article 53(1) of Patent Act, prior to the publication of the patent application, only the applicant, his representative, the expert, or the body called upon to give an expert opinion furthermore – if it is necessary for performing their tasks prescribed in this Act – the court, the prosecutor or the investigation authority may inspect the files. The inventor may inspect the files even if he is not the applicant. After publication – subject to paragraph (2) –anyone may inspect the files of the patent application.

584. According to Art. 85 (1) (1) b) to e) of Patent Act upon request, the court may review the Hungarian Intellectual Property Office's
(b) decisions suspending procedure or furnishing a basis for entries in the Patent Register;
(c) orders excluding or limiting the inspection of files, against which independent legal remedy is admissible under the provisions of the Public Administration Procedures Act;
(d) orders denying persons the legal status as a party to the procedure apart from those who have submitted request for the commencement of a procedure;
(e) decisions imposing procedural fines or ruling on the amount and on the apportionment of procedural costs and their payment.

Upon payment of a fee, the Hungarian Intellectual Property Office shall issue copies of documents that may be inspected if they were not asked by the court, prosecutor, or investigation authority.[585]

§5. Ownership and Transfer (Assignments & Licenses)

196. Patent protection entitles the inventors or their legal successors exclusively to utilize their inventions. Just like ownership, this right with an absolute structure, which can be transferred, inherited, and pledged, because propriety rights arising from a patent may be separated from inventors' moral rights. Special rules may apply to inventions that are created in the course of employment, to assignment of patents, and to license agreements.

The person who has created an invention shall be deemed to be the inventor. In accordance to Article 8 section (1) of the Patent Act, the right to a patent shall belong to the inventor and his or her successor.[586]

Unless a final court decision or other official decision rules to the contrary, the right to a patent shall belong to the person who filed the application with the earliest date of priority.

If two or more persons have created an invention jointly, the right to the patent shall belong to them or their successors in title, jointly. When two or more persons are entitled to the right, it shall be deemed to belong to them equally unless otherwise provided.[587]

197. By virtue of the provision of the Patent Act, a service invention is an invention made by a person, who by reason of his or her employment, is under the obligation to develop solutions in the field of the invention.[588]

An employee (dependent) invention is an invention made by a person, who without being under obligation by reason of his or her employment, makes an invention, the exploitation of which falls within the field of business of his or her employer.[589]

Under current regulations, both a service invention and an employee invention can be created only within the framework of a labour relationship. The provisions concerning service and employee (dependent) inventions shall apply if the invention was created by civil servants, professional members of the armed forces or the police, or members of a cooperative whose legal relationship to the cooperative is one of employment. If an agency or research contract is concluded covering the creation of an invention, thus presuming that it will result in a patentable invention, the regulation allows the parties to specify, when concluding the contract, the person, physical or legal, who will have the right of disposition or the patent claim concerning the intellectual solution to be created.

198. The conceptual criteria of a service invention according to the Patent Act are as follows:

---

585. Article 53(3) of Patent Act.
586. The inventor or his or her successor in title shall be entitled to the patent.
587. Article 8(3) of the Patent Act.
588. Article 9(1) of the Patent Act.
589. Article 9(2) of the Patent Act.

(a) an existing relationship between inventor and employer;
(b) within the required labour relationship, the inventor shall be obliged to develop new technical solutions and products;
(c) the elaboration or creation of new procedures or products to be realized by the inventor should be in the field of invention concerned.[590]

The inventions of employee can be deemed to be of a service nature only if it is unequivocally clear that is within the very domain of employment, that is, research and development, and the labour contract or the actual specification of the task laid down within the performance requirements it implies. Thus, the inventor in terms or his or her labour relationship shall develop a solution within the scope of invention.[591]

The new regulation offers the possibility of a clear delimitation of service inventions[592] and employee inventions.[593] The differences between the two types of inventions can be summarized as follows:

(a) in case of a service invention, the employer is entitled to the right to a patent from the moment of the creation of the invention;
(b) in case of an employee (dependent) invention, the right to a patent remains with the inventor with the limitation that the employer is entitled to a non-exclusive rights of exploitation with respect to the invention from the moment of its creation.

The rights and obligations related to the acquisition of protection concerning service and employee (dependent) inventions have being regulated by the Patent Act. Article 11(1) states that the inventor shall notify the employer of a service or employee (dependent) invention immediately following its creation.

199. In accordance with Article 11(2) of Patent Act, the employer shall make a declaration within ninety days from the receipt of the notification as to whether he or she does or does not claim title to service invention and state his or her intention concerning the exploitation of the employee (dependent) invention.[594]

The employer shall file a patent application within a reasonable time following the receipt of the notification of a service invention; he or she shall furthermore proceed with all due diligence to obtain a patent.[595] The employer would be acting with due diligence if, following his or her decision to apply for a patent, he or she entrusts the organization or a patent attorney to file the application.

590. Csécsy, *A Szellemi Alkotások joga*, 108.
591. In connection with service inventions, patent entitlement shall be vested in the employer, as the inventor's successor in title.
592. In connection with employee inventions, patent entitlement shall be vested in the inventor; the employer, however, is entitled to exploit the invention. The employer's right of exploitation is non-exclusive; the employer may not grant a license of exploitation. The right of exploitation shall be transferred upon the successor in title in case of the winding-up of the employer, or the separation of its department; otherwise, it may not be transferred or assigned to any other person. In connection with service inventions, patent entitlement shall be vested in the employer, as the inventor's successor in title.
593. Csécsy, *A Szellemi Alkotások joga*, 110–112.
594. Article 11(2) of the Patent Act.
595. Article 12(1) of the Patent Act.

Prior to taking any action that excludes the grant of a patent or prior to a wilful omission to this effect, in the cases of a service invention the employer is obliged to offer to assign the patent rights to the inventor free of charge. In the case of an employee invention, the employer is obliged to offer to assign the patent rights to the inventor without stipulating the right of exploitation.[596]

The employer can forego the filing for a patent application or may withdraw it, if the invention is kept secret and exploited within the trade as such, provided that the patentability of the invention at the date of its disclosure has been acknowledged by the employer. Nevertheless, the employee shall notify the inventor of such a decision.[597]

An employer who has a right of disposition for a service invention may have a legitimate interest in not disclosing the invention and may thus forego a patent application. The inventor is entitled to royalties if the employer keeps his or her invention secret as well. Furthermore, the law stipulates that when an invention is kept secret, the disadvantages caused to the inventor by the failure to obtain protection shall also be considered.[598]

The inventor of a service invention is entitled to remuneration on the basis of the utilization of a protected invention.[599] As for the amount, duration, and the remittance of remuneration, the contract between the parties shall be the most decisive. Accordingly, legal proceedings concerning remuneration are settled within by civil law contracts.

The Patent Act provides for: particular cases in which the inventor is entitled to remuneration. In accordance with Patent Act (Article 13 of Patent Act), upon the sale of a service invention, the inventor shall be entitled to royalty if:

(a) the invention is protected by patent, from the commencement of the sale until the termination of definitive patent protection, or the termination of the supplementary protection (Article 22/A of Patent Act) when applicable;
(b) the definitive protection of the invention, or the supplementary of protection (Article 22/A of Patent Act) if applicable, terminated due to being surrendered by the employer, or due to the failure to pay the renewal fee, from the commencement of sale until the date when the patent or the supplementary protection would have been terminated due to expiry;
(c) the invention is held secret, from the commencement of sale until the publication of the invention, or for a period of twenty years from the time of presentment of the invention to the employer whichever is later.[600] In connection with employee inventions, patent entitlement shall be vested in the inventor; the employer, however, is entitled to exploit the invention. The employer's right of exploitation is non-exclusive; the employer may not grant a license of exploitation. The right of exploitation shall be transferred upon the successor in title in case of the winding-up of the employer, or the separation of its department; otherwise, it may not be transferred or assigned to any other person. In connection with service

596. Article 12(4) of the Patent Act.
597. Article 12(2) of the Patent Act.
598. Article 13(9) of the Patent Act.
599. Article 13 of the Patent Act.
600. Article 13(1) of the Patent Act.

inventions, patent entitlement shall be vested in the employer, as the inventor's successor in title.[601]

200. The application of a patent and patents granted also can be transferred (assignment):

(a) before filing; if a patent application is filed by someone other than the inventor, a deed of assignment, signed by the inventor and assignee without legalization, must be lodged. In case of starting the national phase of a PCT application, the assignment is not needed provided that the applicant in the national procedure is the same as in the international application. In case of transfer of Convention priority rights, an assignment of these rights is also required.
(b) the application of patent can be aliened during examination.[602]
(c) the patent granted can be transferred through an assignment of a contract, signed by assignor. An assignment must be recorded in order to be valid against third parties.

201. Chapter III of the Patent Act regulates the license agreements (exploitation contracts). The Patent Act defines the concept of license agreement: Under a contract of exploitation (patent license contract), the patentee licenses the right to exploit an invention and the person exploiting the invention (licensee) is required to pay royalties.[603] The license agreements have great economic importance. The Patent Act sets out only the most important rules of the license agreement.

The patentee shall guarantee, for the whole duration of the license contract, that no third parties hold rights in the preventing or limiting exercise to the right of exploitation.[604]

The patentee shall also guarantee the technical feasibility of the invention.[605] By creating rules that are like guiding principles in connection with the implied warranty and establishing that it is the patentee who is responsible for the technical execution of feasibility of the invention, the interpretation previously established by jurisprudence was thus promoted to the status of an act. It is necessary to emphasize that the patentee has only to answer to the technical feasibility of his or her invention, and that he or she is not the guarantor for the economy and profitability of the use carried out by the licensee.

Amongst the auxiliary obligations of the patentee, the Patent Act lists the warranty as well as the obligation to provide information – this should not extend to the transference of know-how. By virtue of Article 28 section (5) of the Patent Act, the patentee shall inform the license of any third-party rights in relation to the patent and of any other important circumstances. However, he or she shall be obliged to transfer

601. Csécsy, *A Szellemi Alkotások joga*, 111–114.
602. Lontai et al., *A Szellemi Alkotások joga*, 202–203.
603. Article 27(1) of the Patent Act.
604. Article 28(1) of the Patent Act.
605. Article 28(2) of the Patent Act.

economic, technical, and organizational know-how once this has been expressly agreed.[606]

A right of exploitation of licensee may be exclusive or non-exclusive. A right of exploitation shall be exclusive only if expressly stipulated by contract. In the case of an exclusive exploitation license, the patentee may also exploit the invention to the licensee who has acquired the right of exploitation, unless expressly excluded in the contract. The patentee may terminate the exclusivity of a license, subject to proportional reduction of royalty, if the licensee does not begin the exploitation on time.[607]

By virtue of Article 28 section 7, the patentee shall maintain the patent.

The license contract shall terminate, with effect for the future, when the contractual period expires or when retain specified circumstances occur or when the patent expires.

The licensee generally may not assign the license and give a sub-license.[608]

The person enjoying exploitation rights may assign the license to a third party – or he or she may re-license exploitation to a third party – only if this has been expressly permitted by the holder of the patent.

The contract of exploitation shall terminate for all future considerations at the end of the term stipulated in the contract, or upon the occurrence of the circumstances defined in the contract, as well as when the patent protection has terminated.[609]

According to Article 25(1) of Patent Act, rights deriving from an invention and from patent protection, with the exception of moral rights, may be transferred, assigned, and pledged.

A right of pledge shall only be constituted if the mortgage contract is made in writing and the right of pledge is entered in the Patent Register.[610]

§6. Scope of Exclusive Rights

202. Since the industrial revolution, society has respected inventions by giving appreciation to inventors; in addition to moral recognition, society provides material compensation through the legal institution of the patent protection.

Rights attached to the person and pecuniary rights result from the creation of an invention. The Patent Act regulates the personal rights attached to the inventor. These rights ensure the moral recognition of the inventor; they are related to the inventor as a person, and for this reason they are inalienable.[611] Moreover, rights attached to the person – as opposed to pecuniary patent rights – are unlimited in space and time, existing and also enforceable even in the absence of patent protection. Since pecuniary rights arising from a patent, may be separated from inventor's moral rights. Special pecuniary rights of inventor and patentee have absolute structure, which can be transferred, inherited, and pledged. The Act not only marks out the limits of exclusive

606. Pintz, *Találd fel magad*, 32–34.
607. Article 28(4) of the Patent Act.
608. Article 28(6) of the Patent Act.
609. Article 29 of the Patent Act.
610. Article 25(2) of Patent Act.
611. Article 25 of the Patent Act.

patent rights by listing in a positive fashion acts of use, but it also indicates, in an unambiguous way, the acts for which exclusive rights of use are not valid.

203. Chapter II of the Patent Act regulates the rights and obligations deriving from an invention and from a patent. The rights of inventors are defined in Article 7 of the Patent Act.

The person who has created an invention shall be deemed as the inventor, and unless a final court decision rules to the contrary.[612] The moral rights of an inventor consist of several different elements:

(a) the right to acknowledgement of authorship related to invention;[613]
(b) the inventor shall have the right to be mentioned as such in patent documents;[614]
(c) the right to disclosure of application;[615]
(d) the right to keep secret his or her invention and authorship.[616]

The name and address of the inventor must be mentioned in the request part of the patent application; as stated above, if there is more than one inventor, the proportion of authorship must be mentioned if this is non-equal.

The inventor is entitled to be mentioned as such in the documents related to patent; however, an inventor may request not to be mentioned in the patent documents to be published.[617]

The person mentioned as the inventor in the application on the application date shall be regarded as the inventor unless a final court decision has ruled otherwise.

If the subject of a patent application has been taken unlawfully from the invention of another party, such a third party or his or her successor may claim compensation for damages in accordance with the provisions of civil liability.[618]

Under Article 7 section (6) of the Patent Act, the inventor shall be entitled to instigate a legal proceeding under the Civil Code against any person contesting his or her authorship or otherwise infringing his or her moral rights deriving from an invention.

204. Articles 8, 13, 14, 15, 16, 17, 19, and 27 state the right to a patent and rights conferred by the patent economic (pecuniary) rights of the inventor.[619] The economic (pecuniary) rights of an inventor are as follows:

(a) right to a patent (patent claim) that is, the right to a patent shall belong to the inventor;[620]
(b) exclusive right to exploit the invention;[621]

612. Lontai, *A Szellemi Alkotások joga*, 167–169.
613. Article 7(5) of the Patent Act.
614. Article 7(2) and (3) of the Patent Act.
615. Article 60 of the Patent Act.
616. Article 7(1) and (5) of the Patent Act.
617. Csécsy, *A Szellemi Alkotások joga*, 101.
618. Lontai et al., *A Szellemi Alkotások joga*, 54–59.
619. Tattay, *A Szellemi Alkotások joga*, 228.
620. Article 7(1) of the Patent Act.
621. Article 8(1) of the Patent Act.

(c) the right to conclusion of exploitation of contracts;[622]
(d) the right to assignment, transfer and pledge of patent;[623]
(e) a right of pledge shall only be constituted if the mortgage contract is made in writing and the right of pledge is entered in the Patent Register;[624]
(f) on the basis of the exclusive rights of exploitation the inventor, the patentee shall be entitled to prevent any person not having his or her consent to exploitation of patent;[625]
(g) the right to royalty.[626]

205. The inventor or his or her successor in title, that is, assignee (an individual, body corporate or state, the joint inventors or their successors) in title barring any final court or other official decision to the contrary have the right to a patent if they were the first to apply. When two or more persons are entitled to a patent, such a right shall be deemed to belong to them equally, unless provided otherwise. If two or more persons have made the same invention independently of each other, the right to a patent will belong to the inventor who filed the application having earliest priority date.[627]

206. The Patent Act allies the concept rooted in the tradition of Hungarian patent law, which considers the patent protection confers exclusive rights upon the (rightful) claimant of the patent – the holder of the patent – for the exploitation of the invention.

On the basis of exclusive right of exploitation, the holder of the patent shall be entitled to prohibit anybody, who, without his or her authorization:

(a) manufactures, uses, distributes, or offers for distribution the product that is the subject matter of the invention or keeps stocks of this product or imports it into the country for such purposes;
(b) uses the process that forms the subject matter of the invention or offers the process for use to others when he or she is aware – or it is evident on the basis of the relevant circumstances – that the process cannot be used without the authorization of the holder of the patent;
(c) manufactures, uses, distributes, offers for distribution, keeps stocks of, or imports into the country for such purposes the product produced directly through the process that forms the subject matter of the invention.

The patentee being entitled to a patent as a legal position entailing an exclusive authorization to carry out certain acts, with a more extensive international approach that views the substance of patent protection of forbidding the carrying out of certain acts by others. The Patent Act displays both sides of protection incorporated into an absolute legal relationship.

The Patent Act defines the criteria of legal and illegal exploitation of patents.[628]

622. Article 27 of the Patent Act.
623. Article 25 of the Patent Act.
624. Article 25(2) of Patent Act.
625. Articles 19(2) and 8(1) of the Patent Act.
626. Articles 13–17 and 27 of the Patent Act.
627. Article 8(1), (2) and (4) of the Patent Act.
628. Lontai et al., *A Szellemi Alkotások joga*, 196–198.

By virtue of Article 19 section (1) of the Patent Act, the patent protection shall grant the holder of the patent (patentee) the exclusive right to exploit the patent. The Patent Act defines the criteria of exploitation of patent related to the products and processes.

The right to utilization of the invention related to a product includes the rights to making, using, putting on the market, offering for sale a product that is the subject matter of the invention, or using stocking or importing the product for such purposes.

The right to utilization of an invention related to a process includes the right of and offering process for use and making, using, putting on the market, offering for sale or stocking or importing for such purposes, a product obtained directly by a process that is the subject matter of the invention.[629]

207. The Patent Act defines acts submitted to the effect of exclusive rights of utilization due to the patentee, in a manner that is more detailed, precise, and broad than was the case in the previous Patent Act. It deals separately with rights resulting from product[630] and process.[631]

Patents, furthermore, define the offer for circulation as an act of utilization as well as the offer for utilizing a procedure.

On the basis of the exclusive right of exploitation, the holder of the patent may take action against any person, who – without the holder's authorization – delivers a thing (tool, appliance, equipment) related to an essential element of the invention, or offers it for delivery with the purpose of the implementation of the invention, provided that he or she knows – or it is evident on the basis of the relevant circumstances – that the thing is suitable for the implementation of the invention, or serves this purpose.[632]

This provision may not be applied if the object of patent delivered or offered is an ordinary article that may be purchased in commercial circulation.[633]

However, the exclusive right of the patentee does not include such an indirect use if the object transferred or offered is an item of merchandise that is commonly obtainable in trade, except in the case in which the person transferring or offering such a good intentionally induces the recipient to carry out such an act of direct use.[634]

Under Article 19 sections (2), (3), and (4) of the Patent Act, the criteria of illegal use of a patent is defined.

208. On the basis of the exclusive right of exploitation, the patentee shall be entitled[635] to prevent any person not having his consent:

(a) from making, using, putting on the market, or offering for sale a product that is the subject of the invention, or stocking or importing the product for such purposes;

629. Article 19(2) a), b), c), of the Patent Act.
630. Article 19(2) a) of the Patent Act.
631. Article 19(2) b) of the Patent Act.
632. Article 19(3) of the Patent Act.
633. Article 19(4) of the Patent Act prescribes that the provision contained in the foregoing paragraph may not be applied, if the thing delivered or offered is an ordinary article that may be purchased in commercial circulation, except for the case in which the deliverer or the offeror of such article induces the recipient intentionally to carrying out these acts.
634. Pintz, *Táláld fel magad*, 31.
635. Csécsy, *A Szellemi Alkotások joga*, 102.

(b) from using a process that is the subject matter of the invention or when such another person, knows, or it is obvious from the circumstances, that the process cannot be used without the consent of the patentee, from offering the process for use;
(c) from making using, putting on the market, offering for sale, or stocking or importing for such purposes, a product obtained directly by a process that is the subject matter of invention.[636]

By virtue of Article 19(3) of the Patent Act, on the basis of the exclusive right to exploitation, the patentee shall also be entitled to prevent any person not having his or her consent from supplying or offering to supply a person other than a person entitled to exploit the invention, with means (instruments, appliances) relating to an essential element of the invention for carrying out the invention, when such person knows, or it is obvious from the circumstances, that those means are suitable and intended for carrying out the invention.

On the basis of the exclusive right of exploitation, the patentee is not entitled, when the supplied or offered means are staple commercial products, except when the supplier or offer deliberately induces his or her client to commit the acts of unlawful exploitation of patent.

209. The exclusive right[637] of exploitation shall not extend to:

(a) acts done privately or not involved in an economic activity;
(b) acts done for experimental purposes relating to the subject matter of the invention, including experiments and tests necessary for the marketing authorization of the product constituting the subject matter of invention or the product obtained through the process constituting the subject matter of the invention;
(c) preparation for individual cases, in a pharmacy, of a medicine in accordance with a medical prescription, or acts concerning the medicine so prepared.[638]

210. The Patent Act provides several obligations for applicant and holder of patent protection as follows:

description of patent. This means that the applicant must disclose the invention in such manner and with such details so that the invention can be carried out by a person skilled in the art on the basis of description and drawings.[639]

use of patent[640]

636. Lontai, *A Szellemi Alkotások joga*, 169–152.
637. Lontai, *A Szellemi Alkotások joga*, 171.
638. Article 19(6) of the Patent Act.
639. Csécsy, *A Szellemi Alkotások joga*, 104.
640. Articles 30 and 31 of the Patent Act.

maintenance of patent. For the maintenance of patent protection, annual fees are payable annually in advance in respect of each year from filing.[641]

the patentee shall guarantee the technical feasibility of invention[642]

acquire the permission from authorities if it is necessary[643] (e.g., for registration of pharmaceutical products).

§7. Limitations and Exceptions to the Scope of Patent Protection: Compulsory Licenses

211. The balance between public interest and the rights of patentees is principally ensured by several rules of patent protection. There are some limits of exclusive rights of the patentee in the interest of private parties or the public.

In the first place, a time limit of patent protection must be mentioned. The term of protection has developed over the years under consideration of the aspects that patentees shall have sufficient time to exclusive and therefore more profitable use and that other members of society shall still be interested in utilizing the invention after the expiration of the patent. The first Patent Act of 1895 fixed a maximum term of protection of fifteen years, which was later changed to twenty years by an amendment of 1932. In accordance with the current Patent Act, patent protection shall have a term of twenty years.

The effect of the patent does not extend to non-commercial and experimental purposes relating of subject matter of patented invention.[644]

The prior use is another barrier to patent protection. The general legal principle that an activity performed legally and in good faith cannot later become illegal is embodied in the right of prior use. By contrast, the rights acquired through creating an invention, unless followed by utilization or serious preparation to do so, will perish if another diligent inventor files an application for the same invention earlier.[645]

Article 6 of the Patent Act establishes exceptions to the right granted by a patent. The prescriptions of the Patent Act requesting exclusions to the scope of patent production may be mentioned.[646]

641. Article 29(7) of the Patent Act.
642. Articles 5 and 28(2) of the Patent Act.
643. Tattay, *A Szellemi Alkotások joga*, 263.
644. Article 19(6) of the Patent Act.
645. Article 21(1), (2) and (3) of the Patent Act.
646. For example, according to Art. 6(2): Inventions shall be considered unpatentable when their commercial exploitation would be contrary to public order or morality; however, this type of exploitation shall not be deemed to be so contrary merely because it is prohibited by law or regulation.

The exceptions related to the exclusive right of exploitation of patent, that is, the free utilization of patents also can be considered as limitation to the scope of patent protection.[647]

212. The main institutions[648] of limitation and exception to the scope of patent protection according to the current legislation are as follows:

(a) exhaustion of the exclusive right of exploitation conferred by patent protection;[649]
(b) right of prior use;[650]
(c) right of further use;[651]
(d) favour of transit concerning products;[652]
(e) compulsory licenses.[653]

213. The exhaustion of patents rights[654] means a new feature of limitation of rights of patentee. The exclusive right of exploitation conferred by patent protection shall not extend to acts concerning a product put on the market in the territory of the European Economic Area by the patentee or with his or her express consent, except when the patentee has legitimate interest in opposing the further marketing of the product.

214. In accordance with section 21(1) of Patent Act, entitlement for pre-exploitation shall be vested in the person who commenced the production or the use of the subject matter of the invention before the priority date within Hungary, in good faith and within the sphere of his or her economic activities, or has made effective and genuine arrangements in the interest thereof.

A person, who in good faith, before the date of priority, in the territory of the country and within the framework of his or her economic activities started to produce or use the subject matter of invention, or made serious preparations with the view to doing so.

The main criteria of prior use of an invention are as follows. The holder of the right of prior use should have begun before the date of priority, or should have made considerable preparations for that purpose:

(a) preparations with a view to doing so;
(b) to use or to make the subject matter of the patented invention in the territory of country;
(c) in good faith; and
(d) in the framework of his economic activities.[655]

647. Article 19(6) of the Patent Act.
648. Lontai et al., *A Szellemi Alkotások joga*, 206–213.
649. Article 20 of the Patent Act.
650. Article 21(1), (2) and (3) of the Patent Act.
651. Article 21(4) of the Patent Act.
652. Article 21(5) of the Patent Act.
653. Articles 31–33 of the Patent Act and Articles 83/A-83/G of Patent Act.
654. Tattay, *A Szellemi Alkotások joga*, 271–272.
655. Lontai, *A Szellemi Alkotások joga*, 183.

Patent protection shall have no effect against the prior use at the extent of the making, using, or the preparations existing at the date of priority.

The right of the prior user may only be transferred together with an entitled economic organization.[656]

215. According to Article 21 section (4) of the Patent Act, a right of further use shall belong to any person who, in the period between the declaration of the patent protection lapse and revalidation of patent protection and within the framework of his or her economic activities, has started to make use of subject matter of invention, or made serious preparations with a view to doing so, with respect to the rights of further use, patent protection shall have no effect.

A further user shall be considered a bona fide user until it is proved that the further use based on the inventive activity led to patented product. Good faith, that is, 'bona fide', is a behaviour with respect to which the person who behaves likewise is convinced that his or her conduct is right. Acting in good faith shall be supposed unless bad faith is proven. This means that the person who acquired his or her knowledge from the creator, who makes use of the subject matter of the creation without the creator's preliminary permission cannot rely upon the right of prior use. The criteria of making serious preparations are as follows: With respect to adequate preparations, merely forming or declaring intent is not sufficient, as additional proofs are to be furnished with respect to conduct showing that some economic activity will be started or that assure the conditions of starting such activity.

The extent of preparation should be evaluated in connection with the question, whether the offer to produce, use or merchandise the subject matter of the invention is to be qualified as an 'infringement' and further if the procedure covered by the patent is offered for the use by a third party. Preparation might be, e.g., to begin planning filing of a credit application and many other activities.

The holder of the right to prior and further use is not a licensee; he or she has no license for the use of production or merchandising of the subject matter of the protection.

The status does not assure him or her exclusively; this right cannot be assigned and applies only to the economic organization, or with part economic organization, in which such preparations to make or use the invention has been made.

In accordance with Article 21(5) of the Patent Act subject to reciprocity, patent protection shall have no effect with respect to means of communication and transport which are in transit in the territory of the country or to foreign goods which are not intended to be put on the market in the country. The president of the Office shall be competent in giving a ruling on matters of reciprocity.[657]

216. The law of intellectual property and the patent law create a monopolistic situation for the owner with respect to authorization of the use of the invention. The pure fact of being in a monopolistic situation with respect to creation or knowledge secured by such protection does not implicate an economic predominance in that relevant field.[658] In fact, it is an inherent element of use of patents the absolute character of rights resulting from patent law. As a result of the privileged situation granted for

656. Csécsy, *A Szellemi Alkotások joga*, 118–119.
657. *Ibid.*
658. Lontai, *A Szellemi Alkotások joga*, 184–186.

this particular purpose for the delay of protection, the inventor was free to decide to give a license to use of invention or to reject the request for a license. The authorized owner of an intellectual creation decides at his or her discretion, how and under what circumstances to use or utilize this right, and the only limit is that the use should remain within the framework of the other relevant legal statutes and should be not prejudicial to other legal statutes or the lawful interests of third parties.[659]

The compulsory licenses play a pre-eminent role in the limitation of patent protection. The term and institution of compulsory licenses was introduced into Hungarian law by the 1932 revision of the Patent Act of 1895.

The compulsory license may be granted:

(a) due to the non-utilization or delayed utilization of the invention in question;[660] or
(b) because of the dependence of patents concerned;[661] or
(c) to the manufacture of pharmaceutical products for export to countries with public health problems.[662]

If, within four years from the date of filing of the patent application or within three years from the grant of the patent, whichever period was last, the patentee has not exploited the invention in the territory of the country to satisfy the domestic demand or if he or she has undertaken serious preparations or has not granted a license for such purpose, a compulsory license shall be granted to the applicant for the license, unless the patentee justifies the lack of exploitation.[663]

217. If the patented invention cannot be exploited without infringing another patent,[664] a compulsory license shall be granted on request and to the extent necessary for the exploitation of the dominant patent, to the holder of the dependent patent, provided that the invention claimed in the dependent patent involves an important technical advance of considerable economic significance in relation in the invention claimed in the dominant patent.[665]

When a compulsory license has been granted because of dependence of patents with respect to a dominant patent, the holder of such a patent shall be entitled to reasonable terms of a license to exploit the invention claimed in the dependent patent according to the common provision of non-compulsory licenses.[666]

The Office shall grant a compulsory license for the exploitation of an invention in the cases and on the terms laid down in Regulation (EC) No. 816/2006 of the European Parliament and of the Council of 2007 on compulsory licensing of patents relating to the manufacture of pharmaceutical products for export to countries with

659. Lontai et al., *A Szellemi Alkotások joga*, 211–213.
660. Article 31 of the Patent Law.
661. Article 32(1) of the Patent Law.
662. Article 33/A(1) of the Patent Law and Articles 83/A-83/G of the Patent Act.
663. The patentee shall begin the use of his or her patent within four years from the date of filing of the patent application or within three years from the grant of the patent.
664. This patent called dominant or impeding patent.
665. Tattay, *A Szellemi Alkotások joga*, 274–276.
666. Article 32(2) of the Patent Act.

public health problems. The procedural prescriptions of Regulation No. 816/2002 to find in Article 83/A–83/H of Patent Act.

218. Article 33 of the Patent Act involves the general provisions on compulsory licenses grantable for lack of exploitation and in respect of dependent patents.

An applicant for a compulsory license shall be required to prove that the requirements for a compulsory license have been complied with and further that:

(a) the patentee was unwilling to grant a voluntary license to exploit the patent under appropriate conditions and in a reasonable period of time;
(b) he or she is able to exploit the invention to the required extent.[667]

The compulsory license shall not afford an exclusive right of exploitation. The holder of a compulsory license shall have the same rights as the patentee in regard to the maintenance of the patent and the exercise of the rights deriving from protection.[668]

The extent, scope, and time limit of a compulsory license shall be established by the court, taking into account the purpose of the exploitation that was made possible through the compulsory license. A compulsory license may be granted with or without restrictions. A compulsory license shall remain in effect until the end of the period established by the court or until the exhaustion of patent protection. Compulsory licenses shall be registered in the patent register.[669]

The holder of a compulsory license ceases to exist, or if any of its organizational units are separated the compulsory license shall be transferred to the successor in title. A compulsory license granted with respect to a dominant patent may only be assigned together with a dependant patent. However, a compulsory license may not be assigned or transferred to any other person. The holder of a compulsory license may not grant a license of exploitation.[670]

The holder of the patent shall be entitled to appropriate remuneration for the compulsory license.[671]

219. According to the rules respecting compulsory licenses, the holder of a prohibited patent may claim, if possessing a compulsory license for his patent, of being licensed for the exploitation of the patent as part of the depending invention under equitable conditions. The extent and the period of validity of the compulsory license are laid down by the competent court; the royalty due to the patentee will also be determined by the court, taking the circumstances specified by the law as a basis. The granting of a compulsory license is within the competence, and the royalty due to the patent holder for the compulsory license also fixed by the court.[672] The compulsory license shall be transferred upon the successor in title in case of the winding-up of the holder or the separation of its department. The compulsory license granted for the impeding patent may only be transferred together with the dependent patent. The

667. Article 33(1) of the Patent Act.
668. Tattay, *A Szellemi Alkotások joga*, 274.
669. Article 33(2) of the Patent Act.
670. Article 33(5) of the Patent Act.
671. Article 33(3) of the Patent Act.
672. Article 33(7) of the Patent Act.

compulsory license may not be assigned or transferred by any other means. The holder of a compulsory license may not license exploitation.[673]

Actions bearing upon the modification of a grant of a compulsory license or its revocation, respectively, pertain to the competence and jurisdiction of the Metropolitan Court, which proceeds in these cases as a three-member council. Accordingly, the way is free to grant a compulsory license if the patent holder fails to use his or her right for a specified period, fails to exploit the patent, or prevents another patentee in an unjustified way to exploit his or her rights.

When the normative conditions of granting a compulsory license are present, it can be granted regardless of the market behaviour of the patentee or the given situation in the market respectively. Thus a compulsory license is understood to represent a limit to the extent of rights flowing from patent law as set forth under positive patent law.[674]

However, the quasi-abusive application of absolute rights may bring the patentee into conflict with the requirements related to the freedom of competition. Notwithstanding, the typical element in these cases is not that the party, which enjoys a monopolistic position refuses to grant a license but, instead, subjects this grant to conditions that are incompatible with the requirements of competition.[675]

§8. Duration of Protection: Maintaining and Termination of Patent Protection

220. The duration of a definitive patent protection is unchanged twenty years counted from the filing date. In accordance with Article 22 of the Patent Act, definitive protection shall have a term of twenty years beginning on the filing date of the application.

This is also required by the duties of legal harmonization of the state as well as the European Patent Convention.

The term of the final plant variety right shall be thirty years, calculated from the year of grant, in the case of varieties of vine and tree species and twenty-five years for other plant varieties.[676]

By virtue of Articles 38 and 39 of the Patent Act, patent protection shall cease within a period of twenty years in the case of surrender, annulment, or because the maintenance fees have not been paid. Article 38 of the Patent Act also states that provisional patent protection shall lapse:

(a) if the patent application definitively rejected;
(b) if the annual fees have not been paid by the end of period grace;
(c) if the applicant has surrendered protection.

In accordance with Article 39 of the Patent Act, definitive patent protection shall lapse:

673. Article 33(5) of the Patent Act.
674. Csécsy, *A Szellemi Alkotások joga*, 231.
675. Lontai et al., *A Szellemi Alkotások joga*, 212.
676. Article 111 of the Patent Act.

(a) if the annual fees have not been paid by the end of the period grace, on the day, following the date;
(b) if the patentee surrenders the protection, on the day following receipt of the surrender or at an earlier date specified by the person surrendering of protection;
(c) if the patent is revoked, with retrospective effect to the filing date of protection.[677]

221. Twenty years from the filing date, the inventor shall pay annual fees. Annual fees are due for the maintenance of patent protection, both in respect of a published application and for a granted protection. The first payment of annuities becomes due on the date of the publication of the patent application. Further annuities are payable on the anniversaries of the filing date. If patent protection has lapsed by reason of failing to pay annual fees, protection shall be restored at the request of the applicant or patentee.[678]

Restoration of patent may be requested within three months following the expiry of the period of grace. If the patent protection has terminated due to non-payment of the renewal fee, the protection may be revalidated upon the request of the applicant or the holder of the patent.[679] An application for the revalidation of patent protection shall be submitted within three months following expiry of the grace period.[680] Within this time limit, the fee shall be paid.[681]

222. The applicant entered in the register of patent applications or the patentee entered in the patent register may surrender patent protection by a written declaration addressed to the office.[682]

The surrender affects the rights of third parties deriving from legislation from ruling of an authority, from a license contract or any other contract recorded in the patent register, or if a lawsuit is recorded in patent register, it shall take effect only with the consent of the parties concerned.[683]

It shall also be possible to surrender certain patent claims.[684] Surrender may be made of certain specific claims as well.[685] The withdrawal of the surrender of patent protection shall have no legal effect.[686]

223. Article 42 of the Patent Act regulates the revocation of patents. The patent shall be revoked *ex tunc*:

(a) if the subject matter of the patent does not satisfy the requirements of patentability;
(b) if the description does not disclose the invention in a clear and complete manner;

677. Pintz, *Táláld fel magad*, 53.
678. Article 40(1) of the Patent Act.
679. Lontai, et al., *A Szellemi Alkotások joga*, 240.
680. The grace period is six months following the anniversaries of filing date.
681. Article 39(b) of the Patent Act.
682. Article 41(1) of the Patent Act.
683. Lontai, *A Szellemi Alkotások joga*, 195.
684. Article 41(3) of the Patent Act.
685. *Ibid.*
686. Article 41(4) of the Patent Act.

(c) if the subject matter of patent extends beyond the content of the application as a field at the recorded filing date or – in the case of division – beyond the content of the divisional application;[687]
(d) if the patent has been granted to a person who is not entitled to it under the Patent Act;
(e) if the grounds for revocation affect the patent in part only, revocation shall be pronounced in the form of a corresponding limitation of the patent.[688]

Should the request for revocation be rejected by a final decision, a new procedure for the revocation of same patent on the same ground may not be instituted by any person.[689]

§9. Infringement and Remedies

224. The Patent Act distinguishes between infringement of inventions and infringement of patents. By virtue of Article 34 of the Patent Act, an infringement of an invention means the subject matter of a patent application, or a patent has been taken unlawfully from the invention of another.

Infringement of patents is defined below.[690] Any person who unlawfully exploits a patented invention commits patent infringement.[691] The patentee may, according to the circumstances of the case, have recourse[692] to the following civil remedies:

(a) he or she may request that the fact of infringement to be declared by the court;
(b) he or she may request an injunction that the infringer cease his infringement or any acts directly threatening with it;
(c) he or she may demand that the infringer give information on the identity of a person involved in the production and distribution of the infringing goods or the provision of infringing services and of their channels of distribution;
(d) he or she may demand satisfaction from the infringer by way of a declaration or by other appropriate means; if necessary, the declaration shall be made public by the infringer or at his expense. At the request of the patentee, the court may order that its decision be made public at the expense of the infringer. The court shall decide on the manner of the publicity. Publicity shall mean, in particular, publication in a national daily newspaper or on the Internet;
(e) he or she may require surrender of the enrichment obtained by the infringement of the patent;
(f) he or she may request the seizure, the transfer to a specific person, the recall and the definitive removal from the channels of commerce, or destruction, of the

687. Lontai, *A Szellemi Alkotások joga*, 195.
688. Article 42(2) of the Patent Act.
689. Article 42(3) of the Patent Act.
690. Lontai, *A Szellemi Alkotások joga*, 197.
691. Article 35(1) of the Patent Act.
692. Article 35(2) of the Patent Act: (1) 'Patent infringement' means the unauthorized exploitation of an invention that is under patent protection.

infringing products, as well as of the means and materials exclusively or principally used for infringement;

(g) the patentee may also claim damages under the rules of civil liability.[693]

Seizure of the means and material used in infringing activities and of the infringing activities and the infringing goods shall be admissible even if they are not in the possession of the infringer, but the holder knew or had reasonable grounds to know about the infringement.

225. Law CLXV of 2005, effective since 15 April 2006, has introduced changes in the legal system, whereby compliance with the IP Enforcement Directive has been implemented. The main elements of the changes in the enforcement of patent rights following the adapted Directive 2004/48 are as follows:

> The effective Patent Act define the concept of the patent infringement[694] and has a regulation according to which the infringer can be obliged to provide information[695] on manufacturers and use of the services on commercial scale or infringing goods as far as far business relationship.[696]

In case of patents, the obligation to provide information also covers infringing services.

The new rule in Article 35 section (5) provides that a third person can be obliged to provide the above information. Such an obligation can be imposed against any third person, who:

(a) was found in possession in the infringing goods on a commercial scale;
(b) was found to be using the infringing services on a commercial scale;
(c) was found to be providing on a commercial scale services used in infringing activities;
(d) was indicated by the person referred to in (a), (b), and (c) as being involved in the production, manufacture, or distribution of being involved or the provision of the services.

In accordance with above-mentioned amendment, the holder of the patent may seek the provision of information against a person whose services are being used in connection with the infringement.[697]

The delivery of the information can be claimed on an objective basis against third parties as well. Thus, the obligation which can be imposed irrespectively of the fact whether the person in question knew or should have known that his or her corresponding activity was connected with an infringement or either patent right.

693. Pintz, *Találd fel magad*, 34.
694. 'Patent infringement' means the unauthorized exploitation of an invention that is under patent protection.
695. Article 35(4) of the Patent Act.
696. Article 35(2) c) of the Patent Act.
697. Article 35(4) of the Patent Act.

226. The Patent Act includes definition of commercial scale.[698] The above obligation related to a person who committed patent infringement on a commercial scale.[699]

The acts of infringement are carried out on a commercial scale if it is obvious from the nature or quantity of the infringing goods or services that these acts are carried out for direct or indirect economic advantage. In the absence of proof to the contrary, acts carried out by consumers in good faith shall not be regarded carried out in commercial scale.

In accordance with Article 35(7) of the Patent Act, the following information[700] can be requested:

(a) the names and address of the producers, distributors, suppliers, and holders of the infringing goods or services, as well as the intended or involved wholesalers and retailers;
(b) the quantities produced, delivered, received, or ordered of the infringing goods and services, as well as the prices obtained or given for the goods or services in question.

At the request of the patentee, the court may rule that the infringing nature of the means, materials, and goods seized, recalled or definitively removed from the channels of commerce be removed, or where this is not possible, that they be destroyed. In justified cases, the court may order, in place of destruction, that the means and materials seized be auctioned according to the procedure of judicial execution; in such cases, the court shall decide how the sum obtained is to be used.[701]

227. According to Article 156 the Code of Civil Proceeding, preliminary injunctions could be requested after patent infringement proceeding was started. This is a very substantial measure, as owners of rights can obtain such basic information well before the infringement proceeding is finished if they succeed in obtaining the preliminary injunction from the court.[702]

228. Article 104 of the Patent Act has been amended and prescribes a legal presumption concerning the existence of a specially preferred legal protection of the right holder. In patent litigation, provisional measures – until the contrary is rendered probable – shall be considered necessary to protect the plaintiff's rights deserving special appreciation if the plaintiff proves that the invention is patented, and he or she is the patentee or an exploiter is entitled to institute proceedings for infringement in his or her own name.[703]

---

698. Article 35(6) of the Patent Act.
699. Paragraph 14 of the Preamble of IP Enforcement Directive gives quite a broad definition for commercial scale, according to which, acts carried out on a commercial scale are those carried out for direct or indirect economic or commercial advantage. This would normally exclude acts carried out by end consumers acting in good faith.
700. Article 35(7) of the Patent Act.
701. Article 35(8) of the Patent Act.
702. Tattay, *A Szellemi Alkotások joga*, 197.
703. Article 104(2) of the Patent Act.

In rendering the contrary probable, all circumstances shall be taken into consideration, in particular that the patent was revoked by the Office or by the Court of First Instance, or the European patent effective also in Hungary was revoked by an opposition division of the EPC or in another Member State of the EPO.

The provision relating to the presumption substantiating the necessity of protecting the plaintiff's right deserving special appreciation shall not apply when six months have already elapsed from the beginning of patent infringement or sixty days from the date on which the plaintiff became aware of the infringement and the identity of the infringer.[704]

A request for provisional measures may be lodged before filing for court action in connection with a patent infringement, and it shall be adjudged by the Metropolitan Court of Justice in non-judicial proceedings. Measures to preserve evidence may be implemented before court proceedings are instituted if the holder of the patent has already substantiated the infringement or threat of infringement to a reasonable extent. The measures to preserve evidence shall be carried out by the Metropolitan Court of Justice.[705]

229. A request for provisional measures may be lodged before filing for court action in connection with a patent infringement, and it shall be adjudged by the Metropolitan Court of Justice in non-judicial proceedings.[706]

The new amendment of the Patent Act has introduced a special expedited procedure in the case when the validity of patent is questioned on the basis where an infringement proceeding started. The Office has to process such nullity or cancellation quickly, and the parties should respond in fifteen days and no extension term can be granted. By such an expedited proceeding, the validity can be decided earlier, and the suspension of the infringement will last for a shorter period.

Preliminary measures – preliminary injunction – can be initiated before the start of the main infringement process, and this latter process must be started in fifteen days counting back from the issuance of a decision of preliminary injunction.

In accordance with Article 105 of Patent Act, the holder of the patent – apart from the civil claims available in connection with infringements – may request the court to order, under the conditions applicable to provisional measures:

(a) protective measures in accordance with the provisions laid down in the Act on Judicial Enforcement, if able to verify that any subsequent attempt for the recovery of profits made by the infringement or the payment of damages is in jeopardy;
(b) the infringer to notify of and present bank, financial, or commercial information and documents for the purpose of ordering the protective measures referred to in paragraph (a);
(c) the provision of security if in exchange – in lieu of demanding the termination of the infringement – the holder of the patent agrees for the infringer to continue the alleged acts of infringement.[707]

704. *Ibid.*
705. Article 104(10) of the Patent Act.
706. Article 104(4) of the Patent Act.
707. Article 104(5) a), b), and c) of the Patent Act.

These provisions have introduced the possibility of requesting the lodging of a counter guarantee from the defendant instead of requesting discontinuation of the infringement, which is intended to ensure the compensation of the holder. In addition to civil remedies applicable in the case of infringement, the patentee may request the court, on conditions relating to provisional measures to order the lodging of security, if in place of demanding discontinuance of the patent infringement, the patentee consents to the continuation, by the infringer, of the allegedly infringing activity. The court may order the lodging of security even in the absence of a request of the patentee to this effect, provided that the patentee filed a request for the discontinuance of patent infringement, which the court does not allow.[708]

230. The mentioned amendment of the Patent Act has introduced a special expedited process. According to Article 104(7), the court shall decide on the provisional measures taken, but not later than within fifteen days from the filing of a request to this effect.

The court of second instance shall decide on the appeal filed against the decision on the provisional measures taken, but not later than within fifteen days from the filing of an appeal.[709]

When any delay would cause irreparable harm, it should be regarded as a case of extreme urgency and – taking this into account – provisional measures including the lodging of security may be taken without the defendant having been heard. Decisions taken without the defendant having been heard shall be communicated to the defendant on execution. After communication of the decision, the defendant may request a hearing, and the review of the annulment of the decision ordering provisional measures or the preliminary production of evidence.[710]

When a party in a patent infringement action has already substantiated its statements to a reasonable extent, upon the request of the party providing proof, the court may require the other party:

to present and allow for review the documents and other physical evidence in his or her possession;

to notify of and to present bank, financial or commercial information and documents in his or her possession.[711]

The court shall, upon request of the other party, revoke its decision for ordering measures to preserve evidence if the holder of the patent does not file charges for patent infringement within fifteen days from the date of the resolution ordering measures to preserve evidence.[712]

708. Article 104(6) of the Patent Act.
709. Article 104(7) of the Patent Act.
710. Article 104(12) of the Patent Act.
711. Article 104(9) of the Patent Act.
712. Article 104(11) of the Patent Act.

The court may require the provision of security in connection with ordering measures to preserve evidence and – with the exception of the provision of security – in connection with the ordering of provisional measures.[713]

231. The patents are also protected from infringement by the Criminal Code (Violation of industrial Property Rights). According to Article 388 of new Criminal Code (Law No. 100 of 2012), a person who violates the right of the holder of a patent, (plant variety, certification of supplementary protection, trademark, geographical indication, design rights, utility models, or topographies conferred on the basis of an act, promulgated international convention or Community legislation) by imitating or copying the subject matter of protection, and thereby causing financial injury, is guilty of a misdemeanour:

(a) punishable by imprisonment of up to two years, community service work, or a fine;[714]
(b) The punishment for a felony shall be imprisonment between one year to five years if the violation of patent rights results in a pattern of business operation;[715]
(c) The punishment for a felony shall be imprisonment between two years to eight years if the violation of patent rights results in particularly substantial financial injury.[716]

§10. Overlapping and Relations to Other Intellectual Property Rights

232. The admissibility of the parallel protection of different objects of intellectual property belongs to the fundamental principles of Hungarian intellectual property rights. According to this basic principle, the cumulative protection of several objects is generally permissible. The protection of patents may overlap with protection of copyrighted works, trademarks patents, and utility models. The overlap between the protection of patents and utility models has a practical importance.

233. The Patent Act defines the notion of patentable invention: Patents shall be granted for any inventions in any field of technology that is new, involves an inventive activity, and is susceptible to industrial application.[717]

Protection may be granted to a technical invention by utility model relating to the construction, structure or arrangement of components or an article, provided that they are new, involve an inventive step and are capable of industrial application. Only one article is registerable in one application.[718]

The possibility of overlap of the patent protection and utility model protection is immediately noticeable, since the main criteria of protection of both objects (novelty,

713. Article 104(13) of the Patent Act.
714. Article 388(1) of the new Criminal Code (Law No. X of 2012).
715. Article 388(2) of the new Criminal Code (Law No. X of 2012).
716. Article 388(3) a) of the new Criminal Code (Law No. X of 2012).
717. Article 1(1) of the Patent Act.
718. Article 1(1) of UM Act.

inventive step at utility model, inventive activity at the patents and capacity of industrial application) are almost identical.

234. A patent application can be transformed into utility model application and vice versa.

According to the UM Act and Patent Act, parallel utility model and patent protection may be granted for the same object, however the same object shall not be protected in parallel at the same time. An invention may not be protected exclusively by patent or utility model simultaneously. In the interest of applicants, the Act assures, however, a possibility to file such a utility model application on an earlier patent application. The derived application may keep the priority and application date of the former.[719]

If an applicant has filed a patent application for a certain utility model, he or she may file a utility model application relating to the same subject matter claiming the filing and priority dates of the earlier patent application.

This provision prescribes an opportunity for saving a rejected pending regular patent.

Accordingly, any applicant who has previously filed a patent application may submit a statement within two months from the date of application for a utility model for the same subject matter to claim the day and priority for the patent application (act of derivation).

The day and priority for the patent application may be claimed for an application for a utility model by an act of derivation if the derived application for a utility model is submitted to the Hungarian Patent Office:

(a) during patent registration proceedings, before the decision for the grant of patent protection becomes final and operative. This provision prescribes an opportunity for saving a rejected pending regular design;[720] or
(b) within three months from the operative date of the decision on the refusal of the patent application. The UM Act provides a possibility to receive protection in the form of utility model during a pendency of patent application;[721] or
(c) if the patent is declared cancelled because of non-compliance with the requirements of novelty and the inventive step, within three months of the date a decision of[722] cancellation of the patent. The rule of legal derivation ensures further a possibility for the applicant to obtain a utility model protection, when his or her patent is cancelled.[723]

---

719. In accordance with Art. 30 of UM Act, any applicant who has previously filed a patent application may submit a statement within two months from the date of application for a utility model for the same subject matter to claim the day and priority for the patent application (act of derivation).
720. Article 2 a) of UM Act.
721. *Ibid.*
722. Article 2 b) of UM Act.
723. Article 30(3) of UM Act.

A utility model application may only be derived within ten years from the date of the patent application. Such derivation will be not possible after expiration of ten years from the date of filing of the earlier patent application.[724]

The priority from the earlier patent application is to be claimed on filing the utility model application in the request for grant of protection, indicating the serial number, filing date of the priority date of the original patent application documents evidencing the derivation must accompany the application.

In order to avoid double protection, the utility model protection shall be qualified lapsed – in the case of abandonment with retroactive effect to the beginning of protection – if a patent is granted for the patent application which was derived from the utility model application, or from which the utility model application was derived.[725]

The admissibility of the parallel protection of different objects of intellectual property belongs to the fundamental principles of Hungarian intellectual property rights. According to this basic principle, the cumulative protection of several objects is generally permissible. The protection of patents may overlap with protection of utility models. The patent applications may be transformed utility model application and vice versa.

Internal priority may also be claimed from the earlier patent application filed in Hungary, for an application filed within twelve months of the filing date of such an earlier application.[726] For claiming internal priority, it is required that publication of whose priority is claimed is still pending and that it has not yet served as a basis for claiming priority right. If an internal priority has been claimed, the earlier application whose priority was claimed shall be considered withdrawn. Derivation from utility model application is allowed when the applicant has already filed a utility model application at an earlier date, and he or she may, in the declaration of priority filed within two months after the date of filing of patent application for the same subject matter, claim the filing date of the utility model application and the right of priority relating to such application.[727]

Under Article 62 (2) of Patent Act, derivation of a patent application shall be admissible within three months from the date when the decision on the grant of utility model protection becomes final, but not later than twenty years from the filing date of the utility model application.

Partial priority may also be allowed.

---

724. Article 30(2) of UM Act.
725. Tattay, *A Szellemi Alkotások joga*, 292–293.
726. According to Art. 61(6), internal priority shall be claimed within four months from the date of filing the patent application. If claiming internal priority, the earlier patent application shall be deemed to be withdrawn.
727. Article 62(1) of the Patent Act.

Chapter 3. Utility Models

§1. Sources: Legislations

235. Utility models have been protected since 1992 in Hungary. This form of protection was introduced by Act XXXVIII of 1991 in order to foster a market economy and promote domestic innovation.[728]

The utility model protection is a legal protection for the new technical solutions not reaching the level of a patentable invention. By virtue of utility model protection, the owner of the said protection has, as provided for by legislation, the exclusive right to exploit the utility model or to license another person to exploit it. The protection has a term of ten years, and then the utility model becomes part of the public domain.

The utility model is considered as a kind of petty patent. The utility model has a role to fulfil in the case of national inventions of minor or local importance; in particular, in Hungary it is/was a means to join the European patent system.

According to the historical concept of utility models (Gebrauchmuster), the invention must relate to working tools or other useful commodities, which means, according to established case law, the inventive concept must be embodied in three-dimensional form.[729]

> The utility model protection can be obtained through the granting procedures set out in law before the Office.[730] By virtue of Act CXLVIII of 2010 the name of Hungarian Patent Office was changed to Hungarian Intellectual Property Office (hereinafter referred as Office) as of 1 January 2011 to better reflect its competence extending to activities related to all form of industrial property protection as well as to the field of copyright.

In Hungary, it is also possible to obtain a valid utility model protection through an international application within the frame of Patent Cooperation Treaty (PCT). Foreign applicants have to be represented by an authorized representative residing in Hungary in procedures started before the Office. In case of obligatory representation, only an attorney or patent attorney is entitled to perform it.[731]

Several provisions of the UM Act refers to the corresponding prescriptions of the Patent Act: e.g., assignment, license contracts, procedural aspects, and court procedure. Other provisions are comparable in structure to the relevant provisions of the Patent Law.

The new Civil Code, the Law V of 2013. is one of the most significant achievements of the twenty-first century in Hungary. The Code omits detailed regulation of intellectual

728. Annual report of National Office of Inventions (Budapest: NOI, 1992), 7.
729. Beier & Schricker, *German Industrial Property*, 9.
730. Csécsy, *A Szellemi Alkotások joga*, 142.
731. Guide to Utility model Protection (Budapest: Hungarian Patent Office, 2009), 12.

property. The new Civil Code shall apply in respect of intellectual property, if these issues directly fall within its scope, which are not governed by the legislation on copyright and industrial property rights of Hungary.

236. The national legal sources[732] of utility model protection are as follows:

- The utility models are protected by Act XXXVIII of 1991 on the Legal Protection of utility models (hereinafter: 'UM Act') in Hungary.
- Act XVI of 2013 on the Amendment of certain Acts relating to Intellectual Property.
- Government Decree 556/2013 (XII 30) on customs authority measures against goods, infringing certain intellectual property rights.
- Decree No. 18/2004 (IV 28) IM on the detailed formal requirements of the application for utility model protection.
- Government Decree No. 147/2007 (VI 26) on the detailed rules concerning electronic filing of certain documents in industrial property procedures.
- Decree No. 19/2005 (IV 12) GKM on the fees for administrative services in industrial property procedures before the Hungarian Patent Office.

§2. Protection of Utility Models

237. Protection may be granted to a technical invention by utility model relating to the construction, structure or arrangement of components of an article, provided that they are new, involve an inventive step, and are capable of industrial application. Only one article is registerable in one application.[733] The UM Act allows such a protection only for solutions pertaining to the shaping of some object in its structure or arrangement of its parts; of course, the aesthetic shaping of a product is excluded, because it is subject matter of industrial design protection; animal breeds and plant varieties are also excluded.[734]

238. The criteria of legal protection are the novelty, inventive step, and industrial applicability. A utility model shall be considered to be new if it does not form part of the state of the art. The requirement for novelty, which is less strict than in the case of patents in connection with the novelty concept does not require worldwide novelty but is satisfied with relative novelty, since the novelty is destroyed by written communication anywhere or domestic use by anyone prior to the priority date.[735]

On the one hand, it does not form part of the state the art, which means that it is not made available to the public by means of a written description anywhere in the world or by public use in Hungary before the filing or priority date. On the other hand, the public use in Hungary is a bar of novelty. The following may not be considered as detrimental to novelty:[736]

732. Pintz, *Találd fel magad*, 211.
733. Article 1(1) of UM Act.
734. Article 1(2) of UM Act.
735. Article 2(2) of UM Act.
736. *Guide to Utility Model Protection*, 9.

(a) verbal communication anywhere;
(b) foreign use.

Additionally, the content of utility model and patent applications filed under the PCT with earlier priority and designating Hungary but announced much later provided the national phase of such application in Hungary has been properly entered into, and shall be considered as comprised in the state of the art.[737] Accordingly as part of the state of the art, they are considered patent and utility model application is filed in Hungary but announced by the Hungarian Intellectual Property Office (hereinafter: 'Office') later.

239. A grace period of six months preceding the priority date is provided in UM Act. (Article 2(4) of UM Act) that is, the following are not a bar of novelty:[738]

(a) when an invention is made available to the public or used by or with the consent of the applicant or his or her predecessor in title within six months prior to the filing or priority date; or
(b) in consequence of an infringement of the lawful rights of the applicant or his or her predecessor in title before the priority date by not more than six months.

In the case of patents is required inventive activity of patentability. In contrast to the inventive activity at patents in relation of utility models the inventive step must be only.

240. A utility model shall be considered to involve an inventive step if, having regard to the state of the art, it is not very obvious to a person skilled in the art. The solution based on an inventive step if it is not obvious to a technician is skilled in the art.[739]

A utility model shall be considered as susceptible of industrial application if it can be made or used in any kind of industry, including agriculture. The extent of utility model protection is determined by the claims; the claims may be interpreted only on the basis of description and the drawing.

Utility model protection will cover not only a product in which all the characteristic of the claim are realized, but also a product in which one or more characteristic of the claims are realized, but also a product in which one or more characteristic of the claim are replaced by an equivalent characteristic; an element in this context may be deemed equivalent if it solves the same problem in essentially the same manner and with the same result.[740]

241. The following, in particular shall be excluded from protection:

(a) aesthetic creations;
(b) plant varieties;
(c) processes;
(d) powder or liquids, chemical composition, pharmaceuticals, or foodstuffs.

737. N. Buzás, *Innovációmenedzsment a Gyakorlatban* (Budapest: Akadémiai Kiadó, 2004), 124.
738. Article 4(2) of UM Act.
739. Article 3 of UM Act.
740. Pintz, *Találd fel magad*, 211.

Utility models shall be refused protection when their commercial exploitation would be contrary to law or to accepted principles of morality, except if statutory restriction applies only to the movement of production.[741]

242. The provisions of the Patent Act shall be applied as regards to the priority and date of filing of applications for a utility model, the examination, withdrawal of and disclosures from such applications, as well as the lapse of the protection and revalidation of utility models and the procedure for the granting of protection for utility models.[742] The Office shall have powers to handle the following:

(a) granting protection;
(b) declaration of termination and revalidation of protection;
(c) declaration of invalidity of a utility model;
(d) declaration of non-infringement;
(e) interpretation of utility model descriptions;
(f) maintenance of protection and records of protection.[743]

243. Proceedings for the granting of utility model protection shall commence upon submission of an application to the Hungarian Intellectual Property Office.

The utility model applications may be filed electronically too.

The application for a utility model shall contain the application for registration, a description of the model, as well as other related documents. The description shall disclose the invention in a manner sufficiently clear and complete for the invention to be carried out by a person skilled in the art. At the end of the description, one or more claims shall be inserted to define the scope of protection in accordance with other parts of the description.

The requirements for filing an application are basically the same as in the case of patents, provided that the description and drawings are to be filed in duplicate only, and no abstract need be filed. The description must be sufficiently clear as to enable a person skilled in the art to execute the subject matter of the utility model on the basis of the specifications and drawings. At the end of the description, one or more claims must be given defining, with reference to description and drawing, the scope of protection applied for.

There is no provisional protection as in the case of patents. An application for a utility model shall be deemed to be withdrawn where patent protection is granted by final decision on the patent application:

(a) that was derived from a patent application;
(b) from which the patent application was derived. The prescriptions of priority are the same as in the case of patents.

In Hungary, it is also possible to obtain a valid utility model protection through an international application within the frame of *PCT*. Foreign applicant has to be represented by authorized representative residing in Hungary in procedures started before the

741. Tattay, *A Szellemi Alkotások joga*, 289.
742. Article 36 of UM Act.
743. Article 26 of UM Act.

Hungarian Intellectual Property Office. In case of obligatory representation, only attorney or *patent attorney* is entitled to perform it.

A utility model application filed in Hungary can be transformed into a European patent application within the union priority range of twelve months, if the utility model application meets the requirements of European patent applications.

244. Procedure for processing utility model application may be divided into three sections:

(a) formal examination;
(b) substantive examination;
(c) grant of utility model protection.

The Office shall conduct the substantive examination of applications for a utility model based on the following criteria:

(a) the object of the application must be a utility model;
(b) the object of the application must be susceptible of industrial application;
(c) the object of the application must not be refused protection;[744]
(d) the description must comply with the conditions prescribed by law (section 32);
(e) the utility model must have unitary character;
(f) the application for priority must be filed in due form.

According to the UM Act[745] only a restricted examination procedure takes place, which does not cover novelty and inventive step. The following conditions apply in case of dispute.[746]

The applicant shall be granted protection for his or her model if:

(a) it meets the main essential conditions set out in UM Act, namely of the novelty, of inventive step and industrial applicability;
(b) it is not excluded from the protection of utility models; and
(c) there are no grounds for refusal on the basis of their commercial exploitation that would be contrary to law or to accepted principles of morality, except if statutory restriction applies only to the movement of products;
(d) the application is in compliance with the formal conditions stipulated in the UM Act.

The decisions of the Office may not be appealed, and no petition for reopening the case, for special consideration or oversight proceedings, or objection by the prosecution may be filed.

---

744. According to Art. 5 §(2) of the UM Act, utility models shall be refused protection where their commercial exploitation would be contrary to law or to accepted principles of morality, except if statutory restriction applies only to the movement of production.

745. Article 35 of the UM Act.

746. J. Pakucs & G. Papanek, *Az Innovációs Folyamatok Szervezése* (Budapest: Magyar innovációs Szövetség, 2006), 176.

The decisions of the Hungarian Intellectual Property Office adopted in connection with utility models may be reviewed by the court.

If the application of utility model is rejected, an appeal with the office is not possible, but a request for reconsideration of the decision of the office by The Metropolitan Court of Justice can be filed within thirty days of the notification of decision. The request may be submitted to the office which will forward it to the court with the documents of the patent case within fifteen days. The Metropolitan Court of Justice shall act through a division of three members, two of these members having a technical university degree or equivalent qualification.[747]

An appeal to the decision of the Metropolitan Court of Justice can be lodged with the Metropolitan Court of Appeal within fifteen days.

245. The rights of the inventor and claims for entitlement to a utility model shall fall within the scope of the provisions of the Patent Act pertaining to the rights of the inventor to be cited and to patent claims.

Chapter I of the UM Act regulates the rights conferred by utility model. The creator and holder of utility model have moral rights and economic rights. The moral rights of inventor consist of several different elements:

(a) the right to acknowledgement of authorship related to utility model;
(b) 'inventor' means the person who has created the utility model;
(c) the right to the utility model shall vest in the inventor or his successor in title.

Article 7(2) of the UM Act regulates joint authorship of utility model:

> If two or more persons have jointly developed a utility model, entitlement shall be vested jointly in them or their respective successors in title. If two or more persons have developed a utility replica independently, entitlement shall be vested in the person – or his successor in title – who has filed an application to the Hungarian Intellectual Property Office previously for claiming a right of priority.

246. A utility model application can be transformed into patent or design application and vice versa. According to the UM Act and Patent Act, no parallel utility model and patent protection may be granted for the same object. In the interest of applicants, the Act assures, however, a possibility to file such a utility model application on an earlier patent application or on a design application. The derived application may keep the priority and application date of the former.[748]

If an applicant has filed a patent application for a certain utility model, he or she may file a utility model application relating to the same subject matter claiming the filing and priority dates of the earlier patent application.[749]

This provision prescribes an opportunity for saving a rejected pending regular patent.

747. Csécsy, *A Szellemi Alkotások joga*, 152; István Molnar, Szellemi Tulajdon Menedzsment and Technologia Transzfer (Kecskemét: InnovAID, 2008), 41.
748. Tattay, *A Szellemi Alkotások joga*, 292.
749. Article 30 of UM Act.

A utility model application may only be derived within ten years from the date of the patent application. Such derivation will be not possible after expiration of ten years from the date of filing of the earlier patent application.

247. In the interest of the applicant, the UM Act assures, however, the possibility to file such a utility model application which is based on an earlier design application. If an applicant has filed a design application for a certain subject matter, he may file a utility model application relating to the same subject matter claiming the filing a priority dates of the earlier design application.[750]

This provision prescribes an opportunity for saving a rejected pending regular design application. Any interested party may request from the office the cancellation of a utility model.

A utility model shall be cancelled in the following cases in accordance with Article 24 of UM Act:

(a) if the utility model lacks required novelty;
(b) if the utility model lacks the prescribed inventive step;
(c) if the model is not applicable in industry;
(d) the description fails to give sufficient disclosure in the specification and drawings comply with the conditions prescribed by law;
(e) if the utility model is broader than the one represented in the application that was submitted on the registered date of application or – in case of division – in the application for division.

Where the grounds for invalidity apply only in part, the utility model right shall be appropriately restricted.[751]

248. The rights of the inventor and claims for entitlement to a utility model shall fall within the scope of the provisions of the Patent Act pertaining to the rights of the inventor to be cited and to patent claims.[752]

Chapter I of the UM Act regulates the rights conferred by utility model. The creator and holder of utility model have moral rights and economic rights. The moral rights of inventor consist of several different elements:

(a) The inventor of utility model has right to acknowledgement of his or her authorship.
(b) Inventor means the person who has created the utility model.
(c) The right to the utility model shall vest in the inventor or his or her successor in title.

The Article 7(2) of UM Act regulates joint authorship of utility model:

> If two or more persons have jointly developed a utility model, entitlement shall be vested jointly in them or their respective successors in title. If two or more persons have developed a utility model independently, entitlement shall be vested

750. Article 31 of UM Act.
751. Csécsy, *A Szellemi Alkotások joga*, 162.
752. Article 6 of UM Act.

in the person – or his successor in title – who has filed an application to the Hungarian Intellectual Property Office previously for claiming a right of priority.

The creator of a utility model shall be entitled to institute legal proceeding against any person contesting his authorship or otherwise infringing his moral rights deriving from invention:

(a) the inventor of a utility model shall have the right to be mentioned as such in utility model documents. The person mentioned as the inventor of a utility model in the application on the application date shall be regarded as the inventor unless a final court decision has ruled otherwise. If there is more than one inventor, the proportion of authorship must be mentioned if this is non-equal;
(b) the right to disclosure of application of utility model;
(c) the right to keep secret his or her model and authorship of utility model, as an inventor may request not to be mentioned in the utility model documents to be published.[753]

249. A registered utility model shall confer on its holder the exclusive right – within the framework of law – to use it and to authorize (license) others to use it. The aforementioned use shall cover, in particular, the making, offering, putting on the market, importing, exporting or using of a product in which the utility model is incorporated or to which it is applied.

The economic (pecuniary) rights of inventor of utility model are as follows:

(a) right to utility model protection, the right to legal protection shall belong to the inventor;
(b) exclusive right to exploit the invention;
(c) the right to conclusion of exploitation of contracts;
(d) under a contract of exploitation (licensing contract), the holder of the invention shall give authorization for the exploitation of the utility model, and the licensee shall be required to pay a fee therefore;
(e) the right to assignment, transfer and pledge of patent;
(f) the rights conferred by an invention and a protected utility model may be assigned, transferred and encumbered, with the exception of the rights of the inventor stemming from the invention;
(g) on the basis on the exclusive rights of exploitation the inventor (patentee shall be entitled to prevent any person not having his or her consent to exploitation of patent).[754]

The provisions governing service inventions and employee inventions shall apply *mutatis mutandis* to utility models that have been developed by a person in employment, public service, or in a civil servant's or a service legal relationship, or by a member of a cooperative employed within the framework of an employment relationship.

753. Csécsy, *A Szellemi Alkotások joga*, 155.
754. *Guide to Utility Model Protection*, 17.

250. Permission of a compulsory license for lack of use of utility model is not provided for.

The varieties of limitations of utility model protection are as follows:

(a) Prior use.
(b) Transit traffic.
(c) Exhaustion.
(d) Mandatory license because of dependence of utility model. If utility model cannot be used without another utility model, a compulsory license may be granted under this latter utility model. If the utility model cannot be exploited without infringing another invention, a compulsory license shall be granted, to the extent necessary, for the exploitation of the impeding invention. The holder of such a utility model shall be entitled on reasonable terms to a license to exploit the model claimed in the dependent utility model according to the common provision of non-compulsory licenses laid down in Patent Act.
(e) Needs of national defence: At the request of the Minister of National Defence, the President of Hungarian Intellectual Property Office may order that an invention covered by utility model shall be exploited against appropriate convention, for the needs of national defence.[755]

251. A utility model shall be protected for a period of ten years as from the date of the filing of the application.[756] For the duration of protection, an annual renewal fee shall be paid. The utility model shall be protected from the date when legal protection is granted, with retroactive effect to the date of filing of the application.

252. The utility model protection shall lapse:

(a) when the term of protection expires, on the day following the expiry of the term of protection;[757]
(b) if the renewal fee is not paid, on the day following the due date; in this case, the revalidation of protection is permissible. When protection was terminated due to non-payment of the renewal fee, the Office shall, upon request, restore protection if the default occurred due to an excusable reason;
(c) if the holder of the protected utility model surrenders the protection, on the day following receipt of the surrender or at an earlier date specified by the person surrendering of protection;
(d) if the utility model has been cancelled with effect retroactive to the date of application.[758]

A utility model shall be terminated in case of derivation with effect retroactive to the date when granted where patent protection is granted by final decision on the patent application:

755. Csécsy, *A Szellemi Alkotások joga*, 156.
756. é. Nagy & D. Pecze, *Polgári Jog I* (Pécs: Dialog Campus, 2003), 129.
757. I. Molnár: *Szellemi Tulajdon Menedzsment és Technologia Transzfer* (Kecskemét: Innovaid Kft, 2008), 124.
758. Article 21(1) of UM Act.

(a) that was derived from a patent application;
(b) from which the patent application was derived.[759]

253. Any interested party may request from the office the cancellation of utility model protects. A utility model shall be cancelled in the following cases:

(a) if the utility model lacks required novelty;
(b) if the utility model lacks the prescribed inventive step;
(c) if the model not applicable in industry;
(d) if the description fails to give sufficient disclosure in the specification and drawings comply with the conditions prescribed by law;
(e) if the utility model is broader than the one represented in the application that was submitted on the registered date of application or – in case of division – in the application for division.[760]

254. Chapter II of UM Act regulates infringement of a utility model and utility model right. The UM Act makes a distinction between infringement of utility model and infringement of utility mode rights. In connection with any infringement of utility model and of utility model rights, the relevant provisions of the Patent Act shall apply to the rights of the licensee authorized by the right holder.

The plagiarism concerning utility models is forbidden. If the subject matter of an application for the protection of a utility model or a protected invention has been appropriated without authorization from another person, the injured party or his successor in title may demand satisfaction concerning his entitlement for the patent in full or in part.

In contrast to utility model infringement, infringement of utility model rights means the unauthorized use of a utility model under protection. The following acts carried out by a third party without the permission of the holder of utility model are qualified as infringement: the manufacture, use or importation for commercial purpose or the marketing of the subject matter of the protected utility model.

The right holder of utility models shall have the right to demand satisfaction from the infringement under civil liability, as afforded to patent holders under the Patent Act. Civil remedies for infringement of utility model rights are available by analogy to Patent Law.

The utility model protection extends to products, in which all characteristics of the claims are realized, or the ones in which for one or more characteristics of the claims equivalent are substituted. An element in this context may be deemed equivalent if it solves the same problem essentially in the same manner and with the same result.[761]

The UM Act deviates in this relation from the Patent Act with the introduction of principle of equivalence. The utility model may not be circumvented by the use of equivalent characteristics, and the exploiter of products embodying of such characteristics shall also be considered as an infringer.

759. Article 21(2) of UM Act.
760. Csécsy, *A Szellemi Alkotások joga*, 162.
761. Pintz, *Találd fel magad*, 79.

The claim to remuneration in connection with a utility model is not affected by one or more features of the claims regarding the product that have been substituted by improved features made available by the holder or the inventor of the utility model.[762]

255. The admissibility of the parallel protection of different objects of intellectual property belongs to the fundamental principles of Hungarian intellectual property right.

According to this basic principle, the cumulative protection several objects is generally permissible. The protection of utility models may overlap with protection of copyrighted works, trademarks, patents, and designs.

The overlap between the protection of utility models and designs is a regular phenomenon.

Protection may be granted to a technical invention by utility model relating to the construction, structure or arrangement of components of an article, provided that they are new, involve an inventive step and are capable of industrial application. Only one article is registerable in one application.

A design shall be protected to the extent that it is new and has individual character design means the appearance of the whole or a part of a product resulting from the features of, in particular, the lines, contours, colours, shape, texture, and/or materials of the product itself and/or its ornamentation.

The shape and appearance of a product may be protected simultaneously by utility model and design.

---

762. Csécsy, *A Szellemi Alkotások joga*, 157.

Chapter 4. Trademarks

§1. Sources: Legislations

256. The current trademark statute is Act XI of 1997 on the protection of trademarks and geographical indications (hereinafter: 'Trademark Act').

Brand names, packaging, and publicity play an increasing important part in business life. By means of known marks, the consumer could identify the preferred firm, the products, goods and goods quality, high-level services, or could distinguish them from the similar products and services of other undertakings.

The first legal regulation on trademarks was born in 1858. However, it must be mentioned that this Act was not yet a result of the autonomous Hungarian legislation; in 1858, a so-called Austrian Imperial and Royal Trademark Letters Patent, having also effect in Hungary, provided for the protection of trademarks.

The first Trademark Act – creating the basis of the legal regulation is still effective today in many respects – was Act No. II of 1890. This Act defined the notion and main kinds of trademarks and laid down the conditions of protection.

The second Hungarian Trademark law was Act IX of 1969. This Act can be considered a result of the reforms of the socialist economic system. The enactment of Act IX of 1969 on trademarks had questioned the efficiency of a socialist planned economy.

The political changes that occurred in 1990 – broad-scale privatization, the creation of different enterprises by foreigners in Hungary, the transition to a market economy and the abolishment of import restrictions – are all economic changes that have completely modified the economic environment. Furthermore, the revision of the trademark law was necessary rather in order to fulfil obligations of Hungary resulting from international agreements.

The most important was the obligation under the Association Agreement between the European Community and Hungary to improve industrial property protection – including trademark protection – to the level of the European Union. In this way, the EC Directive 89/104 (Community Trademark Directive) providing for the harmonization of the most important provisions of substantive trademark law, further the Regulations on the Community Trademark, have to be taken into consideration. The TRIPS Agreement and the bilateral Agreement on the Protection of Intellectual Property concluded between the governments of USA and Hungary in 1993 also contained essential provisions on the protection of trademarks.

The enactment of the legislation in force of Hungarian trademark law, Act XI of 1997 (hereinafter: the 'Trademark Act') and the related decrees, was necessitated by the legal harmonization perspective and the social and economic needs rising from the change of regime as well.

257. The main changes of Hungarian trademark law laid down in the Trademark Act are as follows:

(a) protectable subject matter;
(b) abolition of limitations applied to particular persons who could acquire trademark protection;
(c) registerability of marks, grounds of refusal;
(d) introduction co-ownership of trademarks;
(e) rights conferred;
(f) the doctrine of exhaustion;
(g) the rules of transfer;
(h) the possibility of the transfer of protection partly;
(i) regulation of infringement;
(j) procedural issues are modernized.

The Hungarian Trademark Act was reviewed and amended by Act LII of 2003. This Act introduced the opposition system into Hungarian trademark law. Hungarian Intellectual Property Office examines applications after 1 May 2004 on absolute grounds only and a whole new chapter was added to the Trademark Act, dealing with issues such as filing of a Community Trademark application via Office and rights conferred by Community trademarks.

The Trademark Act also was amended by Act CLXV of 2005. This Act implemented Directive 2004/48/EC of the European Parliament and of the Council of 29 April 2004 on the enforcement of intellectual property:

> By virtue of Act CXLVIII of 2010 the name of Hungarian Patent Office was changed to Hungarian Intellectual Property Office (hereinafter referred as Office) as of 1 January 2011 to better reflect its competence extending to activities related to all form of industrial property protection as well as to the field of copyright.

The new Civil Code, the Law V of 2013 is one of the most significant achievements of the twenty-first century in Hungary. The Code omits detailed regulation of intellectual property. The new Civil Code shall apply in respect of intellectual property, if these issues directly fall within its scope, which are not governed by the legislation on copyright and industrial property rights of Hungary.

The trademarks are stipulated by Hungarian laws and regulations and Community laws and regulations, as far as international treaties and conventions.[763]

258. Hungarian laws and regulations:

- Act XI of 1997 on the Protection of Trademarks and Geographical Indications (hereinafter: 'Trademark Act').
- Act CL. of 2005 on Enforcement of Industrial Property Rights and Copyrights.
- Act XVI of 2013 on the Amendment of certain Acts relating to Intellectual Property.
- Act CLIX of 2013 on the Amendment of certain Acts relating to Intellectual Property.
- Government Decree 556/2013(XII 30) on customs authority measures against goods, infringing certain intellectual property rights.

763. Lontai et al., *A Szellemi Alkotások joga*, 233–235.

- Decree No. 16/2004 (IV 27) IM on the detailed formalities of trademark applications and applications for the protection of geographical indications.
- Decree No. 19/2005 (IV 12) GKM on the fees for administrative services in industrial procedures to the Hungarian Patent Office.
- Government Decree No. 371/2004 (XII 26) government concerning custom action against goods infringing certain intellectual property rights.[764]
- Government Decree No. 147/2007 (VI 26) on the detailed rules concerning electronic filing of certain documents in industrial property procedures.
- Act No. CXXX. of 2016 on the Code of Civil Procedure.

259. Community laws and regulations:

- Directive 2004/48/EC of the European Parliament and of the Council of 29 April 2004 on the enforcement of intellectual property rights.
- Directive 2008/95/EC of the European Parliament and of the Council of 22 October 2008 to approximate the laws of the Member States relating to trademarks.
- Council Regulation (EC) No. 207/2009 of 26 February 2009 on the Community trademark (codified version).
- Commission Regulation (EC) 2868/95 of 13 December 1995 implementing Council Regulation (EC) 40/94 on the Community trademark.
- Commission Regulation (EC) No. 355/2009 of 31 March 2009 amending Regulation (EC) No. 2869/95 on the fees payable to the Office for Harmonization in the Internal Market (Trade Marks and Designs) and Regulation (EC) No. 2868/95 implementing Council Regulation (EC) No. 40/94 on the Community trademark.
- Commission Regulation (EC) 216/96 of 5 February 1996 laying down the rules of procedure of the Boards of Appeal of the Office for Harmonization in the Internal Market.
- Directive 2004/48/EC of the European Parliament and of the Council of 29 April 2004 on the enforcement of intellectual property (hereinafter: 'IP Enforcement Directive').
- Directive (EU) 2015/2436 of the European Parliament and of the Council of 16 December 2015 to approximate the laws of the Member States relating to trademarks.
- Regulation (EU) 2015/2424 of the European Parliament and of the Council of 16 December 2015 amending Council Regulation (EC) No 207/2009 on the Community trademark and Commission Regulation (EC) No 2868/95 implementing Council Regulation (EC) No 40/94 on the Community trademark.

260. International treaties and conventions:

- Paris Convention for the Protection of Industrial Property (1883) – Promulgated by the Law Decree No. 18/1970 (hereinafter: 'Paris Convention').
- Madrid Agreement for the International Registration of Marks (1891) – Promulgated by the Law Decree No. 29/1973 (hereinafter: 'Madrid Agreement').[765]

764. Pintz, *Találd fel magad*, 211.
765. Tattay, *A Szellemi Alkotások joga*, 405–409.

- Madrid Agreement for the repression of False or Deceptive Indications of Source of Goods and Services (1891) – Promulgated by the Law Decree No. 19/1970.
- Nice Agreement for the International Classification of Goods and Services for the Purposes of Registration of Marks (1957) – Promulgated by Law Decree No. 29/1973 (hereinafter: 'Nice Classification Agreement').
- Protocol Relating to the Madrid Agreement Concerning the International Registration of Marks (Madrid Protocol 1989) – Promulgated by Act No. LXXXIII of 1999 (hereinafter: 'Madrid Protocol').
- Common Regulations under the Madrid Agreement Concerning the International Registration of Marks and the Protocol Relating to that Agreement Promulgated by the Decree 4/2005 (III 11) IM.
- Agreement on Trademark Law Treaty (1994) Promulgated by Act LXXXIII of 1999.
- Arrangement on Trade-Related Aspects of Intellectual Property Rights 1993 (hereinafter: 'TRIPS Agreement' – Promulgated by Act IX of 1998 (hereinafter: 'TRIPS Agreement').[766]
- Nairobi Treaty on the Protection of the Olympic Symbol – promulgated by the Act LX of 2008.

§2. Subject Matter of Protection

I. Signs That May Serve as Trademarks

261. The Hungarian Parliament adopted the Trademark Act in 1997 in order to promote the development of the Hungarian market economy, to strengthen the conditions for fair competition that is based on the ability of distinguishing different goods and services, and to improve the level of consumer information, in harmony with the international commitments of the Republic of Hungary regarding the protection of intellectual property rights.[767]

In accordance with Article 1 section (1) of the Trademark Act, trademark protection shall be granted for any signs capable of being represented graphically, provided that these are capable of distinguishing goods and services from those of another undertaking.

The definition is very broad and does not limit the types of signs that may be considered as trademarks. Another key element of definition is that it also extends to service marks.

A mark is appropriate for distinguishing itself from competitors if it gives the covered goods and services a special and different character. The main criterion for protection is the capacity to distinguish.

The criteria of trademark protection are as follows:

(a) a sign;
(b) capacity to distinguish;

766. Pintz, *Találd fel magad*, 212.
767. Lontai et al., *A Szellemi Alkotások joga*, 254.

(c) graphic representation;
(d) undertaking;
(e) registration of trademark.

262. A trademark may consist[768] of any of the following signs:

(a) a word, combination of words, including personal names and slogans;
(b) letters, numerals;
(c) designs, graphics;
(d) flat or three-dimensional figures, including the shape of the goods or packaging;
(e) a colour, a combination of colours, a light signal, a hologram;
(f) a sound; as well as
(g) a combination of the signs listed in paragraphs (a)–(f).[769]

263. The distinctiveness is absolutely important for merchandise of standard products. The capacity to distinguish is always a relative feature of the trademark. Many marks which were unregisterable under earlier Trademark Law (Act IX of 1969) are now registered, e.g., colours, holograms, and slogans.

A sign shall be excluded from trademark protection if it is devoid of any distinctive character, in particular, if it consists exclusively of a sign or indication that may serve, in trade to designate the kind, quality, and quantity of intended purpose, value, geographical origin, or the time of production of the goods or of rendering of the service or other characteristic of the goods or services, or which have become customary in the current language or in practices of trade.[770]

A sign shall be not excluded from trademark protection if, either before or after the date of priority, it has acquired a distinctive character. The legal institution of acquired distinctiveness through use was introduced to the Hungarian trademark law by current Trademark Act. There are some circumstances, however, that shall be taken into account if an applicant wishes to refer to acquired distinctiveness through use, in this respect shall be mentioned:[771]

(a) the evidence of use in order to judge whether that use has produced a situation where a mark which would otherwise have to be refused on one or several absolute grounds listed in the Trademark Act has become distinctive;
(b) the use must relate to the goods and services being the subject of trademark application;
(c) the use must be of the mark applied and not for a significantly different variation of it;

768. Lontai, *A Szellemi Alkotások joga*, 229.
769. Article 1(2) of the Trademark Act.
770. Article 2(2) of the Trademark Act.
771. According to Art. 2(3) of Trademark Act, a sign may not be refused trademark protection because the absence of distinctiveness if it has acquired a distinctive character through its use either before establishment of priority or subsequent to the establishment thereof.

(d) the mark must have acquired distinctiveness at the time of the filing date; and the distinctiveness must be still present at the time of decision of registerability.[772]

The loss of the distinctive character is provided for grounds of trademark protection.

The rule concerning the publication of trademarks in a manual or handbook aims to prevent the dilution of a trademark into a generic name. Accordingly, the reproduction of a trademark in a dictionary, lexicon, encyclopaedia, or similar reference work gives the impression that it constitutes the generic name of the goods or services for which the trademark is registered, the publisher of the work shall, at the request of the holder of the trademark, indicate – on the next edition of the publication at the latest – that the trademark has been registered and is under trademark protection.[773]

264. Trademark protection shall be granted for any sign that can be graphically represented limited;[774] the sign is excluded from trademark protection if it is not graphically representable. As a consequence, the exhaustive and not exemplificative character of the list of signs capable of distinction that the olfactory signs (smells) may not be granted trademark protection in Hungary despite their possibility of being represented graphically.[775]

265. The trademark should distinguish goods or services from those of other undertakings. Any natural or legal person or a company without legal personality, irrespective of pursuing economic activities, may apply for trademark protection.[776]

Undertaking, that is, the trademark owner may be any natural person, firm, or other kind of legal entity. A trademark may have several proprietors (joint applicants or joint owners). The Trademark Act makes it possible for any physical or moral person, as well as economic companies having no moral personality, to obtain trademark protection independently and regardless of whether they display economic activities.

The Trademark Act defines the sphere of persons who could acquire trademark protection. Generally, everyone could acquire such protection.[777] Applicants not residing in Hungary must appoint a patent attorney or attorney-at-law in Hungary.

266. The Trademark Act invariably ties the acquisition of trademark protection to registration.[778] The right to the legal protection of a trademark shall belong to the person who has made the trademark registered according to the trademark procedure.

Certification of use or having the intent to use a trademark cannot be required to this end. The Trademark register provides evidence, that is, certifies the rights related to trademarks, in an authentic way and is accessible to everybody.

In the case of unregistered marks, it is already uncertain and contestable whether the mark, as a result of its use, has in fact acquired real protection without having been

772. Pintz, *Találd fel magad*, 83.
773. Article 13 of the Trademark Act.
774. Tattay, *A Szellemi Alkotások joga*, 331.
775. Article 1(1) of the Trademark Act.
776. Article 9(2) of the Trademark Act.
777. Pintz, *Találd fel magad*, 86.
778. Article 9(1) of the Trademark Act.

registered, when the rights related to mark as well as its circumstances are not certified by a given authentic recording system.[779]

Use in the country without registration results in exclusion from trademark protection of the latter sign only if use without consent of the prior user would in itself be contrary to the law.[780]

II. Different Categories of Trademarks

267. Trademarks have several categories.[781] The most important kinds of trademarks[782] are as follows:

(a) product marks;
(b) service marks;
(c) well-known marks, trademarks having a reputation;
(d) national marks;
(e) Community trademarks;
(f) international marks;
(g) collective marks;
(h) certification marks.[783]

268. By virtue of Article 1(1) of the Trademark Act, service marks may be registered. The provision relating to marks in principle apply to service marks as well.

269. The legal protection of well-known marks was addressed in Article 6 of the Paris Convention. Trademarks having a reputation in a particular country enjoy an enforced protection.[784]

By virtue of the Paris Convention of 1883, the countries of the Union undertake ex officio if their legislation so permits, or at the request of an interested party, to refuse or to cancel the registration, and to prohibit the use, of a trademark which constitutes a reproduction, an imitation or a translation liable to create confusion of a mark considered by the competent authority of the country or which used to be well known in that country as being already the mark of a person entitled to the benefits of this convention and used for identical or similar goods.[785]

The well-known marks can be characterized by a very high degree of notoriety, such expressions as 'famous mark', 'exceptionally well-known mark', 'mark of high

779. According to Art. 5(2) a), a sign may not be granted trademark protection that has actually been used previously by others in the domestic territory without registration, if use of the sign without the consent of the earlier user would be deemed unlawful.
780. Pintz, *Találd fel magad*, 85.
781. Csécsy, *A Szellemi Alkotások joga*, 196.
782. Lontai et al., *A Szellemi Alkotások joga*, 256.
783. Tattay, *A Szellemi Alkotások joga*, 327–328.
784. Article 4(1) of the Trademark Act.
785. Article 6 s. (1) of the Paris Convention.

repute', and 'highly renowned mark' have been used for such marks, whereas the Trademark Act uses the term 'mark having a reputation in country'.[786]

The problems the proprietors of such marks confront are the use of such marks by third parties for dissimilar products or services.

The Trademark Act uses the expressions 'trademark having a reputation in the country' or 'trademark enjoying a good reputation in the domestic market'.

A sign may not be granted trademark protection with respect to dissimilar goods or services if the later trademark identical with or similar to an earlier trademark having a reputation in the country, where the use without due case of the latter sign would take unfair advantage of or be detrimental to the distinctive character or repute of the earlier trademark.[787]

270. National trademarks are registered according to the Hungarian Trademark Act. By virtue of Article 8 of the Trademark Act, national signs enjoy a trademark protection if they are distinctive and are capable of being represented graphically, not excluded from trademark protection and satisfied procedural requirement laid down in the Trademark Act.[788]

271. Part III of the Trademark Act involves provisions concerning the Community Trademark system. The Hungarian applicants may file a Community trademark application.

A Community Trademark Application is an application for the registration of a Community, filed in accordance with the Community Trademark Regulation.[789]

Extension of the Community trademark system results in a flow of a couple of hundred thousand new registrations into the Hungarian registry from 1 May 2004 (Accession of Hungary to the European Union)[790] automatically extended Community trademarks and constitute earlier rights in Hungary against any trademark registration and application with a filing date on or after effective date of accession, a national right.

The Trademark Act contains the prescriptions related to Community trademarks[791] and Community trademark applications:

(a) filing of a Community trademark application via the Hungarian Patent Office;
(b) rights conferred by Community trademark;
(c) conversion;
(d) seniority of Community trademarks;
(e) infringement of Community trademarks;
(f) conformity with the EU directives;
(g) the amendments of the competence of Metropolitan Court and the Metropolitan Court of Appeals.

786. Csécsy, *A Szellemi Alkotások joga*, 196.
787. Article 4(1) of the Trademark Act.
788. By virtue of Art. 8 of Trademark Act, a sign shall be granted trademark protection, if it corresponds to concept of trademark, not excluded from protection and complies the requirements laid down by Trademark Act.
789. According to Art. 76/A s. (c) of the Trademark Act.
790. Act XXX of 2004.
791. Chapter X/A of the Trademark Act.

272. International marks by virtue of Article 76(1) of the Trademark Act are protected in Hungary. Hungary acceded to the systems of Madrid Agreement[792] in 1909 and Madrid Protocol 1999.[793] International trademark application means an application filed under the Madrid Agreement or Madrid Protocol. The International register is the registry maintained by the International Bureau of trademarks under the Madrid Agreement.

273. In accordance with Chapter XIII, collective marks may be registered and protected in Hungary. By virtue of Article 96 section (1) of the Trademark Act, collective marks are the marks that are capable of distinguishing goods or services of the members of social organizations, public body or association from the goods and services of other undertakings according to the quality, origin or other characteristics of goods or services bearing the collective mark.[794]

The holder may not use the collective mark; he or she shall however, authorize the use with respect to the goods or services complying with the prescribed quality requirements or with other characteristics.[795]

A sign shall be excluded from trademark protection as a collective mark:

(a) if the public is liable to be misled as regards the character or the significance of the mark, in particular if it is likely to be perceived as other than a collective mark;
(b) if the regulations governing its use contain provisions contrary to public policy, accepted principles of morality or law.[796]

Protection of collective trademarks is granted to associations and the members of such organization are entitled to use the mark.[797]

The association functioning as the proprietor of the trademark may not itself use the collective trademark; however, it controls its use by its members.[798]

The holder of a collective mark shall have a regulation which shall include the condition of membership and the conditions of the use of the collective mark. The application for a collective trademark shall contain this regulation.[799]

The regulation of the collective mark shall include:

(a) the name and registered office of the association registered as the proprietor of the collective trademark;
(b) a list of the members of the association, their names, addresses, and/or registered offices;

792. Madrid Agreement for the International Registration of Marks (1891) – Promulgated by Law Decree No. 29/1973.
793. Protocol Relating to the Madrid Agreement Concerning the International Registration of Marks (Madrid Protocol 1989) – Promulgated by Act. LXXXIII of 1999.
794. Csécsy, *A Szellemi Alkotások joga*, 202–204.
795. Lontai et al., *A Szellemi alkotások joga*, 268–269.
796. Article 96(3) of Trademark Act.
797. Article 96(4) of the Trademark Act.
798. Article 96(5) of the Trademark Act.
799. Tattay, *A Szellemi Alkotások joga*, 349.

(c) conditions of membership;
(d) conditions of use of the trademark;
(e) regulations governing control of the use of the trademark.[800]

In case of any change to the data indicated in the regulation, the holder of a collective mark shall submit an amended regulation to the Hungarian Intellectual Property Office. Amendments to the regulation shall take effect only from the entry in the Trade Mark Register. The amendment shall not be entered in the Register if

(a) the amended regulation does not satisfy the prescribed formal requirements;
(b) due to the amendment, the requirements prescribed in Article would not be met or it would involve one of the grounds for refusal.[801]

274. According to the Chapter XIV of the Trademark Act, certification marks may be filed and registered in Hungary. Article 10(1) involves the notion of the certification mark:[802] Certification marks are trademarks that distinguish goods or services of specified quality or of other characteristics from other goods or services by attesting to such quality or characteristic.[803]

The Proprietor of certification mark is entitled to grant the right to its use with respect to goods or services complying with the prescribed quality or other requirements. The Trademark Act protection of certification may not be obtained if:

(a) an undertaking that produces, puts on the market, or imports the goods or supplies the services for which the trademark is registered;
(b) an undertaking that – pursuant to the Competition Act – is not independent from the user of certification mark;
(c) an undertaking with which the user of certification mark is in a permanent relationship in respect of the goods or services for which the mark registered.[804]

The trademark proprietor may not use the certification trademark; he or she may, however, license the use of the mark in connection with goods and services meeting the prescribed quality conditions or other characteristics.[805]

The certification mark should be accompanied by regulation, which includes the main criteria of the use of mark: The quality requirements relating to the goods or services for which the mark is registered, and also the rules attesting to the quality, as well as, the provisions relating to the control of the use of the mark.

The regulations shall contain:

(a) the name and registered office of the trademark proprietor;

800. Article 97(2) of the Trademark Act.
801. Article 97(5)of the Trademark Act.
802. Lontai et al., *A Szellemi Alkotások joga*, 268–269.
803. Csécsy, *A Szellemi Alkotások joga*, 202–204.
804. Article 10(2) of the Patent Act.
805. Article 101(3).

(b) the quality requirements for the goods and services contained in the specification of goods and services;
(c) the regulations governing quality certification;
(d) conditions of use of the trademark;
(e) regulations governing the control of trademark use;[806]
(f) procedure for taking action against unauthorized use of the trademark.

§3. Conditions of Protection

275. In accordance with Article 8(1) of the Trademark Act, trademark protection shall be granted for a sign if:

(a) it satisfies the requirements of trademark protection (sign capable of distinction and graphically representable);
(b) it is not excluded from trademark protection;
(c) the relevant application complies with the procedural requirements of the Trademark Act.

The Trademark Act establishes a system of obstacles to registration, making a distinction between absolute and relative exclusion.[807]

The absolute grounds of refusal of trademark protection[808] relate to inherent objections to distinctiveness, graphic representation, and certain public-interest objection. The relative grounds of refusal of the trademark protection[809] arise because some other trade or proprietor has an earlier conflicting right.

The absolute grounds of refusal exclude the sign in relation to all products and services, and the relative grounds of refusal limits the trademark protection and may concern partly the list of products and services.[810]

The absolute grounds of refusal establish absolute prohibition without exception. When relative grounds of refusal are examined, a sign may be not refused trademark protection if the holder of earlier rights consents to the registration of the latter sign.[811] Consent declarations are not likely to overcome official actions based on absolute grounds of refusal.

In relation to absolute grounds of refusal, the Hungarian Intellectual Property Office shall carry out a substantive examination of the trademark application ex officio. The relative grounds of refusal are examined only by opposition of the interested party.[812]

806. Article 101(5).
807. Csécsy, *A Szellemi Alkotások joga*, 196–201.
808. Articles 2 and 3 of the Trademark Act.
809. Articles 4 and 5 of the Trademark Act.
810. Lontai, *A Szellemi Alkotások joga,* 257–261.
811. Article 7(1) of the Trademark Act.
812. Pintz, *Találd fel magad*, 86–91.

276. The mark is excluded from trademark protection[813] (absolute grounds of refusal) if:

(a) it is not graphically representable;
(b) it lacks distinctive character, as the distinctive character is a fundamental requirement for the registration of a trademark;
(c) in particular, the mark is descriptive or it results directly from the nature of goods; the shape of goods protected by trademark concerned is just necessary for obtaining a given technical effect, or it represents the essential value of the goods. This ground of refusal shall not apply if the mark has acquired distinctive character in relation to the claimed goods and services through its use in Hungary, either before or after the priority of the application;[814]
(d) it uses conflicts with public order or public morality;
(e) it is capable of deceiving consumers with regard to any feature of the goods or services. The sign shall not be to deceive consumers particularly in respect to quality and geographical origin of the goods;
(f) it was filed for registration in bad faith;

In accordance with Article 3(2) of Trademark Act, a sign shall be excluded from trademark protection if:

(a) it consists of, or contains any of the emblems listed in Article 6ter(1) of the Paris Convention for the Protection of Industrial Property, provided that:

(aa) such a sign – if it is not a national flag – has been communicated according to Article 6ter(3) and;

(ab) the sign – if it consists of or contains an official sign indicating control and warranty or a hallmark – its registration was applied not in respect of identical or similar goods as indicated with the official sign,

(b) it consists of badges, symbols, or escutcheons, not covered by point; (a), which are of public interest, or if it contains such badges, symbols, or escutcheons;

(c) it consists exclusively of symbols having a close relation to religious or other beliefs.

Trademark protection shall be granted with the consent of the competent authority to signs which consist of or contain the emblems defined under paragraph 2 (a) and (b).

813. Articles 2 and 3 of the Trademark Act.
814. Article 2(3) of the Trademark Act.

A sign may not be granted trademark protection if it consists of or contains a geographical indication registered pursuant to Trademark Act or to the law of the European Union. This provision shall apply to signs:

(a) which shall not be registered as trademarks pursuant to the law of the European Union;

(b) which are used in connection with goods;

(ba) which do not originate in a geographical area corresponding to the geographical indication; or

(bb) to which the geographical indication shall not be used for any other reason on the basis of the provisions of this Act or of the law of the European Union.[815]

277. The relative grounds of refusal are examined by opposition. The relative grounds of refusal of the trademark protection arise because some other trade or proprietor has an earlier conflicting right:

(a) The first group of relative grounds for exclusion are related to earlier trademark rights according to which the identity of the signs and of the goods and services excludes without any further condition, protection of latter sign.
(b) A sign not be granted trademark protection if, because of its identity or similarity of the goods or services, there exists a likelihood of confusion on the part of consumers.
(c) A sign with respect to dissimilar goods or services if the sign with the later date of priority is identical or similar to an earlier trademark having a reputation in Hungary where the use without due cause of the latter sign would take unfair advantage of or be detrimental to the distinctive character or the repute of the earlier trademark excluded from protection.

Signs that have a reputation in the case of detriment to their repute acquired in the country exclude the protection of a latter sign with respect to different goods and services as well.

Earlier trademarks naturally include those registered in a national or international way to the Madrid Agreement and Madrid Protocol. Community trademarks have the same effect as the national trademark after the accession of Hungary to the European Union.

The trademarks that have not been used do not constitute an obstacle to registration.

The further relative grounds of refusal are as follows:

815. Article 3(4) of Trademark Act.

(a) if it would infringe earlier personal rights, in particular a right in name or of personal portrayal;
(b) if it would conflict with an earlier copyright and industrial property right of others including conflict with the name of protected plant variety;
(c) if it has been used effectively in the country without registration where the use of the sign without the consent of the prior user would be contrary to the law;
(d) if with respect to identical or similar goods or services, it is identical or similar to a trademark whose protection has lapsed by reason of expiration and less than two years have elapsed since that time, unless the earlier trademark had been not used;
(e) if the representative or agent applies for registration in his own name without the holder's authorization, unless the representative or agent justifies his action.[816]

§4. Formalities (Procedure for Obtaining, Establishing, and Maintaining of Trademarks)

278. Besides the material legal rules, the provisions on procedure were also modernized in order to enhance their efficiency in accordance with the effective trademark regulation.

By virtue of Article 37 of the Trademark Act, the Hungarian Intellectual Property Office (hereinafter: 'Office') shall have competence in the following trademark matters:

(a) registration of trademarks;
(b) renewal of trademark protection;
(c) revocation of trademark protection;
(d) cancellation of trademarks;
(e) division of trademark protection;
(f) keeping the records of trademark applications and trademarks;
(g) official information.[817]

In compliance with the requirements of legal safety, the Trademark Act provides for the procedures related to the renewal or division of protection, the decision on lapse and the cancellation of the trademark as well also fall under the competence of the Hungarian Intellectual Property Office.[818]

The trademark applications; requests for renewal requests for recording of the changes in the facts may also be filed in electronic form.[819]

TMe Filing

Since 4 September 2014, the trademark E-filing system serving for filing national trademark applications electronically has been available for the clients of HIPO. The

816. Articles 4 and 5 of the Trademark Act.
817. Lontai et al., *A Szellemi Alkotások joga*, 263–267.
818. Articles 37(2) of the Trademark Act.
819. Article 46/D(2) of Trademark Act.

implementation of the trademark E-filing system developed by EUIPO has been accomplished within the frameworks of the cooperation with EUIPO.

The new trademark E-Filing system, which operates parallel with the already know E system, offers user-friendly supporting functions for the trademark applicants. Special feature is the preliminary search made automatically for the sign to be filed, through which the applicant can immediately be informed on the earlier conflicting trademarks, if any; furthermore, the TMClass tool supporting the creation of the list of goods and services of the trademark application, which helps form the list of goods and services of the trademark application in accordance with the common EU classification practice.

The Office shall also have competence in matters deriving from the applications of provisions relating to the Community trademark system and to the international registration.[820]

The Office shall proceed in trademark matters failing with its competence by applying the provisions of Act CXL of 2004 on the general rules of administrative procedures and services.[821]

The language of trademark procedures is Hungarian. The trademark application shall be drawn up in Hungarian.

279. The information to the public in the Gazette of the Office can be recognized as an important guarantee of legal security related to trademarks.

The following data and facts relating to trademark application and trademarks shall be published in the Gazette of the Office:

(a) on publication of trademark application, the name and address of the applicant and the representative, the reference number of application, the filing date, and the date of priority where the latter is different, the sign and the list of goods and services;[822]
(b) after registration of the trademark, the registration number and the address of the holder, name and address of the representative the reference number, the filing date, and the date of priority where the latter is different, the trademark, the list of goods or services and the date of the ruling of the registration.[823]

280. The main steps in the examination and registration procedure related to trademarks are as follows:

(a) filing;
(b) examination of filing, communication of the filing date of marks for applicant;
(c) research into formal requirements;
(d) the possibility of observations;
(e) research of earlier rights, research report;
(f) the substantive examination related to the absolute grounds of refusal only;
(g) opposition;

820. Pintz, *Találd fel magad*, 89.
821. Article 45(1) of the Trademark Act.
822. Article 49(a) of the Trademark Act.
823. Article 49(b) of the Trademark Act.

(h) registration of the trademarks;
(i) supervision by the courts.

281. Under Article 50(1) of the Trademark Act, the procedure for the registration of a trademark shall begin with a trademark application with the Hungarian Intellectual Property Office.

Since 2007, a trademark application can also be filed electronically by using an electronic form drawn up by the Hungarian Intellectual Property Office for this purpose.[824]

The Hungarian Intellectual Property Office shall confirm receipt of trademark applications by way of electronic means by sending a notice to the applicant – in accordance with specific other legislation – by an automated reply system containing an electronic file number.[825]

The date of filing is the day upon which the application received by the Hungarian Intellectual Property Office contains at least the following:[826]

Minimum requirements to obtain filing date are as follows:

(a) information suitable for the identification (name and address) of the applicant;
(b) representation of the sign;
(c) list of goods and services;
(d) request; (reference to a claim for trademark protection);
(e) a trademark application shall be subject to the payment of a filing fee. The fee shall be payable within two months after the date of filing.

When the enclosures of trademark application have been prepared in a foreign language, the list of goods or services shall be filed in Hungarian within four months[827] after the date of filing.

In the list of goods or services, the goods or services shall be grouped according to the classes of the Nice Agreement. The specification of goods contains a list of goods or services for which trademark protection is claimed under the mark. An additional fee surcharge shall be paid for the second and each additional class of goods and services.[828] The Trademark Act describes the unitary character of trademark application.

The unitary character of trademark application means that the trademark protection may only be claimed for an individual mark in a trademark application.[829]

282. The date establishing priority shall be:

(a) in general, the date of filing of the trademark application (application priority);

824. Article 51/A(1) of the Trademark Act.
825. Article 50/A(2) of the Trademark Act.
826. Article 51(1) of the Trademark Act.
827. Article 51(5) of the Trademark Act.
828. Nice Agreement for the International Classification of Goods and Services for the Purposes of Registration of Marks (1957) – Promulgated by Law Decree No. 29/1973.
829. Article 52(1) of the Trademark Act.

(b) in cases defined by the Paris Convention, the date of filing of a foreign application (Convention priority);
(c) in cases defined in the communication of the president of office published in the Official Gazette, the first day of displaying the sign at an exhibition shall not be earlier that six months prior to the date of the filing of the application (Exhibition priority);
(d) the date of prior or pending trademark application for the same sign, which is not earlier than the six-month period prior to the date of application in question (internal priority).

Convention, exhibition, and internal priority shall be claimed within two months after the filing of the application. The document establishing convention priority and the certification of exhibition shall be filed within four months after the date of the filing.[830]

283. Following the filing of a trademark application, the office shall examine for accomplishment of filing date whether:

(a) the application satisfies the requirements for granting a filing date;
(b) the filing fee has been paid;
(c) the list of goods or services has been filed in the Hungarian language.[831]

The applicant must be informed on the obtaining of filing date.

284. After granting the date of filing, the Hungarian Intellectual Property Office shall examine whether the formal requirements (the request, the sign, list of goods and other enclosures, and detailed formal requirements) have been satisfied and whether the sign is uniform.[832]

If the application does not comply with the above requirements, the applicant shall be invited to rectify the irregularities or to divide the application. The trademark application shall be rejected if compliance with the prescribed requirements is not achieved upon the necessary corrections or upon provision of a statement.[833]

An application may only be refused on the grounds specifically and clearly stated in the request. If the applicant fails to respond to the request within the prescribed time limit, or fails to divide the application, the application shall be considered withdrawn.[834]

285. During the procedure for the registration of a trademark, any person may file an observation with the office to the effect that the sign may not be granted trademark protection because of existence of the absolute ground of refusal. Observations can be filed against a pending application by any person. Observation shall be taken into consideration when the requirement objected to in the observation examined. The observation shall be communicated to the applicant.[835]

830. Article 53(2) of the Trademark Act.
831. Article 55 of the Trademark Act.
832. Article 59(1) of the Trademark Act.
833. Article 59(3) of the Trademark Act.
834. Article 59(4) of the Trademark Act.
835. Article 58 of the Trademark Act.

The person submitting the observation shall not be party to the procedure for the registration of the trademark officio substantive examination to relative grounds of refusal.[836]

Appeal against the decisions of the Hungarian Patent Office can be filed with the Metropolitan Court within thirty days of the decision.[837,838]

286. The research of earlier rights follows the formal expertise. Probably, the major shift in the regulation of trademarks in the course of the last years is that the Hungarian Patent Office examines applications filed after 1 May 2004 on absolute grounds only. Observation by third parties in pending trademark application remains in use, but applicable.

If a trademark application satisfies the minimal requirements (request, name and address of the applicant, representation of the sign, and a list of goods) the Hungarian Intellectual Property Office shall examine whether the formal requirements have been satisfied.

If the trademark application satisfies the formal requirements, the Office shall carry out a research of earlier rights and, on the basis of the mark with due consideration of the specification of goods and services, shall draw up a search report.[839]

The research report shall be indicating those data which may be taken into consideration in deciding whether the sign to which the trademark application relates is registerable. The Office shall send the research report to the applicant.[840]

The applicant, the holder, and the license recorded in trademark register may request the Office to notify him or her of the later trademark application in the search report of which his or her earlier right was indicated by sending him a copy of search report. The Office shall only fulfil the request after payment of the fee. The request may be submitted for a period defined in calendar months, not exceeding one year.[841]

287. The absolute ground of refusal shall be examined by the Hungarian Intellectual Property Office ex officio. After the examination of formal requirements, the Hungarian Intellectual Property Office shall carry out a substantive examination of the trademark protection.[842]

The substantive examination shall access:

(a) whether the sign meets the requirements of graphically representing and distinctiveness;
(b) whether or not it is excluded from trademark protection relating to absolute grounds of refusal for trademark protection; and
(c) whether the application complies with the requirements laid down in the Trademark Act.[843]

836. Article 58(3) of the Trademark Act.
837. Pintz, *Találd fel magad*, 89.
838. Csécsy, *A Szellemi Alkotások joga*, 218–220.
839. Article 60(1) of the Trademark Act.
840. Article 60(3) of the Trademark Act.
841. Article 61(1) of the Trademark Act.
842. Article 61(1) of the Trademark Act.
843. Pintz, *Találd fel magad*, 89.

If the trademark application does not meet the requirements of substantive examination, the applicant shall be invited according to the nature of the objection, to rectify the irregularities or to submit comments.[844]

Trademark application shall be rejected in whole or in part if it does not meet the examined requirements even after the rectification of irregularities or the submitting of comments.

An application may be rejected only on grounds that have been precisely and expressly stated and duly reasoned in the invitation of applicant.[845]

The trademark application shall be published after the examination of formal requirements one month after the research report has been sent to the applicant at the earliest.

The trademark application shall be considered withdrawn if the applicant fails to respond to the request within the prescribed time limit.[846]

In accordance with 61/A(1) of the Trademark Act, the Hungarian Intellectual Property Office shall publish the application for registration after one month from sending the search report to the applicant if the application is found in compliance with the requirements of formal examination in the Gazette of the Office.[847]

The applicant shall be notified of the publication.

The withdrawal, invalidation, rejection, modification, or division of an application after publication shall be officially communicated.[848]

288. The opposition system has been introduced into the Hungarian trademark law in 2004. Within a period of three months following the publication of trademark application, the owner of prior rights can file a notice of opposition to the Office on the grounds that a mark may not be registered due to conflict of earlier rights:

(a) by the holder of the earlier trademark and the licensee recorded in trademark register thereof;
(b) by the holder of personal rights earlier copyrights, industrial property rights and names of protected plant varieties;
(c) by prior user;
(d) by the holder without whose authorization the agent or the representative has applied for the registration of a sign in his or her own name.[849]

The international trademark applications and community trademark applications may also be opposed.

By virtue of Article 7(1) of the Trademark Act, a sign may not be refused the trademark protection related to relative grounds of refusal of trademark protection if the holder of the earlier right consents to the registration of the latter sign.

844. Article 61(3) of the Trademark Act.
845. Article 61(4) of the Trademark Act.
846. Article 61(5) of the Trademark Act.
847. Article 61/A(3) of the Trademark Act.
848. Article 61/A(4) of the Trademark Act.
849. Article 61/B(1) of the Trademark Act.

Opposition will be subject to payment of a fee within one month from filing notice. The opponent shall be a party to the procedure for the registration of a trademark in the subject matter of the opposition.[850]

Opposition procedure involves the examination of the use accordingly to Trademark Act. If within a period of five years following the date of registration, the holder has not commenced genuine use of the trademark in the country in connection with the goods and services for which it is registered, the earlier trademark shall not be considered as relative grounds of refusal.[851]

The requirement of use of trademark is outlined in paragraph 303 below.

During the procedure of the opposition, the registration of the mark shall be suspended. If the opposition is based on conflict with an earlier trademark, an opponent will have to furnish proof on prior use, as trademark application may not be refused on the basis of an opposition in respect to the furnishing of which proof was unsuccessful.[852]

When an objection is lacking any of the requirements, the objector shall be advised to bring it into compliance; if the objector did not pay the fee, he shall be advised to do so within the prescribed time limit. In the event of any further failure to comply, the objection shall be deemed withdrawn.[853]

The opposition shall be adjudged by the Opposition Senate of the Hungarian Intellectual Property Office in an oral proceeding.

The Office shall invite the applicant to submit comments on the opposition. Following the written preparatory work, the Office shall hold a hearing of the applicant and the opponent must be heard together in order to clarify the facts or if any of the parties so request.

In accordance with Article 61/C of Trademark Act, the person lodging the objection shall participate in the proceeding for the registration of a trademark – to the extent of the objection – as a party.[854]

The opposition may be rejected by the decision of the office. The opposition shall be considered withdrawn:

(a) if the opponent fails to reply to the invitation within the fixed time limit, fails to appear at the hearing, and has not requested in advance to hold in his or her absence;[855]
(b) if the opponent furnishes proof of prior use, the filing of the trademark will be rejected.

In the trademark procedure, a decision rejecting the application becomes final, the opposition in respect of which the procedure have been suspended shall be considered withdrawn.

289. If the trademark application and the sign to which it relates meet all the requirements of the examination, the Office shall register the subject matter of the

850. Article 61/C of the Trademark Act.
851. Articles 4(3) and 18 of the Trademark Act.
852. Article 61/E(2) of the Trademark Act.
853. Article 61/B(5) of the Trademark Act.
854. Article 61/C of the Trademark Act.
855. Article 61/D(7) of the Trademark Act.

application as a trademark.[856] The date on the ruling of registration shall be the date of the registration of the trademark.[857]

According to Article 64 of Trademark Act, the registration shall be recorded in the trademark register and relevant information shall be given thereon in Gazette of the Hungarian Intellectual Property Office. After registration, the Office shall issue a trademark certificate to which the extract from the registration shall be annexed.

290. The legal security system requests the supervision of decisions of the Office by the court. Under the legislation in force, there are three kinds of judicial procedure in trademark matters:

(a) extra judicial procedures for the review of decisions taken by the Office;
(b) court procedure for trademark infringement; and
(c) any other litigation concerning trademarks.

The above-mentioned decisions of the Office could be changed by the Metropolitan Court of Justice on request. The court shall hear requests for the review of decisions taken by the Office in accordance with the rules of a non-contentious nature of the procedure. The appeals against the decision of the Metropolitan Court of Justice Metropolitan Court are to be heard by the Metropolitan Court of Appellation.

The Office may withdraw or modify its decisions terminating the procedure taken in the following matters only if a request for review is filed and only until such request is transmitted to the court:

(a) registration of trademarks;
(b) renewal of trademark protection;
(c) division of trademark protection;
(d) lapse of trademark protection by reason of surrender;
(e) cancellation of trademarks;
(f) declaration of revocation of trademark protection.[858]

The Hungarian Intellectual Property Office may withdraw or modify its decision – terminating the procedure – taken in the matters referred to in paragraph 46/A (3)(e) and (f) and (4) on the basis of a request for review only if it establishes that its decision is contrary to law or if the parties request unanimously the modification or withdrawal of the decision[859]

§5. Ownership and Transfer (Assignment & Licenses)

291. Pursuant to Article 9 section (1) of the Trademark Act, the right to legal protection of a trademark shall belong to the person who has registered the trademark.

856. Pintz, *Talald fel magad*, 90.
857. Csécsy, *A Szellemi Alkotások joga*, 224.
858. Article 46/A(3) of Trademark Act.
859. Article 46/A(4) of Trademark Act.

Any natural or legal person or a company without legal personality may apply for a trademark protection that is, the owner a trademark may be any Hungarian physical or moral person as well and their successor in title irrespective of pursuing economic activities.[860]

There is a possibility in the Hungarian Trademark Act[861] to acquire the right of co-ownership if several persons commonly require the registration of a mark; the trademark protection will be acquired in co-ownership: In the case of several rightful claimants – if no contrary indication given – the rights to trademarks may be considered as an equal, undivided share in the mark.

The owner of a collective mark is the social organization, whose members are entitled to use the collective mark. The holder shall not use the collective mark; however, the members of the organization concerned may use the mark.[862]

The owner of a certification mark has an undertaking which produces, puts in market, or imports the goods or supplies the services for which the trademark registered.[863] The holder may not use the certification mark; he or she shall, however, authorize its use with respect to the goods or services complying with the quality requirements or with other characteristics.

By virtue of Article 12 section (1) of the Trademark Act, trademark protection shall confer on its holder the exclusive right to the use of the trademark.[864]

292. Joint rights to trademark protection and joint trademark protection are regulated by Article 21 of the Trademark Act.

When there are two or more holders of the same trademark, each of the joint holders may exercise the rights conferred by trademark protection over his or her share.[865]

When the joint holder wishes to exercise the rights over his or her share, the other joint holders shall enjoy a right of pre-emption with respect to third parties.

The trademark may be used by any of the joint holders. He or she shall be obliged to pay appropriate remuneration to the other joint holders, in proportion to their shares.[866]

A license for the use of a trademark may only be granted to a third party jointly by the joint holders.[867]

Any of the proprietors may independently take action for the renewal, invocation, or protection of the trademark – with the exception of concluding settlements, and recognizing or renouncing rights – for the renewal, invocation or protection of the trademark.[868]

Costs relating to joint trademark protection shall be borne by the joint holders in proportion to their shares. If, despite being ratified, a joint holder does not pay the

860. Article 9(2) of the Trademark Act.
861. Article 9(3) of the Trademark Act.
862. Article 96(4) of the Trademark Act.
863. Article 101(2) of the Trademark Act.
864. Pintz, *Találd fel magad*, 92.
865. Article 21(1) of the Trademark Act.
866. Article 21(2) of the Trademark Act.
867. Article 21(3) of the Trademark Act.
868. Csécsy, *A Szellemi Alkotások joga*, 208.

costs for which he or she is liable, the joint holder who has paid those costs may claim assignment of the share belonging to the joint holder having not met his or her obligation.[869]

293. Pursuant to Article 19 section (1) of the Trademark Act, rights deriving from a trademark and from trademark protection may be assigned.

The assignment of a mark may be with or without enterprise.

The assignment may be recorded in the Office and the record of assignment is not obligatory.[870]

The successor in title to a legal person or to a company without legal personality shall also acquire the trademark, unless otherwise provided by the parties or the circumstances clearly dictate otherwise.

Trademark protection may be assigned by contract. Trademark protection may also be assigned in respect of some of the goods or services for which the trademark is registered.[871]

The contract for the assignment of trademark protection shall be null and void where the assignment is likely to mislead the public.[872]

The rights deriving from a trademark and from trademark registration may be pledged. A right of pledge shall only be constituted if the mortgage contract is made in writing and the rights of pledge are entered in the trademark register.

The co-ownership of trademarks is admissible in Hungarian trademark law.[873]

294. Pursuant to the Article 19(1) of the Trademark Act, rights deriving from a trademark and from trademark protection may be licensed. Trademark license is regulated in Chapter IV Articles 23–26 of the Trademark Act. The statutory legal rules on licensing agreement are primarily compact. The main reason is that the licensing agreement is adapted to extremely diverse circumstances; it may assume very different forms and can include individual variable contents.

Under a licensing contract (trademark licensing contract), the proprietor of the trademark may grant permission for the use of the trademark and the party using the trademark assumes the obligation to pay a fee for such use. The contents of the licensing contract may be established freely by the contracting parties.[874]

In accordance with Article 26(1) of Trademark Act, if both parties agree, they may deviate from the regulations pertaining to a licensing contract, to the extent that such deviation is not prohibited by law. A licensing contract might lead to deception of consumers; it shall be deemed null and void.

The holder may control the licensee as to the quality of the goods bearing the trademark or of the services supplied under the trademark.[875] The owner of the mark may stipulate that the licensee may use the licensed mark only for goods complying with certain quality standards. In such case, the owner of the mark shall be entitled to

869. Article 21(7) of the Trademark Act.
870. Rights associated with a trademark and rights conferred by trademark protection are transferable and negotiable.
871. Article 19(2) of the Trademark Act.
872. Article 19(4) of the Trademark Act.
873. Lontai, *A Szellemi Alkotások joga*, 233.
874. Article 23(1) and (2) of the Trademark Act.
875. Article 24(3) of the Trademark Act.

carry out quality controls, even if not explicitly upon the grant of exclusive and non-exclusive trademark licenses allowed.[876]

The Trademark Act disposes two kinds of exclusive license. In one of these, the trademark owner assumes only the obligation not to grant to anyone else – except the licensee – the right of use, however he or she maintains the right to use the trademark. In the other case, the trademark owner not only renounces his or her right to grant further licenses of use but also agrees not to use the trademark.

The right of use shall be exclusive only if expressly stipulated by contract. In the case of an exclusive license, the holder may also use the trademark in addition to the licensee who has acquired the right of use, unless expressly excluded by contract. The holder may terminate the exclusivity of a license, subject to a proportional reduction in the royalty if the licensee does not begin the use of the trademark within a reasonable period of time.[877]

The licensing contract shall terminate for the future upon the expiration of the duration of the contract or upon the occurrence of the circumstances specified in the contract, as well as upon termination of trademark protection.[878]

295. There is a rule that offers a possibility to remedy an anomaly that occurs not rarely, namely the case of an exclusive license that authorizes the trademark owner to revoke the exclusivity of the license if within an acceptable delay, the licensee does not begin using the trademark.

The holder shall guarantee for the whole duration of the license contract that no third parties hold rights in the trademark preventing or limiting the right of use. This guarantee shall be subject to the rules applicable to a vendor who transfers propriety rights, except that the licensee may, instead of cancellation terminate the contract with immediate effect.[879]

Under a trademark license contract, the holder of trademark protection licenses the right to use a trademark and the licensee is required to pay royalties. The Trademark Act regulates the warranty of title, which additionally clarifies that the obligation of the party granting the license to provide information does not extend to the transfer related to the trademark.

The trademark holder shall be obliged to transfer economic, technical, and organizational know-how, only if this has been expressly agreed.[880]

The licensee may transfer the license or grant sub-licenses to third parties only with the express consent of the holder.[881]

The register of a license is not mandatory; however, that register is suggested in order to avoid difficulties and disputes in connection with the use and enforcement of trademarks.

876. Csécsy, *A Szellemi Alkotások joga*, 242–243.
877. Lontai et al., *A Szellemi Alkotások joga*, 288.
878. Article 25 of the Trademark Act.
879. Article 24(1) of the Trademark Act.
880. Article 24(2) of the Trademark Act.
881. Article 24(6) of the Trademark Act.

§6. Scope of Exclusive Rights

296. Trademark protection shall confer on its holder exclusive rights:

(a) to the transfer of the trademark;[882]
(b) to the assignment of the trademark;[883]
(c) to the encumbrance of rights deriving from a trademark;[884]
(d) to the use of trademark.[885]

The use of a trademark shall be considered:

(1) affixing the sign on the goods or to the packaging thereof;
(2) putting on the market or offering for sale the goods under that sign or stocking them for such purposes;
(3) offering or supplying services under that sign;
(4) importing or exporting the goods under that sign;
(5) using the sign in business correspondence and in advertising;
(6) license the use of trademark;[886]
(7) the holder of a trademark has the right in case of infringement to the remedies of civil and trademark law where a trademark is infringed, the holder may request measures by the customs authorities to prevent infringed goods from being placed on the market.[887]

297. Rights deriving from a trademark and from trademark protection may be pledged. A right of pledge shall only be constituted if the mortgage contract is made in writing and the right of pledge is entered in the Trade Mark Register.[888]

The Trademark Act authorizes the trademark owner to interdict the use of the trademark in the course of trade:[889]

(a) with those for which the trademark registered;
(b) with any sign where, because of its identity or similarity to the trademark and the identity or similarity of the goods or services, there exists a likelihood of confusion on the part of the public;
(c) any sign identical with or similar to the trademark in relation to goods and services that are not identical with or not similar to those for which the trademark is registered, provided that the trademark has a reputation in the country and the

882. Article 19(3) of the Trademark Act.
883. Article 22 of the Trademark Act.
884. Article 20 of the Trademark Act.
885. Article 12(2) of the Trademark Act.
886. Articles 23–26 of the Trademark Act.
887. Article 12(2).
888. Article 20 of Trademark Act.
889. Article 12(2) of the Trademark Act.

use of that sign without due cause would take unfair advantage of, or would be detrimental, to the distinctive character or the repute of the trademark.[890]

298. The provision, related to initiate proceedings proprietor against any party who, without his consent, uses in its business operations, of course, only applies in respect to registered trademarks having good reputation in the domestic market:[891]

> This provision may actually be considered a highly effective example of the symbols of prohibition occurring in trademark law, since such additional or enhanced protection of trademarks with a reputation is essentially the protection of the repute, and serves to prevent third parties from taking unfair of the repute of the trademark, thus obtaining an unfair competitive advantage.[892]

By virtue of the Trademark Act, the trademarks with reputation may enjoy the additional protection,[893] if marks the use of the sign without due cause would be detrimental to or unfairly exploit the trademark's distinctive character or reputation.[894]

By the Trademark Act, a more effective protection of marks having a reputation is provided for. The Trademark Act allows that when the registered trademark has a reputation, its owner shall be entitled to prevent third parties not having his or her consent from using an identical or similar sign in relation to goods or services that are not similar to those for which the further mark for goods or services that are not identical or similar in connection with which the mark has became well known.[895] It does not seem to be justified to make possible that a well known but not registered sign being prevented to the registration or use of a further mark for goods or services that are not identical or similar in connection with which the mark has became well known.

This rule of the Trademark Act embraces all cases of confusion. This means it extends to any confusion generated because of a connection occurring by means of association of ideas; consequently, it allows intervention against non-authorized use of a mark that builds on the effect of that association.

---

890. Article 4(1) c) of the Trademark Act.
891. Pintz, *Találd fel magad*, 93.
892. By virtue of Art. 4 of the Trademark Act, the following may not be granted trademark protection:
(a) a sign with later priority which is identical to an earlier trademark and is registered for identical goods or services as the earlier trademark;
(b) a sign which, due to its identity with or similarity to an earlier trademark or the identity or similarity of the goods or services covered by the trademark, consumers may confuse with the earlier trademark;
(c) a sign with later priority registered for different goods or services that is identical or similar to an earlier trademark enjoying a good reputation in the domestic market, where the use of the later trademark without due cause would take unfair advantage of, or be detrimental to, the distinctive character or the repute of the earlier trademark.
893. Article 12(1) c) of the Trademark Act.
894. Csécsy, *A Szellemi Alkotások joga*, 201.
895. Tattay, *A Szellemi Alkotások joga*, 323.

§7. The Limitations of the Scope of Trademarks Protection

299. The limitation of the trademark protections are as follows:

(a) territorial limitation of the protection;[896]
(b) limitation to prohibition of use the trademark; Article 15(1) of the Trademark Act;[897]
(c) exhaustion of the rights conferred by trademark protection;[898]
(d) acquiescence.[899]

First may be mentioned, the territorial limit the trademark protection from the effect of Trademark Act extends only to the territory of Hungary. According to the reasons for the Trademark Act, the determination of the exceptions from the exclusive rights arising from trademark protection enhances the foreseeability of adjudication of acts relating to trademarks and improves trade safety.

300. By virtue of Article 15 section (1) of the Trademark Act, trademark protection shall not entitle the holder to prohibit a third party from using in the course of trade in accordance with the requirements of fair trade practice:

(a) his or her own name or address;
(b) indication concerning the kind quality, quantity intended purpose, value, geographical origin, the time of production of the goods or of the rendering of the service, or other characteristics of the goods or service;
(c) the trademark when it is necessary to indicate the intended purpose of the goods or services in particular in the case of accessories or spare parts.

In respect of affixing the name and address of users, only a natural person may invoke his or her own name or address against the holder of a trademark.[900]

301. Another novel feature relating to provisions of the Trademark Act was introduced by prescription of acquiescence. The provision on acquiescence reflects the civil law principle according to which persons must act in accordance with the requirement of good faith in the course of the exercise of their rights.[901]

If the trademark proprietor has acquiesced,[902] for a period of five successive years, in the use of a later trademark in the country, while being aware of such use, the trademark proprietor shall no longer be entitled to challenge the use of this later trademark in the country, nor may he or she apply for a declaration that the later trademark is invalid on the basis of the earlier trademark

896. Csécsy, *A Szellemi Alkotások joga*, 207.
897. Article 15(1) of the Trademark Act.
898. Article 16 of the Trademark Act.
899. Article 17 of the Trademark Act.
900. Tattay, *A Szellemi Alkotások joga*, 339.
901. Lontai et al., *A Szellemi Alkotások joga*, 254.
902. Article 17(1) of the Trademark Act.

The provisions of acquiescence shall only apply to goods and services in relation to which the latter trademark was put into genuine use.[903]

The prescriptions of acquiescence shall not apply when the latter trademark was applied for in bad faith.[904]

The holder of a later trademark shall not be entitled to oppose the use of the earlier trademark, even though the holder of the earlier trademark may no longer oppose, on the basis of the acquiescence.[905]

The provisions of the acquiescence shall apply in relation to earlier trademarks, having a reputation, to trademarks that have become well known in the country at an earlier date. The Trademark Act extended rules of the acquiescence to prior well-known trademarks to a trademark that had become well known in the past and well known in the county.[906]

It does not seem to be justified that, from the point of view of the trademark law, unregistered marks or brands, as well as geographical denominations of goods should enjoy a stronger protection, that is, a protection that is exempt from the legal consequences of acquiescence.

The provision on acquiescence is also in accordance with the principle of extinction, which would be not directly applicable. The rule on acquiescence is to enable the prevalence of quasi-extinction by means of the said special provision.[907]

302. The exhaustion of the rights conferred by trademark protection is an institution of European law, namely of the Community Trademark Directive.[908] The concept of exhaustion of rights is relevant to goods which emanate initially from an intellectual property owner or associated enterprise.[909] The European Court of Justice has established that the exhaustion of trademark rights applies in a community-wide basis, rather than a purely national one.[910]

The doctrine of the exhaustion of trademark rights was created by the Directive of the European Community interpreting the relations between the free movement of goods and the territorial protection of intellectual property rights.

The rule of exhaustion of rights was introduced consequently to all branches of intellectual property rights (Patent Act, Copyright Act, and Design Acted).

In accordance with Article 16(1) of the Trademark Act, trademark protection shall not entitle the holder to prohibit the use of the trademark in relation to goods that have been put on the market in the European Economic Area by him or her or by expressed consent. The Trademark Act settles the rule of exhaustion of rights at Community level.[911]

This prescription in respect of exhaustion shall not apply when the holder has legitimate reasons to oppose further commercialization of the goods, in particular

903. Article 17(2) of the Trademark Act.
904. Article 17(3) of the Trademark Act.
905. Article 17(4) of the Trademark Act.
906. Csécsy, *A Szellemi Alkotások joga*, 206.
907. Pintz, *Találd fel magad*, 86.
908. Article 7 of the Community Trademark Directive.
909. Other subsidiaries, licenses, distributors, etc.
910. Csécsy, *A Szellemi Alkotások joga*, 207.
911. Tattay, *A Szellemi Alkotások joga*, 340.

when the condition of the goods has been changed or impaired after they have been put on the market.[912]

§8. Use Requirements

303. The criteria of use are defined by Article 12 section (3) of the Trademark Act. The use of a trademark shall be considered:

(a) affixing the sign on the goods or to the packaging thereof;
(b) putting on the market or offering for sale the goods under that sign or stocking them for such purposes;
(c) offering or supplying services under that sign;
(d) importing or exporting the goods under that sign;
(e) using the sign in business correspondence and in advertising.

The genuine use of the trademark can be considered the most important obligation the trademark owner has. In the Trademark Act is given the concept of genuine use.

The genuine use of a trademark means: use of the trademark in a form differing from only in elements that do not alter the distinctive character;[913] and affixing of the trademark to goods or to the packaging thereof in the territory of country solely for export purposes.[914]

Use of the trademark with authorization of the holder shall be deemed to constitute use by the holder.[915]

When the new product appears on the market, the producer may find that the mark that is given comes to be used as a description of the product itself. The new names of goods newly marked generally have characters to distinguish and may be registered as trademarks.

The use of a trademark is an obligation important for the trademark holder,and the lack of use has several negative consequences.

In accordance with Article 18(1) of the Trademark Act, if within a period of five years following the date of registration, the holder has not commenced genuine use of the trademark in the country in connection with the goods and services for which it is registered, or if such use has been suspended during an uninterrupted period of five years, trade mark protection to by virtue of Trademark Act shall be subject to negative consequences.

(a) relative grounds of registration of trademarks. A sign shall not be refused trademark protection if it is in conflict with an earlier trademark, which the proprietor has not used;

912. Article 16(2) of the Trademark Act.
913. Article 18(2) of the Trademark Act.
914. The genuine use shall be occurred in generally in territory of Hungary (Art. 18(2)b) of Trademark Act).
915. Article 18(3) of the Trademark Act.

(b) termination of protection. The trademark protection shall terminate if the trademark proprietor has failed to put the trademark to actual use;[916]
(c) cancellation of trademark protection. A trademark may not be cancelled, if it conflicts with an earlier trademark, non-registered sign or other right, the proprietor of which was aware of the later trademark registration and acquiesced to the use of such for a period of five successive years, unless the proprietor of the later trademark acted in bad faith;[917]
(d) the proceedings of opposition. If the objection concerns an earlier trademark, the objector shall be obliged to prove that his or her use of the trademark was in compliance with the requirements set out in Article 18 on the day of publication of the application for registration of the same trademark. The Hungarian Intellectual Property Office[918]

The questions of use are affected in paragraphs 296–297 *supra*.

§9. Duration of Protection, Renewal, and Termination

304. According to the Article 11(1) of Trademark Act, the trademark protection shall be valid for a period of ten years from the date of filing for registration. Trademark protection commences from date of registration, and it is effective retroactively to the date of filing for registration.[919]

Pursuant to Article 10(2) of the Trademark Act, the trademark protection may be renewed for further periods of ten years. In the event of renewal, trademark protection commences from the day following the date of expiration of the previous trademark protection.[920]

305. The renewal of trademark may be requested by the trademark proprietor.[921] A trademark renewal application may be submitted twelve months prior to the date of expiration of the protection period at the earliest and within six months of such date of expiration or of the date of registration at the latest.[922]

In the course of renewal proceedings, the mark itself may not be changed and the specification of goods and services may not be expanded.[923]

The renewal application shall be rejected if compliance with the requirements specified in the request is not achieved upon the necessary corrections or upon provision of a statement.[924] If the applicant fails to respond to the request within the prescribed

916. Article 30(d) of the Trademark Act.
917. Article 33(2) b) of the Trademark Act.
918. Article 61/E(1), (2) of the Trademark Act.
919. Article 10 of the Trademark Act.
920. Lontai et al., *A Szellemi Alkotások joga*, 264.
921. Article 65(1) of the Trademark Act.
922. Article 65(3) of the Trademark Act.
923. Article 65(5) of the Trademark Act.
924. Lontai et al., *A Szellemi Alkotások joga*, 265.

time limit or the renewal fee is not paid, the renewal application shall be considered withdrawn.[925]

Renewal of the trademark shall be entered in the Trademark Register, and official publication of such shall be made in the Official Journal of the Hungarian Intellectual Property Office.[926]

306. Under the Hungarian Trademarks Act, trademark protection may lapse by expiration, surrender, cancellation, by means of non-use, and by reason of the trademark losing its distinctive character or becoming deceptive.

The dissolution of the proprietor enterprise without a successor in title does not in itself result in the lapse of protection. In accordance with Article 35/A of the Trademark Act, following a final ruling rejecting an application for termination due to the trademark proprietor's dissolution, no new application shall be accepted for the termination of protection under the same trademark on the same grounds.

Lapse may have effect in respect of the whole trademark or of only some goods or services for which the trademark is registered.[927]

Trademark protection lapses, according to the reason of lapse, with respect to the future (*ex nunc*) or with retroactive effect (*ex tunc*).

The Trademark Act has largely developed substantial provisions related to the cancellation concerning the requirements of registerability, mainly in consequence of harmonization with the Community Trademark Directive. Accordingly, each obstacle to registration constitutes at the same time a ground for cancellation. As a result of cancellation, trademark protection lapses with retroactive effect (*ex tunc*) to the date of its establishment, that is, to the filing date of the application in all cases.

In the case of lapse by reason of non-use,[928] the five-year period is to be calculated from the date of registration (and not the filing date of the application). The lapse has a retroactive effect to the starting date of the procedure for a decision on the lapse of protection. The requirement of using the trademark must be interpreted strictly also from the perspective of lapse. Therefore, the use of a trademark cannot be proved by presenting some peripheral advertising. The lapse of protection has retroactive effect to the starting date of the procedure also in the cases of lapse by reason of losing the distinctive character[929] or becoming deceptive.[930]

925. Article 66(2) of the Trademark Act.
926. Article 67(2) of the Trademark Act.
927. Lontai et al., *A Szellemi Alkotások joga*, 231.
928. Article 30(d) of the Trademark Act.
929. In accordance with Art. 35(1) of the Trademark Act, the protection shall terminate, if:
(a) as a result of the actions of the trademark proprietor, the trademark has become a common name in the trade of those goods or services for which the trademark is registered; or
(b) as a result of its use, the trademark has become liable to mislead, in particular in respect to the nature, quality or geographical origin of the goods or services.
930. In accordance with Art. 35(2) of the Trademark Act, the trademark protection may terminate due to lack of distinctive character or liability to mislead for all or for a portion of the goods or services for which the trademark has been registered, depending on whether the grounds for termination of the trademark applies to all the goods or services for which the trademark was registered or only to a portion of such.

§10. Infringement and Remedies

307. By virtue of Article 27 section (1) of the Trademark Act, any person who unlawfully uses a trademark in contravention of the provisions of the Trademark Act[931] commits trademark infringement.

The trademark holder may according to the circumstances of the case have recourse:

(a) on the basis of the Trademark Act;[932]
(b) on the basis of the new Hungarian Penal Code;[933]
(c) when a trademark is infringed, the holder may request – under the provisions of special legislation – measures by the customs authorities to prevent infringing goods from being placed on the market remedies.[934]

The holder may accord the circumstances of the case; have recourse to the following civil remedies:

(a) he or she may request that the fact of infringement be declared by the court;
(b) he or she may request an injunction that the infringer cease his or her infringement or any acts directly threatening with it;
(c) he or she may demand that the infringer give information on the identity of persons involved in the protection and distribution of the infringed goods or the provision of infringed services and of channels of distribution;
(d) he or she may demand satisfaction from the infringer by way of declaration or by other appropriate means; if necessary the declaration shall be made public by the infringer or at his or her expense.

At the request of the holder, the court may order that its decision be made public at the expense of infringer. The court shall decide on the manner of publicity. Publicity shall mean, in particular, publication in a national daily newspaper or on the internet:

(a) he or she may require surrender of the enrichment obtained by the infringement of the trademark;
(b) he or she may request the seizure, the transfer to a specific person, the recall and the definitive removal from the channels of commerce, or destruction, the infringing products, and the packaging thereof, as well as of the means and materials exclusively or principally used for infringement, seizure of the means and materials used in the infringement;
(c) the trademark holder may also claim damages under the rules of civil liability.[935]

---

931. Article 27(2) of the Trademark Act.
932. Article 27(2)(a–f) of the Trademark Act.
933. Article of 388 of new Hungarian Penal Code(Law No. C of 2012-Violation of industrial Property Rights.
934. Act CXXVI of 2003 on the Implementation of Community Customs Law.
935. Article 27(1)-(11) of the Trademark Act.

In court proceedings on trademark infringement, the legal consequences laid down in Articles 27(2) – recourse to the civil remedies-- and (3)-- claim damages under the rules of civil liability – shall not apply in respect of the period when the grounds for revocation of trademark protection existed based on this Law, provided that the defendant refers to this fact in his defence as to the merits.[936]

Seizure of the means and material used in infringing activities and of the infringing activities and the infringing goods shall be admissible even if they are not in the possession of the infringer, but if the holder knew or had reasonable grounds to know about the infringement.

308. Law CLXV of 2005, effective since 15 April 2006, has introduced changes in the legal system, whereby compliance with the Directive 2004/48[937] of the IP enforcement has been implemented. The main elements of the changes in the enforcement of trademark rights following the adapted form of the Directive 2004/48 are as follows.

The effective Trademark Act, in harmony with IP Enforcement Directive, has a regulation according to which the infringer can be obliged to provide information on distributors of infringing goods and business relationship.[938]

In case of trademarks, the obligation to provide information covers infringing services too.

Such obligation can be imposed against any third person, who:

(a) was found in possession of the infringing goods on a commercial scale;
(b) was found to be using the infringing services on a commercial scale;
(c) was found to be providing on a commercial scale services on a commercial used in infringing activities;
(d) was indicated by the person referred to in (a), (b), and (c) as being involved in the production or distribution of being involved or the provision of the services.

The delivery of the information can claimed on an objective basis against third parties as well; thus, the obligation can be imposed irrespectively of the fact whether they knew or should have known that their corresponding activity was connected with an infringement or either trademark right.

309. According to the IP Enforcement Directive, the Trademark Act includes definition of commercial scale.[939] The above obligation related to the person who committed the trademark infringement on a commercial scale. Paragraph 14 of the Preamble of the Directive 2004/48 gives quite a broad definition for commercial scale, according to which, acts carried out on a commercial scale are those carried out for direct or indirect economic or commercial advantage, which would normally exclude acts carried out by end consumers acting in good faith. The prescription of the Trademark Act is as follows:

936. Article 95 (14a) of Trademark Act.
937. Preamble of IP Enforcement Directive.
938. Article 27(2)(c) of the Trademark Act.
939. Article 27(6) of the Trademark Act.

(a) the acts are carried out on a commercial scale if it is obvious from the nature or quantity of the infringing goods or services that these acts carried out for direct or indirect economic advantage;
(b) in the absence of proof to the contrary, acts carried out by consumers in good faith shall not be regarded carried out in commercial scale.

In accordance with Article 27(7) of the Trademark Act, the following information can be requested:

(a) the names and addresses of the producers, distributors, suppliers, and holders of the infringing goods or services, as well as the intended or involved wholesalers and retailers;
(b) the quantities produced, delivered, received, or ordered of the infringing goods and services, as well as the prices obtained or given for the goods or services in question.

At the request of the holder of the trademark, the court may rule that the infringing nature of the means, materials and packaging goods seized, recalled or definitively removed from the channels of commerce be removed, or when this is not possible, that they be destroyed.

In justified cases, the court may order, in place of destruction, that the means and materials seized be auctioned according to the procedure of judicial execution; in such cases, the court shall decide how the sum obtained is to be used.[940]

The court shall order the seizure at the expense of infringer.

310. An important procedural instrument against trademark infringement is the preliminary injunction which may be ordered by courts.[941]

They have introduced a statutory presumption in favour of intellectual property holders that there is a need to protect a right deserving special appreciation, if the applicant certifies that the trademark is legally protected, and that he or she is entitled to that protection; that is, he or she is the owner, or the duly authorized licensee of the trademark protection in question.[942]

Preliminary injunction may only be requested within six months following the beginning of trademark infringement and within sixty days from the date on which the petitioner became aware of the infringement and of the identity of infringer.[943]

The court decides on the provisional measures out of turn, but not later than within fifteen days from the filing date of the request to this effect.[944]

According to Article 156 of the Code of Civil Proceeding, preliminary injunctions could be requested after trademark infringement proceeding was started.[945] This is a very substantial measure, as owners of rights can obtain such basic information well

940. Article 27(8) of the Trademark Act.
941. Pintz, *Talàld fel magad*, 93–96.
942. Lontai et al., *A Szellemi Alkotások joga*, 267–268.
943. Tattay, *A Szellemi Alkotások joga*, 368–369.
944. Article 27(8) of the Trademark Act.
945. Lontai et al., *A Szellemi Alkotások joga*, 237–238.

before the infringement proceeding is finished if they succeed in having the courts order a preliminary injunction.[946]

311. The conditions were examined after the injury of the trademark right and they include four preconditions as follows:

(a) the injunction is necessary to prevent the occurrence of imminent damages; or
(b) the injunction is necessary to prevent the situation giving cause for lawsuit; or
(c) the interlocutory injection is necessary to the specifically preferred legal protection of the plaintiff;
(d) the disadvantages caused by the measure do not exceed the advantages achieved therewith.[947]

The facts must be supported with a certain level of certainty that the applicant is the right holder and that the applicant's right is being infringed, or that such infringement is imminent. Ordering a provisional measure can be made subject to the payment of an appropriate security deposit.[948]

§11. Overlapping and Relation to Other Intellectual Property Rights

312. The admissibility of the parallel protection of different objects of intellectual property belongs to the fundamental principles of Hungarian intellectual property rights. According to this basic principle, the cumulative protection several objects is generally permissible. The protection of trademarks may overlap with protection of geographical indications, trade names,[949] design, names of plant varieties, and as far as domain names.

Domain names are indications, which are necessary for correct functioning of the internet, for identifying the server and the person setting in action the server and as far as the forwarding of information to all servers.

A very practical question and a problem very new is the overlap between the protection of trademarks and domain names.

A trademark protection shall be granted for any signs capable of being represented graphically, provided that these are capable of distinguishing goods and services from those of other undertakings.[950] The main function of trademarks is the marking of goods or services of a natural or legal person in order to distinguish them from other goods, services or activities of this person.

Under the signs which may be registered as trademarks are items such as; combinations of words, personal names and slogans, letters and numerals.[951] Domain

946. Csécsy, *A Szellemi Alkotások joga*, 209–213.
947. Tattay, *A Szellemi Alkotások joga*, 374.
948. Csécsy, *A Szellemi Alkotások joga*, 222.
949. Particularly may be overlapping the protection of trade names an trademarks, while the trade names may be registered as trademarks.
950. Article 1(1) of the Trademark Act.
951. Article 1(2) of the Trademark Act.

names are words consisting exclusively of Roman letters, without accents, numerical characters, or hyphenated compounds.[952]

313. Domain names have different features as trademarks:

(a) domain names shall have exclusively one owner, but by virtue of Article 21 of the Trademark Act, more persons can own the same trademark;
(b) the holder may not grant a license of use of domain name and are not transferable; on the contrary, the trademarks are transferable and may be licensed;
(c) the owner of a domain shall use his denomination immediately after registration; the trademark holder may commence the use of trademark within a period of five years following the date of registration.[953]

According to the decision of Hungary's Council of Internet Service Providers, any Hungarian natural person or legal entity may register a domain name directly under the 'hu', Hungarian Top Level Domain. Company names, their abbreviations, trademarks and names of periodicals may be registered as domain names. This possibility is granted also for all Hungarian trademark owners. The main function of domain names is for the identification of any legal or natural person on the Internet and for the display of goods, services, or activities of this person.[954]

Accordingly, the cumulative protection of domain names and trademarks is permissible.

The domain name applications have two main types:

(a) with priority, in this case, the chosen name is identical with the officially registered whole or abbreviated name of the applicant;
(b) without priority, when the application includes a new name in the application.[955] The majority of applicants so far have registered their own trademarks and names as domain names under the name 'hu', and many pirates since 2000 have jumped in and have filed hundreds of applications such as disney.hu, britishtelecom.hu, mastercard.hu, billgates.hu, rolls-royce.hu, and pepsicola.hu. The Hungarian Intellectual Property Office in 2000 issued a statement according to which any unauthorized registration of registered trademarks, as domain names will be considered as trademark infringement.[956] The trademarks may be registered as domain names only in favour of trademark owners.[957]

952. Pintz, *Találd fel magad*, 142.
953. Pintz, *Találd fel magad*, 139.
954. *Ibid.*, 140.
955. K. Szamosi, 'A domain név és a védjegyek ütközésének problémái', *MIE Közlemények* 41, no. 1 (2000): 161–167.
956. L. Tattay, 'Hazai domain nevek – nemzeti védjegyek', *Magyar Jog* 50 (2006): 617–626.
957. Pintz, *Találd fel magad*, 137.

Chapter 5. Trade Names

§1. Sources: Legislations

314. By virtue of the Paris Convention, trade names are protected as objects of industrial property. Trade names are listed between the objects of industrial property in Article 1(2) of the Paris Convention.[958]

The legal protection of trade names is protected by several national legal sources: by Civil Code,[959,960] by Firm Act,[961] and Competition Act.[962]

By virtue of Act CXLVIII of 2010, the name of Hungarian Patent Office was changed to Hungarian Intellectual Property Office (hereinafter: 'Office') as of 1 January 2011 to better reflect its competence extending to activities related to all form of industrial property protection as well as to the field of copyright.

The new Civil Code, of Hungary the Law V of 2013 is one of the most significant achievements of the twenty-first century in Hungary. The Code omits detailed regulation of intellectual property. The new Civil Code shall apply in respect of intellectual property, if these issues directly fall within its scope, which are not governed by the legislation on copyright and industrial property rights of Hungary.

By means of known trade names, the consumer could identify the preferred firm and the undertaking or may distinguish them from other firms and other undertakings.[963]

Several Hungarian trade names can be mentioned that have survived forty-five years of a socialist regime: Hercz, Pick, Chinoin, Dreher, Ganz, Richter-Gedeon, Chinoin, Ganz, Biogal Egis, Tungsram, and Taurus. These companies have become well known in a number of countries.

There is a strong contact between the family name and trade name: A natural person may use his or her own name as a trade name.[964] When someone makes a trade name from his or her family name, the name of the legal entity becomes fully independent from the person, or founder of the undertaking.[965] After several years, natural persons may also have trade names.

315. Trade names may be protected:

958. According to Art. 1(2) of the Paris Convention, the objects of industrial property are as follows: patents, utility models, industrial designs, trade marks, appellation of origin, indication of provenance, trade names, prohibition of unfair competition.
959. Civil Code, Act LIX of 1959 on the Civil Code of the Hungarian Republic.
960. Act IV of 2006 on Business Associations.
961. Act V of 2006 on Public Company Information, Company Registration and Winding-up Proceedings.
962. Act LVII of 1996 on the Prohibition of Unfair Trading Practices and Unfair Competition.
963. Csécsy, *A Szellemi Alkotások joga*, 189.
964. J. Fehérvári, 'Személyhez fuzodo Jogok-Védjegy-és Cégnévhasználat', *Védjegyvilág* 3, no. 3 (1993):10.
965. *Ibid.*

(a) without registration, as name of a natural or legal persons, private entrepreneurs the names of magazines and restaurants, the titles and figures copyrighted works and slogans::pursuant to rules of new Civil Code (Law No. V of 2013);
(b) as registered corporate names of business companies (firms, firm names) according to provisions of The new Civil Code, of Hungary and Firm Act;
(c) firms and other trade names, as registered trademarks with accordance of prescriptions of the Trademark Act.

The essential resources of protection of the trade names are as follows:

- Paris Convention; Paris Convention for the Protection of Industrial Property – Promulgated by Law Decree No. 18/1970 in Hungary.
- The new Civil Code of Hungary (Law No. V of 2013).
- Act LVII of 1996 on the Prohibition of Unfair Trading Practices and Unfair Competition (hereinafter: 'Competition Act').
- Act XLVII of 2008 on the Prohibition of Unfair Business-to-Consumer Commercial Practices prohibits the misleading commercial practices.
- Act V of 2006 on Public Company Information, Company Registration and Winding-up Proceedings (hereinafter: 'Firm Act').

§2. The Protection of Trade Names

316. In spite of the fact that the trade names belong to the domain of industrial property by virtue of Article 1(2) of the Paris Convention, trade names are protected by civil law and specific rules relating to companies and company names.[966]

Trade name protection shall be granted for any signs, provided that these are capable of distinguishing undertakings from other undertakings.

A trade name is different from a company name, corporate name, or firm name. Any name that is not protected by the company register and distinguishes private and legal business entities will fall under this category too.

The definition is very broad and does not limit all types of trade names. Trade names may be accepted as collective nouns, which involves all categories of these denominations.

317. The main varieties of trade names[967] are as follows:

(a) the names of natural persons, private entrepreneurs, establishers, or proprietors of undertakings: Zwack, Törley, Dreher, Jacobs, Opel, etc.;
(b) the catchwords of economic companies: Stollwerck, Videoton and Tungsram;
(c) the acronyms of the names of companies: BMW= Bayerische Motor Werke; HP=Hewlett Packard; KERMI= Kereskedelmi Minoségellenörző rz Intézet;[968]
(d) the names of business associations: Nevikén Kft, Stollwerck Édesipari Kft;

966. Tattay, *A Szellemi Alkotások joga*, 68.
967. *Ibid.*, 362.
968. L. Tattay, 'Gondolatok a kereskedelmi nevek oltalmáról', *Védjegyvilág* 11, no. 3 (2001): 44.

(e) the names of magazines and restaurants: Muskátli, Fortuna, Országház, Gerbeaud (names of restaurants);
(f) slogans: 'Legendary Harley Davidson'; Pannon GSM – 'the Front Rank' (Forefront); Westel (Hungarian Company); 'the Connection';
(g) the titles and figures copyrighted works: 'Casablanca', 'Bonnie and Clyde', 'Piedone' pizzeria;
(h) the names of economic operators The 'economic operator' shall mean state-owned companies, other state-owned economic agencies, cooperatives, housing cooperatives, European cooperative societies, business associations, European public limited-liability companies, groupings, European groupings of territorial cooperation, European economic interest groupings, public-benefit organizations, companies of certain legal entities, subsidiaries, water management organizations, forest management associations, court bailiffs' offices, and private entrepreneurs. The civil relations of the state, local governments, budgetary agencies, and societies are also included.

318. By virtue of Article 2:49. of new Civil Code of Hungary (Law No. V of 2013) the trade names are protected. The new Civil Code of Hungary protects the names of persons and of legal entities without registration.

Pursuant to Article 2:49: of the new Civil Code, everyone has the right to bear a name. The application of the name may not offend the right of any other natural and legal person bearing the same name. This principle based on the new Civil Code, which protects the right to bear a name, not only in the base of natural persons but also legal persons. The name of a legal person must be different from the names of other previously registered legal persons who are engaged in similar activities in the same field of the endeavour.

Inherent rights shall be honoured and respected by everyone. Inherent rights are protected by law.[969] The provisions on the protection of inherent rights shall also apply to legal persons, unless such protection, by virtue of its very nature, can only be given to private persons. Accordingly, the illegal use of another trade name or a trade name similar to that of another person shall be deemed a violation of the right to bear a name.

A person whose right to a trade name has been violated shall have the following options open under civil law, depending on the circumstances of the case:[970]

(a) demand a court declaration of the occurrence of the infringement;
(b) demand to have the infringement discontinued and the perpetrator restrained from further infringement;
(c) demand that the perpetrator make restitution in a statement means and, the perpetrator, at his own expense, make an appropriate public disclosure for restitution;
(d) demand the termination of the injurious situation and the restoration of the previous state by and at the expense of the perpetrator and, furthermore, to have the effects of the infringement nullified or deprived of their injurious nature;

969. Article 2:42 of new Civil Code (Law No. V of 2013).
970. Article 2:51 an 2:52 of new Civil Code (Law No. V of 2013).

(e) demand to require surrender of the enrichment obtained by the infringement of the patent;
(f) file charges for punitive damages in accordance with the liability Regulations 2:51.

319. The prescriptions of prohibition of the unfair competition shall apply, where a non-registered trade name is infringed. Civil law, particularly the Civil Code and the Firm Act protects generally the registered names. Accordingly, the names which used, but not registered are protected by rules of Competition Law.

By virtue of the general clause of unfair competition, it is prohibited to conduct economic activities in an unfair manner, in particular, in a manner violating or jeopardizing the lawful interests of competitors, business partners, and consumers, or in a way which is in conflict with the requirements of business integrity. In the Competition Act given interpretation concerning a business partner: A business partner shall mean persons other than consumers.[971] Without the consent of a competitor, it is prohibited to utilize a name or designation by which third parties normally recognize the competitor and not the party using it.

The use of a false or deceptive trade name may infringe the lawful interest of competitors, particularly business partners and consumers. The unlawful use of a trade name may infringe upon or jeopardize of good reputation or credibility of any competitor too.

The Competition Act emphasizes the importance of protection of trade names even more. Article 6 of the Competition Act says:

> Without the express prior consent of the competitor, goods or services may not be produced, placed on the market or advertised with such typical external appearance, packaging or marking (including the indication of origin) by which the competitor or its goods are normally recognized; furthermore, any such name, marking or indication of goods may not be used by which the competitor or its goods are normally recognized.

320. The Act XLVII of 2008 on the Prohibition of Unfair Business-to-Consumer Commercial Practices prohibits the misleading commercial practices.

In accordance with Article 6(1) of this Act, a commercial practice shall be regarded as misleading if it contains false information and is therefore untruthful or in any way, including overall presentation, deceives or is likely to deceive the average consumer, even if the information is factually correct, in relation to one or more of the following elements, and in either case causes or is likely to cause him or her to take a transactional decision that he or she would not have taken otherwise:

> A commercial practice shall also be regarded as misleading if it involves a commercial practice which creates confusion with any business entity or its

971. Article 2/A(2) of the Company Act.

corporate name, or with any products, trade marks, trade names or other distinguishing marks of such business entity.[972]

Conducting the proceedings due to the violation of the aforementioned provisions shall fall within the competence of the court. The county courts and the Metropolitan Court of Justice in Budapest shall have jurisdiction in respect of legal proceedings instituted on the basis on infringement of trade names according to the Articles 2 and 6 of the Competition Act.[973]

The plaintiff: shall have the options under civil law.

Moreover, the plaintiff shall have other actions based on the Competition Act:

(a) may demand the termination of the injurious situation, to have the former status quo reinstated, and the deprivation of the goods manufactured or placed on the market illegally, or, if this is not possible, the destruction thereof, and the destruction of any special devices and facilities used for the manufacture or production thereof;
(b) may demand that the defendant disclose information on the parties participating in the manufacturing and marketing of the products involved in the case as well as on the business relations it has established to distribute such products.

Legal proceedings may be instituted on the grounds of conduct infringing of trade names within six months from the time of commission of the infringement mentioned previously. If the infringement is constant, the time limit shall commence at the time the infringement is terminated.[974]

To assert the civil claims of consumers regarding any infringer whose illegal action results in a grievance that affects large number of consumers, or if a considerable magnitude, the Chamber of Commerce on behalf of its members, or the organization providing representation for consumers from the Office of Economic Competition, may take court action, even if the identities of the consumers who have suffered the infringement may not be determined.

321. The most essential types of trade names are corporate names, that is, names of business companies, firm names or firms (hereinafter: 'corporate names'). Corporate names are regulated by the Civil Code of Hungary and the Firm Act. Business corporations may operate as legal persons.[975] Business associations may only be founded in the forms regulated in the Civil Code of Hungary.

Business associations with legal personality are general partnerships (Kkt.) and limited partnerships (Bt.), private limited-liability companies (Kft.) and public and private limited companies (Rt.).[976] Business' company means a legal entity that is

972. Article 6(2) of the Act XLVII of 2008 on the Prohibition of Unfair Business-to-Consumer Commercial Practices prohibits the misleading commercial practices.
973. Article 86(1) of the Competition Act.
974. Article 88(1), (2) of the Competition Act.
975. J.A. Gál, 'Cégeljárási Szabályok Változása', *Védjegyvilág* 3, no. 1 (1998): 25.
976. Article 2(2) of the Company Act.

brought into existence when entered into the register of official company records for the purpose of engaging in business operations.[977]

Each business association shall have a corporate name. Business associations have legal capacity under their corporate names; they may obtain rights and undertake commitments, such as acquire property, conclude contracts, and may sue and be sued.

The name of a company must contain the selected company form and at least a lead word. The corporate names shall be written in Roman letters.

The lead word is meant for better identification of the company, or to help distinguish the company from other companies engaged in similar activities. The lead word is placed at the beginning of the corporate name. The lead word may be a foreign expression, an abbreviation, or an acronym written in Roman letters. Other than the lead word, the corporate name may only consist of Hungarian words, in conformance with the rules of Hungarian grammar.[978]

The corporate name (concise name) of a company must clearly differ from the name of any other company already registered in the country – irrespective of the company form – and it must not suggest any misleading implications, in particular as relating to the scope of activities and the form of the company.[979]

322. There are three principal requirements relating to corporate names. Names meeting these requirements may be registered.[980] If the corporate name does not correspond with the following requirements, the court of registry will reject the petition. The requirements regarding the name are:

(a) authenticity, requiring that the name reflect the basis activity and actual form of a company and not create an impression – especially not giving the false impression to the contrary – that its activities and existence are connected to those of another legal person;
(b) exclusiveness, requiring that the name of company be different and not similar to the names of other companies operating in a similar sphere of activity and in the same area; and[981]
(c) precision, requiring that the name be characteristic, and distinguishable from the names of other legal persons and grammatically correct.[982]

A corporate name may contain the words 'state' or 'national' only if the government has majority control in the company whether directly or by way of its organizations, or if the company falls within the category of inalienable state ownership in accordance with another act.

The names of outstanding historical figures may only be included in a corporate name by authorization of the Hungarian Academy of Sciences, and name the rights of which are owned by others may be included in a corporate name only with the consent of the party holding such rights.

977. Article 2(1) of the Firm Act.
978. Article 3(2) of the Firm Act.
979. Article 3(4) of the Firm Act.
980. Tattay, 'Gondolatok a kereskedelmi nevek oltalmáról', 45–46.
981. Csécsy, *A Szellemi Alkotások joga*, 191.
982. Lontai et al., *A Szellemi Alkotások joga*, 251.

The lead word is used for better identification[983] of the company, or to help distinguish the company from other companies engaged in similar activities. The lead word is placed at the beginning of the corporate name. The lead word may be:

(a) the name of the company's owner;
(b) name of the company's members in due application;
(c) family name;
(d) Hungarian compound noun;
(e) Hungarian fantasy word;
(f) foreign expression;
(g) an abbreviation or;
(h) an acronym;
(i) the name of an outstanding historical figure.[984]

The abbreviated name of the company may also be entered in the Companies Register, which must contain the catchword and an indication as to the form of the company.

323. The corporate name of the branch office of a foreign company or the direct commercial representative office of foreigners will include the name of the parent company. The name must comply with the rules of the Hungarian language and orthography. If the name is entered in the document in Roman script, it must be entered in the Companies Register into Roman letters.

When two or more companies bear the same name, the company that first submitted its registration application shall have the right to use that name[985] (concise name).[986] This provision shall not apply to the part of the name of the company, which is identical to the surname of the natural person who is the owner of the company.

Legal persons obtain their legal capacity by official acknowledgement. A company acquires its legal capacity by registration. Only those firms may be registered that are established in a form determined in the Company Act. The Companies Register certifies the authenticity of the data contained therein, the prevalence of the rights and facts registered, and any changes thereto.

Companies are registered in the Companies Register by the county court (Metropolitan Court). The courts of registry keep records of companies and the data related to these companies in the companies register.[987] The court of registry is the court in whose area of competence the registered office of the company is located.

The process of registration is non-litigious. The document, serving as a base for the application for the registration, will be examined by the court of registry to determine if it complies with the legal requirements.

The Companies Register is public; therefore, no one may claim a legal excuse that the existence of any details, rights or facts indicated in the Companies Register was unknown.

983. Sasvári, 'Cégnevek és Védjegyek', 4.
984. Articles 3 and 4 of the Firm Act.
985. J. Gál, 'A cégnév bejegyzésével kapcsolatos problémák', *Védjegyvilág* 6, no. 3 (1996): 35.
986. Article 6(1) of the Firm Act.
987. Article 23(1) of the Firm Act.

All data (current and previous) of the companies register and the company documents – including those submitted by way of electronic means and the company documents converted into electronic format – shall be made available to the public.[988]

Publicity of company records shall be ensured by the courts of registry, the information service, and by way of publication in the Cégközlöny (Company Gazette).[989]

324. The trade names may be registered as trademarks.

In accordance with Article 1(1) of Trademark Act, any sign that can be graphically represented and is suitable for distinguishing goods and services from other goods and services can be protected by trademark.

A trademark may consist of any of the following signs: a word, combination of words, including personal names.

Accordingly, corporate names, names of natural persons, private entrepreneurs, or establishers or proprietors of undertakings; catchwords of economic companies; acronyms of the name of companies; names of business associations: names of magazines and restaurants; titles and figures copyrighted works; names of economic operators set out in Article 585(1)C of the Civil Code may be protected as trademarks.

988. Article 10(2) of the Firm Act.
989. Article 11 of the Firm Act.

Chapter 6. Industrial Designs

§1. Sources: Legislations

325. The current design statute is Act XLVIII of 2001 on the Legal Protection of Designs (hereinafter: 'Design Act'). Design law does not concern technical but aesthetic creations; it protects the outer appearance, the appealing shape of industrial products.[990]

The legal regulation of designs has more than a century-old tradition in Hungary.[991] The first Hungarian legal regulation was Decree 107.709 of 1907, which settled questions of designs. A further Act was enacted in 1978, that is, the decree law on the protection of Designs No. 28 of 1978, entered into force on 1 January 1979.

A revision of the former Design Decree of 1978 was deemed necessary in view of several considerations in 2001. The new Design Act is aimed to:

(a) improve the compatibility of the Hungarian economy internationally;
(b) refine the common approach in Hungary to designs in general;
(c) refine the moral and financial appreciation of designers.[992]

The most important factor of Hungarian design law is the process of association and accession of Hungary to the European Union. The Agreement of Association (hereinafter: 'the European Agreement') between Hungary and the European Community was signed in Brussels on 16 December 1991, and the European Agreement entered into force on 1 January 1994. The European Agreement was promulgated by Act I of 1994.

By virtue of Article 65 of the European Agreement, Hungary shall continue to improve the protection of intellectual, industrial, and commercial property rights in order to provide, by the end of the fifth year, a level of protection similar to existing in Community, including comparable means on enforcing such rights. This essential demand also concerned the design law. The Hungarian design law was harmonized on the basis of Directive 98/71/EC of the European Parliament and of the Council of 13 October 1998 on the legal protection of designs.[993]

The Design Act entered into force on 1 January 2002 before the accession of Hungary to the European Union.

Hungary became a Member State of the European Union in 2004. Act XXX promulgated the accession of the Hungarian Republic to the European Union on 1 May 2004:

990. Beier & Schricker, *German Industrial Property*, 10.
991. Cs-Gy, Benko, 'Az ipari formatervezés helyzete Magyarországon', *Iparjogvédelmi Szemle* 103, no. 6 (1998): 26.
992. Preamble of the Design Act.
993. Gy. Kovári, 'Az Európai Ornamentális Minták a 98/71/EC/EC Directive után', *Védjegyvilág* 9, no. 2 (1999): 9.

By virtue of Act CXLVIII of 2010 the name of Hungarian Patent Office was changed to Hungarian Intellectual Property Office (hereinafter referred as Office) as of 1 January 2011 to better reflect its competence extending to activities related to all form of industrial property protection as well as to the field of copyright.

The new Civil Code, the Law V of 2013. is one of the most significant achievements of the twenty-first century in Hungary. The Code omits detailed regulation of intellectual property. The new Civil Code shall apply in respect of intellectual property, if these issues directly fall within its scope, which are not governed by the legislation on copyright and industrial property rights of Hungary.

The sources of design protection[994] in Hungary can be divided into three categories: Hungarian laws and regulations; Community laws and Regulations; and international treaties and conventions.

326. Hungarian Acts and Regulations:

- Act No. XLVIII of 2001 on the Legal Protection of Designs (hereinafter: 'Design Act'), Act XVI of 2013 on the Amendment of certain Acts relating to Intellectual Property.
- Act CLIX of 2013 on the Amendment of certain Acts relating to Intellectual Property.
- Government Decree 556/2013 (XII 30) on customs authority measures against goods, infringing certain intellectual property rights.
- Government Decree No. 147/2007 (VI 26) on the detailed rules concerning electronic filing of certain documents in industrial property procedures.
- Decree No. 19/2001 (XI 29) IM (Minister of Justice) on the detailed formal requirements of the application for design protection.
- Decree No. 19/2005 (IV 12) GKM on the fees for administrative services in industrial property procedures before the Hungarian Patent Office.
- Government Decree No. 266/2001 (XII 21) on the Hungarian Design Council.
- Schedule of fees concerning design applications and granted protection as in force from 16 May 2008 by virtue of Decree No. 19/2005 (IV 12) GKM.
- Schedule of fees concerning design applications and granted protection as in force from 20 April 2005 by virtue of Decree No. 19/2005 (IV 12) GKM (PDF format).

327. Community laws and regulations:

- Directive 2004/48/EC of the European Parliament and of the Council of 29 April 2004 on the enforcement of intellectual property rights.
- Directive 98/71/EC of the European Parliament and of the Council of 13 October 1998 on the legal protection of designs; (hereinafter: 'Design Directive').
- Council Regulation 6/2002 (EC) of 12 December 2001 on Community Designs.
- Commission Regulation (EC) No. 2245/2002 of 21 October 2002 implementing Council Regulation (EC) No. 6/2002 on Community designs.

994. Pintz, *Találd fel magad*, 213.

- Commission Regulation (EC) No. 2246/2002 of 16 December 2002 on the fees payable to the Office for Harmonization in the Internal Market (Trade Marks and Designs) in respect of the registration of Community designs.[995]

328. Treaties and conventions:

- Paris Convention for the Protection of Industrial Property – Promulgated by Law Decree No. 18/1970 in Hungary (hereinafter: 'Paris Convention').
- Hague Agreement Concerning the International Deposit of Industrial Designs – Promulgated by the Law Decree No. 29/1984.
- The Hague Agreement Concerning the International Registration of Industrial Design, Geneva Act of the Hague Agreement Concerning the International Registration of Industrial Designs – Promulgated by Act XLIII of 2001 (hereinafter: 'Hague Agreement').
- Regulation under the Hague Agreement Concerning the International Deposit of Industrial Designs.
- Locarno Agreement Establishing an International Classification for Industrial Designs, Agreement signed at Locarno on 8 October 1968 – Promulgated by the Law Decree No. 29/1993 (hereinafter: 'Locarno Agreement').[996]

§2. Subject Matter of Protection

329. In accordance with the Design Act, the appearance of the whole or a part of industrial and craftsmanship products can be protected.

Design means the appearance of the whole or a part of a product resulting from the features of, in particular, the lines, contours, colours, shapes, textures, and/or materials of the product itself and/or its ornamentation.[997]

Besides the shape and colour, all features affecting the appearance of the product shall be considered as part of the design, including the characteristics of the material used, features resulting from processing the surface, and decoration disposed on the product.[998]

The protection is not limited to traditional three-dimensional products, plane, shapes, textiles, graphic symbols, and typographic typeface may be protected as well.

Product means any industrial or handicraft item, including *inter alia* parts intended to be assembled into a complex product, packaging, get-up, graphic symbols and typographic typefaces, but excluding computer programs.[999]

The appearance of sets of matching components may also be subject to protection, which means tableware, furniture, and chess pieces may be protected as design.

995. Tattay, *A Szellemi Alkotások joga*, 405–409.
996. Pintz, *Találd fel magad*, 213.
997. Article 1(2) of the Design Act.
998. A. Orbán, 'Az Eropai Unió Formatervezési Mintarendszere és a Magyar Formatervezési Mintarendszer' *Külgazdaság* 50, no. 6 (2006): 63–78, 76.
999. Article 1(3) of the Design Act.

The appearance of components that are part of a complex product may also be protected. In this case, essential criterion of the protection shall be deemed that the component should have the capacity of being installed and removed without damage and should be visible if properly used.

Complex product means a product that is composed of multiple components that can be replaced permitting disassembly and re-assembly of the product.[1000]

330. The subject matter of the protection conferred by a design shall include any design which does not produce on the informed user a different overall impression.[1001] Article 20 of the Design Act states:

> The subject matter of protection conferred by a design shall be determined by the appearance of the whole or a part of a product resulting from the features of, in particular, the drawing or graphic or photographic reproduction of the design deposited in the Register of Designs, and the disclaimer if any.

Computer programs cannot be protected as designs, although visual elements, icons, and screen protectors occurring when the program is in function may be protected.

The design cannot be protected if it:

(a) subsists in features of appearance of a product that are solely dictated by its technical function;[1002] accordingly, features of appearance of product exclusively deriving from its technical function shall not be protected. Article 6(2) of the Design Act allows an interpretation on design subsisting in features of appearance which are solely dictated by its technical function. Accordingly, these features must be reproduced in their exact form and dimensions in order to permit the product in which the design is incorporated or to which it is applied to be mechanically connected to or placed in, around or against another product so that either product may perform its function;
(b) the sign is excluded from design protection if it is contrary to public policy or to public morality;[1003]
(c) constitutes an unauthorized use of state emblems or other emblems of an authority or international organization as defined in Paris Convention for the Protection of Industrial Property;[1004]
(d) if its design contains any decoration, badge, or escutcheon, or any official warranty or authentication sign which is not regulated in Paris Convention and whose use is of public interest;[1005]

1000. Article 1(4) of the Design Act.
1001. Article 20(2) of the Design Act.
1002. A. Orbán, 'Az Eropai Unió Formatervezési Mintarendszere', 71.
1003. Article 7 of the Design Act.
1004. Article 8(1) a) of the Design Act.
1005. Article 8(1) b) of the Design Act.

(e) is identical with a design that has been made available to the public after the date of priority[1006] and to which protection has been granted with an earlier date of priority;[1007]
(f) uses a distinctive sign that would be in conflict with an earlier industrial property right of third persons, or has been used by others effectively in the country from an earlier date, provided that the use of the design without the consent of the prior user would be contrary to law;[1008] or
(g) infringes an earlier copyright.

Design protection shall be granted with the consent of the competent authority to designs which consist of or contain any of the emblems defined under paragraph (d) and (e).[1009]

§3. Conditions of Protection

331. A design shall be protected to the extent that it is new and has individual character.[1010] A design shall be considered new, if no identical design has been made available to the public before the date of priority. A design shall be deemed to have been made available to the public:

(a) if it has been published following registration or otherwise;
(b) or exhibited;
(c) used in trade;
(d) or otherwise disclosed by way of application to any patent office at both national and international level,[1011] except when these events could not reasonably have become known in the normal course of business to the circles specialized in the sector concerned, operating within the Community.[1012]

A disclosure shall not be taken into consideration:

(a) if the design has been made available by the designer to a third party under obligation of official secrecy;[1013] or
(b) if the design is made available by the designer in less than a twelve-month period proceeding the filing date of application as a consequence of an abuse in relation to the designer or his or her predecessor in title; or

1006. Any registered design of earlier priority shall be understood as protection granted in Hungary or a protection covering Hungary as well.
1007. Article 9(1) of the Design Act.
1008. Article 9(2) of the Design Act.
1009. Article 8(2) of the Design Act.
1010. Article 1(1) of the Design Act.
1011. 'Comments on the Design Act', *Szabadalmi Közlöny és Védjegyértesítö* 106, no. 12 (2001): 13.
1012. Kovári, 'Az europai ornamentális', 8.
1013. A. Orbán, 'Az Eropai Unió Formatervezési Mintarendszere', 79.

(c) if the design is made available by the designer, his or her predecessor in title, or a third person in less than a twelve-month period proceeding the filing date of application as a result of information provided, or action taken by the designer, or his or her predecessor in title, the designs shall be deemed to be identical if their features differ only in immaterial details.[1014]

332. A design shall be considered to have individual character if the overall impression it produces on the informed user differs from the overall impression produced on such a user by any design, which has been made available to the public before the date of priority.[1015]

In assessing individual character, the degree of freedom of the designer – taking into consideration the nature of the product to which the design is applied or in which it is incorporated,[1016] and in particular, the industrial or handicraft sector – in developing the design shall be applied.[1017]

The individual character of a component of a complex product should be judged from another standpoint. A design applied to or incorporated in a product, which constitutes a component part of a complex product, shall only be considered new,[1018] and to have individual character:

> If the component part, once it has been incorporated into the complex product, remains visible during normal use (use by the consumer or end user, excluding maintenance, servicing or repair work) of the latter; and to the extent that those visible features of the component part fulfil in themselves the requirements as to novelty and individual character.[1019]

§4. Formalities (Procedure for Grant and Obtaining Protection)

333. The Hungarian Intellectual Property Office (hereinafter: 'Office')shall have powers to handle the following design related matters:

(a) granting of design protection;
(b) renewal of designs;
(c) division of a multiple design into separate designs;
(d) declaration of termination of design protection;
(e) declaration of invalidity of a design;
(f) declaration of non-infringement;
(g) registration of design applications and registered designs;
(h) provision of official notice.[1020]

1014. Article 2(2) of the Design Act.
1015. Article 3(1) of the Design Act.
1016. Lontai et al., *A Szellemi Alkotások joga*, 240, 241.
1017. Article 3(2) of the Design Act.
1018. Pintz, *Találd fel magad*, 143.
1019. Article 5(1) a), b) of the Design Act.
1020. Article 30 of the Design Act.

The Office is vested with competence to enforce the provisions relating to the Community protection of designs and to the international registration of industrial designs.

The duration of procedure of granting design protection may be thirteen to fifteen months.

334. Proceedings for the granting of design protection shall commence upon submission of an application to the Hungarian Intellectual Property Office. Applications for a design may be filed by way of electronic means, using the standard electronic form prescribed for this purpose by the Office.[1021]

The application for a design shall contain the application for registration, a representation of the design, a description of the product in which the design is incorporated or to which it is applied, as well as any other documents as they are deemed necessary.

The representation enclosed with the application for a design shall be prepared in such a way as to indicate clearly the nature of the design for which protection is requested.[1022]

The application for a design shall indicate – when possible – the class of international classification of the Locarno Agreement[1023] to which the product and design is incorporated or to which it is applied

, including the corresponding description.

335. An application fee shall be paid for the application for a design within two months falling the date of filing the application. The filing fee shall be paid to the budgetary account of the Office by indicating the reference number and the function. Payment without a reference number is not effective.[1024]

The date of filing an application for a design[1025] shall be the day on which the application is received by the Hungarian Intellectual Property Office and it contains *inter alia*:

(a) reference to a claim of the design;
(b) data that can be used to identify the applicant or make contact with the applicant if possible;
(c) a representation of the design, regardless of whether or not it complies with the prescribed requirements.

To have a date of filing accorded, it is sufficient to make reference to a priority document in lieu of submitting a representation of the design.

336. The priority rights[1026] have several varieties: application priority, exhibition priority, internal priority, and priority within the Community.[1027]

1021. Article 36A(1) of the Design Act.
1022. Pintz, *Találd fel magad*, 106.
1023. Locarno Agreement establishing an International Classification for Industrial Designs Agreement signed at Locarno on 8 Oct. 1968 – was promulgated by Law Decree No. 29/1993.
1024. Pintz, *Találd fel magad*, 108.
1025. Article 37(1) of the Design Act.
1026. Article 40(1) of Design Act.
1027. Csécsy, *A Szellemi Alkotások joga*, 175.

Concerning the priority within the Community, the right of priority of an application shall be determined in the cases specified by the Paris Convention, by the filing date of the foreign application.

Convention, exhibition, and internal priority shall be applied for within two months calculated from filing the design application. The document establishing the convention priority and the certification of exhibition shall be filed within four months calculated from the day of filing. If internal priority is claimed, the earlier design application shall be deemed to be withdrawn. The Convention priority shall be demanded within six months calculated from filing date of the national application.[1028]

337. Several designs being part of the overall impression may be combined in one application. The products incorporating the designs shall belong to the same class of the Locarno Agreement. A common feature may be any decoration disposed on each design, and any formal or substantive uniformity, however may connect the designs. Moreover, several designs may be combined in one multiple application where the products contain similar ornamentation features, which are likely to produce an overall impression on the informed user.[1029]

338. The procedure for registration of the design may be divided into following sections:

(a) preliminary examination;
(b) formal examination;
(c) novelty search;
(d) publication of application;
(e) observations;
(f) substantive examination;
(g) grant of design protection.

The Gazette of Office gives information to the public relating to the design application (bibliographic data) and certain data and facts relating to the grant of designs after obtaining a patent. A patent application shall also be published after the expiry of eight months from the earliest.

339. The preliminary examination[1030] is the first section of procedure. Following the filing of the design application, the Hungarian Intellectual Property Office examines whether the application is in conformity with the conditions prescribed for according the date of filing, that is, whether it contains the reference to the right to design protection, the data suitable for identifying the applicant, the representation of the design, the description of the product according to the design or the reference to the priority document, as well as whether the filing fee has been paid.

The Office notifies the applicant about the accorded date of filing. If the date of filing cannot be accorded, the Office invites the applicant to remedy the deficiencies within thirty days. In a case in which the deficiencies are remedied on the deadline,

1028. Pintz, *Találd fel magad*, 107.

1029. Gy. Kovari, 'Az ipari mintaoltalmi jog az Europai Unióban', *Védjegyvilág* 8, no. 2 (1998): 6, 7.

1030. Article 41(1) of the Design Act.

the date of filing will be the day when the remedy is received. In a contrary case, the application shall be regarded as withdrawn.

The applicant may withdraw the application for a design in due observation: The Office shall acknowledge such withdrawal.

Examination as to formal requirements[1031] follows the preliminary examination. If the design application satisfies the requirements prescribed for according the date of filing, the filing fee has been paid, the request, the design representation, the description of the design according to the product as well as other necessary attachments have been filed, the Office examines the application in order to establish whether the filed documents satisfy the prescribed formal requirements.

If deficiencies are noted when examining the formal requirements of the design application, the Office invites the applicant in the form of a decision to remedy the deficiencies and conducts the procedure on the basis of the remedy. Should the applicant fail to respond to the invitation to remedy the deficiencies by the set deadline, the design application shall be regarded as withdrawn.

340. The novelty search[1032] is an essential part of the examination procedure. If the design application satisfies the requirements prescribed for according the date of filing, and the filing fee has been paid, as well as the design representation and the description of the design according to the product have been filed, then the Office shall conduct a novelty search. As well as they shall prepare a novelty search report on the basis of the representation of the design, having regard to the description of the product in which the design is incorporated or to which it is applied.

Also, the Hungarian Intellectual Property Office shall draw up a search report on the basis of the representation of the design. The search report shall mention those documents (designs, representations, as well as data) that may be taken into consideration in connection with the design or design group represented in the design application upon consideration.

341. The design application shall be published by the Hungarian Intellectual Property Gazette of Office[1033] after the expiry of nine months from the earliest date of priority in the Gazette, and the applicant shall be notified thereof.

At this time, the following data and facts are released in connection with the design protection application:

(a) over and above the data disclosed upon the communication of data;
(b) the name of the author;
(c) the international classification of the product according to the design;
(d) as well as the representation of the design.[1034]

The publication shall become final with a retroactive effect to the date of filing, by granting provisional design protection. The rights deriving from the design protection may only be enforced on the basis of the definitive design protection.

1031. Article 43, *ibid.*
1032. Article 44, *ibid.*
1033. Article 45, *ibid.*
1034. Pintz, *Találd fel magad*, 109.

Upon request by the applicant, the Hungarian Intellectual Property Office may also publish the design application at an earlier date, (at nine months) if it meets the conditions of the formal examination.

The Office defers the publication upon request by the applicant if the request is submitted by the applicant two months before the expiry of nine months calculated from the earliest priority date or the period of previous deferment. The publication may not be deferred beyond the thirtieth month calculated from the earliest priority. That means the publication can be deferred within thirty months.

342. The observations[1035] may be filed by any person after the publication with the Office to the effect that the design or the application therefore fails to meet any of the requirements for protection. Also, observations may be submitted in the case of an earlier right or earlier domestic use by the holder of an earlier right.

Observations

Section 46

(1) Following publication, in design protection proceedings any person may submit observations – subject to the exceptions set out in Subsection (2) – to the Hungarian Patent Office to the effect that the design – or the application therefor – fails to meet any of the requirements governing the validity of designs as prescribed in this Act.
(2) Where Section 10 applies observations may be submitted by the holder of an earlier right only.
(3) The Hungarian Patent Office shall acknowledge that a design is refused protection pursuant to Section 10 only if the right holder submits an observation thereof.
(4) The observation shall be taken into account in the course of the examination covering the condition objected to, except if it is submitted by a person other than the right holder.
(5) The person submitting the observation - other than right holder mentioned in Subsection (2) – shall not be a party to the design proceedings. This person shall be notified of the outcome of his observation, with the decision on the granting of protection enclosed.

In accordance with Article 46 (4) the Hungarian Intellectual Property Office shall take into consideration the observations in the course of the examination covering the condition objected to, except if it is submitted by a person other than the right holder. The Office shall notify the person making the observations about the result of the observations. Design Act.

343. The substantive examination may be considered as the last section of design examination. If the design application satisfies the requirements laid down for according the date of filing and the filing fee has been duly paid, the Office shall perform a substantive examination of the design application in order to ascertain whether it satisfies the requirements set forth by law.

In Article 47(2) of the Design Act, the substantive examination shall include inquiries:

1035. Article 46 of the Design Act.

(a) as to whether the design meets the requirements of novelty and individual character;
(b) if it is not refused of protection because of exclusion of protection;
(c) if it has conflict with registered propriety industry right or other earlier rights stemming from any observation of the right holder therefore;
(d) as to whether the application therefore is in compliance with the formal and other conditions set out in the Design Act.

In the course of the substantive examination of the design application, the Office invites the applicant – according to the nature of the objection – to remedy the deficiencies, to submit comments or, as the case may be, to divide the application. The Hungarian Intellectual Property Office rejects the design application in whole or in part if it does not meet the examined requirements even after the remedy of deficiencies or the submitting of comments.

If the applicant fails to reply to the invitation or to divide the application, he or she shall be deemed to have withdrawn the application or, after publication of the application, to have surrendered provisional protection.

The Design Act states that the application may only be rejected on the basis of reasons indicated clearly and categorically and properly explained in the notice. If necessary, a new notice shall be issued.[1036]

344. If the design and the design application meet all requirements of the examination, the Office shall grant protection for the subject matter of application after the expiry of at least one month from the date of publication. After granting the design protection, the Office shall issue a design protection certificate to the holder, to which the extract from the register shall be annexed, and the grant of design protection shall be announced in the Gazette of Office.

In case of rejection of an application for design registration, a request for review of the decision by the Office may be filed with the Budapest Metropolitan Court within thirty days of the notification of the decision. An appeal to the court decision with the Metropolitan Court of Appeal should be lodged within fifteen days.

The Hungarian Intellectual Property Office may withdraw or modify its decisions terminating the procedure taken in the design matters only if a request for review is filed and only until such request is transmitted to the court.

§5. Ownership and Transfer: Assignment & Licenses

345. The protection of the design is rightfully due to the designer or legal successor, with the exception of the moral rights.

In the case of a design that has been created by several persons, any of the co-authors may utilize it, but the one who utilizes the design is obliged to pay appropriate royalties to the co-authors in proportion of their share in a license for utilization. The user may transfer the license to a third party only if this has been expressly permitted by the licensor.

1036. Article 42(5) of the Design Act.

The rights conferred by a design may be assigned, transferred, and encumbered, with the exception of the rights of the designer stemming from the design.[1037] A written document is required for the filing of a lien, and such a lien shall be entered in the Register of Designs.[1038]

The basic form of utilization is the license agreement[1039] (industrial design licensing agreement). Under a contract of exploitation, the holder of the industrial design gives authorization for the exploitation of the design, and the person enjoying exploitation rights is required to pay a fee therefore.[1040] The holder of the patent shall guarantee for the entire life of the contract of exploitation that no third party has any right relating to the patent, which would impede or restrict exploitation. In such a case, the licensee may give immediate notice and claim damages. Design licensing contracts shall be governed by the relevant provisions of the Patent Act pertaining to patent license contracts.

The licensing agreement must extend to every mode and measure of utilization, without any restriction of time and space. The contract of exploitation shall confer an exclusive right only if expressly stipulated. In case of an exclusive license of exploitation, in addition to the person enjoying exploitation rights the holder of the patent may also exploit the invention, except when this has been expressly prohibited in the contract. The holder of the design may terminate the exclusivity of the license – subject to a proportionate reduction of the royalty – if the person enjoying exploitation rights fails to commence exploitation within a timeframe that may reasonably be expected in the given situation.[1041]

The person enjoying exploitation rights may assign the license to a third party – or he or she may re-license exploitation to a third party – only if this has been expressly permitted by the holder of the design. The holder of the design shall provide for the renewal of the design protection.

346. Service design means any design developed by a person in the execution of his or her duties stemming from employment that includes working out solutions within the domain of the design.[1042] In connection with service designs, the right to the design shall vest in the employer, as the designer's successor in title.[1043] Employee design means any design developed by a person who is not required to do so under his or her contract of employment; however, the utilization of such design falls within the sphere of the activities of his or her employer.

In connection with employee designs, the right to the design shall vest in the designer; the designer is entitled to file the design at the Office that the employer has economic rights to design. The employer shall be entitled to exploit the design. The employer's right of use is non-exclusive, and the employer may not license the use of the design. The right of use shall be transferred upon the successor in title in case of

1037. Lontai et al., *A Szellemi Alkotások joga*, 242.
1038. Article 21(1) of the Design Act.
1039. Csécsy, *A Szellemi Alkotások joga*, 243.
1040. Article 21(2) of the Design Act.
1041. Pintz, *Találd fel magad*, 102.
1042. Kovari, 'Az europai ornamentális', 6.
1043. Articles 14(1) and (2) of the Design Act.

the winding-up of the employer, or the separation of its department; otherwise, it may not be transferred or assigned to any other person.

The designer of a work for hire is due to appropriate royalties according to the royalty given for the utilization of an employee's invention and service invention are indicated in the Patent Act.[1044]

347. The provisions of the Patent Act governing service and employee inventions shall also apply[1045] to service and employee designs and to the appropriate remuneration of designers, subject to the following exceptions:

(a) the provisions relating to the confidential treatment of service inventions and to exploit them as solutions comprising a trade secret shall not apply to service designs;
(b) in connection with service designs, failure to pay the renewal fee shall constitute failure to renew the term of protection while in case of design the owner shall not pay an annual fee of maintenance but may renew the design protection relating to expiry shall mean the time beyond which the term of protection may not be renewed (twenty-five years);
(c) the designer shall be entitled to appropriate remuneration only in connection with the sale of a service design that falls within the scope of the protection conferred by a design right.[1046]

The rules of service and employee designs shall apply, if the design has been developed by a person in public service, or in a civil servant's or a service legal relationship, or by a member of a cooperative employed within the framework of an employment relationship.[1047]

In connection with employee designs, the design entitlement shall be vested in the inventor; the employer, however, is entitled to exploit the invention.[1048]

The creator of a design may dispose over the service design if the employer consents thereto, or if the employer fails to make declaration within ninety days if he or she wants to lay claim to the service invention, or if he or she wishes to exploit the employee invention. For the employee invention, design entitlement shall be vested in the inventor free of the exploitation right of the employer, if the employer consents thereto, or if the employer fails to make the declaration in foregoing paragraph.

If the employer ceases to exist or if any its organizational units are separated, the right of exploitation will be transferred to its successor in title; it may not be assigned or transferred in any other way.

1044. Orbán, 'Az Eropai Unió Formatervezési Mintarendszere', 77.
1045. Article 14(5) of the Design Act.
1046. Pintz, *Találd fel magad*, 101.
1047. Article 14(6) of the Design Act.
1048. Pintz, *Találd fel magad*, 104.

§6. Scope of Exclusive Rights

348. The creators of designs have moral rights and economic rights. Rights attached to the person and pecuniary rights result from the creation of a design. The Patent Act regulates the personal rights attached to the creator of industrial design. These rights ensure the moral recognition of the creator of design; they are related to the inventor as a person, and for this reason, by virtue of Article 2:49 new Civil Code (Law No. V of 2013),[1049] they are inalienable. Pecuniary rights arising from a patent may be separated from the moral rights of the design creator. Special pecuniary rights of the owner of a design have absolute structure that can be aliened, inherited, and pledged.[1050]

The scope of protection is essential for the rights of the absolute nature of a designer.

The scope of the protection conferred by a design shall be determined based on the appearance of the whole or a part of a product resulting from the features of, in particular, the drawing or graphic or photographic reproduction of the design deposited in the Register of Designs and the disclaimer. The scope of the protection conferred by a design shall include any design that does not produce on the informed user a different overall impression.[1051]

Chapter II of the Design Act regulates the rights and obligations conferred by the design and by design protection.

The beneficiaries of industrial design are:

(a) the designer or his or her legal successor;
(b) the co-designers;
(c) in the case of a work for hire, the employer or the claimant, on the basis of different relationship.[1052]

349. The rights of the creator to design are defined in Articles 13(1), (2), and (3) of the Design Act: The right to the design shall vest in the designer, or the right to the design shall vest in the person identified in the application that has been accorded a date of filing as the designer, insofar as a final court verdict does not find otherwise, or if two or more persons have jointly developed a design and there are no conflicting signs, the right to the design shall vest in them jointly.

The person who has created a design shall be deemed as the designer. Unless a final court decision rules to the contrary, the person mentioned as such in the application filed at the accorded filing date shall be deemed to be the creator of a design.

The moral rights of the inventor consist of several different elements:

(a) the right to acknowledgement of authorship related to design;[1053]

1049. Any contract or unilateral statement that restricts inherent rights is null and void.
1050. Csécsy, *A Szellemi Alkotások joga*, 172.
1051. Lontai et al., *A Szellemi Alkotások joga*, 243.
1052. *Ibid.*, 242.
1053. Article 12(6) of the Design Act.

(b) the designer shall have the right to be mentioned as such in design documents;[1054] this rule is in compliance with the rules of the new Civil Code (Law No. V of 2013) relating to right to name;[1055]
(c) the right to make the design available to the public (disclosure) of application;[1056] Before the publication of the application for a design, the design may be made available to the public subject to the consent of the designer or his or her successor in title.

350. Articles 13–20 of the Design Act state the right to a design and rights conferred by the design protection that is economic (pecuniary) rights of the designer. The economic (pecuniary) rights of creator of design and designer are as follows:

(a) the right to design protection shall belong to the creator of a design. If two or more persons have created the design[1057] in cooperation, the protection is due to the designers or their legal successors jointly. If two or more persons have created a design independently from each other, the right to design protection will belong to the designer or his or her successor in title, according to whoever filed the application with the earliest date of priority, as the case may be;
(b) the right to remuneration. The designer is entitled to remuneration[1058] relating to the service designs, the employer designs, the license agreements, and assignments;
(c) exclusive right to exploit the designs, which will cover, in particular, the manufacture, use, putting on the market, offering for sale, importation, exportation of the product according to the design, and the stocking of such products for those purposes;[1059]
(d) the right to conclusion of exploitation of contracts;[1060]
(e) the right to assignment, transfer and pledge of design.[1061]

Based on the exclusive exploitation right, the holder of the design shall have the right to prevent any third party not having his consent from using it. That means an infringement of design protection is committed when a person utilizes the design under protection without authorization.[1062]

The protection of designs may overlap with copyright protection.[1063] Several artistic creations, e.g., creations produced by drawings, painting, sculpturing, applied art creations, and designs and engineering structures, may be also protected as designs.

1054. Article 12(5), *ibid.*
1055. By virtue of Article 2:49 of new Civil Code (Law No. V of 2013), everyone has the right to bear a name.
1056. Article 12(7) of the Design Act.
1057. Article 13(5) of the Design Act.
1058. Article 14(5), *ibid.*
1059. Article 16(3), *ibid.*
1060. Article 21(2), *ibid.*
1061. Article 21(1), *ibid.*
1062. Lontai et al., *A Szellemi Alkotások joga*, 242.
1063. J. Batta, 'Ipari termékek külso megjelenésének védelme', *MIE Közleményei* 42, no. 1 (2001): 71.

By virtue of Article 64[1064] of the Design Act, these objects may enjoy copyright protection and design protection parallel.[1065] Accordingly, the designer may choose merely copyright protection or both design protection and copyright protection.

§7. Limitation of the Scope of Protection

351. The balance between public interest and the rights of designers is principally ensured by the several rules of design protection.[1066] There are some limits drawn to exclusive rights of the designer in the interest of private parties or the public.[1067]

The limitations and exceptions in respect to exclusive rights of design owners may be permissible:

(a) to create and maintain a balance between the interests of authors and other right holders users and the public at large;
(b) to take account of the requirements and demands school education, of experiments, culture, scientific research;
(c) to diminish the monopoly law of authors.[1068]

In respect of industrial designs, compulsory licenses for utilization are not granted. The main types of the limitation of design protection are as follows:

(a) acts done privately, non-commercial, experimental, and school education purposes;
(b) prior use;
(c) limitation of design protection to repair of a complex product so as to restore its original appearance;[1069]
(d) favour concerning transit products;
(e) exhaustion of design rights.

352. The rights conferred by a design shall not be exercised in respect of:

(a) acts done privately and for non-commercial purposes;
(b) acts done for experimental purposes, including experiments and research necessary for the authorization of the distribution of a product in which the design is incorporated or to which it is applied;

1064. By virtue of Art. 64 of the Design Act, protection granted for a design by the Design Act shall not concern the copyright protection afforded for artistic works under specific other legislation, if applicable to the design.
1065. Tattay, *A Szellemi Alkotások joga*, 305.
1066. Tattay, *A Szellemi Alkotások joga*, 312.
1067. Lontai et al., *A Szellemi Alkotások joga*, 243.
1068. Tattay, *A Szellemi Alkotások joga*, 312.
1069. Gy. Kovari, 'Az Eurpai ornamentális', 6.

(c) acts of reproduction for the purpose of making citations or of teaching, provided that such acts are compatible with fair trade practice and do not unduly prejudice the normal exploitation of the design, and that mention is made of the source.[1070]

The prior use is a possibility generally permitted on the domain of industrial property. If several persons created the design irrespective of one another, the design protection is due to its creator – the designer – or legal successor who announced the design with earlier priority to the office. Rights to prior use are not governed by the Design Act.[1071] The prior use is another barrier to design protection. The general legal principle that an activity performed legally and in good faith cannot later become illegal is embodied in the right of prior use.[1072] By contrast, the rights acquired through creating a design, unless followed by utilization or serious preparation to do so will perish if another diligent designer files an application for the same invention earlier.[1073]

Limitation of design protection to repair a complex product so as to restore it to its original form is a limitation on protection of design protection.[1074] The Design Directive prescribes the so-called Repair Clause in Articles 14 and 18. Accordingly, a protected design shall not entitle the holder to prohibit a third party from using such a design for the purpose of the repair of a complex product so as to restore its original appearance, when the design is applied to or incorporated in a product that constitutes a component part of a complex product upon whose appearance the protected design is dependent, provided he or she uses it in accordance with honest practices in industrial or commercial matters.[1075]

The favour concerning transit products is a general legal institution of limitations of industrial property rights by virtue of the Paris Convention. This means:

> In case of reciprocity, the rights conferred by a design shall not be exercised in respect of the equipment on ships and aircraft registered in another country when these temporarily enter the territory of Hungary, the importation to Hungary of spare parts and accessories for the purpose of repairing such craft, and the execution of repairs on such craft. As to whether reciprocity applies, this shall be determined on the basis of the opinion of the President of the Hungarian Intellectual Property Office.[1076]

The exclusive exploitation right conferred by a design shall not extend to acts relating to a product in which a design included within the scope of protection of the design is incorporated or to which it is applied, when the product has been put on the market in the European Economic Area by the holder of the design or with his or her consent.[1077]

1070. Article 17(1) of the Design Act.
1071. Lontai et al., *A Szellemi Alkotások joga*, 209.
1072. Article 17(2) of the Design Act.
1073. Tattay, *A Szellemi Alkotások joga*, 312.
1074. Article 17(3) of the Design Act.
1075. This limitation concerns the producers of the spare parts of cars considerably.
1076. Article 17(4) of the Design Act.
1077. Article 18, *ibid.*

§8. Duration of Protection

353. The term of design protection is generally five years and may be provisional and final. The term of provisional design protection prescribed in Article 25 of the Design Act states that a design shall be protected from the date of publication of the application, with retroactive effect to the date of filing of the application. Provisional design protection shall lapse with a retroactive effect to the date of filing if the design application is definitely rejected, or the applicant surrenders protection.

Final design protection shall last for a period of five years calculated from the date of filing.[1078] The term of duration of definitive protection of design protection is maximally twenty-five years. Protection may not be renewed beyond twenty-five years as from the date of the filing of the application.[1079]

The design protection may be extended for further five-year periods and at most, up to four times.[1080] In the case of renewal, the new period of protection shall commence on the day following the day of expiry of the previous period of protection.[1081]

The renewal of the design protection may be requested at the earliest six months prior to the expiry of the term of protection, and at the latest within six months calculated from the day of expiry of filing.[1082]

The request for renewing the design protection is subject to the payment of a fee and the said fee shall be paid within two months following the submittal of the request. If the renewal fee is not paid even despite the invitation by the Office, the request shall be considered as withdrawn.[1083]

354. The unregistered design shall be declared terminated with retroactive effect to the date when granted if: the application for a design is rejected by final decision; or the applicant surrendered the protection.[1084]

Definitive design protection shall lapse[1085] if:

(a) the term of protection expired without renewal, on the day following the expiration of the term of protection;
(b) the holder of the design protection surrendered protection, on the day following the date of receipt of the surrender, or at an earlier date specified by him or her; the applicant or the right holder indicated in the Register of Designs may surrender design protection by way of a written declaration addressed to the Hungarian Intellectual Property Office[1086] When several designs are combined in one multiple protection, surrender may be declared for parts of such design;
(c) the term of protection expired (twenty-five years), on the day following the expiration of the term of protection.;

1078. Article 19(1) of the Design Act.
1079. Article 19(3), *ibid.*
1080. Article 19(2), *ibid.*
1081. Orbán, 'Az Eropai Unió Formatervezési mintarendszere', 78.
1082. Article 51(3) of the Design Act.
1083. Article 52(3), *ibid.*
1084. Article 25 of the Design Act.
1085. Article 26, *ibid.*
1086. Article 27(1), *ibid.*

(d) the design protection is invalidated with retroactive effect to the date of filing.[1087]

Design shall be invalidated[1088] in the following cases:

(1) if the design fails to comply with the requirements of novelty and individual character; and
(2) if it is excluded of protection;
(3) if the representation deposited in the Register of Designs fails to demonstrate the design;
(4) the way prescribed by Act 9, while the representation enclosed with the application for a design shall be prepared in such a way as to indicate clearly the nature of the design for which protection is requested;[1089]
(5) the design differs from the one represented in the application that was submitted on the registered date of application or – in case of division – in the application for division;
(6) protection was granted to a person other than the person legally entitled to it;
(7) the application for international registration of an industrial design under the Hague Agreement was submitted by a person without proper entitlement.

When several designs are combined in one multiple protection, and the grounds for invalidity apply only to some of them, the design right shall be appropriately restricted.[1090]

The term of design protection is generally five years. The design protection may be extended for further five-year periods. The term of duration of definitive of design protection is maximally twenty-five years as outlined in paragraph 353.

§9. Infringement and Remedies

355. Chapter III of the Design Act regulates infringement of a design and a design right. The Design Act makes distinction between infringement of design and infringement of design rights. In connection with any infringement of design and of design rights, the relevant provisions of the Patent Act shall apply to the rights of the licensee authorized by the right holder.[1091]

The Design Act states:

> Where the object of an application for a design or a design product in which the design is incorporated, or to which it is applied is copied without authorization from the design of a third party, the holder of such a design or his successor in title may file for court action to declare that he is entitled to the whole or a part of that design, and may demand compensation for damage under civil liability.

1087. Pintz, *Találd fel magad*, 101.
1088. Article 28 of the Design Act.
1089. Article 39, *ibid.*
1090. Article 28(3), *ibid.*
1091. Article 22 of the Design Act.

The aforementioned 'plagiarism' concerning industrial designs is forbidden. If the subject matter of an application for the protection of a design has been appropriated without authorization from another person, the injured party or his or her successor in title may demand satisfaction concerning his entitlement for the design in full or in part.[1092]

The following acts carried out by a third party without the permission of the holder of the industrial design are qualified as infringement: in particular, the making, using, offering, putting on the market, importing or exporting of a product in which the design is incorporated or to which it is applied, or stocking such a product for those purposes.[1093]

356. In respect of infringement of a design right, the scope of protection shall be taken into consideration. The scope of the protection conferred by a design shall be determined based on the appearance of the whole or a part of a product resulting from the features of, in particular, the drawing or graphic or photographic reproduction of the design deposited in the Register of Designs, and the disclaimer if any.[1094] The scope of the protection conferred by a design shall include any design that does not produce on the informed user a different overall impression. This means that the scope of the design protection extends to all similar designs that do not produce a different overall impression on the informed user. The drawings or photographs recognizably representing the subject matter of the design on the whole, in details or in various aspects are indispensable to properly determine the scope of the right to protection. The drawings and photographs shall enable precisely determine the subject matter and scope of design protection and to give clear and concise information for third parties.

The designer may according to the circumstances of the case have recourse:

(a) on the basis of the Design Act;
(b) on the basis of the Hungarian Penal Code;[1095]
(c) when a design is infringed, the holder may request – under the provisions of special legislation – measures by the customs authorities.[1096]

The designs are also protected from infringement by the Criminal Code (Article 329/D of Criminal Code).

357. The designer shall have the right to demand satisfaction from the infringement under civil liability, as afforded to patent holders under the Patent Act. Civil remedies for infringement of design rights are available by analogy in Patent Law.[1097] In the case of infringement of the stipulations of a design license agreement, the relevant provisions of the Patent Act related of claimants and licensees shall apply.[1098]

In cases of infringement of design rights, the holder of the design may, under the provisions of specific other legislation, require the customs authority to take

1092. Csécsy, *A Szellemi Alkotások joga*, 174.
1093. Article 16(3) of the Design Act.
1094. Article 20, *ibid.*
1095. Pintz, *Találd fel magad*, 103.
1096. *Ibid.*
1097. Article 35 of Patent Act.
1098. Article 23(3) of the Design Act.

measures to prevent the dutiable goods affected by the infringement from being put into circulation.[1099]

The declaration of non-infringement on the domain of industrial property rights (patents, utility models) is prescribed in order to avoid the claims of infringement.[1100]

In accordance with the Design Act, the possibility of declaration of non-infringement[1101] is permissible. Article 24(1) of the Design Act prescribes:

> Any person who anticipates being charged for an alleged design infringement may request, before the proceedings are opened, a finding to the effect that the product exploited by him or her – or proposed to be exploited – does not infringe upon the design he has specified.

A final ruling establishing a negative statement excludes an infringement action on the basis of designated utility models against the product mentioned.[1102]

1099. Article 23(2), *ibid.*
1100. Tattay, *A Szellemi Alkotások joga*, 313.
1101. Orbán, 'Az Eropai Unió Formatervezési mintarendszere', 80.
1102. Article 24(2) of the Design Act.

Chapter 7. Plant Variety Protection

§1. Sources: Legislation

358. The current regulation of plant varieties to find in Patent Act (Part V of the Patent Act on the Protection of Plant Varieties).

In Central and Eastern Europe, Hungary was the first country to provide for the protection of plant varieties in a special chapter of the former Patent Act (Act II of 1969), in accordance with the UPOV Convention of 1961. This Act allowed protection preparation of new compounds (active ingredients, activators, antidotes) compositions containing them and processes for the use of such preparations.

The former Patent Act of 1969 was amended by Act VII of 1997 that enabled new compounds to be patented, while the conditions of patentability remained unchanged. The introduction of product protection made it unnecessary for active ingredient content in claims relating to a process of use.

The UPOV Convention (International Convention for the Protection of New Varieties of Plants) was concluded in 1961 for the international protection of Plant Varieties. It was also necessary to revise it three times in 1972, 1978, and 1991 (hereinafter: 'UPOV Convention'). The UPOV Agreement was promulgated by Act LI of 2002.[1103]

Hungary acceded to the Convention in 1983 and accepted the Act of 1978. Hungary signed the Act of UPOV Convention. The modification of the Patent Act (Part 5, Chapter XIII) has been in force from 1 January 2003 and deals specifically with plant variety protection.

'Protection will be granted for twenty-five, in some cases for thirty years from grant and is restricted to the commercial production and marketing of propagating material of the protected variety. A further restriction is the so-called farmers' privilege and the right of breeders to use propagating material of the protected variety.[1104]

The new regulation of plant varieties is fully compatible with Council Regulation (EC) 2100/94. Finally, the TRIPS Agreement shall be mentioned, an international treaty that contains imported rules referred to plant variety protection.

The new Civil Code, the Law V of 2013. is one of the most significant achievements of the twenty-first century in Hungary. The Code omits detailed regulation of intellectual property. The new Civil Code shall apply in respect of intellectual property, if these issues directly fall within its scope, which are not governed by the legislation on copyright and industrial property rights of Hungary:

> By virtue of Act CXLVIII of 2010 the name of Hungarian Patent Office was changed to Hungarian Intellectual Property Office (hereinafter referred as Office) as of 1 January 2011 to better reflect its competence extending to activities related to all form of industrial property protection as well as to the field of copyright.

1103. M. Fáber, & H. M. Gorkáné, 'Növényfajta oltalom', *MIE Közlemények* 46, no. 1 (2003): 45.
1104. Beier & Schricker, *German Industrial Property*, 12.

The sources of plant variety protection may be divided into three categories: national, European, and international rules

359. Hungarian variety laws and regulations:

- Part V of the Patent Act on the Protection of Plant Varieties.
- Decree 20/2002 (XII 12) IM on the detailed formalities for patent applications, documents filed in relation to European patent applications, European patents, and international patent applications for plant variety protection.
- Government Decree 61/2006 (III 23) on the deposit and handling of biological materials for the purposes of patent procedures.
- Decree 19/2005 (IV 12) GKM on the Fees for Administrative Services in Industrial Property Procedures before the Hungarian Patent Office.
- Enforcement of decision on intellectual property rights infringement – Act LIII of 1994 on Judicial Execution [184/A. §].
- Government Decree 556/2013 (XII 30) on customs authority measures against goods, infringing certain intellectual property rights.

Community Laws and Regulations:

- Council Regulation (EC) 2100/94 of 27 July 1994 on Community plant variety rights.
- Commission Regulation (EC) No. 874/2009 of 17 September 2009 establishing implementing rules for the application of Council Regulation (EC) No. 2100/94 as regards proceedings before the Community Plant Variety Office.
- Commission Regulation (EC) 1238/95 of 31 May 1995 propagating 'material of the protected variety' establishing implementing rules for the application of Council Regulation (EC) 2100/94 in regards to the fees payable to the Plant Variety Office.
- Directive 2004/48/EC of the European Parliament and of the Council of 29 April 2004 on the enforcement of intellectual property rights.

360. Treaties and Conventions: International Convention for the Protection of new Varieties of Plants of 2 December 1961 as revised in 1972, 1978, and 1991 – promulgated by Act LI of 2002 in Hungary (hereinafter: 'UPOV Convention').[1105]

§2. Subject Matter of Protection

361. When speaking about the patent protection of biological inventions, this category of invention may be divided into three groups:

(a) micro-organisms and products connected with them and with other biological materials and microbiological processes;
(b) plant varieties; and
(c) animal breeds.

1105. Pintz, *Talald fel magad*, 216.

Biotechnological inventions have been integrated into patent systems and belong to a wider category of industrial products and industrial processes. The patent law of Hungary involves microbiological processes and products with the scope of patentable inventions.

Microbiological processes include various fermentation processes and products with the scope of patentable inventions.[1106]

The Patent Act excludes patent protection for plants. Plants or animals and processes for preparing plants or animals, which are essentially biological and therefore cannot be patented.[1107] However, an independent variety of patent protection has been established within the Patent Act. Inventions relating to plants or animals can be patented if the technical feasibility of the invention is not confined to a particular plant or animal variety.

The revised text of the international Convention for the Protection of New Plant Varieties (UPOV) was accepted by the Hungarian Parliament by Act LI of 2002. Chapter XIII of the Patent Act regulates plant varieties.[1108]

362. The Patent Act defines the concept of a plant variety.

A plant variety means any plant grouping within a single botanical taxon of the lowest known rank, which grouping, irrespective of whether the conditions for the grant of a plant variety are fully met, can be:

(a) defined by the expression of the characteristics that results from a given genotype or combination of genotypes;
(b) distinguished from any other plant grouping by the expression of at least one of the said characteristics; and
(c) considered as a unit with regard to its suitability for being propagated unchanged.[1109]

'Propagating material' shall mean entire plants, seeds, or parts of plants that can be used to cultivate entire plants or produce them by other means.[1110]

Varieties of all botanical genera and species, including, *inter alia*, hybrids between genera or species, may form the object of plant variety rights.[1111]

Species shall mean species of plants, and also groupings and subdivisions of species of plants.

Plant variety protection valid in Hungary can be obtained by filing a national application or for the territory of the European Union – by filing an application for a Community plant variety right if the plant variety meets the legal requirements.

1106. E. Szarka, 'A Biotechnológia Fejlodése a Szabadalmaztatás Tükrében', in *Biotechnológiai Találmányok Oltalma*, ed. M. Bendzsel (Budapest: Magyar Szabadalmi Hivatal, 2001), 16.
1107. Article 6(4) of the Patent Act.
1108. J. Kürtössy, 'A Biotechnologiai Találmányok Szabadalmi Oltalmának Magyarországi JogiSzabályozása', in *Biotechnológiai Találmányok Oltalma*, ed. M. Bendzsel (Budapest: Magyar Szabadalmi Hivatal, 2001), 91.
1109. Article 105(a) of the Patent Act.
1110. Article 105(b), *ibid.*
1111. Article 106(2), *ibid.*

The application for national plant variety protection can be filed with the office, while the application for a Community plant variety right can be submitted directly to the Community Plant Variety Office (CPVO).

It is important to emphasize that plant variety protection granted by the Hungarian Intellectual Property Office is not identical with state registration granted by the Central Agricultural Office.[1112] The first ensures exclusive rights for its owner, while the second is a precondition for allowing public production of the plant variety and ensures its indication on the national list of varieties. Accordingly, remuneration for the breeder can only be enforced in the case of plant variety protection.

§3. Conditions of Protection

363. The conceptual criteria of plant variety protection are as follows:

(a) Distinctness.
(b) Uniformity.
(c) Stability.
(d) Novelty.
(e) Registerable denomination.

The distinctness, uniformity and stability are the biological preconditions of protection, thus the novelty and of special content and the registerable denomination are requirements of legal character.

Plant variety rights shall be granted for varieties that are distinct, uniform, stable, and new.[1113]

The distinctness, uniformity and stability must be assessed either during state registration or on the basis of experiments that is technical, testing carried out for the purposes of procedure to grant plant variety protection.

In Hungary, the examination of distinctness, uniformity, and stability shall be examined by the National Institute for Agricultural Quality Control in the so-called DUS testing: The requirements of DUS have been involved in the UPOV guidelines. The duration of the examination is:

(a) at least two breeding seasons that can be evaluated (four years);
(b) one growing cycle (perennial plants);
(c) three years after the fruit-bearing period (ligneous plants).[1114]

The variety can be deemed to be distinct if it clearly differs by its characteristic expressed from the given genotype or combination of genotypes from the other variety whose existence is commonly known at the date of priority. The distinctness which separates the plant variety from other varieties is a matter of common knowledge at the date of priority. It may be characterized essentially in a visually observable

1112. Kürtössy, 'A Biotechnologiai Találmányok', 91.
1113. Article 106(1) of the Patent Act.
1114. Fáber & Gorkáné, 'Növényfajta oltalom', 43.

morphological characteristic of the variety, but it may also be expressed in other measurable features as well, such as the azulene content of chamomile varieties.[1115]

The existence of a variety shall be deemed to be a matter of common knowledge particularly if:

(a) it was the object of a plant variety right or entered in an official register of plant varieties;
(b) an application for the granting of a plant variety right in its respect, or for its entering in such an official register, or state approval was filed, or provided the application has led to the granting or entering in the meantime.

The distinctness must always be assessed with respect to the variety that most closely resembles the examined variety.

The important characteristics taken into account on the course of examination of distinctness are principally independent of the effects of the environment and enable a clear and detailed description of the plant variety.

364. A variety shall be deemed stable if the expressions of the characteristics that are included in the examination for distinctness as well as any others used for the variety description remain unchanged after repeated propagation or, in the case of a particular cycle of propagation, at the end of each such cycle. The criterion of stability refers to a demand of temporal sameness.

365. Uniformity is a synonym of heterogeneity and unity. In the course of stability, the propagating materials or seed supplied with the application are put in long-term storage, and then they are sown together with fresh seeds of the last propagation.

The individual plant varieties shall exhibit, after each propagation or, in the case of propagation cycle, after each such cycle, the same distinctive characteristics as those sown by the plants deriving from the propagating material.

A variety shall be deemed to be uniform if, subject to the variation that may be expected from the particular features of its propagation, it is sufficiently uniform in the expression of those characteristics that are included in the examination for distinctness, as well as any others used for the variety description. The uniformity of plant variety refers to spatial steadiness of invention.

The criterion of uniformity shall be deemed as not an absolute requirement. In the case of varieties regarded as uniform, the observed characteristics vary subject to the different types deriving from the peculiarities of propagation and to the conditions of fertilization.

366. The variety is recognized to be new if it has not been offered for sale or marketed with the consent of the breeder or his successor in title:

(a) in the country earlier than one year before the date of priority;
(b) or earlier than six years in the case of trees and vines;
(c) or earlier than four years in the case of other plants.

1115. Pintz, *Táláld fel magad*, 216.

The novelty of the plant variety shall be considered as a commercial novelty. That means the plant variety has not been offered in sale or marketed with the consent of breeder or his or her successor in title within one, four or six years.[1116]

The assessment of novelty of plant variety considerably differs to invention for industrial purposes. The novelty shall be recognized by the office on the basis of the applicant's declaration covering the requirements of the Patent Act.[1117]

The criterion of novelty means whether or not, the breeder or successor in title – after having available the plant variety to the public by sale – files an application for plant variety within a specified time limit.

The sale of the plant variety may be considered as prejudicial, an act prejudicial to the novelty. The offering for sale of a plant variety has no significance in this respect. The display of the plant variety at a fair or exhibition is not prejudicial to novelty.[1118] The advertising of a plant variety in a catalogue of the marketing is not prejudicial to novelty. Any disposition for the purposes of exploitation of the variety is an act prejudicial to novelty after the date specified in the Patent Act.

367. Nevertheless, the plant variety shall have:

(a) a suitable denomination;
(b) it shall be reported in accordance with the conditions prescribed by the Patent Act.

Each plant variety shall have a suitable denomination designated. The variety of denomination shall not be deemed suitable if:

(a) it is identical or may be confused with a variety denomination under which another variety of the same or a closely related species is entered;
(b) its use is likely to violate the prior right of a third party;
(c) it is liable to mislead or to cause confusion concerning the characteristics, the value or the identity of the variety, or the identity of the breeder;
(d) it contains only numerical characters, unless it is common practice for designating the varieties;
(e) it is liable to give offence or is contrary to public policy.[1119]

The variety denomination can consist of:

(1) any word;
(2) combination of words;
(3) words and numbers; or
(4) combination of words and numbers, with or without a meaning, provided that such a denomination makes the identification of the plant variety possible.[1120]

1116. Fáber & Gorkáné, 'Növényfajta oltalom', 51.
1117. Article 19(2) of the Patent Act.
1118. Faber & Gorkáné, 'Növényfajta oltalom', 52.
1119. Article 107(2) of the Patent Act.
1120. Fáber & Gorkáné, 'Növényfajta oltalom', 51.

§4. Formalities (Procedure for Grant and Obtaining Protection)

368. 368. The application for national plant variety protection can be filed with the Hungarian Intellectual Property Office, while the application for a Community plant variety right can be submitted directly in the CPVO.

Protection is established as a result of the granting procedure under the competency of the relevant authority. In the procedure for obtaining plant variety protection, a *patent attorney* or an attorney-at-law can be appointed as representative.

The following procedures shall fall within the competence of the Hungarian Intellectual Property Office concerning plant variety rights:

(a) granting of plant variety rights;
(b) declarations of exhaustion and revalidation of plant variety rights;
(c) declaration of nullity of plant variety rights;
(d) cancellation of plant variety rights and denominations;
(e) registration of applications for plant variety rights and of the rights granted, including matters concerning the maintenance of such supply of official notice in connection with plant variety rights.[1121]

The plant variety application may be filed electronically too.

369. The procedure for the granting of a plant variety right shall commence upon having the application submitted to the Hungarian Intellectual Property Office[1122] An application for the granting of a plant variety right shall contain:

(a) a request for registration;
(b) a statement concerning the novelty of the variety;
(c) a final description based on the results of the technical examination to determine compliance with the provisions of the Patent Act related to distinctness, uniformity, stability and novelty of plant variety;
(d) the denomination of the variety, the Hungarian and Latin name of the species; and
(e) other travel documents as may be required.

Applications for plant variety rights shall be prepared in conformity with the formal requirements laid down in specific other legislation.

Applications for plant variety rights shall be subject to a fee payable within two months following the date of application. With respect to any foreign-language enclosure submitted with an application, the Hungarian translation of, the provisional designation of the variety, and the Hungarian name of the species shall be submitted within four months following the date of application.

370. An application for a plant variety right shall pertain to a single plant variety.[1123]

1121. Article 114/G of the Patent Act.
1122. Article 113/R of the Patent Act.
1123. Article 114/K(1) of the Patent Act.

The date of application for a plant variety right shall be the date on which a valid application is received by the Hungarian Intellectual Property Office and if such application *inter alia* contains the following:

(a) a request for the granting of a plant variety right;
(b) data that can be used to identify the applicant or make contact with the applicant possible;
(c) a provisional designation for the variety regardless of whether or not it complies with the prescribed requirements;
(d) the proposed denomination of the variety;
(e) the Hungarian and Latin name of the species.

The right of priority of an application shall be determined:

(a) in general, by the date of receipt of the application;
(b) the date of application filed outside the domestic territory in cases under the UPOV Convention. Priority under paragraph in conformity with UPOV shall be claimed on the date of application for a plant variety right. The document on which the right of priority is based shall be submitted within four months of the date of application.[1124]

371. Procedure for grant plant variety protection may be divided into five main sections:

(a) preliminary examination;
(b) formal examination;
(c) publication of application and observations;
(d) substantive examination;
(e) grant of patent.

372. Throughout the course of the process, preliminary examination by the Hungarian Intellectual Property Office shall examine whether:

(a) the application satisfies the conditions for confirmation of the date of application (at least the request for grant of protection of the data identifying of applicant, the provisional designation of plant variety, the proposed denomination of variety, the Hungarian and Latin name of species);
(b) the application fee has been paid;
(c) the provisional designation for the variety has been submitted in Hungarian along with the Hungarian name of the variety.[1125]

If the application fee has not been paid and/or the provisional designation for the variety in Hungarian or the Hungarian name of the variety has not been submitted, the Hungarian Intellectual Property Office shall request the applicant to correct these

1124. *Ibid.*, Art. 114/L(2).
1125. Article 114/M(1) of the Patent Act.

deficiencies within the time limit prescribed by this Act failing which the application shall be considered withdrawn.

373. The formal examination[1126] is the second phase of the procedure of the plant variety protection.

If the application for a plant variety right complies with the conditions of preliminary examination, the Hungarian Intellectual Property Office shall, subject to the provisions of the Patent Act examine the application to determine whether it satisfies the formal requirements of plant variety protection, laid down in norm of formalities[1127] related to grant procedure. It is worth mentioning that if the breeder asks in writing to omit the indication of his or her name in the documents, a reference to this effect must be given on a separate sheet. It is checked whether the declaration of novelty of the variety has been filed. It is also examined whether the application has been accompanied by one or more photos of the variety showing preferably the distinctive features and whether the request has been signed by the applicant or his or her representative.

The request for the grant of plant variety protection may also be prepared by completing a form obtained from the office free of charge.

374. The Hungarian Intellectual Property Office shall publish the official notice of applications for plant variety rights.[1128] A plant variety application will be published after expiration of eighteen months from the filing date.

With the publication of the application, a provisional protection starts. Upon publication of the application, the entire file will be open to public inspection. This protection becomes definitive when the definition of grant issued.

If a date of filing can be accorded, the filing fee has been paid, the provisional description in Hungarian and the Hungarian name of the species have been filed, then the application may be published at an earlier date if the applicant so requests.

Payment of the described maintenance fee is due with the publication with the Office notifying the applicant of the publication. Publication shall make by publishing following data in Official Journal of Office:

(a) the name and address of applicant (the representative and the breeder);
(b) the application file number;
(c) the application date and the priority date if the latter is different;
(d) the variety denomination;
(e) the name and Latin name of species; and
(f) the characteristic photo or photos.

After the disclosure of plant variety application, the documents of application may be inspected by anybody. These documents are:

(a) the power of attorney;
(b) the deed of assignment.

1126. Pintz, *Talált fel magad*, 146.

1127. Decree No. 20/2002 (XII.12) IM on the detailed formalities for patent applications, documents filed in relation to European patent applications, European patents and international patent applications for plant variety protection.

1128. Article 114/N of the Patent Act.

The examination report of the variety denomination and the declaration of novelty of variety may be inspected. However, the description of plant variety, documents not communicated to the parties, draft decisions shall not be inspected. Until the publication of the application, only the applicant, his or her representative, and the examining authority can inspect both provisional and final descriptions.

Any person may file with the office observations with regard to the patentability of the plant variety protection, that is, that the plant variety or the relevant application does not satisfy any requirement of protectability. Such observations will be taken into consideration during the substantive examination.

375. The Substantive Examination of Applications for Plant Variety Rights is the most essential part of the examination procedure section.[1129]

The Office shall examine the application for a plant variety right to determine whether:

(a) the requirements of distinctness, uniformity stability and novelty are complied with;
(b) the proposed variety denomination is suitable;
(c) the application is in compliance with the conditions prescribed in the Patent Act.

The requirements of distinctness, uniformity, stability, and novelty shall be determined in the course of state approval or on the basis of the results of the technical examination conducted for the purpose of the granting of a plant variety right.[1130]

The technical examination to examine the distinctness, uniformity, stability, and novelty shall be conducted throughout the country by an agency designated in other specific legislation (examination office).

The results of a technical examination conducted by a foreign office may be taken into consideration upon the consent of that office. If the applicant files an examination report drafted by a foreign office, the Hungarian Intellectual Property Office shall forward this report to the examination office with the statement of consent of the foreign examination office attached. The examination office shall use this examination report subject to the provisions of specific other legislation.

The costs of a technical examination shall be borne by the applicant.[1131]

376. The examination report shall be filed with the Hungarian Intellectual Property Office within four years of the priority date or within three months of the date on which the examination report is communicated, testing whichever expires later.

If the results of the technical examination are not submitted within the three-month period preceding the end of the fourth year from the priority date, the Hungarian Intellectual Property Office shall request the applicant to submit the results within the time limit of four years or provide proof that the examination report has not yet been conveyed. Failure to comply shall be treated as if the applicant has surrendered the temporary plant variety right.

1129. Article 114/R of the Patent Act.
1130. *Ibid.*, Art. 114/R(1).
1131. Guide to Plant Variety Protection (Budapest: Hungarian Patent Office, 2004), 15.

If the application for a plant variety right fails to comply with the requirements of distinctness, uniformity, stability, novelty, and suitable denomination, the Hungarian Intellectual Property Office shall invite the applicant to make the necessary corrections, issue a statement, or divide the application depending on the nature of the transgression.

377. If the plant variety and the relevant application meet all the requirements of the examination, the office shall grant plant variety protection for the subject matter of application. The protection starts on the date of filing with retroactive effect.

The granting of a plant variety right and the denomination of the variety shall be entered into the register of plant variety rights and shall be published in the Official Journal of the considered granted as of the date of the decision on granting. The Hungarian Intellectual Property Office shall send to the examination office a copy of its decision on the granting and on the entry of the denomination into the register.[1132]

The Hungarian Intellectual Property Office shall issue a certificate on the granting of a plant variety right with the official definitive description attached. After the granting of plant variety protection, the relevant documents are accessible to anyone.[1133]

The Hungarian Intellectual Property Office may withdraw or modify its decisions terminating the procedure taken in the plant variety matters only if a request for review is filed and only until such request is transmitted to the court.

§5. Ownership and Transfer: Assignment & Licenses

378. Entitlement to plant variety right shall be vested in the breeder or his or her successor in title. 'Breeder' means the person who bred, discovered, or developed the plant variety. An application for a plant variety right may be filed by a natural or legal person.[1134] Plant variety protection entitles breeders or their legal successors to exclusively exploit plant variety.[1135]

Like ownership of plant variety, this right with an absolute structure can be aliened, inherited, and pledged. Propriety right arising from a plant variety may be separated from breeder's moral rights. Special rules may apply to plant varieties that are created in the course of employment, to assignment of plant varieties, and to license agreements.[1136]

The person who breed or discovered and developed the plant variety shall be deemed to be entitled to the plant variety. The breeder shall be a natural person.[1137]

Unless a final court decision or other official decision rules to the contrary, the right to the plant variety shall belong to the person who filed the application with earliest date of priority.

1132. Kürtössy, 'A Biotechnologiai Találmányok', 94.
1133. Pintz, *Találd fel magad*, 147.
1134. In accordance with Art. 25 of the Patent Act, the rights originating from an invention and from patent protection may be assigned, transferred, and encumbered, with the exception of the rights attached to the person of the inventor. This rule also affects the plant varieties under protection.
1135. Faber & Gorkáné, 'Növémyfajta Oltalom', 21.
1136. *Ibid.*, 22.
1137. *Ibid.*, 44.

If two or more persons have created a plant variety jointly, the right to plant variety shall belong to them or their successors in title jointly. When two or more persons are entitled to the right, it shall be deemed to belong to them equally unless otherwise provided.

The claims for entitlement of a plant variety are the inherent right of breeder.[1138]

379. A plant variety created under employment obligation (hereinafter: 'service plant variety') is a plant variety created by a person, who by reason of his or her employment, is under the obligation to develop solutions in the field of the given species of plant.

Under current regulations, a service plant variety can be created only within the framework of a labour relationship. The conceptual criteria of the service plant variety are as follows:[1139]

(a) an existing relationship between breeder and employer;
(b) within the required labour relationship, the breeder shall be obliged to develop protectable plant varieties;
(c) the elaboration or creation of distinct, uniform, stable and new plant variety to be realized by the breeder should be in the field of the plant concerned.[1140]

As successor in title of the breeder, the employer becomes the holder of plant variety in the case of a service plant variety.

The inventor of an employer plant variety is entitled to remuneration on the basis of the utilization of a protected creation.[1141] As for the amount, duration, and the remittance of remuneration, the contract between the parties shall be most decisive. Accordingly, legal proceedings concerning remuneration are settled within the frame civil law contracts.

380. The inherent rights of the breeder, claims for entitlement to a plant variety right, and the cases when varieties are discovered under any form of employment relationship and the related remuneration shall fall within the scope of the Patent Act, which are related to the moral right of inventors, joint authorship service, and employment invention.

381. Chapter III of the Patent Act regulates the license agreements (exploitation contracts). The license agreement of a plant variety shall be interpreted as follows: Under a contract of exploitation of plant variety (plant variety license contract), the holder of plant variety licenses the right to exploit a plant variety with the person exploiting the invention (licensee) is required to pay royalties. The Patent Act sets out only the most important rules of the license agreement.[1142]

1138. Concerning the moral rights, the claim to plant variety protection and the remuneration of breeder, the rules of the Patent Act shall apply.
1139. According to Art. 108(5) of the Patent Act the rules of service patents shall apply *mutatis mutandis*.
1140. Guide to Plant Variety Protection (Budapest: Hungarian Patent Office, 2004), 22.
1141. Tattay, *A Szellemi Alkotások joga*, 319.
1142. Lontai et al., *A Szellemi Alkotások joga*, 336.

The holder of the plant variety shall guarantee for the whole duration of the license contract that no third parties hold rights in the preventing or limiting exercise of the right of exploitation.

The holder of plant variety shall also guarantee the technical feasibility of the given plant variety and shall maintain the plant variety protection. During the term of the plant variety right, the holder must take measures to ensure the continuing existence of the plant variety is unaltered.

382. A right of exploitation of licensee of plant variety may be exclusive or non-exclusive; the license contract shall terminate, with effect for the future, when the contractual period expires or when specified circumstances occur or when the patent expires.

Under the international norms of patent rights, the economic rights are constituted as generally transferable in contrast with moral rights, which are not transferable. In harmony with Hungarian copyright law, the economic rights of a plant variety may be assigned. Hungarian patent law recognizes the validity of assignment of plant variety protection.

The economic rights of plant variety shall be passed on through inheritance, and the author is free to dispose of them in the case of his or her death.

Transfer of a plant variety right by assignment can only be made to successors on the basis of the Patent Act.[1143] Transfer of a plant variety right by assignment can only be made to Hungarian nationals and other successors listed in Articles 108(3), (4) of the Patent Act.[1144]

If the holder of a plant variety right has obtained Community plant variety rights for the same plant variety after plant variety rights were granted, renewal fees shall not be charged up to the expiry of the Community plant variety rights in question. If the Community plant variety right expires after the expiry of the plant variety rights, the holder shall be entitled to request revalidation of the plant variety rights.[1145]

Contracts for the exploitation of plant varieties and contracts for the assignment of plant variety rights shall be subject to the provisions of the Patent Act relating to license agreements shall apply.

Pursuant to Article 114(1) of Patent Act, rights deriving from plant varieties and plant variety protection may not be transferred to any person who cannot be granted plant variety protection. In any other matters pertaining to the succession in title, the provisions on the transfer of Laws of Patent Act shall apply *mutatis mutandis*.

1143. Articles 10 and 25(1) of the Patent Act.

1144. Plant variety right may be obtained:

(a) Nationals of Hungary or have their private or corporate domiciles in Hungary;

(b) Nationals of a state or of a member of 'UPOV Convention' or have their private or corporate domiciles in such Member State;

(c) on the basis of other international agreements and under the principle of reciprocity.

1145. Article 114(2) of the Patent Act.

§6. Scope of Exclusive Rights

383. The exclusive rights of breeders of plant varieties can be divided into moral and economic rights. Like ownership of plant variety, this right has an absolute structure, which can be aliened, inherited, and pledged. Propriety right arising from a plant variety may be separated from breeder's moral rights.

Entitlement to plant variety right shall be vested in the breeder or his or her successor in title.

Breeder[1146] means the person who bred, discovered, or developed the plant variety. The breeder may be a person who has created the variety in a traditional manner, by breeding, or has developed a new variety from a naturally occurring variety discovered by him or her or by another person. Breeding encompasses the development of varieties both by essentially biological processes (i.e., typically by crossing or selection) and by genetic engineering, by means of molecular biology. Only a natural person may be a breeder.[1147]

384. The moral rights, as inherent rights of breeder are protected by Patent Act.[1148] The moral rights of breeder of plant variety consist of several different elements:

(a) the right to acknowledgement of authorship related to plant variety;
(b) the breeder of plant variety shall have the right to be mentioned as such in patent document;
(c) the right to disclosure of application of the plant variety;
(d) the right to keep secret the plant variety.

Applications for a plant variety right may be filed by natural or legal persons:

(a) provided they are nationals of Hungary or have their private or corporate domiciles in Hungary;
(b) if they are nationals of a state or of a member of the International Convention for the Protection of New Varieties and Plants (hereinafter: 'UPOV Convention') or have their private or corporate domiciles in such Member State;
(c) In addition to national applications and applications obtained from Member States of the UPOV mentioned above plant variety rights may also be obtained on the basis of other international agreements and under the principle of reciprocity.

385. The economic (pecuniary) rights[1149] of holder of plant variety are as follows:

(a) right to a plant variety protection that is, the right to a patent shall belong to the breeder;
(b) exclusive right to exploit the plant variety;
(c) the right to conclusion of exploitation contracts;
(d) the right to assignment, transfer and pledge of plant variety;

1146. Faber.Gorkáné, *Növényfajta oltalom,* 21.
1147. Article 108 of Patent Act.
1148. Lontai et al., *A Szellemi Alkotások joga*, 194.
1149. Csécsy, *A Szellemi Alkotások joga*, 102.

(e) on the basis of the exclusive rights of exploitation the holder of plant variety shall be entitled to prevent any person not having his consent to exploitation of the plant variety.

The right to exploitation of plant variety has special features.

386. The holder of plant variety right shall have exclusive rights for the exploitation of the variety[1150] that is, to the production and multiplication of the propagating material of the protected variety, conditioning for the purpose of propagation, offering for sale, selling or other marketing, exporting, importing and stocking for any of these purposes.[1151]

According to Article 112 of Patent Act, the breeder of the plant variety shall be entitled to a remuneration (remuneration for the breeder) under the provisions relating to remuneration for inventions of maintenance of the plant variety, use of variety denominations.

The holder shall be entitled to prohibit anybody who, without his authorization, is engaged in any of the following acts in respect of the propagation material of the protected variety:

(a) production or reproduction (multiplication);
(b) conditioning for the purpose of propagation;
(c) offering for sale;
(d) selling or other marketing;
(e) exporting from the country;
(f) importing to the country;
(g) stocking for any of the purposes mentioned above.[1152]

The holder may take action against any person who utilizes without his consent the harvested material of plant variety received through unauthorized use of the propagation material and products obtained directly from such harvested material through its unauthorized use.[1153]

The exclusive rights of plant variety protection extends to varieties which are essentially derived from the variety in respect of which plant variety right has been granted, where this variety is not itself an essentially derived variety.

387. A variety shall be deemed to be essentially derived from another variety (hereinafter: 'the initial variety'), when:

(a) it is predominantly derived from the initial variety, or from a variety that is itself predominantly derived from the initial variety, while it retains essentially the expression of the characteristics that results from the genotype or combination of genotypes of the initial variety;
(b) it is distinct, from the initial and protected variety; and

1150. Article 109(1) of Patent Act.
1151. Faber & Gorkáné, 'Növémyfajta Oltalom', 45.
1152. Article 109(2) of the Patent Act.
1153. Faber & Gorkáné, 'Növémyfajta Oltalom', 45.

(c) except for the differences that result from the act of derivation, it conforms essentially to the initial variety in the expression of the characteristics that results from the genotype or combination of genotypes of the initial variety.[1154]

The right of exploitation – as mentioned above – is also due to the holder with respect to essentially derived varieties. This means that the protection of plant variety extends:[1155]

(a) to varieties which are not distinct referring to protected variety;
(b) to varieties whose production requires the repeated use of the protected variety.

Judgment of the essentially derived variety still calls for the clarification of lot of qualifications problems.

By virtue of Article 113(1) of Patent Act, the holder shall be required to maintain the plant variety during the period of plant variety protection.

In accordance with Article 113(2) when a variety is offered for sale or is marketed, it shall be permitted to associate a trademark, a geographical indication, or other similar indication with the registered variety denomination. If such an indication is so associated, the denomination must nevertheless be easily recognizable.

§7. Limitations of the Scope of Protection: Compulsory Licenses

388. The limitations of plant variety protection concern acts made privately outside of economic activity as well as acts done for experimental purposes. The exclusive rights of plant variety protection does not extend to these acts.

The territorial validity and the term of plant variety protection are limited that means the protection is valid only in the country or international organization where it was granted.

The exclusive right of exploitation shall not extend to:

(a) acts done privately and for non-commercial purposes;
(b) acts done for experimental purposes in connection with the plant variety;
(c) acts done for the purpose of breeding other varieties.[1156]

The main categories of delimitations relating to plant variety protection are as follows:

(a) acts done privately, non-commercial and experimental purposes; the use of plant varieties for the purposes of breeding other varieties;
(b) the farmers' privilege;
(c) exhaustion;
(d) mandatory license.[1157]

1154. Article 109(5) of the Patent Act.
1155. Faber & Gorkáné, 'Növémyfajta Oltalom', 46.
1156. Article 109(6)(a), (b), (c) of the Patent Act.
1157. Chapter IV of the Patent Act related to mandatory licenses shall apply.

389. The farmers' privilege shall be mentioned first. First protected plant variety can be used for the purposes of breeding other varieties without the consent of the author.[1158]

For the purposes of safeguarding agricultural production, exclusive right of exploitation shall not extend to farmers using for propagating purposes in the field, on their own holding the product of the harvest which they have obtained by planting, propagating material of a variety other than a hybrid or synthetic variety that is covered by a plant variety right.[1159]

The farmers' privilege protects first of all the interests of small holders and small farmers. The farmers may use the given privilege against an equitable remuneration and in the framework of a strong monitoring system.[1160]

390. Exhaustion of exclusive rights[1161] of exploitation of protected plant varieties has specific features. Exclusive rights of exploitation of protected plant varieties shall not extend to acts concerning any material (propagation material, harvested material, and products directly obtained from harvested material)[1162] of the protected variety, or of the varieties:

(a) that are essentially derived from the variety in respect of which the plant variety right has been granted;
(b) that are not distinct;
(c) whose production requires the repeated use of a protected variety that has been disposed of to others by the holder, or with his or her express consent inside the European Economic Area, or any material derived from the said material.[1163]

The exclusive right of exploitation shall also extend to the acts of exploitation of plant variety, if they involve further propagation of the plant variety in question or if they involve an export of variety constituents for propagation purposes into a third country that does not protect varieties of the plant genus or species to which the variety belongs, except where the exported material is for final consumption purposes.[1164]

391. The Patent Act involves the general provisions on compulsory licenses grantable for lack of exploitation and in respect of dependent plant varieties. An applicant for a compulsory license shall be required to prove that the requirements for a compulsory license have been complied with and further that:

(a) the patentee was unwilling to grant a voluntary license to exploit the patent under appropriate conditions and in a reasonable period of time;
(b) he or she is able to exploit the invention to the required extent.

1158. Article 109(7) of the Patent Act.
1159. Faber & Gorkáné, 'Növémyfajta Oltalom', 46.
1160. Article 47 of the Patent Act.
1161. *Ibid.*, Art. 110.
1162. Exhaustion of rights is a general rule on the domain of the intellectual property, which concerns not only copyright but also the objects of industrial property.
1163. Article 110(1) of the Patent Act.
1164. *Ibid.*, Art. 110(2).

The compulsory license of a plant variety shall not afford an exclusive right of exploitation. The holder of a compulsory license shall have the same rights as the holder of plant protection in regard to the maintenance of the patent and the exercise of the rights deriving from protection.[1165]

When the holder of a protected plant variety cannot exploit it without infringing a prior plant variety right, at the request of the holder of such pending plant variety, a compulsory license shall be granted. In the case of compulsory license the licensee may use the plant variety to the extent consistent with the exploitation right of the dominant plant variety right. The compulsory license shall constitute a significant technical progress of considerable economic interest compared to the plant variety protected under the dominant plant variety right.[1166]

§8. Duration of Protection

392. The term of the final plant variety right shall be generally twenty-five years and thirty years, calculated from the year of grant, in the case of varieties of vine and tree species and twenty-five years for other plant varieties.[1167]

The term of protection is not calculated from the date of application, but from the date of the grant of the protection.[1168]

The holder is obliged to maintain the variety. During the term of the plant variety right, the holder must take measures to ensure the continuing unaltered existence of the plant variety.[1169]

The registered denomination of a protected variety must be used when it is offered or disposed of to others for commercial purposes, even after the termination of the plant variety right, unless such use is likely to violate the prior right of a third party.[1170]

393. The plant variety protection shall cease in the case of surrender, cancellation, or because the maintenance fees have not been paid.

By virtue of Article 38 of the Patent Act, provisional plant variety protection shall lapse:

(a) if the plant variety application definitively rejected;
(b) if the applicant has surrendered protection;
(c) if the fee for the provisional protection has been not paid.[1171]

Definitive plant variety protection shall lapse:

1165. Article 114/B(1) of the Patent Act.
1166. According to Art. 114/B(1) of the Patent Act, from the point of view of exhaustion of plant variety right, the 'material' means propagation material, harvested material and products directly obtained from harvested material.
1167. Article 111 of the Patent Act.
1168. Pintz, *Talál fel magad*, 141.
1169. Article 113(1) of the Patent Act.
1170. Article 113(3), *ibid.*
1171. Faber & Gorkáné, 'Növémyfajta Oltalom', 53.

(a) if the annual fees have not been paid by the end of the period grace, on the day, following the application date;
(b) if the holder surrenders the protection, on the day following receipt of the surrender or at an earlier date specified by the person surrendering of protection;
(c) if the plant variety protection recorded is, with retrospective effect to the filing date of protection;[1172]
(d) if the plant variety cancelled – with retroactive effect to the date instituting the procedure for cancellation or the date at which the conditions for cancellation have already existed, or whichever is earlier.

394. The plant variety right shall be declared null and void retroactively if it is established:

(a) that the conditions of distinctiveness and novelty are not completed;
(b) that when the granting of the plant variety right has been essentially based upon information and documents furnished by the applicant or his or her successor in title;
(c) that the conditions of homogeneity and stability were not complied;
(d) that the right has been granted to a person who is not legally entitled to it, unless it is transferred to the person who is so entitled.[1173]

The plant variety protection shall be cancelled if after the grant of protection, the condition of uniformity and stability are no longer fulfilled,[1174] and if the holder after being requested to do so, does not verify the maintenance of the variety.[1175]

The variety denomination may also be cancelled in the procedure. The registered variety denomination shall be cancelled if the holder, after being requested to do so and within a prescribed period, does not verify that it fulfils the condition of a variety denomination suitable for identification.[1176]

§9. Infringement and Remedies

395. According to Article 114/C of the Patent Act, unauthorized use of protected varieties and the infringement of plant variety rights shall be governed by the provisions of the Patent Act in respect of infringement of patent protection.[1177]

Infringement of plant variety is defined as follows: on the basis of an exclusive right of exploitation, the holder shall be entitled to prohibit anybody who, without his authorization, is engaged in any of the following acts in respect of the propagation material of the protected variety:

1172. *Ibid.*
1173. Article 114/D of the Patent Act.
1174. *Ibid.*, Art. 114/E(1).
1175. *Ibid.*, Art. 114/E(3).
1176. Faber & Gorkáné, 'Növémyfajta Oltalom', 54.
1177. Articles 34–36 of the Patent Act shall be applied.

(a) production or reproduction (multiplication);
(b) conditioning for the purpose of propagation;
(c) offering for sale;
(d) selling or other marketing;
(e) exporting from the country;
(f) importing to the country;
(g) stocking for any of the purposes mentioned in paragraphs (a)–(f).[1178]

The provisions of unauthorized exploitation[1179] shall apply with regard to harvested material obtained through the unauthorized use of the propagation material of the protected variety and to products obtained directly through the unauthorized use of such harvested material, if the holder did not have reasonable opportunity to exercise his right in relation to the said propagation material or the harvested material.[1180]

396. The provisions of unauthorized exploitation of plant varieties shall also apply in relation to:

(a) varieties that are essentially derived from the variety in respect of which the plant variety right has been granted, where this variety is not itself an essentially derived variety;
(b) varieties that are not distinct in accordance with the provisions of the Patent Act from the protected variety;[1181] and
(c) varieties whose production requires the repeated use of the protected variety.[1182]

397. The holder of the plant variety protection may, according to the circumstances of the case, have recourse to the following civil remedies:

(a) he or she may request that the fact of infringement be declared by the court;
(b) he or she may request an injunction that the infringer cease his infringement or any acts directly threatening with it;
(c) he or she may demand that the infringer give information on the identity of person involved in the production and distribution of the infringing goods or the provision of their channels of distribution;
(d) he or she may demand satisfaction from the infringer by way of a declaration or by other appropriate means; if necessary, the declaration shall be made public by the infringer or at his or her expense. At the request of the patentee, the court may order that its decision be made public at the expense of the infringer. The court shall decide on the manner of the publicity. Publicity shall mean, in particular, publication in a national daily newspaper or on the Internet;
(e) he or she may require surrender of the enrichment obtained by the infringement of the plant variety;

1178. Article 109(2) of the Patent Act.
1179. Tattay, *A Szellemi Alkotások joga*, 319.
1180. Article 109(3) of the Patent Act.
1181. Article 106(3) of the Patent Act.
1182. *Ibid.*, Art. 109(4).

(f) he or she may request the seizure, the transfer to a specific person, the recall, and the definitive removal from the channels of commerce, or destruction, of the infringing products, as well as the means and materials exclusively or principally used for infringement;
(g) the plant variety holder may also claim damages under the rules of civil liability.[1183]

Seizure of the means and material used in infringing activities and of the infringing activities and the infringing goods shall be admissible even if they are not in the possession of the infringer, but the holder knew or had reasonable grounds to know about infringement.[1184]

§10. Overlapping and Relations to Other Intellectual Property Rights

398. The Patent Act excludes patent protection for plants. Plants and processes for preparing plants that are essentially biological cannot be patented.

In accordance with Article 6(4) of Patent Act, the following shall not be patentable:

(a) plant varieties[1185] and animal varieties;
(b) essential biological processes for the production of plants or animals.

However, an independent variety of patent protection has been established within the Patent Act. Inventions relating to plants can be patented if the technical feasibility of the invention is not confined to a particular plant variety. This means that the patent protection can overlap with plant variety protection if the technical feasibility of the invention concerns not only a plant but also several plant varieties.

In accordance with Article 6(6) of the Patent Act, plant varieties shall receive variety right protection in accordance with the provisions of Chapter XIII of Patent Act.

The Patent Act defines the concept of a plant variety. Plant variety means any plant grouping within a single botanical taxon of the lowest known rank, which grouping, irrespective of whether the conditions for the grant of a plant variety right are fully met, can be:

(a) defined by the expression of the characteristics that results from a given genotype or combination of genotypes;
(b) distinguished from any other plant grouping by the expression of at least one of the said characteristics; and
(c) considered as a unit with regard to its suitability for being propagated unchanged.[1186]

1183. Article 35(2) of the Patent Act.
1184. Pintz, *Találd fel magad*, 141.
1185. Article 105(a) of the Patent Act.
1186. *Ibid.*, Art. 105(a).

399. The cumulative protection of patents and plant varieties is permissible. The plant variety must be given a variety denomination suitable for identification. The variety denomination can consist of:

(a) any word;
(b) combination of words;
(c) words and numbers or;
(d) combination of words and numbers, with or without a meaning, provided that such denomination makes the identification of the plant variety possible.[1187]

The registered denomination of a protected variety may be associated with a trademark, trade name, or similar indication when it is offered or disposed of to others for commercial purposes. This associated denomination must be easily recognizable as such.

The denomination of plant varieties cannot conflict with name of natural person, registered trademark, or trade name. This means that the cumulative protection denominations of plant varieties and trademarks and trade names may be permissible, if the owner of the trademark (trade name) and plant variety are the same person.

1187. Faber & Gorkáné, 'Növémyfajta Oltalom', 51.

Chapter 8. Chip Protection

§1. Sources: Legislations

400. The current legislation of protection of the chips is Act XXXIX of 1991 on the protection of the topographies of microelectronic semiconductor products (hereinafter: 'Chip Protection Act').

The topographies of microelectronic semiconductor products in property industry have several denominations: layout-designs, topographies, integrated circuits, semiconductor chips, and chips. The topographies of microelectronic semiconductor products are called 'chips' hereinafter in this book.

The intellectual property protection in respect to chip protection has come into the limelight of international interest in the last few years, which unambiguously justified the consideration of different international solutions. The Topography Act considered the following points:

> The Washington Treaty on Intellectual Property in Respect of Integrated Circuits that was accepted within the scope of WIPO; the draft of TRIPS to the General Agreement on Tariffs and Trade, the directives of the Council of European Communities and the national statutory of several European countries and the United States.

Act XXXIX of 1991 on the chip protection (on the protection of the topographies of microelectronic semiconductor products) introduced a sui generis protection for semiconductor chips that follows the Topography Directive.

The legal sources[1188] of chip protection may be divided into three categories:

> Hungarian laws and regulations, European Community laws and Regulations, and international treaties and conventions.

By virtue of Act CXLVIII of 2010, the name of Hungarian Patent Office was changed to Hungarian Intellectual Property Office (hereinafter: 'Office') as of 1 January 2011 to better reflect its competence extending to activities related to all form of industrial property protection as well as to the field of copyright.

401. Hungarian laws and regulations:

- Act XXXIX of 1991 on the protection of the topographies of microelectronic semiconductor products; (hereinafter: 'Chip Protection Act').
- Government Decree No. 147/2007 (VI 26) on the detailed rules concerning electronic filing of certain documents in industrial property procedures.
- Decree No. 19/2005 (IV 12) GKM on the Fees for Administrative Services in Industrial Property Procedures before the Hungarian Patent Office.

1188. Pintz, *Talald fel magad*, 311.

- Decree No. 19/1991 (XII 28) IM (Minister of Justice) on the detailed formal requirements of the application for protection of the topographies of microelectronic semiconductor products.

402. European Community laws and Regulations:

- Council Directive 87/54/EEC of 16 December 1986 on the legal protection of topographies of semiconductor products (hereinafter: 'Topography Directive').

403. Treaties and conventions:

- Paris Convention for the Protection of Industrial Property – Promulgated by Law Decree No. 18 of 1970; (hereinafter: 'Paris Convention').
- Agreement on Trade-Related Aspects of Intellectual Property rights- Promulgated by Act IX of 1998 in Hungary; (hereinafter: 'TRIPS Agreement').

§2. Subject Matter of Protection

404. The subject matter of protection is the topography of microelectronic semiconductor products (chips).

Topography (chip) means the three-dimensional disposition of a microelectronic semiconductor product or such a three-dimensional disposition prepared for a semiconductor product intended for manufacture.[1189]

The topography may be expressed by several elements and shall have at least an active element.[1190] The Article 1(2) of Chip Protection Act defines the concept of topography as:

> Topography (chip) means the three-dimensional disposition, however expressed, of the elements, at least one of which is an active element, and of some or all of the interconnections of a microelectronic semiconductor product, or such a three-dimensional disposition prepared for a semiconductor product intended for manufacture.

The scope of protection shall be determined by illustration of the registered topography. Protection shall extend also to original parts of the topography (chip) which may be used independently and to devices which inseparably bear the topography.[1191]

Protection shall not extend to:

(a) concepts, processes, and systems on which the topography (chip) is based, or any information stored in a semiconductor product;

1189. Lontai et al., *A Szellemi Alkotások joga*, 246.
1190. Pintz, *Találd fel magad*, 164.
1191. Article 7(2) and (3) of the Chip Protection Act.

(b) reproduction of the topography (chip) for purposes of analysis, evaluation, or teaching and original topography created on the basis thereof.[1192]

§3. Conditions of Protection

405. Protection shall be granted to the topography of microelectronic semiconductor products, (chip) if it is original.[1193] A topography (chip) shall be original if it is the result of its creator's own intellectual effort and is not commonplace in the industry at the time its creation.[1194] The simple reproduction of another topography (chip) may not be considered original.

A topography (chip) consisting of an arrangement of commonplace parts shall be eligible for protection, insofar as the arrangement is original. The originality of the topography is not examined by the office.

§4. Formalities (Procedure for Grant and Obtaining Protection)

406. The Hungarian Intellectual Property Office (hereinafter: 'Office') shall be competent to deal with matters concerning:

(a) registration of the topography (chip);
(b) declaration of the lapse of protection;
(c) nullity of protection;
(d) decision of non-infringement;
(e) interpretation of the illustration of the topography;
(f) recording of protection.[1195]

The application of topography may be filed electronically too.

For the procedure of the Office in matters concerning topography (chip) protection, the provision of the Patent Law and of the Implementing Decree[1196] concerning the procedure of the office in patent matters shall apply with certain exceptions.[1197]

Examination concerns only formal requirements of protection. The Office does not examine the originality of the subject of the application.

The procedure for the registration of topography (chip) shall begin with the filing of an application with the Hungarian Intellectual Property Office[1198] The application

1192. Article 7(4) a) and b), *ibid.*
1193. Article 1(1) of the Chip Protection Act.
1194. Article 1(3), *ibid.*
1195. Article 16 of the Chip Protection Act.
1196. Decree No. 19/1991 (XII 28) IM (Minister of Justice) on the detailed formal requirements of the application for protection of the topographies of microelectronic semiconductor products (chips).
1197. Article 17(4) of the Chip Protection Act.
1198. *Ibid.*, Art. 20(1).

shall contain a request, as well as an illustration suitable for identifying the topography, and other relevant documents.[1199]

Rights can only be based on an application that contains at least the name and address of the applicant, as well as an illustration suitable for identifying the essence of the topography.[1200] In any application, protection may only be sought for a single topography (unity of application).

407. The Hungarian Intellectual Property Office shall examine the application in order to ascertain whether it complies with the following requirements:

(a) the foreign person is entitled to the right of protection of topography (chip);[1201]
(b) the application contains the name and address of applicant, a request; and
(c) illustration suitable for identifying the topography (chip), and other relevant documents;
(d) the application contains a topography (unity of protection).[1202]

If the application is so incomplete that no right can be based on it, that the application contains not the name and address of applicant, and an illustration suitable for identifying the essence of the topography, the application shall be rejected without further procedure.

If the application does not comply with the requirements prescribed related to a foreign applicant, the prescription of application, requirements of topography procedure, and unity of application, the applicant shall be invited to remedy the deficiencies, to make a declaration or to divide the application. If the invitation produces no result, the application shall be rejected.[1203]

If the application complies with the prescribed requirements, the Hungarian Intellectual Property Office shall register the topography (chip), shall issue a document concerning the registered topography, and the registration shall be published in the Gazette of the Office.[1204]

408. In case of rejection of an application for topography (chip) registration, a request for a review of the decision by the Office may be filed with the Metropolitan Court of Justice[1205] within thirty days of the notification of decision. An appeal from a court decision with the Metropolitan Court of Appeal should be lodged within fifteen days.

From the date of registration, any person may inspect the illustration of the registered topography (chip) and can obtain copies of it. Parts of the illustration of the registered topography marked by the applicant as secret shall be available for inspection

1199. *Ibid.*, Art. 20(2).
1200. *Ibid.*, Art. 20(4).
1201. Foreign persons shall be entitled to a right to protection only under an international treaty or in the case of reciprocity. In matters of reciprocity the president of the Hungarian Patent Office shall be competent to give a ruling.
1202. Csécsy, *A Szellemi Alkotások joga*, 167.
1203. *Ibid.*
1204. Article 22(4) of the Chip Protection Act.
1205. Lontai et al., *A Szellemi Alkotások joga*, 247.

only to parties participating in the procedure, on the basis of the decision of the Intellectual Property Office or the court.[1206]

§5. Ownership and Transfer: Assignment & Licenses

409. The right to protection shall belong to the creator or his successor in title. Rights deriving from topography (chip) and from its protection, with the exception of personal rights, may be transferred, assigned, and encumbered. Rights deriving from topography (chip) and from its protection, with the exception of personal rights, may be transferred, assigned, and encumbered.[1207]

On the basis of a contract of exploitation, the owner of the protection grants a license for the exploitation of the topography (chip), in exchange, the exploiter pays royalties.[1208] The rights of topography may also be assigned by contract.[1209]

When the creator of the topography (chip) is, on the basis of his or her employment or by virtue of other legal relationships, under obligation to create topographies (employees' topography), the right to protection shall belong to the employer or the person entitled by other legal relationships. The creator of an employee's topography shall be entitled to remuneration.[1210]

The provisions of the Patent Act and of its Implementing Decree[1211] concerning succession in title, the assignment, the contracts of license, service and employees' topographies (chips) shall apply *mutatis mutandis*.[1212]

§6. Scope of Exclusive Rights

410. The creator is the person who has created the topography (chip). The right to protection shall belong to the creator or his or her successor in title. When several persons have jointly created topography (chip), the right to protection shall jointly belong to them or their successors in title. When several persons have created topography (chip) independently of each other, the right to protection shall belong independently to the creators or their successors in title.[1213]

The rights of the topography (chip) creator may be divided into moral (personal) and economic (pecuniary) rights. The rights of topography owner have absolute character and negative contents.

411. The moral rights of topography (chip) creators are as follows:

1206. Article 18 of the Chip Protection Act.
1207. Article 8(1) of the Chip Protection Act.
1208. Article 8(2), *ibid.*
1209. Lontai et al., *A Szellemi Alkotások joga*, 247.
1210. Article 4(1) and (2) of the Chip Protection Act.
1211. Decree No. 20/2002 (XII.12) on the detailed formalities for patent applications, documents filed in relation to European patent applications, European patents and international patent applications for plant variety protection.
1212. Article 5(2) of the Chip Protection Act.
1213. Article 2(1), (2), and (3) of the Chip Protection Act.

(a) the right to acknowledgement of authorship related to topography (chip);
(b) the topography creator shall have the right to be mentioned as such topography documents;
(c) the right to disclosure of application;
(d) the right to keep secret the topography and authorship.

By virtue of Article 5 of the Topography Act, in any other matters, for the personal rights of the creator of the topography (chip), the provisions of the Patent Act shall apply *mutatis mutandis*.

412. The economic (pecuniary) rights of the creator of topography are as follows:

(a) right to protection, that is the right to a topography (chip) shall belong to the creator;[1214]
(b) exclusive right to exploit the topography (chip). On the basis of the protection, the owner shall have, as provided for legislation the exclusive right to exploit the topography commercially.[1215] Exploitation means reproduction, whether by incorporation in a microelectronic semiconductor product or otherwise, importation for commercial purposes or marketing of the topography or of the semiconductor product incorporating the same;
(c) the right to conclusion of license contracts;[1216]
(d) the right to assignment, transfer, and pledge of a topography (chip);
(e) on the basis of the exclusive rights of exploitation, the topography owner shall be entitled to prevent any person not having his or her consent to exploitation of the topography;[1217]
(f) right to remuneration.[1218] In the case of license agreement, employee and service topography and assignment contract, the holder of the topography is entitled to remuneration. Foreign persons shall be entitled to a right of protection only under an international treaty or in the case of reciprocity. In matters of reciprocity, the president of the Office shall be competent to give a ruling.[1219]

413. The exclusive right of topography owner shall not extend to:

(a) concepts, processes, and systems on which the topography is based, or any information stored in a semiconductor product;
(b) reproduction of the topography for purposes of analysis, evaluation, or teaching and original topography created on the basis thereof;
(c) topography identical with the topography concerned, created independently by a third party.[1220]

1214. The right to topography (chip) may belong to the creator, the applicant, and the natural or legal person.
1215. Csécsy, *A Szellemi Alkotások joga*, 166.
1216. Article 7(1) of the Chip Protection Act.
1217. Lontai et al., *A Szellemi Alkotások joga*, 247.
1218. Tattay, *A Szellemi Alkotások joga*, 32.
1219. Article 3 of the Chip Protection Act.
1220. Article 7(4) of the Chip Protection Act.

414. That means that unlawful use of protected topography (chip) in good faith may not be considered as infringement of topography (chip) protection.[1221] Exploitation shall not be considered as unlawful if a person imports for commercial purposes or markets semiconductor products (chips) incorporating topography, or products incorporating the same, without knowing or having reason to believe that these products contain an unlawfully reproduced topography.[1222]

The use granted by the legal law becomes illegal[1223] from the date that the person originally of good faith knows or has reason to know that the reproduction of the topography was unlawful; he or she may put on the market only the stock on hand or ordered, against the usual royalty payable to the owner of the protection.[1224]

§7. Limitations of the Scope of Protection

415. There are no explicit prescriptions relating to limitation of the scope of protection; however, the general provisions of the patent law limit the topography protection, and the rules of effect if scope of protection involve restrictions concerning the topography protection.[1225]

The main limitations of topography (chip) protection are as follows: The exclusive right of exploitation shall not extend to:

(a) acts done privately or not involved in an economic activity or acts done for experimental purposes relating to the subject matter of the topography protection;
(b) reproduction of the topography for purposes of analysis, evaluation, or teaching and original topography created on the basis thereof;[1226]
(c) to topography identical with the topography concerned, created independently by a third party;
(d) time limit and territorial limit of the protection; the parallel creation with always protected identical topography may be used;
(e) the free exploitation of topography identical with the protected chip, developed independently by a third part is permissible;[1227]
(f) exhaustion,[1228] that is, importation and marketing of the topography or of the semiconductor product incorporating the topography, put on the market by the owner or with his or her consent shall be considered as free exploitation of protected topography.[1229]

1221. Pintz, *A Szellemi Alkotások joga,* 169.
1222. Tattay, *A Szellemi Alkotások joga*, 322.
1223. Article 7(5) of the Chip Protection Act.
1224. Pintz, *A Szellemi Alkotások joga*, 165.
1225. Generally, the rules of the limitations of the scope of protection the rules of patent protection shall be apply.
1226. Article 7(4) b) of the Chip Protection Act.
1227. Article 7(4) c) of the Chip Protection Act.
1228. Lontai et al., *A Szellemi Alkotások joga*, 246.
1229. Article 7(4), i) d) of the Chip Protection Act.

Exploitation shall not be considered as unlawful if a person imports for commercial purposes or markets semiconductor products incorporating topography or of the chip, without knowing or having reason to believe that these products contain an unlawfully reproduced topography.[1230]

§8. Duration of Protection

416. Protection of topography (chip protection) is ten years and shall be established by registration of the topography. The protection may be established:

(a) with retroactive effect from the date of application;[1231] or
(b) from the date of the first commercial exploitation in any country, which is earlier than the filing date. If the protection is established by the first commercial exploitation, the priority can be claimed only within two years from the first commercial exploitation in any country of the topography.[1232]

417. Chapter III regulates the lapse of protection. By virtue of Article 12 of the Topography Act, the chip protection shall lapse:

(a) When the period of protection expires, on the day following the date of expiration.
(b) If the owner surrenders protection, on the day following the receipt of the surrender or at an earlier date specified by a person surrendering the right.
(c) The owner indicated in the Topography Register may surrender the protection by written declaration addressed to the Hungarian Intellectual Property Office. If the surrender affects the rights of third parties based on legislation, on decision of an authority, on a license contract recorded in the Topography Register, or if proceedings are recorded in the Topography Register, it shall only take effect with the consent of the parties concerned.[1233]
(d) If the protection is declared null and void, with retroactive effect to the establishment of the protection.

418. The protection of topography shall be declared null and void[1234] if:

(a) the topography does not satisfy the requirements of originality[1235] laid down in Article 1 of Chip Protection Act;
(b) a foreign person has not been entitled to protection under Article 3;[1236]

1230. Pintz, *Találd fel magad*, 165.
1231. Tattay, *A Szellemi Alkotások joga*, 322.
1232. Article 6(2) of the Chip Protection Act.
1233. Article 13 of the Chip Protection Act.
1234. In the industrial property, literature can be used as others expressions also, as cancellation and revocation.
1235. Article 1 of the Chip Protection Act.
1236. Article 3, *ibid.*

(c) an application in the case in which prior commercial use in respect of the topography is not filed[1237] within two years from the first commercial exploitation, in any country;[1238]
(d) the application does not contain any illustration suitable for identifying the topography.[1239]

§9. Infringement and Remedies

419. Chapter II of Chip Protection Act regulates the topography infringement an infringement of chip protection. The Chip Protection Act distinguishes between the infringements of topography and infringement of topography protection.[1240] The topography infringement may be established as follows:

> Where the subject of an application concerning topography or the subject of a protection has been taken unlawfully from another person, the injured party or his successor in title may claim partial or total assignment of the protection.[1241]

The Infringement of topography protection (chip) shall be interpreted as follows:

(a) any person who unlawfully exploits a chip under protection commits infringement of protection. The unlawful exploitation means the illegal reproduction, importation for commercial purposes or marketing of the topography or of the semiconductor product incorporating the same (chip);[1242]
(b) the licensee of a topography license contract may infringe the rules stipulated in license contract.

In the case of infringement of topography protection, the creator of topography protection has several possibilities of recourse:

(a) on the basis of the Patent Act;
(b) on the basis of the new Penal Code (Law No. C of 2012);[1243]
(c) on the basis of customs procedure.[1244]

420. The owner of chip protection may, according to the circumstances of the case, have recourse[1245] to the following civil remedies:[1246]

1237. Csécsy, *A Szellemi Alkotások joga*, 168.
1238. Article 6(3) of the Chip Protection Act.
1239. Article 20(2), *ibid.*
1240. Lontai et al., *A Szellemi Alkotások joga*, 267.
1241. Article 9 of the Chip Protection Act.
1242. Article 7(1), *ibid.*
1243. Article 388, of new Penal Code (Law No. C of 2012) Violation of Industrial Property Rights.
1244. Act CXXVI of 2003 on the Implementation of Community Customs Law.
1245. Article 35(1) of the Patent Act.
1246. Pintz, *A Szellemi Alkotások joga*, 103.

(a) he or she may request that the fact of infringement be declared by the court;
(b) he or she may request an injunction that the infringer ceases his or her infringement or any acts directly threatening it;
(c) he or she may demand that the infringer give information on the identity of any person/s involved in the production and distribution of the infringing goods or the provision of infringing services and of their channels of distribution;
(d) he or she may demand satisfaction from the infringer by way of a declaration or by other appropriate means; if necessary, the declaration shall be made public by the infringer or at his or her expense. At the request of the patentee, the court may order that its decision be made public at the expense of the infringer. The court shall decide on the manner of the publicity. Publicity shall mean, in particular, publication in a national daily newspaper or on the Internet;
(e) he or she may require surrender of the enrichment obtained by the infringement of the patent;
(f) he or she may request the seizure, the transfer to a specific person, the recall, and the definitive removal from the channels of commerce or destruction of the infringing products, as well as of the means and materials exclusively or principally used for infringement.[1247]

421. In the case of an infringement of topography (chip) protection, for the rights of the exploiter authorized by the owner provisions of the Patent Law shall apply.[1248]

The Chip Protection Act also allows the possibility for the decision of non-infringement.[1249] Accordingly, any person who fears that proceedings for infringement of protection will be instituted against him or her, may, prior to the institution of such proceedings, request a decision ruling that the topography exploited or intended to be exploited by him or her, does not infringe the protection of a topography specified by him or her.[1250]

A final decision of non-infringement bars the institution, on the basis of the specified protection, of infringement proceedings in respect of the same topography.

§10. Overlapping and Relation to Others Intellectual Property Rights

422. Protection shall be granted to the topography of microelectronic semiconductor product if it is original. Topography (chip) shall be classed as original if it is the result of its creator's own intellectual effort, as well as not being commonplace in the industry at the time of its creation.

1247. The owner of the protection may have recourse to the same civil remedies against the infringer as the patentee may enforce against the infringer by virtue of the Patent Law by virtue of Art. 16(3) of Topography Act.
1248. The licensee is also entitled to have recourse.
1249. Csécsy, *A Szellemi Alkotások joga*, 167.
1250. Article 11(1) of the Chip Protection Act.

Topography means the three-dimensional disposition, however expressed, of the elements. A topography consisting of an original arrangement of commonplace parts shall be eligible for protection. The scope of protection shall be determined by illustration of the registered topography.

The overlap between the microelectronic semiconductor products (chip) and designs may be verifiable. Pursuant to the Article 20(1) of the Design Act, the scope of the protection conferred by a design shall be determined on the appearance of the whole or a part of a product resulting from the features of, in particular, the drawing or graphic or photographic reproduction of the design deposited in the Register of Designs. The cumulative protection is not prohibited by the Chip Protection Act or the Design Act.

Data is not available in Hungary concerning the registration of topographies and the cases of overlapping of topographies with other objects of intellectual property.

Chapter 9. Trade Secrets: Confidential Information

§1. Sources: Legislation

423. On the basis of several international treaties, the protection of trade secrets and confidential information may be interpreted as a special sphere of protection against unfair competition, which is in the domain of defence of undisclosed information.

In the course of ensuring effective protection against unfair competition as provided in Article 10 of the Paris Convention, members shall protect undisclosed information[1251] in accordance with paragraph 2.[1252]

Article 39 of the TRIPS Agreement provides the protection of undisclosed information. This rule makes reference to Article 10 of the Paris Convention.[1253] A natural or legal person shall have the possibility of preventing information lawfully within their control from being disclosed to, acquired by, or used by others without their consent in a manner contrary to honest commercial practices.

In accordance with the TRIPS Agreement, undisclosed information laid down in TRIPS Agreement. Undisclosed information means:

(a) the secret in a sense that it is not known to anybody or in the precise configuration and assembly of its components, generally known or readily accessible to persons within the circles that normally deal with the kind of information in question;
(b) has commercial value because it is secret; and
(c) has been subject to reasonable steps under the circumstances, by the person lawfully in control of information, to keep it secret.[1254]

424. The conceptual criteria of undisclosed information are the following:

(a) secret;
(b) commercial value;
(c) measures taken to keep it secret.

The new Hungarian Civil Code (Law No. V of 2013) and Competition Act protects business secrets. According to Article 4(1) of Competition Act, it is prohibited to gain access to or use business secrets in an unfair manner, and to disclose such secrets to unauthorized parties or to publish them.

1251. D. Gervais, *The TRIPS Agreement: Drafting History and Analysis* (London: Sweet & Maxwell), 181.
1252. Article 10*bis* (2) of the Paris Convention prescribes: Any act of competition contrary to honest practices in industrial and commercial matters constitutes an act of unfair competition.
1253. J. Bobrovszky, 'Rejtélyek és fortélyok-hozzászólás az üzleti titok és a know-how kérdésköréhez a PolgáriTörvénykönyv reformja kapcsán', in *Fehér könyv a szellemi tulajdon védelméről* (Budapest: Magyar Szabadalmi Hivatal, 2006), 223.
1254. *Ibid.*

Business secrets may be explained directly as trade secrets and confidential information.

Data pertaining to technological procedures, technical solutions, technological secrets manufacturing processes, work organization, logistical methods, know-how, description of patents having legal effect, customer lists and marketing projection, political information, and information relating to personal confidences have all been afforded protection on the grounds of their confidentiality.

Henceforth, computer programs, algorithms, designs for hardware, support documentation, and all new forms of technological information are capable of being classed as confidential information.

Know-how also may be interpreted by the new Hungarian Civil Code (Law No. V of 2013)[1255] and the Competition Act[1256] as undisclosed business information (business secret) by virtue of disclosure being made in an unfair manner to unauthorized parties or to publish them is forbidden.

The protection of confidential information does not give its creator any monopoly right, which can be enforced generally against third parties.[1257]

The essential sources and legislations related to trade secrets and confidential information are as follows:

425. The new Civil Code (Law No. V of 2013) plays an essential part of legal regulation of the trade secrets:

- The new Civil Code (Law No. V of 2013; Act LVII of 1996 on the Prohibition of Unfair Trading Practices and Unfair Competition (hereinafter: 'Competition Act').
- Commission Regulation (EU) No. 316/2014 of 21 March 2014 on the application of Article 101(3) of the Treaty on the Functioning of the European Union to categories of technology transfer agreements (herein after called Commission Regulation (EU) No. 316/2014).
- Paris Convention for the Protection of Industrial Property 1883 – promulgated by Law Decree No. 18/1970 in Hungary (hereinafter: 'Paris Convention').
- Agreement on Trade-Related Aspects of Intellectual Property rights (hereinafter; 'TRIPS Agreement') – promulgated by the Act IX of 1998.
- Directive (EU) 2016/943 of the European Parliament and of the Council of 8 June 2016 on the protection of undisclosed know-how and business information (trade secrets) against their unlawful acquisition, use and disclosure.

1255. The business secrets are protected by Art. 2:47 of the new Civil Code.
1256. Article 4 of the Competition Act.
1257. Pintz, *Találd fel magad,* 156.

§2. The Protection of Trade Secrets/Confidential Information

426. The new Civil Code (Law No. V of 2013) protects personal individual freedom and personal rights[1258] and among these is the right to private[1259] and business secrets.[1260]

The essential variety of secrets is business secrets. The new Civil Code explains the notion of business secret. Business secrets shall comprise all of the facts, information, and other data and their composition, which is not generally known or easily accessible for persons performing economic activities; that, if published or released to or used by unauthorized persons are likely to imperil the rightful financial, economic or market interest of the owner of such secrets, provided the owner has no liability concerning the divulgation of business secret.[1261]

The Civil Code forbids the violation of business secrets. Any person who has come into the possession of a private or business secret and publishes such secrets without authorization or abuses it in any other manner shall be construed as having violated an inherent right.

A person whose right to a business secret has been violated shall have the following options open under civil law, depending on the circumstances of the case:

(a) demand a court declaration of the occurrence of the infringement;
(b) demand to have the infringement discontinued and the perpetrator restrained from further infringement;
(c) demand that the perpetrator make restitution in a statement means and, the perpetrator, at his own expense, make an appropriate public disclosure for restitution;
(d) demand the termination of the injurious situation and the restoration of the previous state by and at the expense of the perpetrator and, furthermore, to have the effects of the infringement nullified or deprived of their injurious nature;
(e) demand to require surrender of the enrichment obtained by the infringement of the patent;
(f) file charges for damage and for punitive damages in accordance with the liability regulations.[1262]

The trade secret may be:

(a) information, such divulgation or publication, however, shall not include any data pertaining to technological procedures;
(b) technical solutions; manufacturing processes;
(c) work organization, logistical methods or know-how that, if made public, would be unreasonably detrimental for the business operation to which it is related.

1258. Article 2: 42(1) of new Civil Code (Law No. V of 2013).
1259. Article 2:46 of new Civil Code (Law No. V of 2013).
1260. Article 2:42(1) of new Civil Code (Law No. V of 2013).
1261. Article 2:47(1) of new Civil Code (Law No. V of 2013).
1262. Articles 251 and 252 of new Civil Code (Law No. V of 2013).

The withholding of such information shall not interfere with the publication of public information in the public interest.[1263]

Information in this context must be used in the widest sense and covers all types of data, including formulas and test data, as long as the information is identifiable. In cases in which the information may not be identified with precision, the legal obligation has no precise object and may not be enforced.[1264]

427. The Competition Act also protects trade secrets and confidential information. Article 2 of the Competition Act prohibits the conduct of economic activities in an unfair manner, in particular, in a manner violating or jeopardizing the lawful interests of competitors, business partners, and consumers, or in a way which is in conflict with the requirements of business integrity.

The Competition Act lists the activities which shall be qualified as work against the rules of unfair competition and prohibits to gain access to or use business secrets in an unfair manner, and to disclose such secrets to unauthorized parties or to publish them.[1265]

428. From the viewpoint of protection of the intellectual property, the violation of trade secret may be particularly significant. The expression 'in an unfair manner' may be interpreted as follows:

> to gain information in an unfair manner that is a manner contrary to honest commercial practices, means which shall include practices such as breach of contract, breach of confidence and inducement to breach, and the acquisition of information by third parties who knew, or were grossly negligent in failing to know, that such practices were involved in the acquisition.[1266]

Article 4(2) of the Competition Act – for interpretation to gain access to or use business secrets in an unfair manner – prescribes:

> It shall also qualify as gaining access to business secrets in an unfair manner where access to such business secrets has been obtained without the consent of the entitled person through a party in a confidential relationship or business relationship with such person at the time of, or prior to gaining access to the secrets.

The conceptual criteria of violation of trade secrets are as follows in this case:

> Business secrets shall comprise all of the facts, information, conclusions or data pertaining to economic activities that, if published or released to or used by unauthorized persons, are likely to imperil the rightful financial, economic or

1263. This means that in case of conflict of two rights, the publicity of information that is the public interest shall have the priority.
1264. Gervais, *The TRIPS Agreement*, 185.
1265. Article 4 of the Competition Act.
1266. Gervais, *The TRIPS Agreement*, 183.

> market interest of the owner of such secrets, provided the owner has taken all of the necessary steps to keep such information confidential;[1267]
>
> Gaining information in an unfair manner that is a manner contrary to honest commercial practice is prescribed in the aforementioned paragraph; 'Confidential relationship' shall, in particular, mean employment relationship, other work-related contractual relationship and membership;
>
> 'Business relationship' shall comprise the provision of information, negotiations and making proposals prior to making a deal, whether or not a contract is subsequently signed in consequence.

429. From the point of view of intellectual property among the undisclosed information and business secrets, the most essential is the know-how. The new Civil Code in Article 2:47(2) makes reference to know-how directly.

Likewise to busóiness secret should be regulated in new Civil Code identifiable (i.e., to say described in a sufficiently comprehensive manner) economic, technical, and organizational knowledge and experience and theirs composition that has pecuniary value (knowledge protected) if its access, use, divulgation or publication happens unfair manner, contrary to honesty.

Know-how does not have a unified, harmonized and in international relations accepted notion. The national legislation does not define the notion of know-how precisely or in a detailed manner. There are several practical explanations for this concept in specialized literature.[1268]

The know-how may interpret as follows in literature of industrial property:

(a) know-how means economic, technical, and organizational knowledge and experience that has pecuniary value;
(b) know-how means a chain of technical resolutions;
(c) know-how is to be understood to be supplementary, of practical experience, connected with technical resolutions.

430. Know-how may be recognized in a narrower sense of the technical experience which has economic value. Know-how may be recognized in a broader sense not only as technical, but also organizational, economical, as well as other information of pecuniary value:[1269]

> Within the sphere of protection provided for intellectual products that do not fall within the scope of other legal regulations and for economic, technical, and organizational knowledge and experience of pecuniary value, may also demand

1267. Bobrovszky, 'Rejtélyek és fortélyok', 223.
1268. Lontai et al., *A Szellemi Alkotások joga*, 176.
1269. Tattay, *A Szellemi Alkotások joga*, 297.

a share of the financial proceeds from persons who have expropriated or used their achievements.

Between the notions of know-how, the European Union definition may be considered relevant.

431. Know-how is from point of view of the economy of industrial property knowledge, which is essential and guarantees a competitive advantage, is hidden, and may be identified with that which may be reproduced.[1270] The conceptual criteria of know-how are related below:

(a) competitive advantage; the information in question shall give a competitive advantage, this may be determined by the fact that the competitor or other person trying to obtain the information may constitute prima facie evidence of this value;[1271]
(b) confidential information may be recognized as secret in the sense that it is not as a body or in the precise configuration an assembly of its components, in general known not quickly accessible to person within the circles that normally deal with the kind of information in question. This can be determined by comparing it with the knowledge of a person, 'skilled in the art' who has access to normal sources Commission Regulation (EU) No. 316/2014 of information concerned. The secrecy is not limited to a particular territory.[1272] The secrecy is essential criterion of know-how; and[1273]
(c) may be reproduced; prima facie evidence of know-how shall be identifiable, that is prescribed, with drawings or in other manner documented. In the cases where the information may not be identified with precision, the legal obligation of protection has no precise object and may not be enforced.

432. The notion of know-how is defined by Commission Regulation (EU) No. 316/2014. According to the EU definition, 'know-how' means a package of practical information, resulting from experience and testing, which is:

(a) secret, that is to say not generally known or easily accessible;
(b) substantial that is to say, significant and useful for the production of contract products; and
(c) identified, that is to say described in a sufficiently comprehensive manner so as to make it possible to verify that it fulfils the criteria of secrecy and substantiality.[1274]

433. Conducting the proceedings due to the violation of the aforementioned provisions shall fall within the competence of the court. The county courts and the Metropolitan Court of Budapest shall have jurisdiction in respect of legal proceedings

1270. Tattay, *A Szellemi Alkotások joga*, 298–299.
1271. Gervais, *The TRIPS Agreement*, 185.
1272. *Ibid.*
1273. Pintz, *Találd fel magad*, 156.
1274. Commission Regulation (EU) No. 316/2014 Art. 1, p. 1 i).

instituted on the basis of infringement of trade names Articles 2–7 of the Competition Act.

The person whose right to trade secrets has been violated shall have options on the basis of a, b, c, and e besides:

(a) may demand the termination of the injurious situation, to have the former status quo reinstated, and the deprivation of the goods manufactured or placed on the market illegally, or, if this is not possible, the destruction thereof, and the destruction of any special devices and facilities used for the manufacture or production thereof;
(b) may demand that the defendant disclose information on the parties participating in the manufacturing and marketing of the products involved in the case as well as on the business relations it has established to distribute such products.[1275]

1275. Article 86(1) of the Competition Act.

Chapter 10. Protection of Geographical Indications and Appellations of Origin

434. The current Act of regulation of geographical indications is the Act XI of 1997 on the protection trademarks and geographical indications (hereinafter: the 'Trademark Act').

As a pioneer in Hungarian law, the Trademark Act provides for the protection of geographical indications.[1276]

The significance of the efficient protection of geographical indications is underlined by the fact that the agriculture and food industry are especially important fields of the Hungarian economy, and the same applies to wine production too. The image of the country is embodied in signs such as: the onions of Makó, the wines of Tokaj, the sausages of Csaba, the salami of Szeged and the red peppers of Kalocsa.[1277]

There is a strong functional link as well between the geographical origin of products and their pre-eminent quality and characteristics of the agricultural products.[1278]

Act XI of 1997 on the protection of trademarks and geographical indications (hereinafter: the 'Trademark Act') contains provisions in respect to geographical indications.

The legal protection of these types of distinctive signs was not adequate in Hungary since there was no special national legislation, although the protection of appellation of origin is ensured.[1279]

The Lisbon Agreement was not sufficient[1280] when we take into account the limited number of states party to that agreement. Legal regulation had become imperative due to our obligations of harmonization with the TRIPS Agreement.[1281] So, it was advisable to bring about harmony with the council regulations all the more, as this makes it possible for the protection of Hungarian geographical indications for agricultural products and foodstuffs recognized within the Community.

With the adaptation of the conception of the Trademark Act, this industrial property category has become part of legislation to the denomination geographic.[1282] The geographical indications are protected in Hungary by Hungarian Acts and European regulations, as far as international treaties.

The new Civil Code, the Law V of 2013 is one of the most significant achievements of the twenty-first century in Hungary. The Code omits detailed regulation of intellectual

1276. Tattay, *A Szellemi Alkotások joga*, 323.
1277. Lontai et al., *A Szellemi Alkotások joga*, 274.
1278. I. Naggyörgy, 'A lajstromozott földrajzi megjelölés garantálja az árú minoségét', *Védjegyvilág* 6, no. 4 (1996): 4.
1279. Lontai et al., *A Szellemi Alkotások joga*, 274.
1280. According to Lisbon Agreement 26, appellations of origin of Hungary are protected.
1281. In accordance with Art. 22(1) of TRIPS Agreement, geographical indications are for the purposes of this Agreement, indications which identify a good as originating in the territory of a Member, or a region or locality in that territory, where a given a quality, or other characteristic of the good is essentially attributable to its geographical origin.
1282. Zs. Klauber, 'A földrajzi árújelzok az Europai Unióban', *Védjegyviág* 14, no. 1–2 (2004): 48.

property. The new Civil Code shall apply in respect of intellectual property, if these issues directly fall within its scope, which are not governed by the legislation on copyright and industrial property rights of Hungary.

By virtue of Act CXLVIII of 2010, the name of Hungarian Patent Office was changed to Hungarian Intellectual Property Office (hereinafter: 'Office') as of 1 January 2011 to better reflect its competence extending to activities related to all forms of industrial property protection as well as to the field of copyright.

435. Hungarian Laws and Regulations:

- Act XI of 1997 on the Protection Trademarks and Geographical indications (Trademark Act).
- Act XVI of 2013 on the Amendment of certain Acts relating to Intellectual Property.
- Act CLIX of 2013 on the Amendment of certain Acts relating to Intellectual Property.
- Government Decree 556/2013 (XII 30) on customs authority measures against goods, infringing certain intellectual property rights.
- Decree No. 16/2004 (IV 27) IM on the detailed formalities of trademark applications and applications for the protection of geographical indications.
- Decree No. 124/2007 (V 31) Government on the detailed rules concerning the protection of geographical indications of agricultural products and foodstuffs and the official control of these products.
- Decree No. 19/2005 (IV 12) GKM on the fees for administrative services in industrial procedures before the Hungarian Patent Office.
- Government Decree No. 371/2004 (XII 26) Government concerning custom action against goods infringing certain intellectual property rights.
- Decision No. 77/2008 (VI 13) of the Parliament on the protection of Hungaricums Government Decree No. 178/2009 (IX 3) on the procedure for the Community protection of designations of origin and geographical indications of wine products as well as the inspection of these products.
- Government Decree No. 158/2009 (VII 30) on the procedure for the protection of geographical indications of agricultural products, foodstuffs and spirit drinks as well as the inspection of these products.
- Act XXX of 2012 on Hungarian national values and Hungaricums.

436. Community laws and regulations:

Agricultural products

Regulation (EU) No. 1151/2012 of the European Parliament and of the Council of 21 November 2012 on quality schemes for agricultural products and foodstuffs.

Commission Delegated Regulation (EU) No. 664/2014 of 18 December 2013 supplementing Regulation (EU) No. 1151/2012 of the European Parliament and of the Council with regard to the establishment of the Union symbols for protected designations of origin, protected geographical indications and traditional specialities guaranteed and with regard to certain rules on sourcing, certain procedural rules and certain additional transitional rules.

Commission Delegated Regulation (EU) No. 665/2014 of 11 March 2014 supplementing Regulation (EU) No. 1151/2012 of the European Parliament and of the Council with regard to conditions of use of the optional quality term 'mountain product'.

Corrigendum to Commission Regulation (EU) No. 668/2013 of 12 July 2013 amending Annexes II and III to Regulation (EC) No. 396/2005 of the European Parliament and of the Council as regards maximum residue levels.

Vines

Regulation (EU) No. 1308/2013 of the European Parliament and of the Council of 17 December 2013 establishing a common organization of the markets in agricultural products and repealing Council Regulations (EEC) No. 922/72, (EEC) No. 234/79, (EC) No. 1037/2001 and (EC) No. 1234/2007.

Commission Regulation (EC) No. 607/2009 of 14 July 2009 laying down certain detailed rules for the implementation of Council Regulation (EC) No. 479/2008 as regards protected designations of origin and geographical indications, traditional terms, labelling, and presentation of certain wine sector products.

Aromatized wine products

Regulation (EU) No. 251/2014 of the European Parliament and of the Council of 26 February 2014 on the definition, description, presentation, labelling, and the protection of geographical indications of aromatized wine products and repealing Council Regulation (EEC) No. 1601/91.

Spirit drinks

Regulation (EC) No. 110/2008 of the European Parliament and of the Council of 15 January 2008 on the definition, description, presentation, labelling, and the protection of geographical indications of spirit drinks and repealing Council Regulation (EEC) No. 1576/89.

Commission implementing Regulation (EU) No. 716/2013 of 25 July 2013 laying down rules for the application of Regulation (EC) No. 110/2008 of the European Parliament and of the Council on the definition, description, presentation, labelling, and the protection of geographical indications of spirit drinks.

Directive 2004/48/EC of the European Parliament and of the Council of April 2004 on enforcement of intellectual property rights.

437. International treaties on the protection geographical indications:

- Paris Convention for the Protection of Industrial Property 1883 – Promulgated in Hungary by the Law Decree No. 18/1970. (hereinafter: 'Paris Convention').
- The Madrid Agreement for the Repression of False or Deceptive Indications of Source on Goods – Promulgated in Hungary by the Law Decree No. 29/1973.

- Lisbon Agreement for the Protection of Appellations of Origin and their international Registration – Modified in 2015
- Agreement on Trade-related Aspects of Intellectual Property Rights – Promulgated in Hungary by The Act IX of 1998.
- Regulation under the Lisbon Agreement for the Protection of Appellations of Origin and their International Registration – Promulgated by the Decree No. 5/2005 (III 11) IM.
- Agreement between the governments of the People's Republic of Hungary and the Swiss Confederation on the Protection of Indications of Source, Appellations of Origin and Other Geographical Names – Promulgated in Hungary by the Decree No. 9/1986 (XI 12) MT.[1283]
- Agreement between the Governments of the People's Republic of Hungary and the Republic of Portugal on the Protection of Indications of Source, Appellations of Origin and Other Geographical Names – Promulgated by the Decree 49/1986 (XI 12) MT.

438. The denomination geographic is used in the course of trade to identify the geographical origin of products.[1284]

The main varieties[1285] of geographical indications are as follows:

(a) appellations of origin;
(b) geographical indications;
(c) traditional denominations;
(d) indication of provenance;
(e) Geographical indications of spirit drinks.

Geographical indications of spirit drinks shall be granted protection if the products bearing the geographical indications comply also with the conditions specified in the product specification provided for by specific legislation.[1286]

439. The denomination geographic may be:

(a) of a geographical name, e.g., Eger, Makó, Kecskemét, Herend;
(b) of a geographical name with an affix 'of' e.g., of Eger, of Makó, of Kecskemét, of Herend;
(c) of a product name and of a geographical name with an affix 'of' Bull's blood of Eger.[1287]

440. Article 103(3) of the Trademark Act states the concept of appellation of origin:

1283. Lontai et al., *A Szellemi Alkotások joga*, 275.
1284. L Tattay, *A Szellemi Alkotások és a Modern Piacgazdaság* (Budapest: Szent István Társulat, 2003), 260.
1285. Tattay, *A Szellemi Alkotások joga*, 357.
1286. Article 104 of Act XI of 1997 on the Protection Trademarks and Geographical indications.
1287. Tattay, *A Szellemi Alkotások joga*, 358.

> Appellation of origin means the geographical name of a region, locality or, in exceptional cases, a country which serves to designate a product originating therein the specific quality, reputation or other characteristics of which are due exclusively or essentially to the geographical environment, with its inherent natural and human factors, and the production, processing and preparation of which take place in the defined geographical area.

An appellation origin comprises two constituent elements:

(a) it is a geographical denomination, that of the place from which the product comes;
(b) it can only be used for products coming from the region referred to and which possess the specific features that are due to natural and human factors present in that region.[1288]

441. Article 103(2) of the Trademark Act defines the concept of geographical indications stating:

> Geographical indication means the geographical name of a region, locality or, in exceptional cases, a country which serves to designate a product originating therein the specific quality, reputation or other characteristics of which are due essentially to that geographical origin, and the production, processing or preparation of which takes place in the defined geographical area.

The Trademark Act makes a difference between geographical indications and appellations of origin depending on the nature of that link, which is taking into account the role both of the natural and the human factors. A product can originate in the defined geographical area if it has been produced, processed, and prepared there.[1289]

Geographical indications also are protected by law on unfair competition and on the protection of consumers.[1290]

442. Indication of provenance means the geographical name of a country, region or locality, which serves to designate a product, originating therein. There is not a strong and functional link between geographical area and quality and other characteristics related to indications of provenance.

In accordance with Article 105 and of the Trademark Act, geographical indication shall not be granted protection:

(a) if, in the course of trade, it has become the common name of a product irrespective of whether the product originates in the place specified by the geographical denomination (e.g., Camembert). It may happen that a geographical indication becomes a generic name of a product in the course of trade. Since such an indication has lost its function of designating a geographical origin, it may not to be granted protection irrespective of whether or not the product for designation of which

1288. Lontai et al., *A Szellemi alkotások joga*, 273.
1289. Csécsy, *A Szellemi Alkotások joga*, 230.
1290. L. Tattay, *A bor és az agrártermékek eredetvédelme* (Budapest, Mezogazda Könyvkiado, 2001), 69.

has become generic originates in the defined place. Whatever a geographic denomination may not be a common or generic name of a product after its registration;

(b) if it is identical to an earlier geographical denomination;
(c) if it is identical or similar to an earlier geographical denomination with respect to identical or similar products;
(d) if it is identical to/or similar to an earlier trademark and its use – due to the knowledge reputation or lasting presence on the market of the trademark – would result in a likelihood of confusion on the part of consumers.[1291] Thus, a trademark has not been used in accordance to the Trademark Act (Article 18(1)) does not constitute a bar to the protection of a geographical denomination;
(e) if it conflicts with the name of an earlier – protected or other – plant variety or animal breed and for this reason it is liable to deceive the consumers.

Geographical indications of agricultural products and foodstuffs shall be granted protection if the products bearing the geographical indication comply also with the conditions specified in the product specification provided for by special legislation, established by the minister responsible for agricultural policy.[1292]

443. Any natural or legal person or a company without legal personality may apply for the protection of geographical indication which produces or prepares in the defined geographical area, a product for which the designation of geographical denomination is used.

Protection shall be granted for a geographical indication if it satisfies the requirements defining subject matter of protection; it is not excluded from protection if the application satisfies the formal requirements laid down in Trademark Act.

The protection of geographical indication shall belong jointly to the person, who: produces, processes, or prepares products.[1293] The protection of geographical indication shall belong jointly to all people, who: produce, process, or prepare the designated item in the place corresponding to the geographical indication. The rights conferred by the protection belong to these persons due to the fact that they produce products of specified characteristic in the given geographic area.[1294]

444. The detailed rules of product specification prescribed in connection with the geographical indication of agricultural products and foodstuffs and those for the inspection of the use. In the course of trade, the geographical indications of such products will be established by a government decree on the basis of authorization of the law. When the inspection authorities are designated and the detailed rules governing their procedures are established, it must be ensured that this activity is incorporated into the inspection structure already functioning in the course of marketing the said products.[1295]

1291. Csécsy, *A Szellemi Alkotások joga*, 231.
1292. Tattay, *A bor és az agrártermékek*, 43.
1293. Tattay, *A Szellemi Alkotások joga*, 354.
1294. Naggyörgy, 'A lastromozott földrajzi megjelölés garantálja az árú minoségét', 6.
1295. Tattay, *A bor és az agrártermékek*, 43.

445. In accordance with Articles 112(1) and (2), the Hungarian Intellectual Property Office (hereinafter: 'Office') shall have competence in the following matters concerning geographical indications:

(a) registration of geographical indications;
(b) cancellation and revocation of geographical indications;
(c) keeping the records of applications for the protection of geographical indications and of registered geographical indications;
(d) official information;
(e) in matters concerning the application of provision relating to the Community protection certain geographical indication;
(f) in matters of international protection of appellations of origins.

446. Applications of a geographical indication are to be filed with the Hungarian Intellectual Property Office. The application for the registration of geographical denomination shall comprise the following:

(a) the name and address of the applicant;
(b) claimed geographical indication (name);
(c) type of geographical indication;
(d) list of goods;
(e) description and specification of goods (in regards to agricultural products and foodstuffs);
(f) power of attorney;
(g) request for the registration of geographical indication.[1296]

The Application of geographical indication may be filed electronically too.

By virtue of Article 113(2) of the Trademark Act, an application shall be subject to a filing fee, which shall be payable within two months from the date of filing.

If the application complies with the requirements mentioned above, the Office shall publish official information thereon in the Gazette of the Office, which shall contain the following data: the name of geographical indication, the date of filing, the list of products.

According to Article 113(4) of the Trademark Act, after communication of data, any person may file an observation with the Hungarian Intellectual Property Office to the effect that the indication or the application does not comply with a requirement of registerability of the indications.[1297]

If an application satisfies all formal requirements, the Office shall carry out a substantive examination of the application.

447. Pursuant to Article 113(5), the substantive examination shall assess:

(a) whether the geographical indication satisfies the legal requirements or not, and whether it is excluded from protection;

1296. Tattay, *A Szellemi Alkotások joga*, 359.
1297. Csécsy, *A Szellemi Alkotások joga*, 234.

(b) whether the application complies with the formal and procedural requirements laid down in the Trademark Act.

In the procedure for the registration of geographical indications as well as matters not mentioned in the foregoing paragraphs, provisions of trademark registration procedure shall apply *mutatis mutandis*.

Inspection of qualification and requirements of the use of geographical indications and agricultural products and food stuffs employed in the trade shall fall within the competence of the minister responsible for agricultural policy.

448. The protection of geographic indications extends:

(a) to the products of agriculture, e.g., onions of Makó;
(b) to foodstuffs such as the peppers of Kalocsa;
(c) wines, spirits, and brandies like those wines of Villány and the apricot brandy of Kecskemét;
(d) art and craft products such as porcelain of Herend;
(e) products of folk art, e.g., lace of Halas.[1298]

Protection shall confer on its holder the exclusive right to use the geographical indication. Only the holders may use the geographical indication and the holder may not grant a license of use of geographical indications.[1299]

In accordance with Article 109(2) of Trademark Act, on the basis of exclusive right of use, any one of the holders shall be entitled to bring an action against any person who in the course of trade uses, if:

(a) the protected geographical indication or a denomination liable to create confusion with respect to products not originating in the defined geographical area;
(b) uses the protected geographical indication with respect to products not included in the list of products, but similar to those and therefore takes unfair advantage of/or infringes the repute of the protected geographical indication. Imitates or evokes in any manner whatsoever the protected geographical indication even if;
(c) the true origin of the product is indicated or if the protected name is translated or accompanied various additions or affixes.

449. Protection shall be ensured against:

(a) any usurpation or imitation, even if the true origin of the product is indicated or its appellation is used in translated form or accompanied by a term such as 'kind', 'type', 'make', 'imitation', or the like;[1300]
(b) uses any false or misleading indication as to the provenance, origin, nature, or essential characteristics of the product, no matter where it is indicated (e.g., on the packaging, advertising material, or documents relating to the product concerned);

1298. Lontai et al., *A Szellemi Alkotások joga*, 237.
1299. Csécsy, *A Szellemi Alkotások joga*, 229.
1300. Zs. Klauber, 'A földrajzi árújelzok az Euórpai Unióban', *Védjegyvilág* 14, no. 1–2 (2004): 50.

(c) performs any other act liable to mislead the public as to the true origin of the product;[1301]

(d) although the enumerated facts include the exploitation of the reputation of a protected geographical indication, the emphasis is placed rather on the prohibition of creating confusion or misleading the consumers[1302] which is in harmony with function of geographical indication.

1301. Tattay, *A Szellemi Alkotások joga*, 359.
1302. Csécsy, *A Szellemi Alkotások joga*, 231.

Selected Bibliography

§1. Books

Blanpain, R. (ed.). *Civil Law in Hungary Contracts*. London, New York: Kluwer Law International, 2003.

Beier, F.K. & G. Schricker (eds). *German Industrial Property, Copyright and Antitrust Laws*. 2nd edn. IIC Studies. Vol. 6. edited by F.K. Beier, G. Schricker & W. Fikentscher. Weinheim: VCH Verlaggesellschaft, 1989.

Benárd, A. & A. Timár. *Szerzöi Jog Kézikönyve* [*Handbook of the Copyright*]. Budapest: Közgazdasági és Jogi Könyvkiadó, 1973.

Bendzsel, M., et al. *Iránytü a mùszaki fejlesztéshez – az iparjogvédelmi tájékoztatás informatikai kalauza* [*Informatory Manual of the Instruction of the Industrial Property*]. Budapest: Magyar Szabadalmi Hivatal, 1997.

Bendzsel, M. (ed.). *Biotechnologiai találmányok oltalma* [*The Protection of the Inventions of Biotechnology*]. Budapest: Magyar Szabadalmi Hivatal, 2001.

Beyer, N. *Die Urheberrechtliche Schutzfrist* [*Duration of the Protection in Copyright*]. München: C.H. Beck, 2001.

Brockman, J. *Az elmúlt 2000 Év legfontosabb találmányai* [*The Most Important Inventions of the Last 2000 Years*]. Budapest: Vince Kiadó, 2001.

Bobrovszky, J. *A tudományos-mùszaki eredmények jogi védelme a szocialista gazdasági Integrációban* [*The Legal Protection Scientific and Technical Achievements in Socialist Economic Integration*]. Budapest: KJK, 1978.

Bobrovszky, J. *Iparjogvédelem és Csucstechnologia* [*The Protection of Industrial Property and the High Technology*]. Budapest: Országos Találmányi Hivatal, 1995.

Boytha, Gy. *Iparjogvédelem és szerzöi Jog az Europai Közösség jogában* [*Industrial Property Right and Copyright in the Law European Community*]. Budapest: PPKE JÁK, 2002.

Cornish, W. & D. Llewelyn. *Intellectual Property*. 5th edn. London: Sweet & Maxwell, 2003.

Drewes, S. *Neue Nutzungarten in Urheberrecht* [*The New Features of Use in the Copyright*]. Baden-Baden: Nomos Verlaggesellschaft, 2001.

Csécsy, G. *Iparjogvédelem* [*Protection of Industrial Property*]. Miskolc: Novotni Kiadó, 1997.

Csécsy, Gy. *Szellemi Alkotások Joga* [*The Right of Intellectual Property*]. Miskolc: Novotni Kiadó, 2007.

Ficsor, M. *Guide to the Copyright and Related Rights Treaties Administered by WIPO*. Geneva: World Intellectual Property Organisation, 2003.

Gazda, I.D. Kövesdi & S. Vida. *Találmányok, szabadalmak* [*Inventions, Patents*]. Budapest: KJK, 1985.

Gervais, D. *TRIPS Agreement Drafting History and Analysis*. London: Sweet & Maxwell, 1997.
Geller, P.E. & M.B. Nimmer. *International Copyright Law and Practice*. New York: Lexis/Nexis, 2007.
Gyertyánfy, P., et al. *A szerzöi jogi törvény magyarázata* [*Commentary to the Copyright Act*]. Budapest: Komplex, 2006.
Hajdu, T., et al. *Europai szabadalmi esetjog* [*European Law of the Patent Cases*]. Budapest: Magyar Szabadalmi Hivatal, 2002.
Hegyi, G. *Rechtschutz und Verwertung von Computrtprogrammen in Ungarn* [*Legal Protection and Use of the Computer Programs*]. München: Max-Planck-Institut, 1999.
Keeling, D.T. *Free Movement and Competition Law: Intellectual Property Rights in EU Law*. Vol. 11, edited by F.G. Jacobs. Oxford: Oxford University Press, 2003.
Király, M., et al. *Az Europai Közösség kereskedelmi joga* [*The Business Law of the European Union*]. Budapest: KJK-Kerszöv, 2003.
Kondricz, P. & A. Timár. *Az elektronikus kereskedelem kérdései* [*The Questions of Electronic Commerce*]. Budapest: KJK Kerszöv, 2000.
Lontai, E. *Szellemi alkotások joga* [*Protection of Intellectual Property Rights*]. Budapest: Eötvös József Könyvkiadó, 2001.
Lontai, E., et al. *A szellemi alkotások joga, Magyar Polgári Jog* [*Protection of Intellectual Property*]. Budapest: Eötvös József Könyvkiadó, 2004.
Mestmäcker, E & Schultze J: Kommentar. zum deutschen Urhaberrecht (Internationale Abkommen) Luchterland Kiadó. 2001. Tom 4.
Milassin, L. *A világháló és az EU szerzöi joga* [*Internet and the Copyright of EU*]. Luxemburg: Az Europai Közösségek Hivatalos Tanulmányainak Hivatala, 2006.
Norman H. *Intellectual Property Law*. Oxford: Oxford University Press, 2011.
Osztovits, A. *EU-Jog, [EU-Law]* budapest, HVGORAC, 2012.
Pfaff, D. & S. Nagel. *International Sources for Licensing of Industrial Property*. München: C.H. Beck, 1992.
Szabó, Á., et al. *Fehér könyv a szellemi tulajdon védelméröl* [*White Book on the Protection of Intellectual Property*]. Budapest: Magyar Szabadalmi Hivatal & Magyar Szellemi Tulajdon Védelmi Tanács, 2005.
Penyigei, K. & M. Kiss. *Fehér könyv a szellemi tulajdon védelméröl* [*White Book on the Protection of Intellectual Property*]. Budapest: Magyar Szabadalmi Hivatal & Magyar Szellemi Tulajdon Védelmi Tanács, 2007.
Penyigei, K. & M. Kiss. *Fehér könyv a szellemi tulajdon védelméröl* [*White book on the Protection of Intellectual Property*]. Budapest: Magyar Szabadalmi Hivatal & Magyar Szellemi Tulajdon Védelmi Tanács, 2008–2009.
Penyigei, K., P. Sümeghy & M. Kiss. *Fehér könyv a szellemi tulajdon védelméröl* [*White Book on the Protection of Intellectual Property*]. Budapest: Magyar Szabadalmi Hivatal & Magyar Szellemi Tulajdon Védelmi Tanács, 2006.
Pintz, G. *Találd fel magad* [*How Obtain Protection*]. Budapest: Akadémiai Kiadó, 2005.
Platt, R. *Your World Explained: Inventions*. London: Marschall Publishing Ltd, 1996.
Ruijsenaars, H. (ed.). *Character Merchandising in Europe*. London, Hague, New York: Kluwer Law International, 2003.

Selected Bibliography

Streber, A.K. *Die Internationalen Abkommen der Bundesrepublik Deutschland zum Schutz Geographischer Herkunftangaben* [*The International Treaties of the Federal Republic of Germany for Protection of Geographic Indications*]. Berlin: Carl Heymanns Verlag, 1994.

Schmidt-Szalevszky, J. & J.L. Pierre. *Droit de la Propriete Industrielle* [*Law of the Industrial Property*]. Paris: Litec, 1996.

Szinger, A. & P.B. Tóth. *Gyakorlati utmutató a szerzöi joghoz* [*Practical Guide to the Copyright*]. Budapest: Novissima Kiadó, 2004.

Stauder, D., et al. *Mélanges offerts á Jean-Jacques Burst* [*Memorial Volume for Jean-Jacques Burst*]. Paris: Litec, 2000.

Szilágyi, J.E. *Eredetvédelmi kérdések a borjogban* [*The Questions of the Protection of Origine in Vine Law*]. Miskolc: Novotny Kiadó, 2009.

Tasnádi, E., et al. *Iparjogvédelmi kézikönyv* [*The Manual of Industrial Property*]. Budapest: KJK, 1974.

Tasnádi, E., et al. *Iparjogvédelmi kézikönyv* [*The Manual of Industrial Property*]. Budapest: KJK, 1978.

Tasnádi, E., et al. *A mùszaki szellemi termékek jogszabályai* [*The Legal Prescriptions of Technical-Intellectual Products*]. Budapest: Magyar Kereskedelmi Kamara Szellemi Termék Szakbizottsága, 1979.

Tattay, L. *A versenyjogok és az ipari tulajdon oltalma az Europai Közösségben* [*The Competition Laws and the Protection of Industrial Property in European Community*]. Budapest: Ozirisz Kiadó, 1998.

Tattay, L. *A bor és az agrártermékek eredetvédelme* [*The Protection of the Origine of Wine and Agricultural Products*]. Budapest: Mezogazda Kiadó, 2001.

Tattay, L. *A tudományirányítás és a szellemi alkotások joga az EU-ban* [The Law of Governance of the Science and the Intellectual Property]. Budapest: MTA Tudomány és Kutatások Jogi és Igazgatási Kérdéseinek Kutatócsoportja, 2003.

Tattay, L. *A szellemi alkotások joga* [*The Law of Intellectual Property*]. Budapest: Szent istván Társulat, 2007.

Tattay L.et al. *Szellemi alkotások joga, [Intellectual Property Law].* Budapest: Szent István Társulat, 2011.

Thouvenin F. *Functionnale Systematisierug von Wettbewerbsrecht (UWG) und immaterialgüterrechten.* Tübingen: Carl Heinz Verlag, 2011.

Ulmer Eitort C. Der Zukunft in der Vervieltältigungs freiheit gungsfreiheit. In: Festschrift für Wilhelm Nordemann. Nomos; Baden-Baden 1999.

Vogel L. *Droit européen des ententes et abus de position dominante.* Paris: Lawlex 2010.

Vida, S. *A Védjegyek és az Ipari Termékek Értékesítése* [*The Trademarks and the Marketing of Industrial Products*]. Budapest: KJK, 1962.

Vida, S. *Az Europai Bíróság védjegy gyakorlata* [*The Practice Concerning the Trademarks of European Court*]. Miskolc: Novotny Kiadó, 2006.

Vida, A., T. Koval-Wolk & G. Hegyi. *Ungarisches Patentrecht* [*Hungarian Law of Patents*]. *Schriftenreihe zun Gewerblichen Rechtsschutz.* Band 114. München: Carl Heimanns Verlag, 2001.

Világhy, M. *A szellemi alkotások joga* [*The Law of Intellectual Property*]. Budapest: Tankönyvkiadó, 1983.

§2. Articles and Studies

Bendzsel. M. '*Védjegy és vesenyképesség*' ['Trademark and Competitiveness']. *Iparjogvédelmi Szemle* 112, no. 4 (2007): 5–12.
Bendzsel. M. '*Fátyoltánc a szabadalmi titok körül*' ['Veil Dance around the Patent Secret']. *Iparjogvédelmi Szemle* 111, no. 1 (2006): 8–21.
Benko Cs, Gy. '*Az ipari formatervezés helyzete Magyarországon*' ['The Situation of Designs in Hungary']. *Iparjogvédelmi és Szerzöi Jogi Szemle* 103, no. 6 (1998): 20–26.
Bobrovszky, J. '*Rejtélyek és fortélyok-hozzászólás az üzleti titok és a know-how kérdésköréhez a PolgáriTörvénykönyv reformja kapcsán*' ['Mysteries and Tricks – Comment to the Questions to the Matter of the Trade Secret and Know-how in Relationship of the Reform the Civil Code']. Fehér könyv a szellemi tulajdon védelmérol. Budapest: Magyar Szabadalmi Hivatal, 2006): 221–238.
Boytha, Gy. '*Az interneten hozzáférheto tartalom szerteágazó védelmének jogi szabályozása*' ['The Legal Ordering of Ramifying Protection on Internet Accessible Content']. *MIE Közlemények* 41, no. 1 (2000): 77–91.
Cserba, V. & Zs. Lendvai. '*A domainnév regisztráció és A domain nevekkel osszefüggo jogérvényesítés*' ['The Registration of Domain Names and Assertation of Claims in Relationship with Domain Names']. In *Fehér Könyv a Szellemi TulajdonVédelméröl*, edited by K. Penyigey, P. Sümeghy & M. Kiss. Budapest: Magyar Szabadalmi Hivatal & Magyar Szellemi Tulajdon VédelmiTanács, 2006.
Dónusz, K. '*Nemzetközi formatervezési minta*' ['International Design']. *Védjegyvilág* 17, no. 2 (2007): 74–78.
Farkas, Sz. & A.E. Touréné. '*Össejtek szabadalmazhatósága:második menet*' ['Patentability of Primordial Germ Cells: Second Round']. *Iparjogvédelm és Szezöi Jogii Szemle* 113, no. 5 (2008): 2–42.
Fáber, M. & H.M. Gorkáné. '*Növényfajta oltalom*' ['Plant Variety Protection']. *MIE Közlemények* 44, no. 1 (2003): 43–55.
Fazekas, J. & A. Gyenge. '*A büntetojogi jogérvényesítés a szellemitulajdon-jogok területén europai és nemzetközi szinten*' ['Criminal Law in the Field of Intellectual Property at the European and International Levels']. *Iparjogvédelm és Szezöi Jogii Szemle* 111, no. 6 (2006): 5–21.
Ficsor, M.Z. '*Törvényjavaslat a formatervezési minták oltalmáról*' ['The Draft of the Statute on the Protection of Designs']. *Védjegyvilág* 11, no. 1 (2001): 1–9.
Gál, J. '*A Cégnév bejegyzésével kapcsolatos problémák*' ['The Problems concerning the Registration of the Firm Names']. *Védjegyvilág* 6, Special Issue (1996): 33–36.
Gonda, I. & Milisits. E. '*Felszólalás tapasztalatai a hazai védjegyeljárásban*' ['The Experiences of Opposition in the Hungarian Trademark Proceeding']. In *Fehér Könyv a Szellemi TulajdonVédelméröl*, edited by K. Penyigei, P. Sümeghy & M. Kiss. Budapest: Magyar Szabadalmi Hivatal & Magyar Szellemi Tulajdon VédelmiTanács, 2006.
Gorkáné, H.M. '*Növényfajta oltalom 2008 a hazai és közösségi jgszabályok változásainak figylembevételével*' ['Plant Variety Protection 2008 Taking into Account the Amendments to Hungarian and Community Regulation']. *Iparjogvédelmi Szemle* 113, no. 5 (2008): 25–42.

Selected Bibliography

Gödölle, I. 'Rosszhiszemuség a védjegyoltalomban' ['Bad Faith in Trademark Law']. *MIE Közlemények* 43 no. 1 (2002): 89–123.

Gyertyánfy, P. 'Az Alkamazandó jog kérdése az internettel kapcsolatos jogvitákban' ['The Question of Applicable Law in Relationship with the Legal Practices Concerning the Internet']. Budapest: MIE Közlemények 41, no. 1 (2000): 9–99.

Kabai, E. 'Müszaki Intézkedés és szabad felhasználás a szerzoi jogban, külföldi megoldások' ['Technical Measurements and Free Use in Copyright Law, Foreign Solutions']. *MIE Közlemények* 43, no. 1 (2002): 167–181.

Kiss, Z. 'A szerzoi jogról szóló törvény 2005. évi módosításai és további tervezett reformjai' ['The Amendment of the Copyright Act of 2005 and the Additional Outlined Amendments of the Copyright Law']. *MIE Közlemények* 45–46, no. 1 (2006): 130–137.

Kiss, Z. 'Az önkéntes munyilvántartás jogi szabályozása – nemzetközi és hazai elozmények' ['Legal Rules Concerning the Voluntary Registration-Hungarian and International Antecedents']. *Iparjogvédelmiés Szeerzöi jogi Szemle* 111, no. 3 (2006): 31–42.

Kiss, Z. 'Könyvkiadás és könyvkereskedelem a szellemitulajdo-védelem célkeresztjében' ['Book Publishing and Book Trade in the Focus of Intellectual Property Protection']. *Iparjogvédelmi Szemle* 113, no. 4 (2008): 109–144.

Kovári, Gy. 'Az ipari mintákra vonatkozó hazai jogi szabályozás' ['The Hungarian Legal Regulation in Relationship with Designs']. *Védjegyvilág* 5, no. 2 (1995): 1–10.

Kovári, Gy. 'Javaslatok az ipari mintaoltalom szabályozás korszerüsítésére' ['Propositions Concerning the Modernisation of Design Regulation']. *Védjegyvilág* 10, no. 1 (2000): 1–10.

Kovári, Gy. 'Az europai ornamentális minták a 98/71/EC Directtive után' ['The European Ornamental Designs after the Directive 98/71(EC)']. *Védjegyvilág* 9, no. 2 (1999): 1–9.

Kömüves, A. 'Hatásos muszaki intézkedések jogi védelmének kérdései' ['The Questions of Legal Protection of the Effective. Technical Measurements']. *MIE Közlemények* 44, no. 1 (2003): 145–173.

Kricsfalvi, A. 'Szerzoi jogdíjak aktuális kérdései a filmszakmában' ['The Current Questions of the Royalties in Motion-Picture-Industry']. *MIE Közlemények* 45–46, no. 1 (2006): 17–184.

Kürtössy, J. 'A Biotechnologiai Találmányok Szabadalmi Oltalmának Magyarországi JogiSzabályozása'. In *Biotechnológiai Találmányok Oltalma*, edited by M. Bendzsel. Budapest: Magyar Szabadalmi Hivatal, 2001.

Liedes, J. 'A szerzoi jog idoszeru kérdései az Europai Unioban és nemzetközi szinten' ['Current Issues of the Copyright in the European Union and at the International Level']. *Iparjogvédelm és Szezöi Jogi Szemle* 111, no. 6 (2006): 23–39.

Markó, J. 'A feltalálói lépés követelménye a használatiminta-oltalmi jogban' ['Requirement of Inventive Step in Utility Model Law']. *Iparjogvédelmi és Szerzöi Jogi Szemle* 112, no. 4 (2007): 12–43.

Mentler, Gy. 'Gondolatok a szabad szoftverek szellemi tulajdonvédelmi vonatkozásairól' ['Suggestions in Relationship with the Protection of Intellectual Property of the Free Softwares']. *MIE Közlemények* 45, no. 1 (2004): 53–67.

Mojzes, I. 'Szellemi tulajdon védelem a félvezeto- és elektronikai technologia iparban' ['Intellectual Property Rights in Semiconductor Manufacturing Industry and Electronics Technology']. *Iparjogvédelmi Szemle* 113, no. 5 (2008): 42–47.
Molnár, I. & G. Németh. 'Egyetemi szellemi tulajdonvédelem és ipaari kapcsolatok a nyilt innovációs közegben: Open Acces vagy Monopoljogok?' ['University IP Protection and Cooperation with Industry in an Open Industrial Environment: Open Acces or Monopollic Rights?']. *Iparjogvédelmi Szemle* 114, no. 5 (2009): 5–27.
Millisits, E. 'Némi élénkülés az eredetmegjelölések nemzetközi oltalma területén' ['An Insignificant Growth on the Domain of International Appellations of Origin']. *MIE Közlemények* 46, no. 1 (2005–2006): 130–137.
Munkácsi, P. 'Aktualitások az adatbázisok nemzetközi szintu sui generis védelmérol' ['Current Informations on the Sui Generis Protection of Databases at International Level']. *MIE Közlemények* 43, no. 1 (2002): 181–193.
Nikodémus, A. 'Hazai tallmányok hasznosítása az iparjogvédelmi támogatási rendszer tükrében' ['The Exploitation of National Inventions in Focus of the System of Assistance Concerning the Industrial Property']. In *Fehér Könyv a Szellemi Tulajdon Védelméröl*, edited by A. Szabó, K. Penyigei & P. Sümeghy. Budapest: Magyar Szabadalmi Hivatal & Magyar Szellemi Tulajdon VédelmiTanács, 2005.
Lantos, J. 'A Szellemi Tulajdojogokkal kapcsolatos vámeljárás, mint a hamisítás elleni küzdelem egyik eszköze' ['Custom Proceeding in Relationship with Intellectual Property Rights, as Effective Appliance of the Fight against the Infringement']. *MIE Közlemények* 46, no. 1 (2006): 108–130.
Orbán, A. 'Az Eropai Unió Formatervezési Mintarendszere és a Magyar Formatervezési Mintarendszer' ['The System of Designs in European Union and the System of Designs in Hungary']. *Külgazdaság* 50, no. 6 (2006): 63–78.
Posteinerné, T.M. 'Visszaszámlálás az Europai Szabaddalmi Rendszerhez való csatlakozás elott' ['Countdown before Joining the European Patent System']. *MIE Közlemények* 43, no. 1 (2002): 31–39.
Posteinerné, T.M. 'Szabadalmi Jogi Harmonizáció az Europai Szabadalmi Egyezmény Szemszögébol' ['Harmonisation of the Patent Law from Point of View of the European Patent Convention']. *MIE Közlemények* 45, no. 1 (2004): 5–13.
Sümeghy, P. 'A földrajzi árujelzok oltalma' ['Protection of Geographic Indications']. *Védjegyvilág* 5, no. 2 (1995): 15–18.
Süle, Á. 'A védjegycsalád, mint kizáró ok' ['The Trademark Family as Relative Reason for Exclusion']. *Iparjogvédelmi és Szerzöi Jogi Szemle* 114, no. 2 (2009): 42–60.
Pakucs, J. 'Az innováció hatása a gazdasági növekedésre' ['The Effect of Innovation to the Economic Growth']. In *Fehér Könyv a Szellemi Tulajdon Védelméröl*, edited by K. Penyigey, P. Sümeghy & M. Kiss. Budapest: Magyar Szabadalmi Hivatal & Magyar Szellemi Tulajdon Védelmi Tanács, 2006.
Szamosi, K. 'A domain név és a védjegyek ütközésének problémái' ['The Conflict of the Domain Name with Trademarks']. *MIE Közlemények* 41, no. 1 (2000): 161–167.
Szilágyi, J. 'Találmánynak nem minosülo elkotások' ['The Achievements Which Shall Not Be Object of Patent Protection']. *Iparjogvédelmi és Szerzöi Jogi Szemle* 106, no. 6 (2001): 7–11.
Tattay, L. 'Hazai domain nevek: nemzeti védjegyek' ['National Domain Names: Hungarian Trademarks']. *Magyar Jog* 50 (2006): 617–626.

Tattay, L. 'A Know-how fogalom fejlodése' ['The Advance of the Concept of Know-How']. *Jogtudományi Közlöny* 57 (2002): 409–413.
Tattay, L. 'A szellemi alkotások europai jogharmonizácioja Magyarországon' ['The European Legal Harmonisation of the Law of Intellectual Property in Hungary']. *Magyar Jog* 51 (2007): 518–531.
Verebics, J. 'A Szellemi tulajdon az információs társaadalomban' ['Intellectual Property in the Information Society']. *MIE Közlemények* 41, no. 1 (2000): 11–77.
Vida, S. 'Olimpiai jelképek oltalma' ['Protection of the Olympic Symbols']. *Iparjogvédelmi Szemle* 113, no. 5 (2008): 25–42.
Vida, S. 'Védjegyhasználat összehasonlító reklámban' ['The Use of Trademarks in Comparative Advertisements']. *Iparjogvédelmi Szemle* 113, no. 4 (2008): 52–61.
Vida, S. 'Licenciaszerzodés megszegése és védjegybitorlás jóhíru védjegynél' ['Outcome of Breach of a License Agreement in respect of a Mark with Reputation']. *Iparjogvédelmi Szemle* 114, no. 5 (2009): 40–55.

§3. Published Reports, Papers and Other Documents

Annual Reports of the Hungarian Patent Office 1990–2012.
Guide to Patent Protection. Budapest: Hungarian Office, 2004.
Guide to Plant Variety Protection. Budapest: Hungarian Patent Office, 2004.
Guide to Utility Model Protection. Budapest: Hungarian Patent Office, 2009.
Manuel of Patent Applications. Budapest: Hungarian Patent Office, 2009.
Report of the XXXVIth Congress Association International of Industrial Property Association (AIPPI). Montreal: AIPPI, 1995.
Report of the Congress of the Association Litéraire et Artistic Internationale (ALAI). New York: ALAI, 2001.
Report of the Congress of the Association Litéraire et Artistic Internationale (ALAI). Budapest: ALAI, 2003.
Report of the Congress of the Association Litéraire et Artistic Internationale (ALAI). Paris: ALAI, 2005.
Report of the Congress of the Association Litéraire et Artistic Internationale (ALAI). London: ALAI, 2007.

Selected Bibliography

Index

The numbers here refers to paragraph numbers

Index

Index

Index

Made in the USA
Monee, IL
18 October 2026

66037577R10177